The Soviet Union and the Middle East

The Soviet Union and the Middle East

BY WALTER Z. LAQUEUR

FREDERICK A. PRAEGER, *Publishers*

NEW YORK

BOOKS THAT MATTER

First published in the United States of America in 1959
by Frederick A. Praeger, Inc., Publishers
15 West 47th Street, New York 36, N. Y.

© 1959 in the United States of America
by Frederick A. Praeger, Inc.

Library of Congress catalog card number 59-7304
Printed in the United States of America

This book is Number 81 in the series of Praeger Publications in
Russian History and World Communism

This study was prepared under grants from the Rockefeller Foundation and
from the Russian Research Center and the Center for Middle Eastern Studies
of Harvard University. Rights of publication by the Harvard University Press
were waived in this instance because of previous contractual obligations of the
author.

"*Wahnsinn ruft man dem Kalchas, und Wahnsinn ruft man
    Kassandren,
Eh' man nach Ilion zug, wenn man von Ilion kommt.
Wer kann hoeren das Morgen und Uebermorgen? Nicht
    Einer!
Denn was gestern und eh'gestern gesprochen—wer hoert's?*"

GOETHE: *Weissagungen des Bakis*

Those who read history with an eye to its continuities only would be inclined to regard the present clash of power interests in the Middle East as being merely the latest recrudescence of the age-old "Eastern Question." They would recall, for example, that Russian interest in that question dates back to the eighteenth century—to go no further—when the Ottoman Empire was already on the defensive. They would invoke the aspirations of the Slavophiles, for whom the Eastern Question became the decisive issue and its solution Russia's manifest destiny. They would remind us how the Slavophiles came to regard the Eastern Question as the dynamic center of Russian history, the main impulse to Russia's social development, almost as being identical with the development of Russia's own national self-consciousness.

And yet, for all the evidence one may adduce from the past, such a view of the present crisis in the Middle East is unhistorical —perhaps dangerously so. The fact is that the Eastern Question of our day has little in common with the Oriental problem that preoccupied the chancelleries of Europe one hundred years ago. To be sure, the conflict between Russia and the West still persists, but it is no longer the same Russia—nor, for that matter, the same West—which contests the area. The center of the conflict has moved southward from the Balkans and Constantinople, and the stakes are vastly different. The question of the nationalities and minorities in the old Ottoman Empire has been solved—or, to be more accurate, shunted aside. The strategic interests of the powers no longer take the same form, involved as they are in such new issues as Arab nationalism and oil, Communism, and the emergence of Israel as a state. In all these respects, not to mention others, Gorchakov, "Dizzy," or the Iron Chancellor would now-adays find the Near and Middle East a problem far more baffling than anything they knew in their day.

The two essays published in this book constitute part of a larger project and represent an attempt to shed light on one of the crucial aspects of an essentially novel problem—i.e., the evolution of Soviet attitudes toward the Middle East, its problems, challenges, and opportunities—in the hope that this may provide a clue to the plans and objectives of Soviet foreign policy in that area. By "attitudes" I mean the complex of analyses, views, and hopes which have taken hold upon the minds of Soviet leaders from Lenin's time until now, particularly as they were embodied in the work of the Soviet Middle East specialists who have supplied the Soviet public and leaders with professional expertise on the area during this period.

A word of explanation and caution is in order at this point. Any survey of the externals of Soviet foreign policy in the Middle East, however important and interesting in itself, is hardly likely to shed much light on Soviet motives and expectations in that part of the world. That policy, like any other, is based on certain fundamental assumptions which seldom, if ever, become apparent from a reading of official documents, speeches, or even day-to-day measures. To understand it, one must turn to the doctrinal discussions and pronouncements frequently ventilated in public in Moscow over the last forty years. But, it may be asked, have these ideologues been really important in the making of Soviet foreign policy? The element of skepticism implied in such a question is based on a misconception. It assumes a strict division of labor between the "ideologists" who haggle over "fundamentals" and the "diplomats" who act merely as the executors of a given line when it has been adopted, and from this the skeptic draws the conclusion that the work of the ideologues is a mere epiphenomenon and that doctrine has no real bearing on the formulation of actual policies. Both the assumption and the conclusion are reinforced whenever it happens, as has been the case in recent years, that the views of the ideologues are belied by some new turn in Soviet policy. Such developments easily encourage the delusion that ideology is no longer of much relevance in

the Soviet Union and that its foreign policy can best be interpreted in traditional terms. Facile comparisons with Tsarist Russia (especially its activities in the Middle East) are, of course,
always available for this purpose. Nevertheless, all attempts to
account for Soviet foreign policy without due regard to the
ideological factor are ultimately sterile; their only effect is to
make a complicated phenomenon even more incomprehensible.
The Soviet Union is not a state comparable to Western states; any
attempt to regard it as such is bound to produce misleading conclusions. If the importance of the "professional ideologues" has
declined over the years in the field of foreign politics as elsewhere, all that has happened is that their monopoly has vanished.
It does not mean that ideological motivation has disappeared.

Soviet policy in the Middle East is more than the history of
official diplomatic relations between the Soviet Union and the
various Middle Eastern countries. If it were that and nothing
more, Soviet policy toward the Arab countries prior to 1944
would be hardly worthy of study, for official diplomatic ties with
such countries as Egypt and Iraq were not established until the
later stages of World War II. But long before all this, the Comintern had been active in these countries, and local Communist
parties had come into existence in all major Middle Eastern countries between 1918 and 1920. These represent activities which
must be taken into account in any general analysis of Soviet
policy in the Middle East, even when such activities were of less
than major importance.*

"The Soviet Image of the Middle East," the first essay in this
book, is an investigation into the sources of Soviet policy in that
area. "The Great Breakthrough" follows, with an attempt to
review the most recent—and the most important—phase of that
policy. Here, too, a self-imposed limitation has been unavoidable.
A full explanation of recent developments would necessarily call
for a detailed analysis of political, social, and economic conditions
in the Middle East and of the entire range of Arab-Western relations. Unfortunately, these can be mentioned only incidentally
in a study of the present scope.

This book was written during a stay at Harvard made possible

---

* See also Appendix I, "China and the Middle East."

by grants from the Rockefeller Foundation, the Harvard Russian Research Center and the Harvard Center for Middle Eastern Studies. I am grateful for this assistance and owe particular thanks to Mr. Marshall Shulman, Associate Director of the Russian Research Center, for the opportunity to undertake this study. Parts of the manuscript were read by Professor George Kirk (of the Center for Middle Eastern Studies), Mr. Morris Watnick (of the Russian Research Center), and Lieutenant Colonel G. Wheeler (of the London Central Asian Research Centre), who offered valuable criticism and suggestions. I also had the benefit of advice on certain specific points from M. Alexandre Bennigsen, Mr. Donald Wilber, Professor Cuyler Young, Dr. Willem van Ravesteyn, Mrs. Jane Degras, Boris Nikolaevski, and Nissim Rejwan. M. Jean Vigneau put at my disposal many of the valuable publications of the Centre de Documentation et de Synthèse (Paris), of which he is the director. Robert Miller, my research assistant in Cambridge, deserves credit for locating and excerpting many now obscure sources from the days of the *Vestnik Evropy* to the time of *Revoliutsionnyi Vostok*. Mrs. Jane Degras, Messrs. M. Mindlin and Philip Mairet suggested improvements in style and rewrote entire passages.

Mrs. Ina Bonnell helped me in procuring some rare books, and microfilms of others. I should also like to thank Mrs. Helen Parsons for her many helpful chores, too numerous to mention. Finally, this list of acknowledgments would be incomplete without a word of thanks to my associates at the *Soviet Survey* in London, who made my stay in America possible by shouldering most of the burden of editing that periodical during my absence.

—W.Z.L.

CAMBRIDGE, MASS.
December, 1958

CONTENTS

The Soviet Union and the Middle East

INTRODUCTION

This is a first attempt to review and to examine critically Soviet views on developments in the Middle East since 1917. It is, of course, impossible to deal with the Middle East entirely in isolation; occasional references to Soviet policy in Asia in general and to the basic conceptions behind it are unavoidable. While making certain allowances for important differences in the various countries, Soviet Asian and African experts have always tended to regard the colonial world and the dependent countries as a whole; Soviet policies in the Middle East have sometimes been decisively influenced by events in India and China. It is impossible to retrace the discussions and disputes about the Middle East except in the wider framework of the great Soviet debate on the coming Asian revolution, a debate that has continued, off and on, for almost forty years.

Some difficulties in method should, perhaps, first be mentioned. It is admittedly easier and more correct to talk about a "Soviet view" on any given subject of public interest—whether modern painting, Tolstoy, or the Middle East—than about, say, an "American" or a "French" view. Nevertheless, there is a danger of exaggerating the uniformity of Soviet thinking; substantial differences of opinion on the Middle East existed up to about 1928; since then, unanimity has not been complete, there are differences of emphasis and there are varying nuances in political appraisal and analysis. The analysis of Soviet views on "Western Asian" topics is further complicated by the frequent changes in the party line in dealing historically with such subjects as the Gilan Republic or the role of the Egyptian Wafd, or Gandhi and Nehru and the non-Communist national liberation movement in general.

1

One cannot say with any exactitude who has actually been shaping Soviet views on the Middle East in the past few decades. There were and are at each stage frequent references to the classics of Marxist-Leninist theory. But in the lifetime of Marx and Engels the Middle East (and Asia in general) was not yet a pivot of world politics, and though they occasionally commented on events in India and China, their *obiter dicta* on the Middle East are fairly infrequent (and not always suitable now). Lenin and Stalin were preoccupied with more urgent issues and never pretended to be Middle Eastern experts. Their references to Turkey, Persia, and Afghanistan were few, and even the most assiduous collector of quotations would find it difficult to fill more than a page with their observations on the Arab world. Lenin and Stalin formulated the general political line with regard to Asia, but the elaboration and application were left to others. True, everybody had to conform to the general line after 1928, but within the wider framework of the "line" there were, on occasion, divergent interpretations. The views expressed by Narkomindel experts on Kemalist Turkey in the twenties and thirties were by no means identical with those of Comintern officials. This, in a sense, was quite natural, for the short-term interests of the Soviet Union could not always coincide with the interests of Communism in Asia. While Soviet Foreign Ministry officials wanted close relations with Kemalist Turkey, Comintern leaders could not quite ignore the fact that Communism was suppressed in Turkey. There were, in addition, other professional observers of the Middle Eastern scene—in the Profintern, the Commissariat for Nationalities, the Komakademia, the All-Union Association of Orientalists, the army general staff, the foreign trade agencies, and, of course, in the secret services, about whom little or nothing is known. In the twenties there were frequent, and sometimes public, polemics between groups as well as between individual experts. "Coordination" has since eliminated most, but not all, of these differences of opinion.

We know about these discussions mainly from books and periodicals; unfortunately, the material available in Western libraries is not complete. An apparent paradox should be mentioned in this context: between 1922 and 1935 a great many books dealing with Middle Eastern and Asian topics were published in the Soviet Union, and there were half a dozen periodicals devoted to these subjects. During that period the revolutionary movement in Asia, and particularly in the Middle East, was not a factor of first-rate political importance. Soviet writers had to deal largely with hopes and expectations and future trends. Between 1935 and 1955, on the other hand, hardly any books on these subjects were published, and all the specialized periodicals had ceased to appear, though it was precisely in these years that the Communist parties in Asia, and the national-revolutionary movement in general, made great advances. Between 1917 and 1955 Soviet interest in the East manifested itself in inverse ratio to the real importance of the Asian revolution. The reasons for this curious development will be discussed in some detail later. It remains to be added that, since 1955, there is again a new literature and that there are specialized periodicals on the contemporary East.

The intrinsic importance of the subject chosen for the present investigation need not be elaborated upon, for recent events in Asia have made this all too obvious. In the course of this survey we shall have to examine predictions that were astonishingly correct and theories that were wildly off the mark, and it may be possible to learn from both. Beyond this, there are larger questions that remain. Did the Soviet Communists expect the revolutionary events in Asia? Were they instrumental in bringing them about, or did they occur quite independently? The revolution in Asia is still going on, and for this reason, if for no other, all that one can do is to provide tentative explanations rather than final answers.

PART ONE

THE SOVIET IMAGE
OF THE MIDDLE EAST

CHAPTER ONE

STORM OVER ASIA

1. *Between West and East*

When the Bolsheviks came to power in November, 1917, their eyes were turned to the West. The revolution had triumphed in Russia, they thought, because the empire of the Tsars had been the weakest link in the capitalist chain. But the revolution in Russia was to be only the prelude to a series of revolutions in the West that would culminate in the emergence of one great Soviet republic of Europe and, eventually, of the whole world. All this was in line with the Marxist expectations that the socialist movement would first come to power in the industrially developed countries of the West. There were some Communists in 1918 who thought that events in the East rather than the West would be decisive for the future of world Communism, but none of these "Asia Firsters" belonged to the top leadership; their opinions were dismissed as the excusable foibles of somewhat provincial Tatar, Turkmen, and Indian comrades. Readers of *Pravda* in 1918 and early 1919 undoubtedly gained the impression that Germany was the most important country in the world, and those who studied *Zhizn Natsionalnostei*, the organ of the Commissariat for Nationalities (the one most intimately concerned with "Eastern questions" in the early days), could be forgiven for reaching the conclusion that events in Ireland and even Luxembourg were as important as developments in China and India—let alone the Middle East. Nobody actually said that Asia did not matter; on the contrary, much lip service was paid to the revolutionary potentialities of the East. But in the early days there was little information and less interest in what really went on in Asia. Zinoviev, in his report to the Third Congress of

7

the Comintern, talked about "our important sections in the
Middle and Far East." But the work of these important sections
was reviewed in precisely two sentences in a document of one
hundred and four pages. Bukharin, at a much later date,[1] complained that, though the Bolsheviks knew all about the Social
Democrats and Liberals in the West, the most elementary facts
about the East remained unknown. It was no mere coincidence
that Stalin, the Commissar for Nationalities, entitled one of his
very first articles "Do Not Forget the East!" For a time the East
was indeed in danger of being forgotten. The reasons for this
apparent neglect are obvious. Russia was in a state of civil war,
the Transcaucasian republics and large parts of Turkestan had
not yet been reunited with Moscow, and when the Russian Communists talked about the East in 1918-19 they were thinking about
Tiflis, Baku, and Tashkent rather than Ankara, Delhi, or Peking.
However important the Middle and Far East, they could not do
much about it in the early days, while there was urgent work to
be done nearer home.

It is important to stress these facts because there has been a
tendency in recent years among both Communists and non-
Communists to ascribe to the early Soviet leaders an Asian
orientation they did not in fact have. Zhordaniia, the Georgian
leader, called the Bolsheviks "Asian Socialists" in contrast to the
Mensheviks, who were the "Europeans," but this was meant to be
an offensive rather than a descriptive remark. Those who then
maintained that the light came from the East were Social Revolutionaries (like Ivanov Razumnik), poets like Alexander Blok, or
the Eurasians. The Bolsheviks had little time for what they considered the wild imaginings of the local Spenglers and Keyser-
lings: "Their East is the mummy of their souls," they said in
derision.[2] And the few non-Russian Communists, such as Ryskulov, Sultan Galiev, or Roy, who maintained that the decisive
battles would be fought in the East, all ended outside the party as
"right-wing nationalist deviationists." Only the recession of the
revolutionary wave in Europe in 1920 evoked a more active
interest in Asia. The Second Congress of the Comintern, which
debated the prospects of the Asian revolutionary movement at
considerable length, was followed by the famous Baku Con-

gress; by that time the idea of the union of the peoples of the East and of the European Communist proletariat had become quite fashionable. Georgi Safarov, an early Soviet authority on Asia, was one of the first to elaborate the theme of Russia as a bridge between East and West; in Europe, he said, Russia was regarded as semi-Asian, but the Asians regarded her as a semi-European member of their family. Russia could, therefore, act as a mediator and introduce to Asia the very latest Western achievement: European Communism.[3]

Of the Bolshevik leaders, Lenin was perhaps the most interested in, and the most knowledgeable on, things Asian. Trotsky did not care much about events in the East, nor did Zinoviev (despite his appearance in Baku), Kamenev, Bukharin, Rykov, and the rest of the old guard. Stalin was interested in Asia *ex officio* as Commissar for Nationalities, but his other activities and the struggle for power in the party soon preoccupied him far more than Eastern affairs. Radek had written occasionally before the revolution on colonial and Asian subjects for *Die Neue Zeit*, and he later became an expert on China, but this hardly exceeded the level of intelligent political journalism. There were some individuals in the left-wing Russian emigration prior to 1917 who had made some specialized studies of certain aspects of Asian or colonial affairs, but neither Pavlovich-Weltman (about whom more below) nor Rotshtein nor Parvus were active members of the Party at the time.

This brings us back to Lenin. A diligent exploration of Lenin's writings on the East, from his very first article on the subject (a comment on China in *Iskra* in 1900) to the essays written between 1908 and 1913 (*Inflammable Material in World Politics, The Awakening of Asia, Backward Europe and Progressive Asia*, etc.) and to his writings after the revolution, reveals much interesting material.

Imperialism, the colonial question, and the national-revolutionary movement in Asia had become issues of cardinal importance in the first decade of the twentieth century. Marx and Engels expected the European colonies and dependencies to become independent one day, but not before the revolution had triumphed in Europe. They assumed that the European proletariat would have to take over the colonies temporarily and lead them as fast as possible toward independence. Engels regarded this prospect with mixed feelings, "for we have enough to do at home."[4] Engels even envisaged the possibility of the liberated countries of Asia and Africa turning against the victorious proletariat in the metropolis. By and large, however, Marx and Engels were preoccupied with Europe and North America, which they regarded as the key areas for the victory of socialism. Only after the turn of the century did colonial affairs and anti-colonial movements come into prominence, the upheavals in China, Persia, and Turkey between 1906 and 1912 attracting general attention in the West. Among the commentators on these events was Lenin, some of whose writings suggest that he regarded the awakening of Asia as the beginning of a new era in world history. A great new storm center had come into being, he thought, and the fate of the world would ultimately be determined by the fact that the majority of mankind was concentrated in China, India, and Russia. The class-conscious workers of Europe now had the support of their Asian comrades, whose numbers were growing not daily but hourly.

This suggests that Lenin attributed decisive importance to the Asian revolution. But quotations can be used to many ends, and Lenin's opinions on Asia have to be placed in the wider context of his writings and in the general political climate in the left-wing movement at the time. Viewed in this perspective, it is difficult to argue that Lenin was much more Asia-conscious than his socialist contemporaries (such as Kautsky, Bernstein, or Rosa Luxemburg); many liberals, too, believed that Asia was gradually emerging as a decisive (and active) factor in world politics. It is true that the Second International virtually ignored events outside Europe; prior to 1914, the Bolsheviks were perhaps more aware of Asia than the rest, but it was a difference in emphasis rather than outlook. The historical fate of the "Asian orientation" in this respect resembles the theory of "Socialism in one country." The *possibility* of having "Socialism in one country" had been mentioned occasionally before 1917, but until well after the revolution hardly anyone assumed that things would really turn out that way. Shortly before the revolution, Lenin formulated his views on imperialism, the "highest stage of capitalism." His theory of imperialism was scheduled to have tremendous revolutionary consequences throughout the awakening East, but it is doubtful whether anyone realized it at the time. Doctrines rationalizing the struggle against the "domination and exploitation" of the West were in the air, and would have emerged anyway, though perhaps on a more primitive and un-Marxist level. Revolutionary Russia gave a strong impetus to the national-revolutionary movement in the East, but it did not create that movement.

As World War I came to an end, Western observers asked whether Communism, victorious in Russia, would next move East or West. According to one school of thinking, Bolshevism would move where it would find least resistance, namely, into Europe. For among Eastern nations, it was argued, foreign interference in the customs and the ways of life was never tolerated. And was not Islam the greatest antagonist of Bolshevism because it offered its adherents "everything that Lenin could promise"?[5] Others had their doubts about this theory, for did not Bolshevism appeal to "proletarian peoples" as well as to proletarian classes? They thought little of the proposal to combat Bolshevism in Asia by an "information campaign"; one of them, a German, argued that Bolshevism could be met in Asia only if the conditions conducive to its spread were changed. "And if that should be impossible, a world-wide bitter struggle will ensue, in comparison with which the terrible last four years may seem child's play and in which the final judgment on Western civilization may be passed."[6]

2. The First Experts

Among the institutions formulating Russia's Eastern policy in the first post-revolutionary decade, the foremost were the Commissariats for Nationalities and Foreign Affairs (Narkomindel) and the Comintern. The head of the Eastern department of the Narkomindel was Arseni Voznesenskii, but his department was not the most active. It took a fairly long time before regular diplomatic relations were established with the various independent Asian nations, and when the first ambassadors had been installed they seem not to have worked through their department chief in Moscow, but apparently communicated directly with

Chicherin or the Party Central Committee. The men in the field (Rotshtein, Shumiatskii, Surits, Raskolnikov, *et al.*) had greater standing at home than the comparatively unknown Voznesenskii.

For some time Stalin's Commissariat for Nationalities played a greater role in Soviet Eastern policies than did the Narkomindel. At that time the borders of the Soviet republic had not yet been definitely fixed; nobody knew whether they would run through Bukhara and Baku—or perhaps beyond Kabul and Tehran. Stalin and his first deputy, Pestkovskii, dealt with internal affairs, but some of the leading officials of his commissariat became involved in various ways in Soviet Middle Eastern policies. Among them was Semen Markovich Dimanshtein, a Bolshevik since 1904 who for a time headed the Jewish section (Evsektsiia) of the party. A native of Vilnius and a locksmith by trade, he had been in the Paris emigration, served as editor of a number of journals after the revolution and became for a while Stalin's right-hand man.* Grigori Isakovich Broido, another deputy commissar, had headed the Tashkent Soviet in 1917 and later became rector of the new Communist University of the Toilers of the East. Nariman Narimanov, a physician from Baku, held high office in both Stalin's and Chicherin's commissariats. Before the revolution he had been the leader of an Azerbaidzhani left-wing group. By inclination a novelist rather than an active politician, his speeches and writings were nebulous and oriental in style, quite unlike those of the old Bolsheviks. Zinoviev compared him, after his death, to Sun Yat-sen. This was a fitting description, for Narimanov was a left-wing nationalist rather than a Communist. But at the time the Bolsheviks did not have many candidates to choose from.†

Sultan Galiev, a Tatar teacher from Kazan, was another of

* S. M. Dimanshtein continued to specialize in the nationalities question. Charged with "right-wing" and "Great Russian nationalist" deviations in the middle thirties, he disappeared in 1937.

† N. Narimanov was posthumously denounced as a "traitor, provocateur, deserter, and slanderer of the Soviet regime" (by Bagirov in *Bakinskii Rabochi*, December 8, 1938). After the Twentieth CPSU Congress he was rehabilitated as a "great revolutionary writer and herald of Leninist ideas in the East" (*Kommunist*, Baku, April 8, 1956).

Stalin's chief lieutenants—and another subsequent nationalist deviationist. He became the protagonist (with Turar Ryskulov—a lawyer of Kirgiz origin*) of a Colonial, rather than a Communist, international (we shall return to the "Sultan Galievshchina"). The Russian Communists faced a difficult dilemma in their search for leading cadres in the East, and (as Stalin wrote) they had to put their trust in the few radicals available, despite their Pan-Islamic or Pan-Turkish background: "There are so few intellectuals, so few thinking people, even so few literate people generally in the Eastern republics and regions, that one can count them on one's fingers."[7]

Most of the early-period stories of the leading Communists from Moslem lands have unhappy endings. There was Mustafa Subhi, one of the founders of the Socialist party in Turkey and subsequently a key figure in the attempt to organize Soviet Moslems and to direct Communist activities in the Near East; he was killed in Trebizond in 1920. There was Haidar Khan Amu-oglu, a prominent Persian revolutionary who had been active in the uprisings ten years earlier and now came again to the fore. He was involved in the ill-starred Gilan Republic and was shot by Persian government troops in 1921. Efendiev, a Turkish officer who had been taken prisoner by the Russians during World War I, became a Bolshevik (or so it seemed at the time) and one of the chief political advisers and commentators on Near Eastern affairs. But his career as a Bolshevik did not last long, either; he joined Enver Pasha and the Basmachi. It is a list that could be prolonged. The Comintern also needed an Eastern department, and its first regular head was Georgi Safarov, still a young man in his late twenties, but already an "old Bolshevik" of some ten years' standing, who had returned with Lenin from Switzerland in the famous sealed train.† Among the early Com-

* T. Ryskulov continued to hold various political posts and to publish books until the middle thirties, despite persistent accusations of nationalist deviationism. In the purges of 1937 he was named as the alleged head of a "Society for the Liberation of Turkestan." His subsequent fate is unknown.

† Safarov belonged to the inner party opposition in 1925-7, and though he recanted and continued to be politically active and to publish, he was under a cloud up to the time of his disappearance in 1935.

intern officials dealing with Eastern affairs there were two of more than average caliber, the Indian M. N. Roy and A. Sultan zade, a Persian from Baku. Roy and, to a lesser extent, Sultan zade had ideas of their own about the future course of the Asian revolution which did not necessarily tally with the views of the Russian comrades. We shall have to deal with both in greater detail.

Other institutions were created and began to be active in the Eastern field. There was the Institute for Oriental Studies in Moscow, which continued the work of the old Lazarev Institute of Eastern Languages. Similar research centers were set up in Petrograd and other major cities. The Red Army had an "Eastern Department" in which specialized training was given to officers. The Profintern, the Communist trade union international, established an Eastern department of its own; some of its early collaborators, such as Kh. Eidus and V. Balabushevich, are still active. The ceiling organization uniting all those with a special interest in the East was the All-Union Association of Orientalists (VNAV). The Party authorities had decided on the establishment of this body in December, 1921, and it began to function the following month. The first issue of the VNAV periodical, *Novyi Vostok* (The New East), was published the same year (1922).

Mikhail Pavlovich (Weltman) became the first president of VNAV; he was undoubtedly the most remarkable personality in the whole field of contemporary Eastern studies and policy planning in the early days. Born in Odessa in 1871, he had been arrested in 1892 as a member of one of the first social-democratic groups in Russia (the Steklov-Ziperovich circle). Pavlovich spent many years in the Paris emigration and was the first Russian Marxist to study the problems of imperialism and colonialism systematically; according to Chicherin, he was the first (even before Lenin) to realize the "potentialities of a link between the struggle of the proletariat in the West and the fight of the oppressed peoples of the East." He published a great many articles on international affairs in both social-democratic and "bourgeois" papers, as well as a number of books of uneven quality. He was interested in a great many subjects and was widely read. But he cannot be described as an original thinker, nor did he apparently ever feel the inclination to specialize within the wide framework of Asian affairs, imperialism, or colonialism. This characteristic he shared with most of his comrades in the emigration, men and women who wanted to make a revolution, not to become university professors.

Pavlovich was a "character" (*"Nemnogo chudak,"* as A. A. Ioffe put it), but universally respected and liked. A man of most unmilitary appearance and bearing, he gave much time to the study of military doctrine and for a while actually served as political commissar in the civil war. When Lenin saw him in uniform at a Party Congress he is reported to have said: "How we have come down in the world when the Entente compels us to put even Mikhail Lazarovich on a horse!" When the Social Democrats split, Pavlovich remained with the Mensheviks. He disarmingly admitted much later that he was much too preoccupied with international affairs: "I had not bothered to read the party documents. . . ." But he became a good Bolshevik after 1917 and was immediately given responsible positions; Trotsky took him to Brest Litovsk as an adviser. He played a leading part in all the organizations and activities concerned with Soviet policy in the East, including the Baku Congress, and when he died in 1926 everybody seemed to agree that there was nobody to replace him. One of his close collaborators, Rafail, wrote that the East would be liberated one day and become Soviet, "and on that day the name of Pavlovich will be mentioned among the first." This prediction was not to come true, however, for soon after his death a cloud passed over his memory; for many years his name disappeared even from most works of reference. Only in 1957, after the Twentieth Party Congress, did the central organ of Soviet Eastern experts carry a short footnote about him, thus reintroducing him to a new generation that had presumably never heard of the man who had earlier been the recognized leader in his field.

Pavlovich and his colleagues made it clear from the beginning that the "East" they were going to deal with was not just the Middle and the Far East but the entire colonial world, including Africa and Latin America. Asia, which was to be the main subject of study, was virtually a terra incognita to the young Soviet republic; it was said that the new diplomats to be sent out to the Asian capitals looked in vain for elementary political and socio-economic guide books.[9] It should be noted in passing that the division of labor between the Soviet Foreign Office, the Comintern, the other agencies, and the VNAV was not clearly marked in the early days. Diplomats such as Surits, Raskolnikov, Tardov, Astakhov,* and others were active in the VNAV and even wrote for its journal while on duty in Ankara, Tehran, or Kabul. These activities were to cease in the middle twenties—a matter of lasting regret to the student of Soviet policy in the East.

None of these new experts was, strictly speaking, an Orientalist. Of the academic Orientalists, a good many remained in Russia after the revolution, and men of the older generation (such as V. V. Bartold or S. F. Oldenburg) as well as the younger Orientalists (such as I. Iu. Krachkovskii and V. A. Gordlevskii) continued their studies at the Academy of Sciences and the universities. But their interest in contemporary affairs was limited, and only a few took part in the new ventures sponsored by Pavlovich. They had their own small niches in the Academy and their own specialized publications, and they were, on the whole, left alone until the late twenties, when stricter controls were introduced.

But even if their knowledge of the East was recently acquired and deficient, their mastery of oriental languages imperfect, and their ideas derived far too often from second-hand material, the achievements of the Pavlovich school should not be belittled. Their discussions were pertinent, and their publications lively; there were experts in the West with more first-hand factual knowledge, but the new Soviet school probably had a better training in the interpretation of socio-economic developments, and a more acute understanding of political trends. In the pre-Stalin days, Marxism had not yet become a petrified doctrine

---

* None of these men stayed in the Eastern field. Surits became ambassador to Paris; Raskolnikov, after working in various ministries and as editor of a literary journal, again joined the Foreign Service, refused to return to Russia in 1938, and died in France the year after. Astakhov was last heard of in Berlin in 1939, when he initiated the negotiations that led to the Soviet-German non-aggression treaty of August, 1939.

but was a method of investigation that could frequently be applied with profit. Some of Pavlovich's close collaborators of VNAV days afterwards ran into serious ideological trouble and disappeared from the scene. Of the younger experts in the Middle Eastern and Islamic fields who received their training in those days, some, such as E. A. Belaev, N. A. Smirnov, B. Dantsig, and I. M. Reisner, succeeded in weathering all storms.*

3. Communism and Bourgeois Nationalism

Two important ideological issues faced the Communists in Asia from the outset, and continue to preoccupy them up to the present day: what should be their attitude toward the national movement in the East? Were they to collaborate with non-proletarian classes and non-socialist parties? If so, in what conditions and to what end? The second major problem was whether the East could possibly skip the capitalist stage of development, passing directly from a precapitalist to a socialist mode of production.

To many Western observers these questions appeared academic, if not downright scholastic: would it not be more logical and practical to examine these problems on the basis of conditions prevailing in the respective countries? But the Communists, especially in the early years, held no brief for empiricism; they insisted on the correct ideological approach before tackling a problem on the practical level. They realized, of course, that conditions in China and Egypt, for instance, were not quite identical, but they believed that the Eastern world had so much

* Evgeni Alexandrovich Belaev (b. 1895) and Nikolai Alexandrovich Smirnov (b. 1896) have specialized in both Islamic studies and the study of the contemporary Middle East. Smirnov, in his history of Islamic studies in the Soviet Union (1954), does not mention Pavlovich once. Boris Moiseevich Dantsig (b. 1896) became one of the leading Soviet authorities on the history and economy of modern Turkey. Igor Mihailovich Reisner (1899-1958) was the son of M. A. Reisner, a professor in Tsarist Russia and an old Socialist who himself originated a theory to explain the emergence and social function of Islam. I. M. Reisner, a first secretary at the Soviet embassy in Kabul at the age of twenty, specialized subsequently in Afghan and Indian studies, but also held the chair of Middle Eastern History at Moscow University between 1945 and 1955. Larissa Reisner (Raskolnikov's wife), one of the best-known Soviet writers in the twenties, was his sister.

in common that the formulation of a general strategy was not merely possible but imperative. The debate between Lenin and M. N. Roy at the Second Congress of the Communist International is of considerable relevance in this respect.[10] Broadly speaking, Lenin was in favor of a temporary alliance with the national movement in the East which he preferred to call "national-revolutionary" rather than "bourgeois-democratic," whereas Roy had grave doubts about the desirability of such an approach. The Comintern Congress adopted Lenin's theses, but it adopted Roy's draft as well (in a somewhat watered-down version), and the whole issue was really left in abeyance. It should be pointed out that neither Lenin's nor Roy's stand was free of inconsistencies. Lenin favored a temporary alliance, but on conditions which, if taken literally, would have made the alliance quite illusory: we should support those bourgeois liberation movements, he said, only if they do not oppose us in our efforts to organize and educate the peasantry and the exploited masses in a revolutionary spirit.[11] But what national-revolutionary movement would agree to have its position undermined by such concessions to the Communists? Roy, on the other hand, found it difficult to discover any common ground between the Communists and the bourgeois-democratic national movement which aimed at the establishment of a bourgeois order. But he had to admit that the Asian revolution would be neither proletarian nor agrarian at first; unless he wanted to condemn the Comintern to a policy of sterility and inactivity, he, too, had to contemplate some form of collaboration with the "bourgeois nationalists."[12] Sultan zade suggested a compromise: the bourgeois-democratic movement should be supported only in those countries where it was still in an embryonic stage. Wherever it had been in existence for ten years or more, the Comintern should create a purely Communist movement in opposition to the bourgeois nationalists.[13] The proposal was scarcely realistic; and Sultan zade soon came to realize—in his own country (Persia)— that, though a bourgeois movement had been in existence for more than ten years, the conditions for creating a strong proletarian party could not yet be found.

Some Western Communist leaders, notably the Italians Seratti and Graziadei, disliked the whole trend of discussion: was it not

extremely likely that the bourgeois-democratic liberation movement in the backward countries would turn imperialist after a
while? This imputation was vigorously rejected as an infringe-
ment of the canons of internationalism, and those who had asked
the question were not to last very long in the Comintern. But it
would be difficult to deny that they had put their fingers on a
problem that was to become relevant many years later.

Communists from Moslem regions and countries differed from
the rest in believing (like Roy) that the victory of Communism
depended on its success in the East. Sultan zade was one of the
few exceptions and he criticized his comrades from Turkestan
who shared what he believed were Roy's illusions.[14] Sultan Galiev,
Efendiev, and others had complained that everybody in Moscow
was interested in events in the West and tended to neglect the
East.[15] Their case was put by Narbutabekov, a lawyer from
Turkestan, at the famous Baku Congress: he reminded the Moscow leaders that for three years they had appealed for the help
of the West European proletariat—and what had been the result?
Soviet Russia had no better ally than the East; there was no other
way for Moscow but to "organize" Asia.[16]

This was not the only important issue on which the Communists from Moslem lands differed from their Great Russian
comrades. They all predicted a brilliant future for Communism
in Asia, on one condition: that the peculiarities of the East were
taken into account. They all agreed that "straight Communism"
would not work in Asia. Ryskulov declared that the Eastern
revolution would be petty bourgeois in character, and that there
was nothing wrong with such a development, since it would be
directed against the Entente and world capitalism. It would be a
revolution for national self-determination, for the unity of the
East, and it would lead to the establishment of a very powerful
"Eastern International."[17] (It is difficult to establish who originated the idea of an Eastern or Colonial International.)* Most

---

* The first suggestion for the establishment of an "Eastern International"
was apparently made at the foundation meeting of the short-lived "Union
for the Liberation of the East" in Moscow (October 31, 1918) by K. M.
Troianovskii (see his *Vostok i Revoliutsiia*, 1918). The proposal did not
fall on fertile ground.

Communists from eastern lands agreed that the class struggle should be played down and the national character of the revolutionary movement emphasized, nor did they regard this as a mere short-term stratagem; they thought, with Narbutabekov, that the "East was entirely different."

The Russian Communist leaders were uncertain. They realized the importance of the nationalist appeal in the East and made use of it in Baku. Zinoviev and his colleagues talked about a holy war; if the East would only begin to move, nothing would remain of Europe but a small area on the map. Radek appealed to that desire to struggle against the West that "inspired your ancestors, your great leaders, in their advance to conquer Europe." Their enemies, of course, would conjure up the ghosts of Genghis Khan and the conquering caliphs of Islam, but such calumnies should not deter them—the purpose of their holy struggle was not to destroy and conquer but to create a new culture under the banner of Communism, a culture a hundred times higher than that created by the slave owners of the West.[18] Radek had perhaps a more astute grasp of the tremendous appeal of nationalism in both West and East than most of his comrades, but neither the friends of Schlageter nor the descendants of Genghis Khan were as yet willing to cooperate.

The effectiveness of these appeals was tempered by too many internationalist ("European") slogans and too much Marxist language; at the opening session of the Baku Congress the "International" was played by the orchestra eleven times in less than an hour.

Not everybody in Moscow was happy about the contemplated alliance with Asia. Maxim Gorky (not yet an enthusiastic supporter of the regime) asked H. G. Wells in an open letter: "Don't you consider this alliance between Russia and the peoples of Asia as a terrible menace to European culture?"[19] Gorky, being clearly out of step, was taken to task for the remark, but even those far more sympathetic to the Asian alliance had strong doubts and reservations. Reporting in November, 1920, to the Executive Committee of the Comintern about the state of affairs in the East, Sultan zade was not very optimistic: experience showed that in the national movement in the East at least some of the national revolutionaries would soon go over to the Entente camp.[20] Sokolnikov, reporting to the same forum several weeks later, also doubted the strength and stability of the pro-Soviet sympathies of the bourgeois and landowning elements in the East. They hated England, but were even more afraid of the masses at home, and would compromise with the enemy at the first opportunity.[21] Sultan zade has been charged by later Soviet historians with left-wing sectarianism and even with treachery,[22] but an examination of the historical record casts doubt on the validity of these accusations. In his *Theses on the Revolution in the East*, Sultan zade advocated the closest alliance with the petty bourgeois elements in the East, and even fusion, which was a farther-reaching concession than most of his contemporaries were ready to make.[23] The Baku initiative was not followed up: the Council for Propaganda and Action set up at the Congress of the Peoples of the East was convened several times but then discontinued its activities; its organ, *Narody Vostoka*, appeared, as far as can be ascertained, only once.

The other ideological issue first discussed in 1920 that had considerable bearing on Communist strategy in the East was the question of bypassing the capitalist stage of development. Prior to 1917, Lenin had rejected such a possibility as a Populist dream, but with the victory of the Bolsheviks in Russia a different situation had been created. At the Second Comintern Congress one of the resolutions adopted on his initiative stated that, with the help of the proletariat of the more advanced countries, the backward countries could indeed proceed directly to a Soviet regime.[24] This discussion, too, was to go on for many years. Historically, it could be traced back to Marx's debates with Russian socialists in the eighteen-seventies about the feasibility of non-capitalist development in Russia. The role of the peasants in the revolutionary movement in the East played a prominent part in this discussion, and the Leninists had to defend themselves against both "left-wing Communist" and Social-Democratic criticism. Some left-wing Communists questioned the possibility of the partial emancipation of the colonial countries. Social Democrats like Otto Bauer or the Mensheviks, on the other hand, accused the Bolsheviks of "Populist deviations" in Asia, saying they wanted to make a revolution in the East only because they could make no headway in the West.[25] The revolution in the backward countries of Asia would then serve as a springboard for the social revolution in the West—an imputation that was then emphatically denied in Moscow.

Reviewing these early ideological discussions in the perspective of almost forty years, one finds Lenin, as usual, taking a more realistic view than his critics of the left and right. Roy was more aware than Lenin of the decisive importance of Asia for the future of world Communism, but the tactics he suggested were hardly conducive to Communist progress in the East. The proposals made by the "Moslem Communists" in 1919-20 are of considerable historic interest and foreshadowed developments in the Arab world in the middle fifties. But even if Moscow had accepted the proposals then outlined by Sultan Galiev, Ryskulov, and others, such a policy would hardly have brought great benefits. The national movement in the East was then only in its initial stage, and the social forces on which a revolutionary movement could be based were either wholly passive (e.g., the peasants) or insufficiently developed (the native intelligentsia and the industrial proletariat). The East had begun to stir but it was not yet in full motion. Moscow was beginning to realize the tremendous possibilities in the East, but was not yet fully aware of them. Time was needed to adjust basic theoretical conceptions to a new world that had not figured prominently in the pre-1917 blueprints.

4. First Contacts—First Comments

Soviet views on the East tended to be erratic in 1918. This is not surprising in view of the general state of the world at that time, the breakdown of communications between countries (and within countries), the difficulty of getting accurate information, the universal dislocation. Just as Western press reports on Russian events were frequently fantastic, comments in Moscow about the outside world, particularly about the East, were at first out of touch with reality, to say the least.

The first step taken by the Soviet government in the East was the publication on November 20, 1917, of an appeal to all

Moslem working people in Russia and the East to support the Russian Revolution. All secret agreements between Tsarist Russia and the Entente on the division of Turkey and Persia were declared null and void: "Constantinople should remain in the hands of the Moslems."[26] But this appeal was not, and could not be, followed up by any practical steps. The only contact with Turkey was on the military level—there was no direct diplomatic contact with either Persia or Afghanistan. Nor could much be done to help the revolutionary movement in the East. In late October, 1918, the "Union for the Liberation of the East" was founded in Moscow, a precursor of the Baku Congress in 1920. There were fiery speeches by Mustafa Subhi, Haidar Khan, and other eastern revolutionaries, but the meeting remained an isolated episode. Meanwhile the first articles on the coming revolution in the East appeared in the Soviet press (written by Bukharin, Radek, and Chicherin), and two books on the subject were published as early as 1918; neither author was an "old Bolshevik."[27]

An astonishing variety of opinions on things Eastern was expressed in these first publications, some of them remarkably shrewd and occasionally prophetic, others extremely silly. Opinions in Moscow at that time were formed on the basis of sporadic and not very reliable reports from informants who frequently exaggerated the extent of the revolutionary wave in Asia. The diversity of views was also due, perhaps, to the fact that in this as in many other fields the Communists had to rely on non-Communist experts; the majority of those who now commented on events in the East and even formulated policy had only the day before been prominent Pan-Islamists or Pan-Turkists, members of Jewish nationalist groups, Tolstoyans, apolitical university professors. Thus, (six years after the Revolution!) a writer could describe Marx and Engels as very good men who, nevertheless, knew remarkably little about the East, and who had apparently not realized that events in the West and in the East were not subject to the same sociological laws.[28] Another observer, an academician, suggested that radical changes were unlikely in Asia, at least for several generations, in view of the hostility of Islam toward all innovations.[29] In this case the professor was challenged; Arthur Young's famous prediction about the French Revolution not being likely to happen was quoted as a warning against an unduly pessimistic approach. Typical of the exaggerated accounts of the revolutionary potential in the East was a report from Egypt according to which 80% of the party membership was "native" and 70% "proletarian"—and this at a time when Egyptian Communists numbered scarcely a dozen, and probably included not a single worker, a fact that was later admitted.[30]

Everybody in Moscow was then looking for the "keys to the East"; some believed they had found them in Turkestan, others in Mongolia and even in Tibet; a third group was convinced that events in Afghanistan would have a tremendous impact on the rest of Asia.[31] Generally speaking, the importance of Central Asia (i.e., Turkestan, Afghanistan, and Sinkiang) for the Eastern revolution was much overrated.

But the Sultan Galievs, Ryskulovs, and Efendievs were not alone in stressing the immense revolutionary potentialities of the world of Islam. At the Fourth Comintern Congress, the main report on the colonial question, given by a Dutchman, Ravesteyn,* makes fascinating reading even now. It was an incongruous performance, a speech with quotations from Shakespeare (*Henry V*) and Lothrop Stoddard rather than Marx and Lenin; one suspects that Ravesteyn had wandered into that society by mistake, and he was indeed to leave the movement very soon. But there he was in 1922 in the Kremlin, engaged in grandiose socio-political speculations and prognostications. In contrast to the West, he said, the Moslem world was capable of real unity, because Islam was much more than a religion. If World War I had not immediately led to a tremendous revolt in the Arab and Moslem world, this was because its leaders were cautious men who preferred not to hurry, and wanted to exploit the conflicts among their enemies. The West was decadent and in a process of disintegration, whereas the world of Islam was young and in the ascendant. In this great, historic struggle for the political libera-

---

* M. Willem van Ravesteyn subsequently made himself a name as a historian of the Socialist and Communist movement in Holland. After World War II he published a study of Jonathan Swift.

tion of the Islamic world, it was the duty of the world proletariat to give the Moslems moral and political support. The liberation of the world of Islam and the breaking of Europe's domination would not only benefit the Arabs and Moslems, but was also
in the best interests of the world proletariat. It would inevitably
lead to the victory of the revolution in Europe.[32]

This was undoubtedly sweet music to the ears of the Moslem
Communists, whose leader, Sultan Galiev, had just been arrested,
and whose ideology, Pan-Islamism, had just been anathematized
by the Party Congress. But Ravesteyn was a voice crying in an
otherwise anti-Islamic wilderness; the Communists had had sad
experiences with Enver and other self-appointed Pan-Islamic
leaders. Almost thirty years were to pass before some of these
ideas became acceptable.

5. The Emergence of Kemalism

Turkey was in very dire straits after World War I: an effective central government had ceased to exist, the non-Turkish
parts of the old Ottoman empire had split away, and even Anatolia was in the process of being occupied by British, French,
Greek, and Italian forces. In the summer of 1919, Turkish partisan groups started a small-scale war against the Entente forces,
and the initiative in this fight subsequently passed to Turkish
regular army units headed by Mustafa Kemal. In March, 1920, a
national assembly was convened in Ankara, beyond the reach of
the Allied forces. Soon after Mustafa Kemal took over, contacts
were established with the Soviet government, and there ensued
a fairly close collaboration that culminated in a treaty of friendship in March, 1921.

The official Soviet attitude towards Kemalist Turkey was
cordial at the beginning, but the ideological approach toward
this new and unfamiliar phenomenon was much more complex;
there was a wide spectrum of opinions, from appraisals that condemned Turkey outright as a "fascist power" to the most favorable judgments, demanding unqualified support for "progressive
Kemalism."[33]

Events in Turkey in 1919 were followed with the greatest
interest in Moscow. Efendiev foresaw that the Turks would ask

Russia for assistance, and another writer described Anatolia's struggle against England as progressive, although it was waged under the banner of Pan-Islamism.[34] Sultan Galiev extended his favorite thesis (about the absence of class differentiation in the East) to Turkey, and found the situation there encouraging on the whole.[35] In this there was remarkable unanimity between him and the Turkish nationalists; for a Kemalist representative at the Baku Congress also said that there were no feudal landowners, nor was there a strong bourgeoisie in his country. Turkish officers, in contrast to army officers elsewhere, were said to be "real proletarians."[36] The general mood in Turkey was reported to be completely favorable to an alliance with Russia; the population was expecting Tatar units of the Red Army to help them.[37] On the other hand, one of the bones of contention between Soviet Russia and Kemalist Turkey in the early days was the existence of a non-Communist Armenian state, which for a while caused considerable tension between the two. At one time, in the winter of 1920-21, some Soviet observers thought that the Kemalists would pass into the Entente camp. But this they attributed, at least in part, to Soviet diplomacy, which had lost six precious months in its negotiations with Ankara: "We should not have been influenced by those Dashnak Armenian views on Turkey." Pavlovich also shared this opinion.[38]

On the whole, Soviet observers did not know what to think of Kemal at first, and these hesitations and vacillations are reflected in Pavlovich's speeches and writings. "Kemal cannot be our faithful ally," he said at one time, stressing the temporary nature of the alliance with Ankara. On another occasion he bitterly complained that Kemal had done absolutely nothing at home, had introduced no reforms, and had only persecuted the local Communists, which explained his military defeats in the summer of 1921.[39] But in the same year (1921) he published a small book that at least one reviewer thought far too pro-Kemalist; was Pavlovich really unaware that nothing, absolutely nothing, had changed for the Turkish peasant and worker? Pavlovich did not recognize the validity of such criticism; Kemalist Turkey was objectively progressive, even revolutionary; and this appraisal remained valid even if the reactionary forces were ultimately to win the upper hand.[40] In 1924 Pavlovich went further and said that some progressive internal reforms had been achieved; he praised in particular Kemal's attempts to solve the national question. Pavlovich's chief assistant at the time, Gurko Kriazhin, took a less favorable view of the Turkish situation, and so the debate went on for years.[41] For a Soviet Communist, the main issue was the class character of the nationalist movement in Turkey. The struggle against the Entente was, of course, considered an extremely progressive course of action, worthy of support. But what would happen once this war of liberation was over? Obviously, national unity would no longer prevail, and the class character of Kemalism would emerge much more clearly. Or would the national movement perhaps split into several factions, each pressing conflicting interests? We know that the Soviet Union continued to support Kemal's statist reforms after the end of the war of liberation, and the explanation given was that such a policy suited Turkey's national interests and helped to keep imperialism out of the Middle East. But the Bolshevik leaders were not particularly enthusiastic about this development, despite the professions of sympathy, and more than once Lenin, Stalin, and others cited the case of Turkey as a revolution that had been "arrested" in the first stage of its development. If support for Turkey continued after 1923, the reasons were not mainly ideological; Turkey was then Russia's only ally in the East.

The whole issue was complicated, especially in the very early days, by the Communist problem in Turkey. Russia was unwilling to refrain from encouraging the Turkish Communists, whereas Kemal opposed the very existence of a Communist Party controlled by Moscow. For a time there existed an "official" Turkish Communist Party that stressed its specifically Turkish character and regarded Communism as a means to a greater aim—the glory and unity of the Turkish nation; it described its political program as "national collectivism." Such a program fitted in very well with the general political climate in Turkey at the time; Kemal himself (in a letter to Chicherin in November, 1920) had denounced the enslavement of both the workers of the West and the oppressed peoples of the East by international capitalism, and had stressed the necessity of overthrowing not only "criminal colonialism but the rule of the bourgeoisie in general."[42] He sounded almost like a Bolshevik, but the Soviets knew it was not the real thing, and while similar talk emanating from the Arab world thirty-five years later was enthusiastically received in Moscow, back in 1920 the Communist leaders looked coldly on this ambiguous solidarity. The Ankara Communists were denounced as fakers, police socialists, imitators of Zubatov, and so forth.[43]

The leaders of the young Turkish Communist Party met a sad fate; in January, 1921, Mustafa Subhi and fifteen of his aides were murdered in Trebizond. According to later Soviet historiography, this murder was planned and executed by "Kemalist gendarmes."[44] In contemporaneous Communist reports, however, the Turkish government is merely accused of not having taken the necessary steps to protect the lives of Subhi and his comrades, of "merely pretending to appear as the defenders of the Bolsheviks."[45] Trebizond, where the Communist leaders were murdered, is not very far from the Russian border, but it took almost ten weeks for the news to reach Baku, and longer to be published in the Soviet press. On March 16, seven weeks after the murder in Trebizond, a treaty of friendship was signed between the RSFSR and Turkey. Whether the news from Trebizond had been received before the middle of March, and whether it had been decided not to release it immediately, is a question of secondary interest. Moscow had to choose between backing the Turkish Communists and support for Kemal. All-out support for the Turkish Communists would have prejudiced their relations with Kemal, and this was clearly not in the best interests of the Soviet Union. So it was decided, with a heavy heart, no doubt, to ignore the Trebizond incident as far as Soviet policy toward Turkey was concerned. The Comintern periodicals and some other Soviet papers published protests against persecution of the Communists in Turkey, but relations between the two countries were not really affected. Some Soviet observers expressed the hope that after signing the treaty, Kemal would modify his attitude towards the Turkish Communists.[46] In these expectations, however, they were disappointed.

The decision to opt for Kemal, with all that it involved for the future of Turkish Communism, was not openly debated at the time in Moscow. But there can be no doubt that such discussions did in fact take place, and one can well imagine, in retrospect, the arguments for and against the decision.

6. Kuchik Khan and Khiabani

The Persian situation in 1918-20 resembled in some respects the state of affairs in Turkey, and the eventual rise to power of a dictator added a further parallel. But for a time Soviet observers were more concerned with events in Northern Persia than in Tehran. The revolutionary movements led by Kuchik Khan in Gilan and Shaikh Mohammed Khiabani in Persian Azerbaijan attracted considerable attention in the Soviet capital and were the subject of much comment. Unfortunately, reliable news about these movements was scarce, and as a result there are wide divergencies in the accounts given, quite apart from the seasonal changes in the political judgments passed on them between 1920 and the present day.

In the summer of 1919 the Soviet public was told for the first time of the existence of the "Forest Brethren" (Jangali), a revolutionary, anti-British movement in the Gilan district of northern Persia, headed by a group of men who had been in revolt against Tehran for several years. Its chances of success were considered to be excellent, despite the vagueness of its social program and its strong Islamic overtones.[47] (Some Western observers denied the political character of the movement and described it as a gang of highway robbers; this was undoubtedly an exaggeration.) In Moscow Kuchik Khan was said to represent the middle class and the "reformist clergy," whereas the left wing, supported by the lower middle class and the peasants, was headed by Ehsanolla. The Gilan movement suffered a temporary setback in January, 1920, but by May of that year the province was again up in arms. Up to this point, most contemporary witnesses and historians seem to be in agreement, but there is a great deal of conflicting evidence and confusion about the events that took place between May, 1920, and the autumn of 1921 when the Jangali were finally suppressed.[48] Until May, 1920, this had been a native rebellion almost entirely unaffected by outside factors, but after May, 1920, several new elements entered the picture. Soviet military forces under Raskolnikov had established contact with Kuchik's movement in Resht and Enzeli, and the newly founded (June, 1920) Persian Communist Party also began to collaborate with the Jangali. In late July the followers of the more radical Ehsanolla rebelled against Kuchik, and for a time took control, with the help of the Persian Communists, who had also come out against Kuchik. According to contemporary Soviet accounts, Moscow preferred Ehsanolla to Kuchik for the simple reason that the "former was closer to Communism," and this account was accepted for several years.[49] According to the version regarded now as orthodox, Ehsanolla was a "terrorist anarchist," and the Communists supporting him were Trotskyite traitors engaged in left-wing putschism. They wanted to introduce Communism in a country totally unprepared for it, and even tried to nationalize horse and camel saddles.[50] Most of the blame is put on Sultan zade; according to the current version, the Persian Communist leaders were ordered to come to Baku during the Congress of the peoples of the East (September, 1920), where the old leaders were replaced by a new group under Haidar Khan Amu-oglu.* This new leadership re-established the "national front" and the alliance with Kuchik.

From what we know from contemporary sources, this later version seems dubious. At the first Congress of the Persian Communist Party (Adalet) in Enzeli, Sultan zade declared that the time for a Communist revolution had not yet come, that the Communists would have to work with and inside the national

---

* According to recent Western studies and some Persian books, Sultan zade reappeared in Persia in the late thirties and, under the name of Jafar Pishevari, became the head of the short-lived Communist regime in Persian Azerbaijan in 1945-46. But Pishevari had worked as a journalist in Tehran in the early twenties, and was in prison in Persia in the early thirties (see his autobiographical sketch in *Azhir*, 15 Azar 1322 [1943]) while Sultan zade was active in Moscow. This version is, therefore, open to doubt. As far as can be ascertained, Sultan zade was executed in Moscow in or about 1935, having been in eclipse since 1931 for both leftist and rightist deviations. Pishevari escaped to Russia after the fall of his republic and was reported killed in a motor accident in Baku in 1948. According to current Soviet historiography, Sultan zade was a "traitor," whereas Pishevari is held in esteem.

movement and that there should be no attacks on the landowners and the bourgeoisie,[51] a policy that can hardly be defined as
left-wing deviationism and Trotskyism. When Ehsanolla's coup
took place, Sultan zade was not in Persia, and there is reason to
believe that he did not return to Gilan until after the Baku Congress, that is, after a new party executive had been appointed and
a new line adopted.[52] Several months later[53] the Persian Communists published new theses on the social and economic situation in Persia, in which a national front was recommended because a mass movement could not yet be based on an industrial
proletariat. It was also repeated that the revolution in Persia was
not yet on the agenda. But all this had been said before, and it
is difficult to discern any difference between the "new" and the
"old" line on Persia.

The descriptions of the end of the Gilan movement are
equally contradictory. According to Soviet sources in the
twenties, Haidar Khan, the new Communist leader, wanted to
overthrow Kuchik, and Kuchik, in self-defense, arrested Haidar.[54]
According to Soviet publications in the fifties, Kuchik, in collaboration with British agents and Persian reactionaries, "entered
the path of open betrayal and treachery." A counterrevolutionary
conspiracy was hatched and carried out, as a result of which
Haidar Khan and other leading Communists were killed.[55] Such
radically contradictory stories make it impossible to reconstruct
the Gilan debate; there obviously were differences of opinion
between the Persian Communist leaders about the tactics to be
followed, and there were conflicts between them and the non-
Communist groups in the Gilan movement. But we cannot be
certain what these issues really were and which leaders should
be identified with which tendency; personal quarrels and ambitions may have been as decisive as tactical or ideological issues.
It remains to be noted that Soviet sources in the twenties tended
to attribute much significance to the Gilan movement, which they
described as a genuine "revolution," a more advanced stage of
the social movement than the Persian revolution of 1906-09 (which
had been led by the upper classes). On the other hand, Soviet
historians today tend to describe the Jangali as a national liberation movement rather than a revolutionary party, and to play

down the importance of Gilan in comparison with the Tehran revolution a decade earlier.[56]

The revolt of Shaikh Mohammed Khiabani in Persian Azerbaijan in 1920 attracted less attention in Moscow, but the confusion surrounding it is, if possible, even worse confounded than that concerning Gilan. Discussions of the nature of the 1920 revolt in Tabriz continue to this day, and there is no agreement on essentials. One Soviet author, writing in 1952, noted Khiabani's attitude of distrust towards the Soviet Union, whereas another Soviet authority, writing in 1956, disputed this view and stressed the Shaikh's "love for Soviet Russia."[57] An early Soviet account (Vishnegradova in 1922) was on the whole approving, but a later appraisal (Ilinskii in 1934) described Khiabani as an "objective obstacle to a revolutionary mass movement." The current approach is more positive, though there is still a wide gulf between the praise lavished on him by Mamedli in 1948 and the rather cool approach displayed by M. S. Ivanov in 1952.

The Gilan and Shaikh Khiabani episodes have been introduced here in order to give some idea of the difficulties facing the historian. We have refrained from trying to put these various appraisals into historical perspective, and from attempting to find out which corresponds most closely to the truth. Neither Gilan nor Shaikh Khiabani is of sufficient intrinsic importance here to warrant independent investigation. Even if they were, it is doubtful whether the attempt would be successful; far too many of the essential sources are unavailable outside of the Soviet Union, and even Soviet historians have complained of the lack of some highly relevant material.[58] No doubt the two episodes will one day be subjected to definitive historical analysis; but this is unlikely under present political conditions.

7. Palestine, Zionism, and the Jews

Jewish problems figured prominently in Communist discussions both before and after the revolution. The Jewish "Bund" had once been the strongest and best-organized workers' organization in Russia, and this may have been the reason for the apparently exaggerated preoccupation with Jewish problems. Here we are not concerned with the Communist attitude toward

Russian Jewry or even Russian Zionism, but merely with Soviet policy on Palestine. Admittedly, this necessary limitation is somewhat artificial, for Communist (and Soviet) views on Palestine were, of course, connected with Soviet Jewish policy in general.

It is a matter of common knowledge that Communism from the very outset opposed the idea of Jewish settlement in Palestine. It is not so well known that Lenin, Trotsky, and Stalin shared this outlook with most Socialist leaders of the day, not only with Kautsky and the "Austro-Marxists," but also with many "revisionists." The general attitude towards Zionism was hostile, and the emigration of Jewish workers to Palestine was regarded as "desertion" from the battlefield of the class struggle. The "Bund," the largest Jewish working-class organization in Eastern Europe, was, if possible, even more anti-Zionist than the Bolsheviks—whatever their other political differences. And yet the vehemence with which Zionism was attacked in the Soviet Union in 1918 and 1919 is somewhat surprising; for those were the days when the Soviet leaders had more urgent preoccupations at home and abroad; why, at a time of grave military danger to the young Soviet republic, should they antagonize people who were not necessarily anti-Soviet? The reason was, presumably, that the anti-Zionist campaign was carried out by men and women who were themselves Jews and therefore much more involved, politically and emotionally, in intra-Jewish quarrels than their non-Jewish comrades, who regarded the whole issue as considerably less important.

Be that as it may, the ideological campaign against Zionism, and in particular against "Labor Zionism," was started in March, 1919, and went on for many years.[59] Dimanshtein, who was both the head of the "Jewish section" of the Party (established against the protests of many Jewish Party comrades), and the editor of the main Yiddish newspaper, as well as Stalin's aide in the Commissariat for Nationalities, particularly disliked the Zionists who wanted to compromise with Communism, namely the left-wing "Poale Zion."[60] Our Moses (Lenin), he predicted, will smash the golden calf. Turkey will become a Soviet republic and liberate Palestine from the British mandate and the Zionist occupation.[61] Pavlovich, writing on the "Zionist Lie and the Palestine

Reality," also took an unfriendly view of Zionist projects in Palestine, but also talked about "pogroms" in Palestine (it was the time of the first Arab-Jew clashes). Generally speaking, Soviet Communist observers, however hostile to the idea of a Jewish Palestine, showed little fondness for the Arabs. One commentator on the 1920 clashes said that "it [was] to the credit of the British that they rejected the Arab ultimatum to deport the Zionist leaders, despite the fact that the Arabs threatened pogroms."[62] This use of the term pogrom was later severely criticized; "national revolutionary struggle" would have been a far better designation, it was said in 1929. But even if the Soviet authorities tolerated a "Communist-Zionist" party in the Soviet Union up to the late twenties, all those in authority in Moscow agreed that Zionism was a reactionary movement, by means of which the big Jewish capitalists planned to exploit their proletarian coreligionists. It was reactionary, too, in wanting to turn back the wheel of history and to establish a national state at a time when the whole world was progressing towards internationalism. It was also reactionary because it served as a tool of British imperialism.

A resolution condemning Zionist activities in Palestine was adopted by the Second Congress of the Comintern in 1920. In the short discussion which preceded its adoption, Ester Frumkin, a former Bundist, demanded a determined struggle against Zionism, that "lie without precedent." She was supported by another speaker (Merezhin),[63] but a group of left-wing Zionists at the Congress made a brave attempt to stem the tide. While dissociating himself completely from "bourgeois Zionism," its spokesman described Zionist Socialism as a progressive and revolutionary movement. Before being reminded by the chairman that his time was running out, he managed to ask some awkward questions: why did the Comintern so bitterly oppose proletarian Zionism when it gave its support to the Emir of Fezzan and similar medieval characters who practiced the worst forms of slavery in their lands?[64]

After 1921 the Palestine debate subsided. It went on within Jewish institutions, but the party leaders, including those in charge of Eastern affairs, were occupied with more urgent problems. The general line remained that "Zionism meant terrible exploitation"; the Jewish proletarians in Palestine, unfortunately not very numerous, were called to put an end to this "phantom."[65] Palestine in those years was a fairly quiet country, not very important even by Middle Eastern standards. As far as the Soviet Union was concerned, Palestine for a while faded from the map; it reappeared only in 1929, with the Arab riots and the debates on the tactics of Palestinian Communism.

8. Pan-Islamism, Pan-Turanianism, Pan-Arabism

The young Soviet republic had to face the Eastern "pan-movements" in both domestic and foreign policy: in the Tatar regions and Turkestan at home, and in both the Middle East and Southeast Asia. The dual character of the issues apparently made it difficult to reach conclusions, and there were considerable differences of opinion on how to approach these movements; Soviet policy during the first decade after the revolution was not entirely consistent.

At first glance, the question seemed very simple: Pan-Islamism was unacceptable because it desiderated the union of various peoples and states under the banner of Islam. And Islam, like all other religions, was reactionary in Soviet eyes. Pan-Turanianism was even more reprehensible, for it would have entailed the secession of certain areas from the Soviet Union. Pan-Arabism was perhaps less dangerous, for it did not directly affect Soviet interests.[66]

But from the point of view of Soviet tactics in the East, the issue was far more intricate. These "ideological remnants of the past" (as they were described) were still deeply rooted in the East; would not the Soviet Union antagonize potentially revolutionary movements by a frontal attack on their most cherished beliefs? Would it not perhaps drive them into the camp of imperialism?

The Comintern's treatment of these problems reflected these doubts. True enough, Zinoviev had declared at the Baku Congress that "Pan-Islamism is not our movement." The Second Comintern Congress, several weeks before, had agreed that the Pan-Islamic movement should be fought, because it aimed at combining the struggle for national liberation with efforts to consolidate the power of Turkish imperialism and the rule of the big landowners, the clergy, etc.[67] Two years later the Comintern again debated Pan-Islamism, and several speakers, such as the Indonesian Communist leader Tan Malakka, came out squarely for collaboration with these groups. Pan-Islamism, he said, was a national struggle for liberation, because Islam was everything to a Moslem—not just religion but state, economy, food. This national liberation struggle by all oppressed Moslem peoples was directed against world capitalism and should, therefore, be supported wholeheartedly.[68] The resolutions adopted by the Fourth Comintern Congress on this issue did not revoke the former decisions, but slightly moderated them. Pan-Islamism, it was now argued, was merely the first ideological expression of the national movement in the East. Subsequently, with the growth and expansion of the national liberation movement, these religio-political slogans would be replaced by more concrete political demands.[69]

Inside Russia the issue was bedeviled by the very complex relationship between Moscow and the Turkestan Communists, whose "ideological weakness" was the subject of frequent complaints by the Russian comrades. Most of them were Pan-Turanians to some degree, and though Moscow combatted these tendencies, it was apparently believed that the time for a frontal assault had not yet come. Stalin had condemned the "reactionary character" of Pan-Islamism, and the "aggressive, chauvinistic content" of Pan-Turkism. Both movements, he stated, had been used by counterrevolutionary elements in the struggle against Soviet rule.[70] But it was only at the Communist Party Congress in 1923 that the two "pan-movements" were officially declared "deviations toward bourgeois-democratic nationalism." For some time after that Congress, it continued to be considered a venial sin: "If Sultan Galiev had confined himself to the ideology of Pan-Turkism and Pan-Islamism, it would not have been so bad," Stalin said on one occasion. "I would have said that this ideology might be tolerated in spite of the veto laid on it . . ."[71] A lesser interpreter of the official line stated in 1928 that despite the reactionary character of the Eastern "pan-movements" they could in certain conditions contribute to the struggle against imperialism.[72]

Pan-Islamism and Pan-Turkism were usually lumped together
(and still are), which hampers ideological clarification, for there
are, of course, great differences between the two. Pan-Turkism
gradually ceased to be a major political issue, for the Turkish
government, from Kemal Ataturk onward, did not indulge in
dreams of a great Turanian empire. The theme was occasionally
revived in the Soviet Union, but mainly for domestic purposes,
such as the purges in the Central Asian republics in 1937-38, and
again in 1948-52 in connection with alleged local national deviations. The problem of Pan-Islamism, on the other hand, continued to exist, though in a form somewhat different from that of
the early years, when it had meant mainly the re-establishment
of the Caliphate. We shall return to this subject when discussing
Soviet attitudes toward Islam.

Pan-Arabism was at the time the least important of these three
Eastern movements; even the name had not yet gained wide currency. Some early Soviet observers (such as Gurko Kriazhin)
tended to regard it as a positive trend and predicted a great
future for Pan-Arabism.[73] Others were less enthusiastic, and de-
plored both its Moslem chauvinism and its lack of a clear social
program. It was said to be split into pro-British and pro-French
wings, at least in its early days, and there was a widespread suspicion that the whole movement was a tactical maneuver of
reactionary forces.[74] Greater interest in the movement for Arab
unity began to emerge only in the late twenties.

9. 1921: The Interim Balance

Addressing the Baku town Soviet on the third anniversary of
the revolution, Stalin presented a rather optimistic picture of the
prospects of the revolution in the East: three years previously
in the East there had been only indifference to the revolution.
Now the East was in motion, and a whole series of liberation
movements directed against imperialism had come into existence.[75]
Nobody in Moscow had hoped for a revolutionary movement in
Asia that would also be Communist in character. But it was generally expected that within the national movement the left wing
would gradually take over, and the national movement would
then turn into a social revolution. By 1921 it was obvious that

this process had been arrested and that the Kemals, Reza Shahs and Amanullahs were the best Moscow could expect for some time to come.

Soviet interest in Asia in 1918-19 had been limited; in 1920, following setbacks in Europe and news about revolutionary ferment in the East, it showed a marked rise. But by 1921 the trend in the East, as well as in the West, was again toward consolidation. The ebbing of the revolutionary wave did not come as a great shock to Moscow; no undue expectations had been attached to it, and there was no acute disappointment when the revolutionary movement in the East failed to make rapid progress. The sincere and emphatic efforts of the Soviet leaders to dissociate themselves from traditional Tsarist foreign policy had made a favorable impression in the East. The immediate impact of the Russian revolution was limited, but the delayed effect was considerable. While the first revolutionary stirrings in 1920 were followed by years of stagnation, the groundwork, however fragmentary, had already been prepared for future collaboration between the Soviet Union and the national revolutionary movement in the East.

NOTES

1. In a report to the 15th conference of the Communist Party of the Soviet Union, *Biulleten* I (Moscow, 1926), p. 25.

2. A quotation from the poet Andrei Beli. I. P. Trainin in *Zh.N.* 14 (149), June, 1922.

3. G. Safarov, "Vostok i Revoliutsiia" in *K.I.* 15, 1920, p. 3128 *et seq*. See also his *Problemy Vostoka*, (Petrograd, 1922).

4. Engels to Kautsky, Sept. 12, 1882, in Bened. Kautsky (ed.): *Friedrich Engels' Briefwechsel mit Karl Kautsky* (Vienna, 1955), p. 63.

5. J. Clive Room, "Lenin's Eastern Dreams" in *Near East*, April 10, 1919.

6. Herbert Mueller in *Der Neue Orient*, Vol. V (1919), No. 1-2, p. 72.

7. Joseph Stalin: *Marxism and the National and Colonial Question* (London, 1936), p. 174.

8. More biographical details about Pavlovich can be found in his autobiographical sketch written for *Entsiklopedicheskii Slovar Granat*, Vol. XLI, in the obituaries by Chicherin, Ioffe, Rafail, and others in *N.V.* 18, 1926, and by Shestakov in *Istorik Marksist* 4, 1927.

9. *N.V.* 1, 1922, p. 16 *et seq*.

10. For further details about this debate see the protocols of the Second Congress of the Comintern and Allen S. Whiting, *Soviet Policies in China 1917-1924* (New York, 1954), pp. 42-58.

11. *Protokoll des Zweiten Weltkongresses der Kommunistischen Internationale* (Hamburg, 1921), p. 140.

12. *Ibid.*, p. 146.

13. *Ibid.*, p. 169.

14. *Ibid.*

15. See Sultan Galiev, "Sotsialnaia Revoliutsiia i Vostok" in *Zh.N.* 36, 39, 42, 1919, and Efendiev, "Revoliutsionnye Perspektivy v Persii," in *Zh.N.* (November 1, 1920).

16. *Pervyi S'ezd Narodov Vostoka. Stenograficheskie Otchëty* (Moscow, 1920), p. 87.

17. *Ibid.*, p. 169.

18. *Ibid.*, p. 72.

19. Quoted in *Zh.N.* 14 (149), June, 1922.

20. *K.I.* 15, 1920, p. 3367.

21. *Ibid.*, p. 3796.

22. M. N. Ivanova in *S.V.* 3, 1955, p. 346 *et seq.*

23. *Zh.N.* 41 (97), December 24, 1920. See also Safarov's reply in *Pravda*, July 16, 1921.

24. Lenin, *Sochineniia*, Vol. XXV, p. 354.

25. *Sotsialisticheskii Vestnik* 13, 1928, p. 5.

26. *Dokumenty Vneshnei Politiki SSSR*, Vol. I (Moscow, 1957), pp. 34-35. See also Trotsky's note to the Persian ambassador in Moscow in January, 1918, declaring the 1907 treaty with Britain concerning the division of Persia null and void. *Ibid.*, pp. 9-12.

27. K. M. Troianovskii: *Vostok i Revoliutsia* (Moscow, 1918). V. A. Gurko Kriazhin: *Sumerki Vostoka* (Moscow, 1918).

28. S. D. Navshirvanov in *N.V.* 4, p. 274 *et seq.*

29. Prof. D. Anuchin in *N.V.* 1, p. 248 *et seq.*

30. In *Zh.N.* 10 (16), May 19, 1922. According to a much later source ("Avigdor" in *R.V.* 6, 1934, p. 65), most of the members of the party in the early period were foreigners.

31. On the supposed importance of Mongolia and Tibet see *Zh.N.* 19 (27), 1919. On Turkestan as a "jumping board for India," *Zh.N.* 17 (25), 1919. On Afghanistan as a "revolutionary nucleus," *Ibid.*

32. *IV Vsemirnyi Kongress Kommunisticheskogo Internatsionala. Izbrannye Doklady, Rechi; Rezoliutsiia* (Moscow-Petrograd, 1923), p. 221 *et seq.*

33. For the "fascist" thesis, see Arslan: *Sovremennaia Turtsiia* (1923); for pronounced pro-Kemalist views, G. Astakhov: *Ot Sultanata k Demokraticheskoi Turtsii* (Moscow, 1926).

34. Efendiev in *Zh.N.* 40 (48), 1919. Sherk Ogly in *Zh.N.*, April 27, 1920.

35. Sultan Galiev in *Zh.N.*, May 23, 1920.

36. Bagardin Shakir in *Pervyi S'ezd Narodov Vostoka* . . . , p. 77.

37. Unsigned report from Turkey, *Zh.N.*, December 2, 1920.

38. A. Sachko in *Zh.N.*, December 8, 1920.

39. M. Pavlovich-Volonter: *Voprosy Kolonialnoi-Natsionalnoi Revoliutsii i Treti Internatsional* (Moscow, 1921), p. 63, and *Zh.N.*, September 16, 1921.

40. M. Pavlovich: *Revoliutsionaia Turtsiia* (1921). See the critical review of Inal Butaev in *Zh.N.*, March 29, 1922, and Pavlovich's reply, *ibid.*

41. See V. A. Gurko Kriazhin: *Blizhny Vostok i Derzhavy* (Moscow, 1925).

42. *Izvestiia*, December 5, 1920. This letter has frequently been reprinted in the Soviet press in recent years—for obvious reasons.

43. M. Pavlovich and Others: *Turtsiia v Borbe za Nezavisimost* (Moscow, 1925), pp. 95-104.

44. *Noveishaia Istoriia Stran Zarubezhnogo Vostoka*, Vol. I (1954), p. 283.

45. Jevad's letter to Pavlovich, originally published in *K.I.* 17, 1921 reproduced in M. Pavlovich and Others: *Turtsiia* . . . , p. 106.

46. M. Pavlovich, *ibid.*, p. 109, and Karl Radek in *Izvestiia*, July 27, 1922.

47. *Zh.N.* 19 (27), 1919. Article by "Ips."

48. There is a detailed comparison of some of the Soviet sources on Gilan in *Central Asian Review*, Vol. IV (1956), No. 3, pp. 303-316 and Vol. IV, No. 4, p. 403.

49. R. Abikh in *N.V.*, 26-27, 1929, and 29, 1929.

50. M. S. Ivanov: *Ocherk Istorii Irana* (Moscow, 1952), p. 266 *et seq.* M. N. Ivanova in *S.V.* 3, 1955.

51. *Die Kommunistische Internationale* No. 14, 1921, p. 2939. On the first Persian Party Congress in Enzeli, see also A. Sultan zade: *Sovremennaia Persia* (Moscow, 1922), pp. 59-60.

52. *Noveishaia Istoriia* . . . Vol. I, p. 258.

53. *Zh.N.* 17 (103), March 17, 1921. These resolutions had been adopted in October, 1920.

54. "Irandust" in *Istorik Marksist* 5, 1927.

55. M. N. Ivanova, *loc. cit.*

56. As shown by a comparison between the studies of Sultan zade and Irandust, on the one hand, and M. S. Ivanov or M. N. Ivanova, on the other.

57. Sh. A. Tagieva: *Natsionalno-Osvoboditelnoe Dvizhenie v Iranskom Azerbaidzhane v 1917-1920 godakh* (Baku, 1956), p. 7. The other relevant Soviet sources quoted are articles by A. Vishnegradova (*N.V.* 2, 1922) and G. Ilinskii (*R.V.* 6, 1934) and the book of G. Mamedli: *Khiabani* (Baku, 1949—in Azerbaijani) and the history of Persia by M. S. Ivanov, quoted above.

58. Tagieva complains that she could not obtain access to Khiabani's program and the newspaper of his movement *Tadjadod*.

59. *Zh.N.* 16, March 9, 1919. Dimanshtein in *Zh.N.* 24 (32) and 25 (33), 1919.

60. Dimanshtein in *Zh.N.* 24 (32) and 25 (33), 1919.

61. Dimanshtein in *Zh.N.* 26 (34) and July 13, 1919.

62. *N.V.* 1, 1922, p. 79.

63. *Protokoll des Zweiten Weltkongresses der Kommunistischen Internationale* (Hamburg, 1921), pp. 198, 204.

64. *Ibid.*, p. 209.

65. V. A. Gurko Kriazhin: *Blizhny Vostok i Derzhavy* (Moscow, 1925), p. 242.

66. For some early views see M. N., "Pod Znakom Islama," in *N.V.* 4, 1923, p. 72, and articles in *Zh.N.*, Jan. 13, 1921, and March 22, 1922 (by Sherif Manatov).

67. *Vtoroi Kongress Kominterna*, pp. 494-95.

68. *Protokoll des Vierten Kongresses der Kommunistischen Internationale*, pp. 188-89.

69. *Kommunisticheski Internatsional v Dokumentakh*, p. 318.

70. I. V. Stalin, *Sochineniia*, Vol. V, p. 403.

71. Joseph Stalin: *Marxism and the National and Colonial Question*, p. 176.

72. M. G. Galkovich: *Vostok i SSSR* (Moscow, 1928), p. 113.

73. V. A. Gurko Kriazhin: *Blizhny Vostok i Derzhavy*, p. 243.

74. L. S. Nekora in *N.V.* 7, 1925, p. 127 *et seq.*

75. Stalin, *Sochineniia*, Vol. IV, p. 393.

CHAPTER TWO

A QUIET INTERLUDE: 1921-1928

1. *Socialism in One Country and the Asian Revolution*

It was in 1924 that Stalin formulated his theory of the construction of socialism in one country, but it had already been obvious since 1921 (and the events in Germany in 1923 only confirmed this) that the "capitalist world" had, for the time being, overcome its crisis and surmounted both the political and economic upheavals in the West and the colonial tensions in the East. Soviet Communists continued to follow with passionate interest the course of events in the outside world, but no longer expected events of great revolutionary significance to occur in the near future, as most had done in 1919 and 1920. There were important developments in Russia: the NEP and the struggle for power between various factions of the Communist Party; in the late twenties, agriculture was collectivized, and the first five-year plan was set in motion. Henceforth attention was chiefly focused on the Soviet home front. Roy and other Asian Communists continued to complain that not enough was being done by the Russian comrades about the Asian revolution.

But what could have been done? In 1921 the Communist University of the Toilers of the East had been founded; by the end of that year it already had more than 700 students of many nationalities and continued to grow.[1] At Comintern Congresses and on other occasions, the problems of the Asian revolution continued to be debated. Everyone now agreed that it had become more difficult to generalize about the East: the tactics to be followed in a very backward colonial country without an industrial proletariat would necessarily have to differ from the political line in more developed Eastern lands. Roy thought that groups and movements that had been potential allies in 1919 could no longer be regarded in this light in 1924. Referring to Turkey, he said that the bourgeoisie and the feudal military clique might temporarily take over the leadership of the national revolutionary movement, but sooner or later they would "inevitably betray its cause and pass to the counterrevolutionary camp."[2] If the Communists would not train their own "cadres," the victory of the national revolutionary movement would become highly problematical.

During these years there was an almost universal lack of appreciation of the potential role of the intelligentsia in the national movement in the East, and a general unwillingness among the Bolsheviks to take advantage of the great appeal of nationalist slogans. Safarov, summarizing the discussions at the Fourth Comintern Congress, complained bitterly about the strength of nationalist influence among the young workers in Asia, which made it so difficult for the Communists to find adherents. He suggested that although the intelligentsia had an important part to play in the initial stages of the working-class movement, Communists could make real headway only after outgrowing this early phase.[3] He mentioned favorably the Egyptian Communist movement for having broken with the "careerists of the intelligentsia." Roy was similarly pessimistic about the revolutionary potentialities of the national movement in the East, but even those who charged him with "nihilism à la Rosa Luxemburg on the national question" had no real alternative to offer. Like Manuilskii,[4] they pointed to the pitfalls to be avoided: Communists should not shun contact with the national movements in such countries as China, Indonesia, or Egypt, since this would mean losing contact with the masses. They should not cooperate too closely, either, because this would blur the differences between the Communists and other parties. This was very good advice, but what did it mean in practice? According to Stalin, the Communists in a country like China or Egypt had to pass from the policy of a united national front to that of a revolutionary bloc of the workers and the petty bourgeoisie.[5] This was all very well, but it did not work even in China, where the Communists were relatively strong; in Egypt such a policy could not even be contemplated.

According to some of the Comintern strategists, the main difference between the national movement in Egypt and Turkey was that in Turkey it had come to power on the crest of a revolutionary wave from below, while in Egypt it had been a "revolution from above." Consequently, the Turkish movement was more "progressive"; about the Wafd everyone was rather caustic, and Roy said that Zaghlul had broken the world record for revolutionary phrases. But the Turkish movement was also more dangerous, because it had misled the Turkish Communists into cooperating far too closely with Kemal.[6] In a country like Morocco, without an industrial proletariat, there was no alternative to supporting the national front. Commenting on Abd el-Kader's revolt, Zinoviev and Ioffe observed that these movements were not without importance, because they gave fresh impetus to world revolution. By themselves, such colonial movements could not be successful, of course, but they would succeed in cooperation with the international working-class movement.[7] This collaboration between the party of the proletariat in the West and the revolutionary movement in the East was apparently not so close as it should have been, for there were continual complaints by Asian delegates about the inadequate assistance given by the European comrades. There was even worse—revelations of "social imperialism" among European Communists. In 1923, for instance, when the Comintern had issued a special appeal summoning the colonial slaves to rise against their masters, the Communist branch in Sidi-bel-Abbès in North Africa had denounced this appeal as an act of sabotage against France's civilizing mission in North Africa. Such incidents apart, everybody seemed to agree that there ought to be a measure of collaboration between the Communists and the national movement in Asia, especially its radical (or "lower middle class") wing. In relatively developed Eastern countries, such as India, the bourgeoisie was to be fought, because its upper, compromising section had already managed to come to terms with imperialism. But these were exceptional cases: by and large, the emphasis was on cooperation, while the specific character of the Communist parties was maintained. In practice, the cooperation frequently tended to be closer than envisaged, for the Communist movement was still small and weak everywhere in Asia, and could not yet negotiate with the national movement as an equal partner; if it wanted to be accepted at all, it had to make concessions.

Some Soviet leaders realized that there was not much sense in trying to split ideological hairs about the precise form and character of the coming revolution in Asia. They were firmly convinced that this revolution would eventually come, but they also felt sure that it would not happen in the immediate future, and that it would be quite different from the European experience. Talking to the teachers and students of the University of the Toilers of the East, Bukharin said in 1926 that this would be "an entirely original form of state power"; a new and original form of the nationalization of the key positions in the national economy. "This will not be, and indeed cannot be, a repetition of what happened in the Soviet Union." Bukharin expressed his belief that there were no historical precedents for the coming Asian revolution and that in view of its peculiarities and of the uselessness of any rigid, preconceived scheme, it was virtually impossible to make predictions—except that the coming revolution in the East would differ from all previous revolutions.[9]

2. Reza Khan and Amanullah

In the chaotic Persia of 1920 it was merely a question of time before the providential strong man would take over. The expected *coup d'état* came in February, 1921, when Reza Khan, a colonel in the Cossack Division, assisted Sayyed Ziauddin to come to power. For some years Reza ruled from behind the scenes, but he gradually legalized his dictatorship and, late in 1925, established himself as the new Shah and the founder of the Pahlavi dynasty.

The Soviet appraisal of Reza Khan has undergone marked changes since he first appeared on the political scene in 1921. At first he was enthusiastically acclaimed as a true national hero, with the dissenters in the minority. After 1926-27 the Soviet attitude became cooler and more reserved, and since the early thirties it has been almost entirely negative and hostile, mitigated only by diplomatic considerations during the lifetime of the late Reza Khan. The changes reflected the gradual disappointment of the

high hopes that had at first been fixed on the new ruler of
Persia.

Despite the Gilan revolt and Shaikh Khiabani's movement,
Soviet observers in the early years were not optimistic about the
prospects of the revolutionary movement in Persia. One commentator said that even if the democratic revolution were to win
out, the victory would not be complete because the left-wing
forces were too weak and the country as a whole was too backward. Another expert stressed the firm hold of the ruling classes,
which he thought was stronger than in any other Eastern country.[10] A third observer warned his readers against attributing too
much importance to the workers' organizations in Persia; while
there were such groups, they mostly continued the tradition of
medieval guilds, which reduced their political value.[11]

Moscow was agreeably surprised when Reza Khan came to
power, for he was believed to head a national revolutionary
movement similar to Kemal's in Turkey. His coup was hailed as
a "historic event"; the Persians were said to be right in considering Reza a "national hero, for his reign [marked] the beginning
of a new era."[12] The military dictatorship, it was assumed, would
be a transient stage toward a national, republican regime.[13] This
optimism was based not merely on such progressive but superficial measures as Reza's expulsion of foreign military advisers.
Some leading Soviet students of Middle Eastern affairs, such as
Gurko Kriazhin,* believed they had uncovered important social
and economic trends that gave cause for optimism. Deep trans-
formations had taken place in Persia after World War I, and the
archaic national ideology was disappearing, they said. Reza's rule
was based on three social groups: the big landowners, whose
position had, however, been weakened; the bourgeoisie; and the

---

* Gurko Kriazhin was Pavlovich's main aide; he published several books
and a great number of articles on Middle Eastern topics in the early
twenties. He first appeared as a student of Eastern affairs with *Belaia
Opasnost* (The White Danger, Moscow, 1914) in which he argued, notably
influenced by Tolstoy, that East is East and West is West, and that a doctrine like socialism, based entirely on reason, had no future in Asia. After
1918 he closely followed the Bolshevik line. His downfall came in 1930
when he was attacked as an "objective apologist of imperialism" (L. Mamet
in *Istorik Marksist*, 17, 1930, pp. 69-85).

"national army," whose influence had increased and who had become more "progressive."[14]

Such an unduly favorable appraisal invited contradiction, and the first "Persian Discussion" started in 1926. (There was a second "Persian Discussion" in the early thirties, which dealt with the revolution of 1906-08 rather than current affairs.) Gurko Kriazhin was said to have greatly exaggerated the progressive and liberal character of Reza Khan's movement; there was no significant industrial or agricultural progress, nor had a "modern bourgeoisie" come into being. The army was not an independent social group but an instrument of the old ruling class. All in all, Reza Khan was portrayed by the dissidents as a rather unsuccessful imitator of Napoleon III.[15] However, Gurko Kriazhin did not give in easily, despite the fact that meanwhile Reza had himself appointed Shah, which made it difficult to maintain the old thesis about the progressive republicanization of his regime. Kriazhin now thought that even if part of the "progressive bourgeoisie" had capitulated, Reza's movement as a whole had not become reactionary.[16] The general impression in Moscow at the time was that Reza Khan was, after all, different from, and presumably better than, a "bourgeois monarch."[17]

After 1927, however, Reza Khan lost favor in Moscow; from then on, the line was that he had originally carried out some progressive measures but had soon retreated from this course and had established a reactionary regime. After 1929, the Soviet attitude became even more negative: Reza Khan was then said to have attained power by "betrayal and lies," and with the assistance of British imperialism; his regime was described as representing the interests of the biggest landowners and the most reactionary circles.[18]

This negative approach has not changed to the present day. Even those of Reza's reforms that would appear to be innocent enough from the Soviet point of view are disapproved of: the emancipation of women is explained as an attempt to obtain cheap labor for the factories[19] and even the measures restraining the influence of the Islamic clergy are criticized.[20] As for Reza's foreign policy, the version claiming that he came to power as a British agent is maintained,[21] and he is accused of obstructing a closer *rapprochement* between the Soviet Union and Persia. His plans for a "Greater Iran," composed of Persia and certain Soviet territories in Turkestan and Transcaucasia, are sharply denounced. These ideological condemnations did not, however, prevent the Soviet Union from maintaining fairly close relations with Persia in various fields up to the middle thirties. Generally speaking, official relations with Persia never deteriorated as they did with Turkey, although Kemalism always appeared to Soviet observers as the more advanced movement. If Kemalism was called a national revolutionary movement that had been arrested during the first stage of its development, Reza Khan would presumably be described as having stopped short even of the first stage.

Amanullah, who ruled Afghanistan from 1919 to 1929, had a better press in Moscow than the first of the Pahlavis. Early Soviet attempts to "reach the masses" in Afghanistan in 1918-19, organized in a rather haphazard way, had produced no results,[22] but when Amanullah came to power as the head of the Young Afghan party, which stood for internal reform and an anti-British foreign policy, expectations rose in Moscow. A treaty of friendship was concluded with Kabul, and Amanullah received a yearly grant; Lenin himself praised the treaty between the "two great peoples," Stalin called Amanullah objectively more progressive than the British Labour party, and there were articles in the Soviet press about the great significance of Afghanistan for the world revolution.[23] Amanullah, who, in a letter to Lenin, had declared his willingness to help spread the revolution in the East, went on a visit to Moscow—the first foreign head of state to do so. The Afghan-British wars in 1919-20 brought a further *rapprochement* between Kabul and Moscow, and the head of the Afghan mission in the RSFSR declared that the proletarian revolution in Russia had brought enormous advantages to the Moslem world and to the exploited East in general.[24]

Amanullah's internal reforms were described at the time as far-reaching, affecting all spheres of life and of great service to the people.[25] His foreign policy was praised almost without reservation. There had been some tension between the two countries in the early twenties over Afghan support for Enver, the Emir

of Bukhara, and the Basmachi. But a contemporary Soviet observer said there was never any danger of armed conflict, for the
Soviet leaders understood that Afghanistan's main enemy was
England, and they were therefore willing to negotiate and compromise.[26] The crisis in Soviet-Afghan relations was eventually
overcome after the death of Enver and the defeat of the Basmachi.

Amanullah, who had perhaps spent too much time outside his
country, was overthrown as the result of a series of revolts that
started in November, 1928; he was deposed in January, 1929.
The first Soviet reaction was to charge the British, and in particular the "notorious adventurer T. E. Lawrence" (at that time
an RAF private in India) with responsibility for these events,[27]
but subsequent comments were more restrained. The revolt
against Amanullah had been reactionary, even if the peasants had
taken part in it. But why had Amanullah failed? Was it not
largely his own fault—had he not removed from power and
responsibility all the sirdars that were capable of ruling?[28] Raskolnikov, who had some first-hand knowledge of the country, went
even further and said that from the start Amanullah's reforms had
been inherently defective; they had been devoid of an economic
basis. In themselves they had been highly progressive, but they
were superficial and of no real benefit to the peasant. While
opposed to feudalism, Amanullah had been reluctant to carry out
a real, comprehensive land reform. In other words, Amanullah
had lacked a social and political basis for his reforms. Much of
this could be explained, not by reference to the shortcomings of
the king, but to the backwardness of the country. Kemal, in
Turkey, had been in a much better position from the very beginning.[29] These views are shared on the whole by later Soviet
historians; there have been no important changes in the appraisal
of the historical role of Amanullah.[30]

Amanullah's reign was followed by a lengthy period of civil
war. One of the chief contestants was Batcha-i-Sakao, a military
leader whom contemporary Soviet sources described as reactionary, and who is now simply dismissed as a tool of British imperialism.[31] Eventually power passed into the hands of Nadir
Khan, a former general and Afghan envoy to France, and the
father of the present King of Afghanistan. At first Moscow was

cautiously optimistic about Nadir Khan; it was believed that he would continue Amanullah's foreign policy. Apparently basing himself on semiofficial information, one commentator wrote, "We are in possession of information to the effect that Nadir Khan will pursue internal and foreign policies in accordance with the cause of Afghan independence."[32] These Soviet hopes were not realized, and later observers came to regard Nadir Khan as a "reactionary and cruel ruler" who re-established the privileges of the feudal chiefs and the clergy, and collaborated with British imperialism.[33]

3. Turkey after the War of Liberation

Following the military victories of Kemal's army, Asia Minor again became Turkish in the autumn of 1922, and the Lausanne Conference in the summer of 1923 restored peace to the Near East. Some Soviet observers had been dubious about the prospects of Kemal's movement: according to a Turkish left-wing paper quoted in *Novyi Vostok*, civil war would soon follow the war of independence.[34] Others were skeptical about the prospects of the Communist movement in Turkey: the self-styled Socialist and Social-Democratic groups were said to be merely gangs of adventurers, while the "Spartacists," a Constantinople left-wing group, were said to be preoccupied with theory rather than revolutionary practice.[35] But these were apparently minority views; the Narkomindel certainly had an open mind with regard to Kemalism, and most other experts were sympathetic. The abolition of the Sultanate and certain other reforms in the economic, educational, and administrative fields made a good impression in Moscow, and the general opinion was that Kemal and his government sincerely tried to get rid of both "Western ideological alignments" and financial dependence on the imperialistic powers. In the disputes between Kemal and his domestic foes in the middle twenties, Soviet opinion was almost unreservedly pro-Kemal.[36] Turkish foreign policy was also described in a highly favorable light: Ankara was the "center of all oppressed Eastern peoples"; diplomatic relations between Turkey and China, Persia, and other Asian nations had been strengthened. Turkey's prestige in the Arab world had increased, and even Ibn Saud had invited the

Kemalists to the (Pan-Islamic) Mecca Congress despite the "dis-establishment" of Islam in Turkey.[37] It was only after the Sixth Congress of the Comintern and the general change in Communist policy that the ideologists had second thoughts about Kemal. But even in 1930 some of the Soviet Middle Eastern experts con-tinued to believe that Kemal should be supported against his domestic adversaries; one wing of the Turkish bourgeoisie had gradually become pro-imperialist, but Kemalism as a whole, and especially its left wing, still had revolutionary potentialities.[38] However, even the pro-Kemal commentators in Moscow ad-mitted, more in sorrow than in anger, that Kemalism was in retreat before what they called an "imperialist onslaught"; it had once been a progressive movement, but it had not been able to complete the bourgeois revolution.* In the full-scale debate on Kemalism which followed, the general tenor of comment veered from mere criticism to open hostility, which, nevertheless, did not affect diplomatic and economic relations between the two countries. Subsequent fluctuations in Soviet-Turkish rela-tions greatly affected Soviet historiography about the early period of Kemalism. Books and articles published in the Soviet Union between 1940 and 1955 display, as a rule, unmitigated hostility toward Kemal's reforms. In one textbook Kemalist policy in the twenties is summarized as follows: "Mortally afraid of their own people, the Kemalists most cruelly suppressed even the slightest manifestation of a democratic movement, not to speak of the class struggle of the workers and peasants. They stamped out without mercy the liberation movement of the non-Turkish nationalities. The exploiting nature of their rule inevitably made the Kemalists enter an alliance with the 'compradores' and the landowners."[39] This was the official line, and the few publica-

* There was strong feeling in Comintern circles in 1927 about the per-secution of Communists in Turkey. "The Kemalist leaders are completely under the spell of Anglo-French imperialist intrigues to detach Turkey from the Soviet Union. . . . The friendship between the Soviet Union and Turkey is losing all significance in the face of the suppression of the workers' movement," wrote Ali Risa, stressing that the fight against the Kemalist government would contribute to the struggle for Turkey's peace and independence (*Inprecorr* No. 69, 1927, p. 1561).

tions that deviated from it came in for sharp criticism. Since 1955, following the general modification in the Soviet attitude toward the national movement in the East and its history, Soviet historians have been considerably less hostile to the early period of Kemalism.[40] Both Kemal's domestic and foreign policies are now held up as a shining example to Turkey's present rulers, who are said to have departed from the political tradition established by Ataturk.

4. The Arabs Appear on the Scene

To Moscow in 1921 the "Middle East" was Turkey, Persia, and perhaps Afghanistan; the Arab countries did not yet figure prominently in the picture. These nations had just seceded from the Ottoman empire but were not yet independent; there still were no diplomatic relations between them and the Soviet Union. Nor could they boast of a strong labor movement or a developed Communist Party, which would have been a redeeming feature. In their frequent political *tours d'horizon* Soviet statesmen and commentators occasionally mentioned the Arab world in passing; they pointed out that the British (and French) had betrayed the Arab people, inasmuch as the promises given to them during World War I had not been kept,[41] but they entertained few hopes of the emergence of a strong left-wing movement in these countries. In the early twenties the Arab world was a side show in the unfolding revolutionary drama. Among the Arab countries the most important was (and is) Egypt, which in 1922 had become an independent kingdom. Soviet observers doubted whether this involved a real political change; they were inclined to think that Egypt had remained an "unofficial colony" and that one form of colonial rule had merely been replaced by another.[42] Nor were they optimistic about the Wafd, the popular movement that had come into being in 1919. Nevertheless, the general consensus of opinion was that a national revolutionary movement of sorts did exist in Egypt, that it had forced imperialism to make some concessions, albeit unimportant ones, and that it would continue to press for more. In the early period the chief Soviet expert on Egypt was K. M. Troianovskii, who had organized the 1918 "Union for the Liberation of the East"; he combined a sweeping vision of the course of the Asian revolution and some remarkable insights with a crude "sectarianism" and an astonishing ignorance about the basic facts of political life in the Middle East. He thought that land in Egypt should be nationalized, but since the peasants were unorganized, weak, and, generally speaking, incapable of revolutionary action, the urban proletariat would have to carry out this task. The proletariat stood for the Soviet system, whereas the bourgeoisie wanted (formal) democracy, but because the middle class was weak in Egypt, the "democratic" slogan was less dangerous from the Communist point of view than in other countries: "In the given situation in Egypt, the democratic slogans obviously lead to the establishment of Soviet rule."[43] The main problem in Egyptian foreign policy then was, and remained, the Suez Canal. Troianovskii had pondered this subject, too: the ideal solution, of most benefit to the world in general and the Egyptian proletariat, was the internationalization of the Canal, but in present circumstances, nationalization of the Canal was the correct slogan. All these considerations were entirely academic, for the Egyptian working class on which Troianovskii based his speculations was still extremely weak in 1921, and certainly showed no inclination to join the Communist party. The only revolutionary group in Egypt at the time was the national movement led by middle-class political leaders, but the Wafd did not figure at all in Troianovskii's schemes.

Other Soviet observers shared this pessimism with regard to the Wafd, which was accused of failing to carry out a single important social or economic reform while in power. Zaghlul was said to be a traitor, a capitulator; after all, what could one expect from a friend of Ramsay MacDonald?[44] Only in 1926 did Akselrod, one of the very few Soviet students of Middle Eastern affairs with some first-hand knowledge of the area, present a somewhat fairer and more realistic appraisal of the Wafd. It was said to be a real mass party, supported, *inter alia*, by the intelligentsia, despite the fact that it did not have a clear political program.[45] At about the same time, Stalin made his remark about the "objectively progressive role"[46] that the Egyptian bourgeoisie was playing in its struggle against Britain, and this helped to set the line for some time to come. When Zaghlul died in 1927, Soviet observers took a more balanced view of him: he had been a great man like Kemal or Gandhi, the personification of the struggle against imperialism.[47] Nevertheless, "Zaghlulism" was impossible to carry out, and his successor, Mustafa Nahas, would be unable to prevent the disintegration of the Wafd (a prediction that was to come true a quarter of a century later); Egypt would attain independence, but under the leadership of another social class. . . .

The Sixth Congress of the Comintern in 1928 and the general change in the Communist line affected Egypt as it did all other Asian countries, and the attitude toward the national movement in the Nile Valley again became much less friendly. The appraisal of the role of the Wafd by later Soviet historians is a subject so intricate as almost to defy description. The Soviet attitude to Kemalism has changed only once or twice since the twenties, but there have been a great many fluctuations in the attitude toward the Wafd. The Wafd has been described in Soviet historical writings after World War II (1947-55) as that part of the Egyptian bourgeoisie that wanted to compromise with British imperialism and was only occasionally prevented from doing so by pressure from below.[48] In 1955, with the general modification of the line on the national movement in the East, the Wafd might have expected to benefit retrospectively. But since by 1955 the Wafd was no longer in existence, Soviet historians saw no compelling reason to make the kind of concessions that had to be made, for instance, to the Indian Congress Party; the appraisal of the Wafd has not, therefore, improved appreciably since 1955.[49]

Egypt was not the only Arab country to emerge from neglect after 1929. Soviet interest in the Arab world was reflected in an appeal to revive the old Russian-Palestine Association that had for many years prior to 1914 engaged in educational and missionary work in the Holy Land; the Soviet government was urged to take over the property of the Association, not, of course, to carry on the Tsarist tradition, but as a basis for economic and scientific activities.[50] (This demand was realized—but only after World War II.) The 1925 revolt in Syria was given some pub-

licity in the Soviet Union, but, by and large, it was overshadowed
by events in China at the same time, and there were some complaints about devoting too much attention to China, and too little
to the Middle East. One economist thought that France would
not hold Syria for long, since it did not yield any economic
profits, whereas the maintenance of a French army in Syria was
a fairly costly business.[51] M. Akselrod, back from his tour of
duty in Arabia, had nothing good to report from Transjordan,
where the situation was said to be tense, and where a strong
opposition had formed, but was more optimistic about Yemen,
which had concluded a treaty with the Soviet Union in 1928;
the Soviet Union (he said) was the only country that could help
Yemen to attain and consolidate its independence.[52] It is somewhat disconcerting now to recall the great importance that was
then attributed to both King Saud and the Imam Yahia of Yemen,
not only by Soviet, but by many Western, experts. They were
regarded as the future rulers of greater Arabian, or even Middle
Eastern, empires. On one occasion Akselrod actually called the
Imam Yahia the Arab Ivan Kalita;[53] it would be difficult to
imagine a more inept historical comparison.

Iraq (or, as it was then called, Mesopotamia) did not figure
in Soviet designs in the twenties. On one or two occasions it was
made clear that Moscow had no liking for the Hashemite family
that had been appointed local rulers by the British, that it regarded them as the "representatives of the upper middle class and
the semifeudal landowners."[54] But they were apparently deemed
too unimportant to call for much comment.

Strange as it may now appear, the attempts to give organizational form to Pan-Islamic tendencies attracted a great deal of
attention at the time in both West and East. Moscow was extremely critical of the various congresses called by this "feudal"
movement (such as the one in Mecca in 1927); the attempt to
establish unity on a religious basis was bound to fail, it was said,
because it ignored the social differences between the various components of the Moslem world. [55] In any case, the new Caliphate
movement was doomed because the British candidates for Caliph
(such as Fuad I of Egypt) lacked support—Ibn Saud in particular
was not willing to cooperate. There was much solicitude for Ibn

Saud in Soviet policy and comment in the middle and late twenties; British "calumnies" against the Wahabi movement were denounced, and it was argued that his rule over the Hejaz was essential to the independence and free development of the area.[56] Subsequently, when Saud reached a *modus vivendi* with Britain, the Soviet attitude toward him became much cooler. But even when the attitude to Ibn Saud was most friendly, there was no enthusiasm for the congresses he called; while colonialism prevailed, it was argued, the meetings of a few privileged representatives of Islam could not possibly have a positive effect.

5. Soviet Attitudes toward Islam

The Soviet approach to Islam is not different, in principle, from the Soviet attitude toward religion in general—it is totally negative. But the relationship between Communism and Islam is more complicated than in the case of other religions. Tactical considerations play their part, as already mentioned; if the Soviet Union sought friends and influence in the Middle East and elsewhere in Asia, active persecution of Islam inside the Soviet Union would have made an unfavorable impression. There were other reasons as well: Islam is not only a religion but also was, at any rate until fairly recently, a way of life. Liquidating Islam does not mean merely closing places of worship, but involves abolishing an entire social system, with its manners, customs, laws, and specific way of life. This peculiarity of Islam was recognized by the Communists; in its resolution on the need for atheist propaganda the Twelfth Party Congress noted that for a variety of historical and social reasons the influence of Islam in Russia was stronger than that of the Orthodox Church.[57]

The struggle against Islam was waged from a number of directions, the general party line being that patient explanation was preferable to stamping out religion by "administrative means." At times, however, good intentions were forgotten and "administrative means" prevailed. While trying for the most part not to offend and antagonize the mass of believers, the party still regarded the mullahs as its implacable class enemies. And how could the mullahs be attacked without offending the religious sensibilities of the believers? There were other such dilemmas, and if the Soviet authorities succeeded in decisively weakening the hold of Islam in Central Asia and elsewhere, this was not so much through antireligious propaganda as by the modernization of these areas, the introduction of a new way of life—and the inability of medieval Islam to adapt itself to modern conditions.

Anti-Islamic propaganda proceeded at various levels. There were popular brochures on such subjects as *Mohammed Never Existed, The Harmful Consequences of Fasting during Ramadan, Against the Veil,* etc.* Perhaps the best known, and certainly the most prolific, producer of this kind of literature, is Lutsian Ippolitovich Klimovich, who has published dozens of books, booklets, and articles on the subject from the middle twenties to the present day. Most of this Islamic or, to be precise, anti-Islamic literature was published in such journals as *Ateist, Bezbozhnik, Anti-Religioznik,* and their equivalents in native languages; all these magazines were discontinued in the late thirties.

At the same time there was a serious attempt to explain (and to refute) Islam on a more sophisticated, ideological level. It soon transpired, however, that in this respect there was no unanimity among Soviet historians and Middle Eastern experts. The discussion was opened by K. Dobroliubskii in a series of articles in *Novyi Vostok* about the early development of Islam;[58] he was followed by M. A. Reisner with a book-length study on the "ideology of the East" (*Essays in Eastern Theocracy*) and the debate went on for about ten years; one of the Comintern Eastern experts, L. Madyar, wrote that though it was undoubtedly useful to study the problems of the origins of Islam, the study of the current revolutionary situation was, after all, more important.[59]

In this Islam debate† most Soviet students of Eastern affairs

---

* The haj was said to be a scandalous reactionary remnant of the past which the national movement (in the Arab world) would abolish when it came to power (*N.V.* 8-9 [1925], p. 230 *et seq.*).

† The Islam debate has been reviewed in *Islam* (a collection of essays published by the journal *Ateist* in 1931) and more recently in N. A. Smirnov, *Ocherki Istorii Izucheniia Islama v SSSR* (Moscow, 1954), pp. 180-202. It has been impossible here to give a full bibliography of Soviet writings on

supported M. A. Reisner's views. By profession a political scientist, who had taught at Tomsk before 1917, he became interested in Islam comparatively late in life. His first contact with these problems had presumably been his assignment, after the revolution, to draft a constitution for Turkestan. Reisner (and with him Belaev, Klimovich, and V. T. Ditiakin) followed in the footsteps of the then fashionable school of M. N. Pokrovskii, which stressed the paramount role of mercantile capital. Islam, according to this theory, served the interests of the Mecca bourgeoisie, which saw its trade routes endangered by Bedouin robbers. The small traders of Mecca suffered no less from the danger of raids on their caravans, and therefore one of them (Mohammed) eventually succeeded in uniting all Arabs and thus restored peace and safety. Reisner went even further in his speculations, and in a passage that almost literally recalls Max Weber on Protestantism, he emphasized the sober rationalism, the dry parsimony, and the general individualist character of Islam, features characteristic not of peasants but of "militant" mercantile capital.[60] Allah was the deification of the merchant, and the main drawback of Islam was (according to Reisner) that it was not at all interested in social classes and the relations between them. It did not want to intervene in the struggles between capital and labor, and therefore developed a new escapist ideology which renounced the material world and thus tried to reconcile the rich and the poor in the realm of the spiritual, in a secret and mystic salvation. M. A. Reisner died in 1928; those who had accepted his ideas about Islam had to revise their concepts in the early thirties, because the Pokrovskii school was banned in 1933-34. Some, however, had realized earlier that Reisner's theories were untenable. N. A. Rozhkov offered as explanation for the birth of Islam the feudal revolution. Before Mohammed, Arabia had all the features of a prefeudal society, and feudalism was introduced by the great organizer, Mohammed. This theory, apart from being factually untrue, was criticized for exaggerating the per-

---

Islam. The fullest available are in *Islam and Russia* (London, 1956, an abridged translation of Smirnov's book), pp. 60-87, and "Russian Materials on Islam and Islamic Institutions, a Selective Bibliography," by Rudolf Loewenthal, published in *Der Islam* (Berlin), 1957-58.

sonal role of Mohammed; Rozhkov was also rebuked for uncritical dependence on foreign authorities.[61]

A completely different interpretation was presented by M. L. Tomar, who tried to prove, not without ingenuity, that Islam, far from representing the interests of either mercantile capitalism or feudalism, had actually been the "ideology" of the poor peasants of the Mecca region.* Mohammed found his social basis not in Mecca (whence he was expelled) but in the predominantly agricultural Medina.[62] This theory had some obvious advantages for there had been a trend in both socialist and communist propaganda to explain the origin of all the great world religions as a movement of protest by the poor against the rich, later taken over by the ruling classes and exploited for their own purposes. These theories pointing to the common ground between socialism and early Christianity, Judaism, and Islam, played a considerable role in early socialist propaganda in many countries. But, factual discrepancies apart, such a conception is not in accordance with the basic Marxist theory of the social function of religion, and it could not, therefore, be accepted by Soviet Orientalists, despite its otherwise attractive features. Still another theory was developed by N. A. Morozov, (d. 1946), a former member of the "Narodnaia Volia," who had spent many years in Schlusselburg prison. According to him, Mohammed never existed at all; the Koran was composed only in the eleventh century, by a sect that was an offshoot of Arianism and practically identical with the Jews until the Crusades.[63] The part of his theory that dealt with Mohammed as a mythical personality gave fresh inspiration to the antireligious experts, but otherwise this version also was soon forgotten.

More acceptable was an interpretation presented by S. P. Tolstov in 1932, which stated that Islam could not be explained by reference to any single social factor, but was the outcome of various processes—the disintegration of "ancient society" in Arabia, the establishment of feudal relations in the Near East and

---

* There were other such attempts to prove that even some of the early religious sects (such as the one founded by Mazdak in Persia) had been Communist in character. See E. Kagarov in the Ukrainian Orientalist organ *Skhidni Svit,* 5, 1928, p. 184.

North Africa, and the collaboration of various classes and social groups in Mecca and Medina.[64] This was certainly the broadest, but also the vaguest, of all explanations, and Soviet interpretations during the last two decades have followed Tolstov in some important aspects. The most recent authoritative version contained in the second edition of the *Great Soviet Encyclopedia* (written, as in the first, by E. A. Belaev) mentions a general economic and social crisis that gave birth to Islam—the wish of the ruling classes to justify the prevailing social and economic inequality and the exploiting character of the regime. But it also lists as additional causes the decline of the Mecca transit trade and the wish of the ruling classes to acquire new territories. This urge found its reflection in a strong, expansive, and monotheistic religion that set out to unite all Arab tribes.[65] There were other discussions about the development and character of Islam in its subsequent states, but the dispute about origins was of more than academic interest—it was an ideological debate with pronounced topical overtones. It may be noted in passing that the leading academic authorities on the subject left it to the younger men, those better trained politically and more *engagé*, to solve these intricate questions.

6. Changes in the Comintern

Toward the end of the twenties an extensive change took place in the Communist general line; the Sixth Congress of the Comintern in 1928 braced itself for a new period of tensions and revolutionary conflict, the so-called "Third Period." The new and more radical course was the result of Communist setbacks in Europe, the crisis in the Far East, and certain internal processes within the Soviet Union. Since these changes frequently affected Soviet attitudes toward the Middle East, it is necessary to review them in some detail. Zinoviev, who had been the head of the Comintern until his replacement by Bukharin, admitted in 1923 that he (and other Soviet leaders) had been wrong in their predictions for the course and timetable of the world revolution. They had expected the revolution to win out first in Germany and then to spread to the rest of Europe, but events had proved them wrong. With the growth of a sizeable Communist movement in China and the emergence of a "revolutionary situation" there, Comintern interest shifted somewhat from Europe to the Far East. Just as Germany stood for the whole of Europe in Communist eyes, so China was regarded as the key to the whole Asian continent.

Communist interest in Asia, as already pointed out, had been strictly limited in the early period. It is always possible to find items of evidence to the contrary, but closer scrutiny (as in the case of Lenin) usually shows that such exceptions do not really affect the over-all picture. Trotsky's biographer, Isaac Deutscher, has drawn attention to a curious document dated August, 1919, implying that Trotsky was convinced for a while that the way to India was nearer and easier than that to Soviet Hungary, and that he played with the idea of an "Eastern orientation." However, a close look at the document in question shows that what Trotsky had in mind was a military adventure rather than a political reorientation: a "serious military expert" had told him that it was quite possible to conquer India with an army of 30 to 40,000 horsemen based on the Urals.[66] It may be just as well for his place in history as a military leader that Trotsky soon forgot about the project. This Indian scheme goes back even further in one form or another. In a letter written by the German ambassador in Bern to Bethmann-Hollweg in September, 1915, reference is made to an eight-point program that Lenin's faction would allegedly carry out if it came to power. Point eight in this document reads: the Russian army will march into India.[67]

The same month that Trotsky, from his armored train, sent his comrades in the Central Committee his observations on the "Indian project," Chicherin, the foreign commissar, published an article on "Russia and the Asian peoples," in which he surveyed the opportunities that had been missed by Russian diplomats fifty years earlier when they had stopped short in their expansion toward India.[68] It may be an exaggeration to regard this as evidence for continuity in Russian foreign policy—though Chicherin had served this very ministry in a junior capacity around the turn of the century. Chicherin, like most other Soviet leaders at the time, regarded England as the main enemy and judged any move in

India or the Middle East mainly by its possible effects on British power rather than in terms of a colonial revolution.

Stalin spoke only infrequently on issues of foreign policy during the middle and late twenties; for a while he followed the lead given by Zinoviev, later that of Bukharin, and when Bukharin was overthrown, the Comintern work was left to three of Stalin's aides: Manuilskii, Kuusinen, and Lozovskii. Stalin himself was preoccupied with internal problems and the struggle for power. He dealt with foreign problems only insofar as they were connected with or brought into the internal struggle for power; such as the war scare of 1927-29, the Chinese debate of 1927, etc. Stalin was the first to issue the slogan of "Social Fascism," having defined Western Social Democracy as the left wing of Fascism in 1924. But if Stalin had fewer illusions about the prospects of Socialism and Communism in Europe, and was therefore psychologically more prepared for a shift to an "Eastern orientation," he put little trust in Asian liberation movements either—especially after Chiang Kai-shek's "betrayal" in 1927.

One should differentiate between Trotsky's views on revolutionary prospects in Asia as they are described in later Soviet writings and as they really were. He was in a sense both more moderate and more radical than the official leadership in 1927-28: he was against close cooperation with Chiang Kai-shek, but was equally opposed to the "adventurist, ultra-radical line" in which the Comintern took refuge after Chiang Kai-shek's "betrayal." These tactical considerations apart, Trotsky differed from the others on certain basic issues. According to Bukharin (and Stalin) the national liberation struggle in the colonies was more progressive than bourgeois-democratic revolutions in the West. But Trotsky argues (and he said that Lenin had shared this view) that it was precisely the other way around. The Chinese liberal-bourgeois movement was not on a higher level than, for instance, liberalism in Tsarist Russia or the Social Revolutionaries: "The Chinese Miliukovs and Kerenskiis are even more vile than their Russian prototypes."[69] For the same reason Trotsky opposed the idea of workers' and peasants' parties for India and other Asian countries, as was proposed at one time by Stalin; such parties, Trotsky thought, could only serve the bourgeoisie. Nor could he accept the Comintern line on "democratic dictatorship" (as distinct from proletarian dictatorship) for the countries of the East, for in the East the national democratic movement could lead to victory only if the social and political relations had ripened sufficiently to bring the proletariat to power later on.[70]

There is not much to choose between Trotsky's line and the official theses on the colonial revolution in the late twenties; both were equally unrealistic. Yet the element of unreality in Trotsky appears to loom somewhat larger; he more consistently underrated the revolutionary potentialities of Asia, which is somewhat surprising, for in the field of foreign political analysis Trotsky was no less farsighted than Bukharin or Stalin, nor was he more doctrinaire.*

There had not been much room for Asia and the colonial revolution in Bukharin's world outlook, for he assumed that the world was moving toward a stage in which a number of state-supertrusts would fight each other. The small nations would get independence for a "historical second," but world history would not be shaped by this "petty bourgeoisie of states" but by the giants of imperialism.[71] In his later works he chided Rosa Luxemburg for having underrated the importance of the colonial question, but he himself did not devote much attention to this issue. Only during his very last appearances as a top party leader in 1928-29 did he modify his stand a bit and give more emphasis to events in Asia. It would be interesting to examine why Bukharin, who had for years opposed an "adventurist course" in the Comintern, came to endorse the hyperradical policy decided upon by the Sixth Congress, but such an investigation would exceed the limits of the present study.

7. From the China Debate to the Sixth Congress

In May, 1927, the plenum of the Executive Committee of the Comintern was convened to perform the disagreeable duty of conducting a post-mortem on China, where Chiang Kai-shek had turned against his erstwhile Communist allies. Not merely China

---

* Or did he perhaps realize the revolutionary potentialities of Asia without considering them "progressive" because he doubted that they would lead to what he would call a socialist regime?

was at stake, but the entire conception of the struggle in the East, and the problem of collaboration with the national movement throughout Asia. Trotsky and Radek (who had predicted Chiang's betrayal) contended that it was extremely naïve to assume that there was an "abyss" between the "compradores" and the national bourgeoisie; that the alliance between the Communists and the Kuomintang had been possible only because the Communist Party had been extremely weak. This thesis was hotly contested by Bukharin, Stalin, Martynov, and others; of interest in the present context is the opinion of the Turkish representative in the Comintern, Ferdi, who obviously had the situation elsewhere in Asia in mind when he reiterated his belief that in the East "national parties and movements like the Kuomintang ought to be exploited by the Communists in order to make the lower middle class, who are deterred by Communism, join the revolution." According to Ferdi, Trotsky had apparently not realized that though there was no difference between the "compradores" and the national bourgeoisie in the West, the situation in the East was another matter. In Asia the industrial proletariat was not strong enough to carry through the struggle for national liberation, but it could join the bourgeoisie in its fight and compel it to intensify the struggle.[72]

Despite the fact that the dire prophecies of the opposition had come true, the Soviet leadership insisted that its line had been right all along; only the application had been wrong. In other words, the people on the spot had not realized that the situation had changed, and had not adjusted their tactics in time. Despite this insistence on the desirability of temporary collaboration with the national movement in the East, especially with its left wing, the shock of the Chinese experience had a lasting effect on Soviet and Comintern policy throughout Asia. While it advocated this collaboration in theory, the attacks launched against the "national reformists" (as the national movement was now called) became so violent as to make any cooperation virtually impossible. True enough, there were the "national revolutionary forces" which should have been the Communists' allies, but the Communists had become so demanding and so critical that hardly anybody in

Asia qualified any longer as a "national revolutionary." The struggle again "social Fascism" in Europe had its counterpart in the fight against "national reformism" in the East. And so the "Third Period" was to be even more sterile than the first and second as far as Communist policy in Asia was concerned, and this despite the fact that the Sixth Comintern Congress had devoted far more attention to Asian affairs than any such meeting before. There was an awareness now of Asia's importance, but the "correct approach" had not yet been found.

Other problems had to be solved in the wake of the general radicalization of Communist policy in Asia. The war scare ought to be mentioned because it had a considerable bearing on the Soviet appraisal of developments in the Middle East. In 1927-28 Stalin in particular had become convinced, or at any rate pretended to believe, that a new world war was just around the corner, and that it would be an attack on the Soviet Union by all the imperialist powers, headed by England. For several years, from 1928 onward, any action by an outside power or a native government in the Middle East was regarded in this light: political and economic agreements, the building of railways and harbors, and many less relevant activities, were considered as part of the preparation for an armed attack. Only in 1934, after Hitler's advent to power, did the war scare abate—perhaps because a real menace compelled Stalin to dispense with an imaginary danger.

On the ideological level, the quarrel about the decolonization theory came to the fore during the Sixth Congress and after. In its most extreme form this thesis had been developed by Sultan zade in 1920; Western imperialism was becoming much more liberal in the colonies, and was largely ready to relinquish its direct political hold and was mainly interested in preserving its economic position.[73] This analysis, however correct, was not Marxist-Leninist in character, and what was to be known in the late twenties as the "decolonization theory" rested on different ideological premises. As developed by Roy, and in another version propounded by several leading British Communists such as Palme Dutt, Bennett, and A. Rothstein, British capitalism had

sown the seeds of its own destruction by industrializing India.*
Colonial methods of exploitation were thus superseded by more
modern relations of production. The former colonies would thus
gradually attain a measure of independence and would even compete with the Metropolis.[74] On the basis of such a theory one
could reach various, and perhaps even conflicting, political conclusions: the British Communists (in contrast to Roy) argued
that it was no longer possible for the bourgeoisie in a country like
India to fulfill a progressive role in the national liberation movement; they would join it only in order to betray it.[75] The Comintern leadership disliked this theory, whatever its conclusions;
Kuusinen and others argued that British imperialism was doing its
best to arrest, rather than develop, India's industry. In the end the
whole conception was rejected, against the opposition of the
majority of the English delegation. Twenty years later, in the
framework of the Varga debate, the issue was to reappear in a
different form: by then India had been politically "decolonized,"
but this was still to be regarded for a number of years as a fic-
titious form of independence.

8. The Turning Point

The concept of the "Third Period," the general radicalization
of Communist policy at home and abroad, had immediate and
far-reaching consequences for the study of the contemporary
East. The first signs of such a change could have been discerned
before the Sixth Congress of the Comintern. In 1927 the "Scientific Research Association" (NIA) at the Communist University of the Toilers of the East had begun to publish a new
magazine (*The Revolutionary East*). This was a clear act of
defiance of the All-Union Association of Orientalists (VNAV),
who did not take it very kindly. In the beginning the VNAV
refused to take the newcomer seriously, claiming that *The Revolutionary East* was a bad copy of already existing publications and
that the articles contained little more than quotations from Lenin,
well known to everybody. Some of the material published was
said to be better fitted for a (student) wall newspaper than a

---

* Bennett (his real name was Petrovskii) disappeared in Moscow in
1937. The other two continue to be (1958) leading members of the C.P.G.B.

scientific journal. There was an article by a comparatively new figure in China, called Mao Tse-tung, not without some interest, but this, too (the critic primly declared), would have been more suited to a daily newspaper.*

But while these lines were written, the storm clouds had already gathered on the horizon. The VNAV was without a leader after Pavlovich's death, and in October, 1928, the party central committee had considered its reorganization. At that time Dimanshtein, who had been appointed to supervise VNAV activities, had protested against such a measure and had won a respite. But as time went on, criticism of the VNAV became more vocal and intense: its members were accused of not being Marxists at all and of being preoccupied with irrelevant problems. They were "bourgeois relics" for which there was no room in a Communist state. A new form of polemic developed: there had, of course, been quarrels and discussions previously, but from then on they were conducted in a much shriller key; the other man was not just mistaken—he was a deviationist, probably a class enemy.

Typical of these new forms of polemics were the attacks on Gurko Kriazhin. Pavlovich's right-hand man was accused of having never sympathized with the cause of revolution in Asia. Instead, he had supported the Pan-Islamic and Pan-Turkish movements, even anticipating Sultan Galiev in his ideas of a great Turanian state. He had praised the bourgeois Orientalist Bartold and regarded him as an authority. Objectively, he had defended imperialism by assigning it a progressive role, for had not imperialism given impetus to the national liberation movement in the East? He had been influenced by such outlandish capitalist theories as the German school of geopolitics. (Gurko Kriazhin had written the preface to the Russian edition of a work on geopolitics by Horrabin.) This last allegation was not altogether

---

* Mao Tse-tung did not have a good press in the Soviet Union in the early years. In March, 1930, his obituary was published in Moscow. He had died (it was reported) of a respiratory disease from which he had suffered for many years. It was a severe loss to the party, the Red Army, and the Communist movement in China in general (*Inprecorr* March 20, 1930, p. 259).

unfounded, for in the Pavlovich era there had been some veiled sympathy in Russia for the conceptions of Karl Haushofer of Munich, who was a bitter opponent of Britain and envisaged a Pan-Asian bloc (Russia, China, and Japan) as a counterweight to the influence of British imperialism.[77] Even so, the attacks on Gurko Kriazhin were only a mild foretaste of the shape of things to come: Gurko Kriazhin was, after all, a man with a non-Communist past and he was out of step with the party line of the late twenties. Afterwards, however, these attacks were directed not merely against real deviationists (however unimportant their deviation) but also against men with a stainless Communist past who had always faithfully followed the party line. The VNAV had certainly done nothing to make the task of its rivals more difficult. It had tried to preserve a certain degree of academic respectability, and had not been astute enough to adapt itself to the Zeitgeist—Stalin quotations and all. In addition, it had neglected the work of younger experts in the field, who had meanwhile been trained and had found work in various institutions. By 1929, the VNAV included only one group of Soviet students of Eastern affairs. Owing to the growing pressure, it had to adopt a resolution in June, 1929, in which it said that its main task in the near future was to fight against the "pseudo-Marxist elements" in its own ranks who took cover behind a revolutionary phraseology.[78] It was somewhat disconcerting to see how all the current slogans had to be applied indiscriminately in the field of Eastern studies. If Soviet industry was called upon to carry out the first Five-Year Plan in four years, Soviet students of Asian affairs were exhorted to do the same. If the Communist party was mobilized for the liquidation of the kulaks as a class, this meant that the members of the association also had to get rid of all bourgeois agents in their ranks.

The spirit of Bolshevik self-criticism was correct procedure, but the Association applied it too mildly and too late. In November-December, 1929, the party central authorities resolved that the Association was to be disbanded and its organ *Novyi Vostok* discontinued. The *Revolutionary East* had triumphed over the *New East*.

Dimanshtein had made a valiant effort to stave off the inevitable; he wanted at least to soften the blow and insure that the young men of the Communist University of the Toilers of the East did not have it all their own way. He also criticized their literary efforts as "seasonal" in character, meaning, presumably, that long-term scholarly projects could not be made to fit exactly the switches in the party line. But the stress now was on self-criticism, and he had to concentrate on the shortcomings of the old VNAV. There were failures of a technical and methodological nature. Eastern languages were not yet sufficiently well known, and the experts had, therefore, depended far too much on secondary, Western sources. Instead of studying the eternal wisdom of the East, the Asian experts should have occupied themselves much more with such contemporary problems as the national and agrarian questions. But worst of all were the ideological weaknesses, the fact that many scholars had not been able to get rid of bourgeois and reformist influences. Of the younger comrades, many had not been interested in politics at all. The real Marxist specialists would be taken over by the Communist Academy, but for the dubious elements there would no longer be any room.[79] Dimanshtein's efforts to soften the blow were in vain. For meanwhile, the Sixteenth Party Congress had been held, and the general process of radicalization had moved one stage further. A new and greater revolutionary wave was said to be approaching in the East—the political prognoses of the Sixth Comintern Congress had been proved correct. Soviet industry and agriculture were undergoing decisive changes and tremendous progress had already been achieved. Only the social sciences were lagging behind—philosophy, economics, and, perhaps worst of all, the study of the contemporary East.

In these circumstances the old Association had to couple its dissolution with a sweeping acknowledgment of political errors. At first, it was stated in its final "Declaration," the VNAV had played a positive role, but subsequently it had not been able to cope with its tasks; on the contrary, it had hampered progress and had been used by "enemy forces," mainly the right-wing deviationists. Among the members of the VNAV the following categories were singled out for denunciation: (1) individuals who posed as Marxists but had nothing in common with Marxism;

(2) academic, non-political specialists who merely wanted to continue the work of the old prerevolutionary Orientalists; and (3) pseudo-scientists, people who had neither a real knowledge of the subject nor the correct ideological approach.[80] This was a rather negative summary of the work done during one decade: if there was anybody who had done better than that, the "Declaration" of 1930 did not mention it.

Meanwhile, the presidium of the Communist Academy had already decided on the establishment of a new body: the Association of Marxist Experts on the East. From then on, the study of the East was to be concentrated at the Communist Academy and at the Communist University of the Toilers of the East.* The assignments of the new Association were twofold: the study of the economics and politics of the East, and of new ways of developing the national revolutionary movement (and the class struggle) in these countries during the "Third Period." The possibilities of non-capitalist development were to be explored, and the struggle against reformism in the East was to be given particular emphasis. The other main task of the new group, not of direct relevance here, was the study of the Soviet East in the light of socialist construction.[81]

In this way one era came to an end, and another, not very happy one opened. It is doubtful whether the full implications of these changes were realized by those directly involved. To them the whole affair might have appeared as a storm in a teacup that would soon blow over. It had only affected a few dozen people; there had been hard words but no one had come to serious harm. How could they know that they had just witnessed in their own field the transition to the Stalin period of Soviet history?

---

* This really meant that the "Association" (VNAV) was to be taken over by the group that edited *Revoliutsionnyi Vostok,* the NIA (Nauchno-Issledovatelskaia Assotsiatsia) founded in 1927. The militant NIA again and again attacked the VNAV, and matters came to a head at the Ukrainian Orientalists' Congress in Kharkov in November, 1929, when the NIA delegates declared that Soviet Oriental studies were in a bad state, and that a fresh Marxist impetus was needed to overcome this "crisis." The NIA spokesmen maintained that the VNAV was "politically bankrupt" and that the only decent course was "self-liquidation" (*R.V.* 9-10, 1930, p. xiii).

9. *The Eurasians*

While the Communists in Moscow and elsewhere racked their brains about how to make the best use of Asia's revolutionary energies, there was one group that thought it had found the philosopher's stone long before. The Eurasians, who had first appeared on the scene in 1921 and flourished in the later twenties,[82] were firmly convinced that Russia's history since Peter I had been one big mistake; everybody had treated Russia as a secular state of the European kind, which to them was a tragic error. They based their new gospel on the "spirit of Russia," the fruit of the marriage of the cultures of Russia and Asia, and stressed the influence of Tsargrad and the Mongols on modern Russia. Thus they claimed that Russia should develop its own distinctive civilization—not on European but on Eurasian lines. They regarded Bolshevism as the evil element in Westernism, but in their blueprint of a future Russia they were prepared to make some allowances for social reforms and declared themselves in favor of a somewhat nebulous "functional character of the right of property." They tended to exaggerate their influence inside Russia: "Most of the second-in-command belong to us or sympathize with us," the Eurasians claimed. The Eurasians were a strictly émigré movement whose spiritual antecedents can be traced back to certain Russian nineteenth-century thinkers such as Khomiakov and Danilevskii. Some observers (e.g., Prince Mirsky) then thought that Eurasianism was in tune with certain important tendencies inside Russia, but the similarity was a very superficial one. Both the Communists and the Eurasians were against "bourgeois Europe," but for very different reasons and from different vantage points. Both Communists and Eurasians toyed with an Eastern orientation, but the latter had in mind the "idea of Asia" rather than the real Asia of 1925. For this and other reasons, Eurasianism as a political movement remained an interesting but inconsequential episode: only its slogan is still remembered.

10. *Political Balance: 1928*

The political diagnosis of the Soviet leaders in 1928 was an extreme one, but in some respects it was remarkably acute. They sensed that a new economic crisis lay ahead and that it would have serious political repercussions. To have recognized this so early was no mean achievement, but it also made them misjudge the situation: they realized that there was trouble ahead, and perhaps a revolutionary situation, but they were looking for it in the wrong direction. In Europe, they came to think of England as the main instigator of the coming war, and Social Democracy rather than Fascism as the main enemy of the Soviet Union. In Asia they predicted an intensification of the anti-imperialist struggle, but thought the Communists would benefit from this development while remaining in bitter opposition to the national movement. They clearly underrated the anti-Western sentiments among the "national bourgeoisie," especially in the Middle East and India. They were unwilling to concede the leadership in the current phase in the struggle for independence to this "national bourgeoisie." Despite these obvious mistakes, Communism continued to take root in Asia, albeit at a slow pace. Between 1928 and 1930, Communist parties were founded in India, Syria, and elsewhere. It could be argued that the intransigence of Soviet and Comintern policy after 1928 stemmed not so much from the mistaken application of a correct thesis as from an inner necessity: the kind of domestic policy that Stalin carried out during those years, forced collectivization in agriculture and rapid industrialization, made it imperative to paint a menacing picture of the state of the world. However that may be, the fact that modest progress was achieved by Communism in Asia despite a line that did not make success easy does tend to show that a prerevolutionary situation did exist, and that a revolutionary party was bound to make some headway.

NOTES

1. Broido on the foundation of the university, *Zh.N.*, May 28, 1921, and January 31, 1922.

2. *IV Vsemirnyi Kongress Kommunisticheskogo Internatsionala*, p. 261 *et seq.*

3. G. Safarov in *N.V.* 2, p. 58 *et seq.*

4. *Fifth Congress of the Communist International. Abridged Report* (London, 1924), p. 185 *et seq.* Also *Pyatyi Vsemirnyi Kongress . . .* (Moscow, 1924), Part I, pp. 589-95.

5. "The University of the Peoples of the East," in *Marxism and the National Question*, pp. 216-17.

6. Manuilskii at the Fifth Congress of the Comintern, *loc. cit.* A Turkish delegate, Fapluk, protested against this criticism and said that the misunderstandings had already been cleared up.

7. *N.V.* 10-11, p. xxxix.

8. Manuilskii, *Abridged Report*, p. 191.

9. *R.V.* 1, 1927, pp. 15-16.

10. G. Torchineni in *Zh.N.*, May 28, 1921, and Gasefusi, *ibid.*, May 1, 1922.

11. V. Osetrov in *N.V.* 2, pp. 568-80.

12. "Iranskii," in *N.V.* 5, pp. 101-13.

13. "Iranskii," *ibid.*

14. Gurko Kriazhin in *N.V.* 12, p. xxxii *et seq.*

15. I. Visanov in *N.V.* 15, p. xxxiii *et seq.*

16. Gurko Kriazhin, *ibid.*, p. 17.

17. "Irandust," *ibid.*, p. 60. The polemics about Persia filled almost 100 pages in that number of *N.V.* Gurko Kriazhin had the last word on that occasion.

18. M. Sendjabi in *M.Kh.M.P.*, March, 1930, p. 100.

19. *Noveishaia Istoriia . . .* , Vol. II, p. 202.

20. M. N. Ivanova, *loc. cit.*, p. 322.

21. *Velikii Oktiabr i Narody Vostoka* (Moscow, 1957), p. 350.

22. *Zh.N.*, June 15, 1919.

23. I. P. Trainin in *Zh.N.*, March 17, 1921. For the early period of Soviet-Afghan relations, see also F. Raskolnikov: *Afganistan i Angliiskii Ultimatum* (Moscow, 1924); I. M. Reisner: *Afganistan* (Moscow, 1929); A. Gurevich: *Afganistan* (Moscow, 1930); E. Veit: *Afganistan* (Moscow, 1929); and F. Raskolnikov, "Rossiia i Afganistan," in *N.V.* 4, 1923.

24. S. S. Golubiatnikov and V. S. Poznanskii in *Istoricheskii Arkhiv* 4, 1956, pp. 249-51.

25. M. N. Reisner in *N.V.* 8-9, p. 40 *et seq.*

26. I. Reisner in *N.V.* 22, p. 67 *et seq.*

27. *Pravda*, December 29, 1928.

28. Arshit in *N.V.* 25, p. xxxiii.

29. F. Raskolnikov in *Inprecorr*, Feb. 8, 1929, p. 106.

30. See, for instance, *Noveishaia Istoriia*, Vol. I, pp. 225-29.

31. *Ibid.*, pp. 230-31.

32. W. Pagmanskii in *Inprecorr*, Nov. 11, 1929, p. 1384. A. Gurevich was more skeptical about Nadir Khan a few weeks later. *M.Kh.M.P.*, January, 1930, p. 84.

33. *Noveishaia Istoriia . . .* , Vol. I, pp. 233-34.

34. *N.V.* 2, p. 642, quoting the newspaper *Siya*.

35. D. Kuzmin, *ibid.*, p. 158.

36. Yoldshu in *N.V.* 16-17, p. 117 *et seq.*

37. Ferdi, representing Turkey at the Seventh (enlarged) Plenum of the Executive Committee of the Comintern, *Puti Mirovoi Revoliutsii* (Moscow, 1927), Vol. I, p. 272.

38. V. I-i in *N.V.* 29, p. xxv *et seq.*

39. From the chapter on Turkey between 1923 and 1928 (written by E. F. Ludshuveit) in *Noveishaia Istoriia* . . . , Vol. I, p. 312.

40. A more moderate approach is revealed in such recent works as B. M. Dantsig: *Turetskaia Respublika* (Moscow, 1956), and A. M. Shamsudinov in *Velikii Oktiabr i Narody Vostoka* (Moscow, 1957), pp. 406-07, and in current articles in Soviet journals (1957-58).

41. Among the earliest Soviet comments on events in the Arab world see "S," in *Zh.N.*, April 18, 1920.

42. K. Troianovskii in *N.V.* 2, p. 94 *et seq.* See also *Zh.N.*, April 14, 1922, p. 20.

43. K. Troianovskii in *N.V.* 2, p. 182 *et seq.* See also his essay in the symposium *Kolonialnyi Vostok* (Moscow, 1924).

44. P. Kitaigorodskii in *N.V.* 7, p. 77.

45. M. Akselrod in *N.V.* 15, p. 302 *et seq.*

46. Stalin, *Sochineniia*, Vol. VI, p. 144.

47. S. Maisel in *Istorik Marksist* 6, 1927, p. 175 *et seq.*

48. *Noveishaia Istoriia* . . . Vol. I. p. 349. See also L. Vatolina (ed.): *Araby v Borbe za Nezavisimost*, p. 140.

49. Kh. I. Kilberg in *Velikii Oktiabr* . . . , pp. 255-61.

50. D. Semenov in *N.V.* 8-9, p. 210 *et seq.*

51. L. Shmorgoner in *N.V.* 22, p. 87 *et seq.*

52. M. Akselrod, *N.V.* 26-27, p. 318 (on Transjordan). M. Akselrod, *N.V.* 28, p. 74 (on Yemen).

53. *N.V.* 23-24, p. 405.

54. *N.V.* 1, p. 45 *et seq.*

55. Ismail Zade in *N.V.* 22, p. 101.

56. Ismail Zade, *N.V.* 20-21, p. 400.

57. *KPSS v Rezoliutsiiakh i Resheniiakh* . . . , Vol. I (seventh ed., 1953), p. 742.

58. *N.V.* 4, p. 346 *et seq.*

59. *R.V.* 9-10, 1930, p. 51. The debate nevertheless went on for several years.

60. *Ideologiia Vostoka*, p. 137; see also Reisner's previously published article "Koran i ego Sotsialnaia Ideologiia," (*Krasnaia Nov*, VIII and IX, 1926).

61. N. A. Roshkov: *Russkaia Istoriia* . . . (third ed., 1928), Vol. I, chapter 18.

62. M. L. Tomar in *Ateist*, No. 58 (1930), p. 47, as quoted in N. A. Smirnov, *loc. cit.*, p. 195.

63. N. A. Morozov, *Khristos* (Moscow, 1930), Vol. VI, quoted in N. A. Smirnov, *loc. cit.*, p. 199.

64. *Sovetskaia Etnografiia*, 2, 1932.

65. *B.S.E.*, 2nd ed., Vol. XVIII, pp. 516-17.

66. Document dated August 5, 1919, in Trotsky Archive, Houghton Library, Cambridge, Mass.

67. This information is given on the authority of the Esthonian Alexander Eduard Keskula ("A. Stein"), one of the left-wing Russian émigré advisers of the German government. The document is in the Public Record Office in London, published in Werner Hahlweg: *Lenin's Rueckkehr nach Russland 1917* (Leiden, 1957).

68. In *Vestnik Narodnogo Kommissariata Inostrannykh Del*, August 12, 1919.

69. *The Draft Program of the Communist International: A Criticism of Fundamentals* (New York, 1929), p. 78, p. 86.

70. L. Trotsky: *Permanentnaia Revoliutsiia* (Berlin, 1930), p. 142.

71. N. Bukharin: *Die Oekonomie der Transformationsperiode* (Hamburg, 1922), pp. 26-27.

72. *Die Chinesische Frage* (Hamburg, 1928), p. 86 *et seq.*

73. *Zh.N.* 41 (97), December 24, 1920.

74. *Compte Rendu Sténographique du VIe Congrès de l'Internationale Communiste*, p. 1226, p. 1286.

75. *Ibid.*, pp. 1501-02.

76. M. Tselishev in *N.V.* 22, p. 288.

77. L. Mamet in *Istorik Marksist* 17, 1930, p. 69 *et seq.*

78. *N.V.* 28, p. 287.

79. S. Dimanshtein in *N.V.* 28, p. viii *et seq.*

80. *N.V.* 29, p. xxii.

81. *N.V.* 29, p. xxiv.

82. The first programmatic publication of this group was *Iskhod k Vostoku*, by P. Savitskii, Prince N. S. Trubetskoi, and G. Florovskii (Sofia, 1921). Their subsequent literature is listed in S. Lubenskii: "Evrasiiskaia Bibliografiia," in *Tridtsatye Gody*, Vol. VII (Paris, 1931), p. 285 *et seq.* An English *Europasian: Russia in Resurrection* (London, 1928) gives an introduction to the aims of the movement.

CHAPTER THREE

THE "THIRD PERIOD"

1. *Against "National Reformism"*

"The vast colonial and semicolonial world has become an un-
quenchable, blazing hearth of the revolutionary mass movement"
—so the Sixth Congress of the Comintern announced in 1928.
The new era that Moscow envisaged in the East was a grim one:
its main features were said to be the intensification of the economic crisis, the pauperization of the masses and of the peasants,
unemployment and starvation, rapacious wars waged by imperialist powers against the remaining independent nations and
among themselves for a new division of the colonial spoils. But
it was predicted that the new era would also witness the strengthening of capitalist, and particularly industrial, development in the
East, peasant risings, workers' strikes, and anti-imperialist revolts.
It would greatly precipitate the awakening of the masses and
thus open the way for a great revolutionary movement and,
eventually, for the dictatorship of the proletariat. *Per ardua ad
astra* would have been a fitting motto for the "Third Period."
But in this grim picture Western imperialism was not the only
enemy of the Communists in the struggle for liberation in the
East. The bourgeois-nationalist movements (the "National Reformists") were vacillating between imperialism and revolution.
They wanted national independence because this corresponded to
their own interests, because there was a conflict of interests between them and Western imperialism. But once independence
was achieved, the danger of a social revolution would overshadow
everything else, they would come to regard Communism as the
main enemy and, to stave off this danger, would surrender to
imperialism. A radical change in the situation in Asia could be

brought about only by an agrarian revolution—which the native bourgeoisie could not carry out because its own interests were closely bound up with landlordism. Instead, it would try to maintain its influence over the petty bourgeois masses by using empty nationalist phrases and gestures; a great show of nationalist firmness would be made, and at the same time it would promote illusions about the possibility of a peaceful compromise with imperialism. But in the end the masses would become impatient, would outlive their reformist illusions, and then the way would be open for the Communists.

These, then, were the prospects for Asia, as seen from Moscow in 1929. Events in China had greatly shocked the Soviets, but these developments alone would not have sufficed to bring about a radical change in Communist strategy in the East. The new policy of the Comintern (as already stressed) was mainly motivated by "European" considerations. In the West, the Communists' struggle against "Social Fascism" went to absurd lengths during the "Third Period" with the chief spokesman of the Comintern declaring that "our chief danger was to oppose Fascism to bourgeois democracy as a matter of principle, to contrast Hitler's party with social democracy."[1] The Social Democrats, in order to deceive the masses, proclaimed that the chief enemy of the working class was Fascism, but this, of course, was a lie. There was no room for a "lesser-evil theory"—Stalin himself had declared that Social Democracy was, objectively, the "moderate wing of Fascism." The exploits of the "Third Period" in the West are well known and need not be repeated in detail. In the East, the Comintern did not go quite so far with this particular brand of radicalism. Even at the height of the "Third Period" it was emphasized that the bourgeois-democratic revolution in Asia was bound up organically with the struggle for national liberation—and was, therefore, more "progressive" than the parallel movement in the West. It was recognized (in theory, at least) that the national factor exerted a considerable influence on the revolutionary process in all colonies and most semicolonies. And the Communists were warned that unless they realized that the "National Reformists" headed a mass movement and were not quite identical with the "feudal, imperialist camp," they would remain a sect, isolated from the workers and the peasant masses.[2]

In practice, however, these commendable insights were frequently ignored, and the Communists turned against the entire nationalist movement, singling out its left wing for attack. At the Tenth Plenum of the ECCI (in July, 1929) it was declared incorrect to assume that the native bourgeoisie was involved in an ever sharpening conflict with the foreign capitalists. On the contrary, the native bourgeoisie was gradually turning into a voluntary assistant of Western imperialism. In such countries as Egypt and Syria, it was even said to be on the way towards a "Fascist dictatorship"; in Egypt and Syria, the parliaments had already been dissolved. . . .[3] As for China, the Communists maintained that the struggle against the Kuomintang left wing and its defeat were the logical counterpart of the destruction of the kulaks as a class in Russia—a prerequisite for the triumph of Communism. In India, they declared war on the Congress, but the left-wing leaders, such as Nehru and Bose, were considered even more dangerous than Gandhi and the official leadership. In the Middle East, the Communists turned against nationalism in general: "The Arab nationalists are trembling with fear of Communism," an *Inprecorr* informant reported from Damascus in September, 1930. A report from Cyprus in 1931 vividly illustrates the self-imposed isolation of the Communists from the nationalist movement. "The nationalists of Cyprus who demand 'Union with Greece' hold annual religious ceremonies and national parades on March 25 at which romantic and fiery speeches are delivered with the object of cultivating the most unbridled chauvinism. . . . When the speaker at the demonstration in Limassol called for cheers for the union of Cyprus with Greece, the workers present replied with the cry 'Down with the union' and 'Long live the Soviet Republic of Cyprus.' "[4] This short report illustrates better than any lengthy theoretical treatise why the Communists found it difficult to make progress during the "Third Period." In addition to this "hard" line, the party cadres had to cope with permanent purges and heretic hunts, frequently carried out on flimsy pretexts. Right-wing deviationists were ousted in India and Palestine. In Egypt, Mohammed Abdel Aziz, one of the party chieftains, was expelled and originally accused of left-wing deviations; afterwards, he was described as a police spy and an "Egyptian Azev." The Turkish poet Nazim Hikmet, a faithful party-liner if ever there was one, even when he had just been released from prison and was about to be rearrested, did not escape the general witch hunt. He was described by the Comintern press in 1933 as a petty bourgeois, a Trotskyite traitor, a member of a group frequently used by the police as spies, and a dangerous renegade who should be exposed.[5] It was a long list.

It has become the fashion to associate the crudities of the "Third Period" in both West and East with Stalin. But this is at best an oversimplification. For the same Stalin who stood for a "hard" line in 1928 to 1934 and again after 1947, sponsored "popular" and "national" fronts between 1935 and 1945, and was willing to make greater compromises than the Communist movement had ever contemplated in pre-Stalinist times. It is difficult to assume that Stalin could have imposed his views on Communists outside Russia unless there was an inherent willingness to adopt these policies. Inside Russia there was a totalitarian state apparatus by means of which people could be compelled to do what Stalin wanted. But there were no such absolute means of compulsion with regard to Communist parties abroad. Compliance with "Third Period" policies was voluntary in both West and East. The history of Communism is a constant shift between "hard" and "soft" policies at fairly regular intervals; sometimes the change came on the basis of tactical considerations, sometimes in accordance with the inner necessities and momentum of the movement. Hard times, as well as free and easy ones, are needed to keep it going.

2. The New Experts

By 1928 Pavlovich and Narimanov were no longer among the living, and most of the other early experts and advisers on Asian affairs had either drifted into other fields or were in disfavor. Some of the old-timers, such as Fëdor Rotshtein (who wrote under the name of "Irandust"),* continued to participate in dis-

---

* Fëdor Rotshtein (1871-1953) worked as a political journalist in London from 1890 to 1920. Author of *Egypt's Ruin* (1910), etc., he was Soviet ambassador to Tehran (1921-22), and a member of the collegium of the

cussions and polemics, but with the beginning of the "Third Period," leadership passed into the hands of a new generation of experts.

The first editor of the *Revolutionary East* was then the head of the University of the Toilers of the East, Boris Shumiatskii, who used the pen name "Andrei Chervonyi." Born in Siberia in 1886, he had joined the Bolsheviks at an early age, had been forced to emigrate to China for a while, and was in the Soviet diplomatic service for some years after the revolution. (Having been ambassador in Tehran, he specialized in Persian affairs.) His guest performance as an Asian expert did not last long, but it deserves to be mentioned, for Shumiatskii was believed to enjoy Stalin's confidence and played a prominent part in the struggle of the NIA against Pavlovich's former organization, the VNAV. In the early thirties he was transferred to a leading position in the Soviet film industry, from which he was purged in 1937 for alleged inefficiency, and was not heard of again.

Shumiatskii's successor, both as head of the university and editor of the *Revolutionary East,* was Y. Raiter, a singularly colorless personality who had been appointed by the party Central Committee to purge these institutions of Trotskyites and other deviationists. Both he and the political commissar of the NIA, P. Zhelesniakov, were typical products of the Stalin era; their speeches and articles were elaborate repetitions of statements made by the leader, devoid of any independent ideas. Raiter's main assignment was organizational; he showed some interest in problems of Soviet Asia (where he had spent some years after the revolution) and occasionally delivered routine reports at Comintern meetings about the situation in the Far East and India.

The planning and management of foreign policy under Stalin was not what it had been in the early and middle twenties. At that time the key positions in both the Comintern and the Commissariat of Foreign Affairs were held by men who belonged to

---

Narkomindel (1922-30). In the early thirties Rotshtein's interests shifted from the Middle East to modern European history. He survived the purge and became a member of the Soviet Academy of Sciences in 1939.

the top party leadership. In the late twenties this began to change; neither Litvinov at the Narkomindel, nor Manuilskii, Kuusinen, and Piatnitskii at the Comintern headquarters were members of the party Politburo. This diminution of status reflected, of course, a decline in independence. Nor were the new heads of the Narkomindel and the Comintern greatly interested in Asia; their past experience had been with Europe, and they continued to deal with Europe almost exclusively. As a result, the responsibility for the management of Near and Far Eastern affairs was shifted to several of their aides and assistants. While Kuusinen was nominal head of the Eastern department of the Comintern after 1928, the actual management of Asian affairs was in the hands of such men as Pavel Mif and L. Madyar.

Pavel Mif (Mikhail Firman), born in 1899 in a little town in the southern Ukraine, had been one of the founders of the Komsomol after the revolution and was a political commissar in the Red Army for a while during the civil war. Having graduated from a party high school, he was sent to Shanghai in 1926 as an adviser to the Chinese Communists, studied Chinese and Far Eastern affairs, and soon made himself a name as one of the leading specialists on the subject. After his return to Moscow he was given an opportunity to address the party Central Committee; his views were warmly applauded by Stalin, and from that time on he became the leading authority on Asian affairs in the Comintern apparatus. He outlasted many of his colleagues in that organization, but in 1937 he, too, was arrested, and executed in the following year. According to one report, he was posthumously rehabilitated in 1956. L. Madyar was another of Kuusinen's "Asian secretaries" after 1928. He had been a left-wing Social Democrat in his native Hungary, and head of the press department in the Karolyi government in 1919. He afterwards joined the Hungarian Communist government, was arrested after its downfall, but succeeded in leaving the country and finding his way to Moscow in the early twenties. There he joined the Hungarian Department of the Comintern, but after a quarrel with Bela Kun he was transferred to the editorial staff of *Pravda*, then sent to China for a while, and in the end became a member of the

Comintern Eastern department. He backed the wrong horse in the factional party disputes in the middle twenties, and also took up a "wrong" position in some of the ideological discussions (on the "Asiatic mode of production"). Thus he was one of the very first to be purged in 1935, and died, or was executed, shortly thereafter in prison.

Pavel Mif and Madyar laid down the general line on Asia and most of the ideological statements made during the "Third Period" were prepared by them. From time to time they had to deal with Middle Eastern affairs, but they had no first-hand knowledge of the area, nor were they very interested in it. Their main attention was devoted to the Far East, not only because their training had taken place there, but also because it was believed to be far more important than the Middle East so far as the march of world revolution was concerned. While Stalin had to rely on Manuilskii (insofar as Stalin put his trust in anybody), Manuilskii received his information from Kuusinen, Kuusinen from Pavel Mif or Madyar, and Mif and Madyar in turn relied on their own advisers on Middle Eastern affairs.

If we follow the Moscow hierarchy downwards with sufficient patience, we at last reach the new experts on Turkey, Persia, and the Arab world. Among the Persian and Turkish specialists—Ilinskii, Rendshbar, Ferdi, and Fakhri—there was a constant turnover; none stayed in office for very long. But the experts and advisers on Egypt ("Avigdor," "Nadab"), Palestine ("Abusiam"), Syria ("Shami"), and the Middle East in general ("Barzilai") remained on the scene throughout the "Third Period," and some even for a year or two after that. A few details of their background and their political biographies may therefore be in place.

"Avigdor" ("Weiss," Yehiel Kossoi) was born in the Ukraine in 1892, joined the revolutionary movement at an early age, and emigrated to the United States on the eve of World War I. In America he joined the "Jewish Legion" that was then organized, went to Palestine for a short time in 1918, stayed in Egypt for eighteen months, and then returned to Russia. "Avigdor" was sent to Egypt twice, in 1922 and in 1924, to organize or, to be precise, to "bolshevize" the local Communist Party.* The second time, he was arrested in Cairo, sentenced to a long prison term, and returned to Moscow only in the late twenties. By then his reputation as an authority on Egypt was established; he became a "Red Professor" and was again sent, in 1932, to tour the Middle East and to inspect the local parties. In 1936 he was arrested in Moscow, accused of being a member of a Trotskyite conspiracy, and given a ten-year sentence. He died in a camp in 1938—and was rehabilitated in 1955.†

One of the most prolific writers and stubborn polemicists on Middle Eastern affairs in the "Third Period" was "Shami" (Iakov Tepper). Born in Russia, he emigrated to Belgium before World War I, where he joined the Jewish left-wing Poale Zion party. "Shami" belonged to the party faction which joined the Communists, and was sent first to Palestine and then to Syria on behalf of the Comintern. In 1927 he returned to Moscow, was involved in various intraparty quarrels, and in the end retreated into the academic life. In 1933 he became rector of the Leningrad Institute for Eastern Studies, but was deposed in 1936 and "liquidated" two years after. Like "Avigdor," he was attacked during the purge as a pro-Zionist and right-wing deviationist, despite (or because of?) the fact that he had been the most extreme anti-Zionist of all, and used to criticize his colleagues in public for lack of anti-Zionist vigor.

"Nadab" (Nahum Leshchinskii) was another of the ex-Palestinians who returned to Moscow and specialized in Egyptian affairs. Born in Krivoi Rog in 1903, he came to Palestine with a

---

* "Avigdor" married the daughter of Josef Rosenthal, the founder of the Socialist-Communist Party in Egypt, who was expelled for "anarchist" deviations in 1922. Mrs. "Avigdor"—Rosenthal was arrested in Moscow shortly after her husband, spent eighteen years in various corrective labor camps, and was released in 1956.

† There is an element of tragicomedy in this otherwise sad but very typical story. In 1928, while on his way back to Russia from Egypt, he was arrested in Rumania by the "Siguranza." The Comintern launched a campaign for his immediate release (see *Inprecorr*, vol. 7, no. 68) under the slogan "The life of Comrade Avigdor is in the greatest danger." The "Siguranza" released him shortly thereafter; if it had held on to him, he might have survived the Moscow purges.

group of agricultural pioneers, joined the Communist Party, and was delegated to work in Egypt. The Egyptian Communist Party then included a fairly large number of police agents, and "Nadab" was soon arrested. After his return to Moscow, he became a member of the NIA executive and a frequent speaker and writer on Middle Eastern topics. Like so many others, "Nadab" was ousted from the party in 1936, arrested the year after, and died on the way to a labor camp.

The oldest, and for a while the most influential of the group, "Abusiam" (S. Averbukh) was a frequent speaker at Comintern Congresses under still another pseudonym ("Haidar"). Like "Shami," he found his way to the Palestinian Communist Party (whose leader he was from 1924 to 1929) via one of the factions of the Poale Zion. His reports on the situation in the Middle East were apparently held in great esteem in Moscow and given wide publicity. But after his return to Russia in 1929 he was criticized for having mismanaged affairs at the time of the Palestine riots. The authorities did not want to employ him again as a Middle Eastern adviser; instead, he was sent as an emissary to Rumania, and after his mission there had failed, he became the political director of a machine-tractor station in the Northern Caucasus. Arrested in 1936, he was one of the few to survive the Yezhov era, but was "liquidated" in a Moscow prison in the autumn of 1941 at the time of the German offensive against the Soviet capital. "Abusiam" was rehabilitated in 1957. Y. Berger ("Barzilai"), another Comintern expert on Middle Eastern affairs, was the last of the group to arrive in Moscow—again via the Palestine Communist Party. He became the head of the Middle Eastern section in Varga's Institute for World Economics and World Politics, was arrested in 1937, somehow survived twenty years of prison and labor camps, and was released in 1956 or 1957. The story of the "Third Period" experts and advisers is a sad one, without exception. All were faithful Stalinists, but this did not make much difference, insofar as their ultimate fate was concerned. On the whole, they were men of lesser stature, of narrower interests, more doctrinaire in approach and on a lower cultural level than the generation of Pavlovich and Rotshtein. But it would be wrong to dismiss them as mere "*apparatchiki*" and bureaucrats. They were all revolutionaries, had worked in conditions of illegality, and had more than once risked their freedom. This intense belief in their mission and their willingness to sacrifice themselves were undoubtedly redeeming features of an otherwise not very attractive group of people. It would be unfair to dismiss their intellectual efforts out of hand; while their polemics were frequently irrelevant and sometimes ridiculous, their Marxist training had given them some insights into Middle Eastern economic, social, and political realities. Their intellectual level does not compare unfavorably with the generation of experts that succeeded them, after an interval of twenty years, in the middle fifties. Neither could it be said that they were purged because they failed, for nobody had expected them to succeed, since it had been realized by 1929 that the attempt to organize a Communist movement in the Arab world had been unsuccessful and would have failed even had those who tried to organize it been Arabs instead of East European Jews and other foreigners. The new native cadres in the Arab world did not fare much better in the thirties, and it was only during World War II and its aftermath that the Arab Communists, in collaboration with the extreme wing of the Arab nationalists, succeeded in making spectacular progress. "Avigdor," "Shami," and the rest of this group continued, nevertheless, to wield considerable influence in Moscow up to the mid-thirties in shaping the Soviet image of the Middle East; books and articles in the specialized and general press were all but monopolized by members of this group. Their views were not necessarily correct and coherent, but they were the only ones who had studied the problems of the area closely and had some first-hand experience of it. They did not influence Soviet foreign policy toward the Arab countries and Palestine, because Moscow did not yet have a policy toward these countries, for they did not yet matter enough.

3. The New Style in Middle East Polemics

One of the characteristics of the "Third Period" was the prevalence of heated polemics between the various Asian experts. There had also been sharp debates in the twenties on a great many subjects, e.g., the character of Kemalism or of Reza Khan's regime. In the early days, the experts enjoyed considerable latitude in their comments and interpretations, while toward the end of the twenties there was a far-reaching *Gleichschaltung*. Nevertheless, the experts quarreled more and more about less and less. Nor was it a debate in the old Marxist fashion: in the "Third Period" there was room only for attacks on colleagues who had strayed from the party line. But had they really deviated? In many cases the polemicists created a deviation artificially by grossly magnifying some unimportant observation in a certain speech, article, or book, or distorted the meaning of a chance remark in order to create a target for attack. The new Stalinist style began to prevail, in this as in all other fields, with the quasi-religious incantations and ecstasies, the chanting of "O altitudo" whenever the name of the greatest of all living beings was mentioned. This is a familiar phenomenon to the student of Soviet history and need not be reviewed in detail. But in the field of Soviet Eastern studies the hunt for heretics was particularly irrelevant and especially divorced from the realities. While one zealous party theoretician attacked another for having insinuated that things in Kemalist Turkey were only 99% and not 100% black, Voroshilov or Litvinov came out with fulsome praise for Kemal and for Soviet-Turkish friendship. Long-term policies and the tactical approach have never been quite identical in Soviet foreign policy. But the quarrel about obscure and frequently irrelevant issues between the ideologists, the struggle for absolute ideological purity, and the unwillingness to put up with the slightest evidence of "rotten liberalism," were too inconsistent with the sweeping concessions that the Soviet leaders were willing to make in their day-to-day contacts with foreign countries. There obviously could not have been perfect harmony between these two approaches, but neither was such disparity justifiable—even during the "Third Period."

Not all the discussions were on issues that had been created artificially. The "second" Turkish and Persian debate (as distinct from the earlier polemics in the twenties) was somewhat unreal in character, but the discussions about the "Asian mode of production" or the policy of the Comintern in Palestine were real enough. As the "Third Period" went on, however, time was running out for both real and unreal discussions. At the Sixth Comintern Congress, when the new line was adopted, there was no unanimity, and some of the Middle Eastern experts and delegates voiced strong criticism. Sultan zade quarreled with Bukharin's (and indirectly with Hilferding's and Lenin's) theory that the domination of finance capital over industry was the most distinctive feature of modern capitalism. He (Sultan zade) had studied the problem for many years, and for a variety of reasons that are of no particular interest here, continued to disagree.[6] Bukharin was on the way out, and it was perhaps not too risky to contradict him. But Kuusinen was very much on the way in and Sultan zade did not accept the opinions of the new boss, either. Kuusinen's theses, he said, were inapplicable because they were far too general. The mere division of the colonial world into four groups was not enough; what did it mean in practical terms with regard to Persia and the Arab countries? Could they skip the capitalist phase of development? Could one establish a Soviet regime immediately after the revolution or should a "democratic dictatorship" of workers and peasants be established? Should one, or should one not, go on with the agrarian revolution?[7] There were no answers to these questions. Nor was Sultan zade the only critic. "Haidar," representing Palestine, flatly disagreed with the demand to establish workers' and peasants' parties in the Arab world and reproached the Comintern leaders for the extreme vagueness of their schemes.[8]

A year later such open dissension had become unthinkable. True enough, at the beginning of the "Third Period" those criticized or attacked were still given a chance to explain and defend themselves. But later on, the polemics assumed the character of progressively fiercer denunciations, and the accused were at best given the opportunity to apologize and recant. In the end, even the denunciations ceased (apart from those that were officially inspired) for, with the beginning of the purge in late 1934, excessive zeal in defending the party line also became suspect.

4. The Debate on Kemalism

Differences of opinion about the real nature of Kemalism had been legion ever since the emergence of the movement. In the middle and late twenties the official attitude toward Kemalism was one of benevolence mixed with constructive criticism. But when the "Third Period" was inaugurated, a re-examination of the attitude to the Kemalist movement was demanded.[9] Comintern spokesmen stressed Turkey's growing dependence on Western imperialism, and the Turkish representative at the Sixth Congress even talked about the traitors (in Ankara) who wanted a war against the Soviet Union.[10]

On the ideological front the offensive was started by one Z. Feridov, who chose as the target of his attack a book, *The Moving Forces of Kemalism* by "Irandust" (i.e., Fëdor Rotshtein), published in 1927.[11] Feridov argued that "Irandust" was wrong in maintaining that Kemalism had destroyed the feudal remnants in Turkey, that its agrarian policy was liberal, that Turkey had not capitulated to the capitalist onslaught, and that, generally speaking, Kemalism was still a revolutionary force. "Irandust" did his best to point out in his reply that his reasoning was in line with the resolutions of the Sixth Congress, but his explanations were not accepted, and Feridov carried the day. The debate continued with attacks on a number of other Turkish experts (such as Melnik, Dantsig, and Skachko) who were all charged with "opportunist deviations" in their appraisal of the social basis and economic policy of Kemalism.[12] They had argued that under Kemal, Turkey, formerly an agrarian country, was becoming an "agrarian-industrial country," and had found other positive features in Kemal's Turkey. The right-wing deviationists had to recant, but their accusers were not to enjoy their victory for long. Feridov, who had led the attack, was himself taken to task in 1932 for having suggested that Turkey had already become Fascist.[13] This was clearly going too far, even for the most radical proponents of the "Third Period." After 1934 the Kemalist debate died down and Moscow became more concerned about the growing German influence in Istanbul than about Ataturk's agrarian policy.

5. Polemics on Persia

The debate on Persia was even more senseless than the one on Turkey, for there were no real differences of opinion between the various participants. In the early twenties there had been conflicting appraisals of Reza Khan's regime. But by 1929 everybody agreed that the new Shah was up to no good. Nevertheless, an "ideological offensive" was considered necessary here, too, and Rendshbar and Ilinskii were called upon, or believed themselves called upon, to rout the opportunist enemy.[14] They charged that the Rightists (above all "Iranskii" and "Irandust") had been mistaken in arguing that the Persian working class had not played an important role in the 1905-08 revolution and that it had not become a decisive political factor even by 1930. Another outrageous deviation was their assumption that national mercantile capital, based on the military and civil bureaucracy, would somehow succeed in making semicolonial countries (like Persia, Turkey, or the Arab countries) independent national states. This petty bourgeois, anti-Marxist view was strongly condemned, and the deviationists were also accused of taking up the wrong position with regard to the agrarian problem in Persia. "Iranskii"* was alleged to have favored the "Prussian"—as against the American "capitalist"—form of development in agriculture. It all ended in utter confusion, with Rendshbar calling Sultan zade in 1933 an essentially right-wing deviationist despite his left-wing phraseology. But Ilinskii, who with Rendshbar had originally spearheaded the attack, now turned against his erstwhile ally and accused him of obfuscating the whole issue and of committing grave political errors. While Sultan zade had been guilty of both left-wing *and* right-wing deviations, the former were far more dangerous, and, by stressing the latter instead, Rendshbar had committed a terrible mistake.[15] Thus the debate on Persia turned into a discussion of Sultan zade's alleged mistakes; even on this point there was unanimity—that he had committed both right- and left-wing deviations—but they could not agree on the minor nuances. The debate went on until Rendshbar recanted in the summer of 1934 and admitted his grievous mistakes. A few months later, they and their hairsplitting were overtaken by the great purge.

* "Iranskii" was a pen name of Vladimir Osetrov, who had been a Soviet diplomat in Persia and was one of Rotshtein's chief lieutenants in the early twenties.

6. Decolonization: Second Round

There was no decolonization debate, strictly speaking, in the Soviet Union in the thirties; like Trotsky's "permanent revolution" and some of Bukharin's theories, it had been banned and could no longer be discussed. But since quite a number of Middle Eastern experts continued to be charged with this decolonialist deviation, the official position ought to be briefly clarified. It will be recalled that on the basis of this theory very different political conclusions could be reached. Some, like the British Communists in 1928, were "ultra-leftists," dividing Asia into a revolutionary and a counterrevolutionary camp, with nothing in between. Others, on the contrary, thought that the "national bourgeoisie" in countries like Persia, Egypt, and perhaps Afghanistan, would be able to gain independence for their nations and should, therefore, be regarded as "progressive" classes.

Moscow rejected both the theory and the possible deductions. According to the official position, it was highly unlikely that one part of the bourgeoisie (in Asia) would temporarily join the national-revolutionary movement—but it was not thought altogether impossible. Kuusinen tried to define the conditions under which such a development could take place, after all. It could happen if the revolution was not making too much progress, and if the bourgeoisie was, therefore, not too afraid of the revolutionary movement. It could happen if the bourgeoisie believed that it would gain concessions from Western imperialism with the help of the masses. And it was possible if the bourgeoisie of a given Asian country had a secret understanding with Western imperialism; in other words, if the fight it put on was merely a sham.[16]

These official explanations remained in force throughout the "Third Period." The idea that Asian countries were moving toward independence under the leadership of the "national bourgeoisie" was completely ruled out, despite factual evidence to the contrary. Any concession in this direction would have been tantamount to giving up the idea of the hegemony of the proletariat in the national-revolutionary struggle—which, after all, was the basic conception of the "Third Period."

7. The Asiatic Mode of Production

At the height of the "Third Period" the struggle against the theory of the Asiatic mode of production became one of the main orders of the day. It was defined as a methodological concept on which all kinds of left-wing Trotskyite deviations were based. Trotsky had no more to do with this concept than Stalin; it had been coined by Marx, and Lenin also used it for many years. (The idea of a specifically Asian mode of production was not invented by Marx either, but can be traced back to the eighteenth century, as Professor K. Wittfogel has shown in his book on oriental despotism.) But it was an admittedly awkward theory for a great many reasons. If in the East there had indeed been a functional state bureaucracy that had been the ruling class for many centuries without owning the means of production, then the entire concept of historical materialism was in need of modification. But there were other reasons for doing away with this pernicious theory, for it was said to endanger the policy of the Comintern in the East. Even more dangerous were the potential repercussions with regard to a Marxist explanation of Soviet society. For if it appeared that there had been bureaucratic class rule before in history, that the nationalization of the means of production could result in state slavery rather than in socialism, then the historical implications would be fairly obvious. For these and perhaps other reasons the Asiatic mode of production had to disappear, and was, in effect, replaced by a new theory of Asian feudalism that was then said to have prevailed in Asia for many centuries. This discussion was less important to the Middle Eastern expert than to the Far Eastern specialist, and is mentioned here because it cropped up in all ideological discussions of the early thirties. The debate on the Asian mode of production in Leningrad in 1931 was a rather one-sided affair,[17] and the adherents of this theory among the Eastern experts (Madyar, for example) were not even invited. Nor were the party authorities content with the outcome of the Leningrad debate. It was said to have been an inconclusive discussion, and the connection between this theory and the Trotskyite ultra-leftist errors had not been pointed out at all.[18] But the Asian experts gradually learned to evade the issue, and it became increasingly a problem to be dealt with by the historians. They had to adjust themselves to the new line and to demonstrate that throughout Asia a slave-holding society had been replaced by a particular (Asian) form of early feudalism in which the soil belonged to the state. Carried to its logical conclusion, this meant that feudalism was introduced to China some three thousand years ago, as Mao Tse-tung indeed now argues. Soviet historians have been somewhat more reserved with regard to the beginnings of feudalism in Asia, a problem that, they say, has not yet been entirely solved.[19] The "bureaucratic apparatus" is now mentioned only as having played a leading role in the "struggle of the superstructure for the formation of a feudal basis," whatever that may mean.[20]

8. Agrarian Revolution

The progress of the "agrarian revolution" in Asia was one of the main theoretical pillars of the "Third Period." There was hardly an Eastern expert who escaped blame at one time or another for neglecting the agrarian issue, for not paying sufficient attention to the revolutionary potential of the peasant movement in the East. But those who paid heed and studied the possible implications of the agrarian movement in the East had their share of criticism, too. Safarov in particular was singled out for attack. He had been excluded by the Fifteenth Party Congress and sent to work in a museum in some provincial town. In the summer of 1928 he was recalled and returned to work in the Comintern. But from then on to his end as a "counterrevolutionary bandit" in 1935, he became an obvious butt for all kinds of attacks, especially as the proponent of the "agrarianization deviation." He was said to have been at fault for neglecting the development of capitalist relationships (in their colonial form) in both town and village. Such a theoretical mistake was bound to have dangerous political effects because of its tendency to regard the peasants as the central force in the colonial revolution and its inclination to underestimate the role of the workers and similar "rightist-opportunist" deviations.[21] Safarov's book (*Problems of the National-Colonial Revolution*), on which these charges were based, afterwards served another function—it involved him in the Kirov murder.[22]

The variety and number of deviations in the "Third Period" were unlimited, for it was an era of compulsive deviationism. Just as God could not exist without the Devil in the medieval picture of the universe, so the faithful adherent of the party line could not live without fighting heretics, and if there were none, they had to be invented. Some deviationists were branded as followers of the semi-Menshevik line of Rosa Luxemburg. Those who had to deal with the Soviet East were attacked either as being prone to Great Russian chauvinism (Zelkin, Karpich, Dimanshtein, Restsov *et al.*) or as giving aid and comfort to local bourgeois nationalism (Mamet, Galuzo, Sadvokasov, and others). Some were charged with being guilty of both deviations at the same time (Moor, Ruchinskii, Butaev, Lavrentiev). Nobody escaped unscathed.

But all this radicalism of the "Third Period" was purely verbal. One might have expected revolutionary action throughout the East in accordance with the official prognosis of 1928 and the detailed instructions concerning the task of Communism in Asia. But no such action was ever tried, and in more than one way the fiery "Third Period" was much quieter than the preceding era. It was not meant to be, but then the Comintern was on the defensive in many countries in the early thirties, and the Communists' self-imposed isolation made it illusory even to contemplate revolutionary action. The witch hunt on the ideological front was coupled with realism in foreign policy.

9. Palestine—The Permanent Deviation

During the early and middle twenties nobody in Moscow cared much about Palestine. But with the Arab revolt in 1929, a polemic got under way, which soon became a *bellum omnium contra omnes*. It was to last, with short interruptions, until 1936, when the critics and their victims were both overtaken by the great purge. It started with a condemnation of the Palestinian Communist Party and of those writers in the Soviet Union and the Communist press of the West who had doubted the revolutionary character of the Arab uprising and who had explained

it in terms of banditry and pogroms. Subsequently, in 1930, the
polemics became more heated; everyone agreed that Zionism was
a most reactionary movement, but there were differences of
opinion about the Arab revolt. Was it mainly an agrarian movement, reflecting the class struggle in the village, as "Shami"
maintained? Or were the leaders of the movement all feudal
landowners who ought to be fought by the Arab masses, as
"Nadab" argued?[23] The exchanges lasted for a long time, and
"rotten opportunist" was one of the mildest epithets used to
describe the other side. So far as the public was concerned, the
last act came in the form of a short notice buried in a book
review in the penultimate number of *Revoliutsionnyi Vostok*
saying that "Avigdor," "Abusiam," Berger, and all the other
Moscow anti-Zionist specialists had been unmasked as imperialist
agents who had engaged in Zionist propaganda under the cover
of anti-Zionist attacks.[24] Three months later the editors of the
magazine and all the members of the editorial board were in
prison, too. And so this debate also came to an end—unless,
which we doubt, it continued in the camps of Vorkuta.

10. Arab Union, Pro or Contra?

Soviet support for the movement for Arab unity is commonly believed to be a recent phenomenon. It is true that this
concept evoked little interest and less enthusiasm in the Soviet
Union between 1935 and 1955. But there was a flirtation with
Pan-Arabism when it was least likely to have occurred, namely,
during the "Third Period." At the Sixth Congress of the Comintern, "Haidar," representing Palestine, had talked with great
confidence about the revolutionary role the Arabs were bound
to play in the East. In 1916, he said (accepting the T. E. Lawrence
version), the Arabs had delivered a "decisive blow" to Germany
and Turkey. But the very same Arabs, the former allies of the
British, would be their bitterest enemies in a future war.[25]

Such optimistic talk about the revolutionary potential of the
Arab world was not universally accepted in Moscow. Other
Middle Eastern experts had reservations. Sultan zade said that the
Arab states had been dismembered to such a degree that there was

not much hope for the creation of a unified Arab state.[26] Others said that the idea of "Arabistan" (as it was then called) should be approached with great caution, for it was probably a British plot rather than a spontaneous movement for national unity.

But Pan-Arabism found some influential sponsors in Moscow. When Madyar gave a talk in 1930 about the impending task of Soviet Middle Eastern experts, he dwelt at some length on the artificial division of the Arab world; he did not think that King Saud would be a new Cavour, and his country a second Piedmont. But he left the question of Arab unity open.[27] Earlier, in 1929, the "League Against Imperialism," a Communist-front organization, had published an appeal, *For the Struggle for Freedom of the Arab People*, in which the Arab national question was defined as one of the most important international issues. The Arabs, it was stated, had the right to overcome the dismemberment of their countries, to form a strong, united, independent, and perfectly free state. To achieve that aim, All-Arab National Revolutionary Councils were to be established throughout the Middle East.[28]

This initiative was followed up in 1931 at a meeting of representatives of the Palestinian and Syrian Communist parties, who produced a curious document on the "Tasks of the Communists in the All-Arab Movement." These resolutions called for a mass campaign for Arab unity that should be coupled with the struggle against imperialism and separatist dynastic interests. A common language, common historical traditions, common current experience, and, above all, the presence of a common enemy were defined as the basis of the new unity. These resolutions envisaged the creation of a number of independent Arab states that would afterwards unite of their own free will on the basis of federal principles. The Communists understood very well the great emotional appeal of the "Arab Union" slogan, the lively response and sympathy it evoked all over the Arab East from Palestine to Morocco. To adjust their propaganda to Pan-Arab nationalism they proposed the formation of an "All-Arab Workers' and Peasants' Federation," the establishment of a central newspaper for all the Arab Communist Parties, and the coordination of

all the Arab and (French) North African Communist parties.*
Neither proposal was followed up; the Comintern could easily
have given the necessary organizational help, but it was apparently felt that the Arab Communist parties had to gain in strength
before more ambitious schemes could be tackled.

During 1933-34 the Pan-Arab motive cropped up from time
to time in the writings of Soviet Eastern specialists, and one
predicted that the Pan-Arab movement would grow stronger as
a result of the pressure of Western imperialism. It was realized,
however, that the hopes put on Ibn Saud had been misplaced:
"The creation of an independent federation of the Arab countries will not be undertaken either by Ibn Saud or by any other
king. It will be the result of the revolutionary fight of the Arab
masses against the imperialists and their native lackeys."[28] Another authority called upon the Arab Communists to fight for the
solution of the Arab national question not only in each Arab
country but also on the All-Arab level.[29]

After 1934 these references to the feasibility and desirability
of Arab unity became more infrequent, and after a while they
disappeared altogether. For in the middle and late thirties the
sponsorship of the movement for Arab unity was largely taken
over by the Germans and Italians; its foreign political orientation
was certainly in the direction of Berlin and Rome. After the
victory over the Axis powers, the Pan-Arab movement was regarded in Moscow as a branch office of British imperialism. It was
not until 1955 that the concept of Arab unity again began to
figure prominently in Soviet thinking on the Middle East.

* This interesting document was not widely publicized at the time, and
I have not been able to find the Arabic original. It was included in a collection of Communist Party programs in Asia published by L. Madyar, P.
Mif, and others in behalf of the Marx-Lenin-Engels Institute in Moscow in
1934—they indicated that their source was the March, 1928 (*sic*), issue of
the Japanese (*sic*) periodical *Marxism*. But the meeting described had not
taken place until 1931; nor had the resolution been published in Japanese.
Prof. I. Spector, in *The Soviet Union and the Moslem World* (1956, p. 64
et seq.), rediscovered the resolution in the Madyar-Mif collection and provided a translation. But there had been an English version before the
Madyar-Mif collection appeared. (See *Inprecorr*, January 5, 1933, p. 16
et seq.) *Habent sua fata resolutiones.*

11. *Russia and Egypt*

"The Wafd is the greatest enemy of the workers and peasants, and the Communists are called upon to deliver a deadly blow to that organization"—according to Vasiliev at the Sixth Congress of the Comintern.[30] It sounded somewhat bloodthirsty but it certainly suited the general political climate. After wavering between outright denunciation and qualified support in the twenties, the Soviet attitude hardened in the "Third Period." In the resolutions of the Sixth Congress, Egypt had been singled out for special mention and treatment. The Communist Party, it was said, would be able to play an important role in the national movement—but only if it based itself on the organized proletariat. The greatest danger then was that the bourgeois nationalists would get hold of the trade unions; without a decisive struggle their influence would not be broken. One of the Communists' main mistakes in the past had been to work exclusively among the urban proletariat, without organizing the broad masses of agricultural workers and peasants.

This was certainly valuable advice, but for the time being it was not too realistic, for the industrial proletariat in Egypt was extremely weak, the trade unions even weaker and without any political influence whatsoever; no Egyptian party, including the Wafd, had so far succeeded in gaining a foothold in the villages. The Egyptian Communist Party, which was to carry out all those ambitious schemes, did not even exist. There were several individual Communists in Cairo and Alexandria, but there was no party.

The weakness of the Communists was extremely frustrating. In Soviet eyes the "revolutionary situation" ripened from day to day. The Wafdists, while in power, had not been able to achieve anything. There was an agrarian crisis that worsened daily, and the masses were said to be ready to fight the foreign imperialists, the local feudal landowners, and the influence of the corrupt nationalists.[31] All the ingredients of a revolutionary situation (*pace* Lenin) were present but one—the force that was to carry out the revolution. What, then, were the causes of this regrettable weakness of Egyptian Communism? "Avigdor," who had considerable first-hand experience of Egypt, tried to provide the answers in 1934: the Communists in Egypt had hitherto failed because the masses believed in the Wafd. Most of the members of the CP were foreigners, the petty bourgeois elements had not been ousted from the party, and, in disobedience to the Comintern instructions, the Egyptian comrades had refused to establish an illegal apparatus; all kinds of "legalist illusions" were rampant among them. Contact with the peasants had been weak, and recurrent arrests had paralyzed the party. Only with the help of the Comintern had it been able to rebuild an organization of sorts.[32]

Then came the crisis of 1930-31: the "revolutionary struggle for liberation" reached an even higher level, and the economic crisis became a political crisis. The Wafd began to show its true physiognomy, its terrible class hatred; it had an "animal horror of the masses." There were strikes and there was agrarian unrest. There was an acute revolutionary situation—but no leadership. Throughout 1930 the Communists had published just one leaflet—and that had called for surrender rather than for the continuation of the struggle. They had remained a sect, isolated from the masses.[33] Subsequently, a scapegoat for all the failures and missed opportunities was found in Mohammed Abdel Aziz, who had allegedly advised the Communists against participation in the great demonstrations of May, 1931.[34] After he had been "unmasked as a police spy," the party at last seemed to be on the road to success: a correct program was adopted, calling for the establishment of Soviet power in Egypt and an agrarian revolution. But then the police again clamped down on the party in 1934, frustrating all further hopes.

But was the Wafd really as bad as all that? Until 1931 at least, some of the Soviet Middle Eastern experts took a more charitable view of the Egyptian national movement. Madyar in 1932 mentions a "great discussion" that had recently taken place to find out whether the Wafd was national-revolutionary or national-reformist.[35] It should have been clear long ago, he said, on the basis of a theoretical analysis, that the Wafd was not national-revolutionary. But some comrades persisted in their mistakes, and changed their mind only after the Wafd had finally revealed its true, despicable character. According to the accepted view in 1932, the Wafd consisted of a gang of traitors who had sold out to British imperialism. Under the Wafd, it was said, Egypt had "finally become a British colony." In the early thirties some Soviet experts noted the crucial importance of the "petty bourgeois intelligentsia" in Egypt, which they regarded as the "transmission belt" by means of which the bourgeoisie was exerting its influence on the masses.[36] It was an acute observation, though it was probably too early then to realize the full implications of the discovery—that the petty bourgeois "intelligentsia" would one day fulfill a very different function.

Only in 1935, with the change in Soviet foreign policy and the Seventh Congress of the Comintern, was there a reappraisal of the role of the Wafd. But it was not a radical change at first. When late in 1935 a writer in the Soviet press drew attention to the growing danger of war in the Middle East and to the aggressive intentions of Italian Fascism, and when he said that it was desirable that Egypt join the democracies in their struggle against Fascism,[37] he was immediately reprimanded and told that it had been a dangerous political error to publish such views at all. Nahas was a pliable tool in the hands of the British, and the greatest contribution the Egyptians could make to world peace was to continue their struggle against British imperialism. To leave no trace of doubt, the writer added that it was amazing that in a Communist organ anybody should have dared to call Italian imperialism "more dangerous"; this was tantamount to advising the Egyptian masses to submit to their fate meekly.[38]

Afterwards, however, Moscow became convinced that the Rome-Berlin Axis was indeed a greater danger than British imperialism. The Wafd was then the only movement in Egypt that supported the democracies in their struggle against the Fascist dictatorships, and thus, for a while, the Wafd was back in favor. But this interlude did not last long, for in August, 1939, with the German-Soviet non-aggression pact, the Axis became the "lesser evil," and the Wafd in view of its pro-Western inclinations, was again highly suspect until Hitler attacked the Soviet Union in June, 1941.

Compared to Egypt, the other Arab countries mattered little

in Soviet eyes. The Arab proletariat was said to be "chiefly agrarian"—which presumably was supposed to explain its backwardness. In addition, there were attempts by the middle class to win over the peasantry by demagogic means; many, it was stated, underestimated the pernicious influence of "Amsterdam" in the Arab world.[39] This was, of course, utter nonsense, for the influence of the Second International in the Middle East had always been virtually nonexistent. But it did not prevent some experts, e.g., Mustafa Sadi, from preparing elaborate theses about the "pact between imperialist Amsterdam and the Arab bourgeoisie against the revolutionary Arab movement."[*]

Other ideologists tried to demonstrate that the Arab bourgeoisie was the most reactionary in the entire East. Tracing the development of the Arab national movement to the early years of the century, "Shami" found that it had always been willing to make the most far-reaching concessions to Western imperialism. In view of its many economic ties with both the imperialists and the feudal landowners at home, the Arab bourgeoisie of Syria and Palestine was hopeless—or very nearly so. Nor were the Communists too successful in their collaboration with the "National Revolutionaries." The case of Hamdi Husseini offers a perfect illustration. Husseini, a Palestinian political leader and left-wing radical nationalist, was staunchly anti-imperialist and pro-Soviet and only too willing to cooperate with the Communists, in contrast to most of his contemporaries. At first, relations between him and the Communists were cordial, but later on, the Communists wanted to impose on him all the rigidities of the "Third Period" instead of making allowances for fellow travelers. At that point Hamdi Husseini refused to follow them, and the Communists bitterly attacked him as a lackey of British imperialism who had become distrustful of the Communist Party, and who,

---

[*] "Mustafa Sadi" was a pseudonym for Sidqi Najati, one of the graduates of the first group of Arab Communists at the University of the Toilers of the East. Some people in Moscow expected him at one time to assume the leadership of Arab Communism, but "Sadi" was a disappointment. Arrested in Jaffa in 1930, he retired from Communist politics after his release. In the forties he became a leading critic of Communist activities in the Arab world.

horribile dictu, entertained police and spies at his home "with biscuits and tea."[40] The political lesson drawn was that instead of cultivating the extreme left wing of the national movement, one should try in the future to cooperate with the left wing of Hamdi Husseini. But Hamdi Husseini had no left wing. . . .

The flirtation with Husseini was resumed in later years, when the line in Moscow again favored a more liberal "national-front" policy. But the episode shows that textbook "National Revolutionaries" like those the Communists were looking for simply did not exist. They should have known that they were looking for conscious and militant Communists who were in absolute agreement with the Comintern line and yet belonged to the bourgeois-nationalist movement.

The Arab countries became of greater interest in Moscow only in 1936, following a swing to the left in Iraq and Syria. The Communists then realized that while the revolutionary slogans of the "Third Period" had not made any impact, the national-front policy of the late thirties might have better results.

12. Riots in Palestine

In August, 1929, riots broke out in Jerusalem and soon spread all over Palestine. They were directed against the Jews, not the British mandatory authorities, lasted for about three months, and claimed several hundred victims. By Asian standards, these were not really large-scale riots, and it is doubtful whether they would have attracted much attention in Moscow had it not been for the fact that this was the very first uprising to occur after the Sixth Comintern Congress had inaugurated the "Third Period." The Palestinian Communists, the only active branch of the Comintern in the Middle East at that time, had several hundred members; whatever line of action they had adopted, it could hardly have influenced the course of events very much. Seen from Moscow, however, it was a matter of principle that the Palestinian Communists have a correct party line. Unfortunately, they were quite unprepared for the revolutionary tasks awaiting them. Instead of heading the Arab revolt and guiding it, they had called for peace between the peoples and published leaflets opposing racial incitement in the name of proletarian internationalism. In the Soviet and Comintern press, too, similar views had been aired during the riots, and some commentators even boasted that the Communists were the only ones to work for fraternization and to denounce murder.[41] In October the Soviet press published a long manifesto by the Palestinian Communist Party[42] in which the masses were called upon not to fight against each other, but with one another against imperialism, Zionism, and the Arab nationalist traitors.[43] Communist organs—not only such Yiddish papers as *Emes* in Moscow and *Freiheit* in New York, but also newspapers in Germany and elsewhere—had denounced the riots as a British provocation and had revealed a large measure of Jewish, rather than anti-imperialist, solidarity. Thereupon the Comintern intervened and in a special resolution sharply denounced the impact of Zionist and imperialist ideas upon certain Communists.[44] Thereafter it was left to the experts to amplify the lessons of 1929. "Abusiam" and Berger had been among the deviationists who failed to recognize the revolutionary character of the August riots. It was left to "Shami" to show them where they had erred. "Shami" interpreted the uprising in terms of a great agrarian movement that reflected the intensified class struggle in the Arab village. But why had this agrarian movement not been directed against the Arab "feudals"? Obviously, because the Jews were a privileged minority (like the Armenians in Syria) and they were, therefore, doubly conspicuous. But there could be no doubt (for "Shami") that this anti-Jewish movement would gradually assume an antigovernment, antifeudal, and anti-imperialist character. There might have been individual excesses, even pogroms here and there, but this did not really affect the basically progressive character of the Arab movement. Leadership in this movement would pass, or had already passed, into the hands of the national revolutionaries; the revolt of the Druse in 1925 had been the last uprising headed by the national bourgeoisie. Since then, their betrayal of the cause of the people had been so manifest that it was inconceivable that they could go on deceiving the masses. "Shami" thus reached the conclusion that the revolt in Palestine was not merely the signal for a new revolution in the

East but also one of the first signs of the end of capitalist stabilization in the West.[45]

It would be tedious to repeat in detail the counterarguments of "Nadab" and others in refutation of "Shami's" theses—that the leaders of the Arab national movement in Palestine, the Husseinis, Muganams, and others were not national revolutionaries but feudals against whom the revolutionaries should fight. What mattered was that Moscow had accepted the version saying that the riots of 1929 had been progressive in character; the experts who disagreed had to adjust themselves to this line. There was a repetition of the 1929 riots, on a somewhat smaller scale, in 1933, but they hardly evoked comment in Moscow;* Hitler's advent to power and other European developments completely overshadowed the events in Palestine. And when the great Arab revolt of 1936-38 broke out, the Soviet purge was already under way, with nobody left in Moscow to give expert advice. As a result, initially favorable Soviet response to the revolt gave way after a while to hostile criticism when it was realized that the Arab nationalists, though anti-Western, were not anti-imperialist, and that their foreign political orientation was toward Rome and Berlin. However, these developments belong to a later phase of Soviet and Comintern policy.

The "Third Period" also brought a stiffening in the Communist line toward Zionism. The attitude toward the Jewish national movement had been negative from the very beginning, but during the twenties there was a certain latitude, and, generally speaking, the problem was not considered sufficiently important to warrant the expenditure of great energies in combatting it. The task of fighting Zionism was left to the Evsektsiia, the Jewish section of the Soviet Communist Party, and with the establishment of a Jewish autonomous region in Biro Bidzhan, the whole issue was believed to be solved. A Communist writer, com-

---

* The only exception was "Avigdor's" lengthy essay on "The Lessons of the Revolutionary Struggles in Palestine" in *R.V.* 25, 1934, pp. 67-85. "Avigdor" maintained that the struggle of the Palestine Communists against the left wing of the Arab national movement had not been intensive enough. He also suggested that Hitler should be elected honorary president of the Zionist movement.

menting on the Seventeenth World Zionist Congress in 1931, declared that a "miserable end had come to a movement which for a time played a role not only in the Jewish community but also in European and Near Asiatic politics."[46] After this Congress Zionism would go on leading a mere sham existence, since it was completely played out as an attempt to solve the Jewish question within the confines of capitalist society.

With the stimulus to Zionism given by the rise of Hitler, the Soviet and Comintern organs intensified their attacks on Zionism. Hitler's anti-Semitism was regarded skeptically; commenting on the April, 1933, boycott in Germany, it was said, "In a few days you will find that all big (Jewish) stores still exist, that Jewish bankers, capitalists, and stock jobbers are still carrying on their business, and that no Jewish industrialist has suffered any damage . . ."[47] All the evidence pointed to the fact that the Nazis and the Zionists had made peace, and that anti-Semitism was "quietly toned down. Foreign political considerations render it impossible for the Third Reich to permit anti-Jewish hysteria for any length of time." And the obvious conclusion: "German Jews may therefore face the future hopefully—provided they have the money."[48] In these conditions the Communists did not think it their main task to combat anti-Semitism, which also would not have been a popular cause in some places (and which could be safely left to Western liberals); a "powerful counter-offensive against Zionism" was demanded, for it had become necessary because of the confusion of Central European Jews, and of the fresh impetus given to Zionism by the events in Germany.[49] In 1933 Moscow had come to view the Jewish question as a remnant of the past or a fossil (*pace* Toynbee) and anti-Semitism as a deliberate attempt to sidestep the crucial issues of the age. There was considerable irritation, since these problems kept cropping up again and again.

13. Turkey

It was comparatively easy to lay down the party line on the Arab world and Palestine, for these countries had not yet attained full political independence, so that relations with the Soviet Union, official or unofficial, did not exist. Nor did anyone in

Moscow then expect anything important to happen there. But Turkey and, to a lesser degree, Persia were in a different category. These were neighboring states, and relations with Ankara and Tehran were clearly believed to be of some importance in Moscow. As a result, the definition of the Communist line on Turkey (in accordance with the "Third Period" concepts) was a far more complicated, and even delicate, task. Political realities mattered as much as, and in the end more than, ideological exigencies. On the one hand, there were the guardians of orthodoxy in Moscow with their magazines, the discussions of the Sixth Congress of the Comintern, the 1929 program of the Turkish Communist Party—all in line with the spirit of the "Third Period." On the other hand, there were favorable comments about Kemalist Turkey by Soviet leaders, and above all, a friendly Soviet foreign policy toward Turkey, with the stress on economic, cultural, and even political collaboration between the two countries.

On the ideological level, the attitude toward Kemalism became sharply critical after 1928. Experts such as Rotshtein ("Irandust"), who argued that this movement had not yet exhausted its revolutionary potential, that it was still "progressive" in character, and had not surrendered to Western imperialism, found themselves under heavy fire. According to the new line, these were just illusions, or at best remnants of a past era; Kemalism had ceased to be a mass movement, and was on the way to total capitulation. It had destroyed some, but by no means all, of the feudal vestiges in the Turkish villages, and its social basis was an alliance between the top layers of the bourgeoisie and the big landowners, plus the "kulaks." Kemal was said to rule by means of a unique mixture of terror and social demagogy, a special Turkish brand of "national fascism" or "agrarian Bonapartism."[50] The attempt to brand Kemal as a fascist was not altogether new and had been tried before in the early twenties. But at that time it was denounced as an aberration, whereas after 1929 it was given serious consideration, and eventually accepted. According to this analysis, Turkey was increasingly drawn into the orbit of Western imperialism, whereas inside the country the course was toward a social, if not political, restoration of the old regime. The political conclusions drawn from such an appraisal were obvious: the Communist Party of Turkey was to wage an irreconcilable and persistent struggle against the Kemalist "People's Party," as the new (1929) party program announced. This struggle was inseparable from the general fight against imperialism, for only as the result of the overthrow of the Kemalists could Turkish independence be safeguarded. Accordingly, the new program provided for a new revolution, to be carried out by a workers' and peasants' bloc directed by the Communist Party, and aiming at the establishment of a Soviet government.[51]

The Turkish government, not altogether surprisingly, did not take kindly to such a policy. It arrested all the Communists who could be seized, and the Turkish party had to retreat into even deeper illegality. The Comintern press summoned world public opinion to protest against these "contemptible persecutions," and Ferdi, in his speech at the Thirteenth Plenum of the ECCI, talked about the "accelerated pace of fascistization and the uninterrupted policy of terror" that had prevailed in Turkey since 1927.[52]

As early as 1933 there were second thoughts in Comintern circles about the wisdom of an ultra-radical line regarding Turkey. One expert denounced the indiscriminate lumping together of Kemalists and the "direct agents of world imperialism."[53] The "fascist" thesis was quietly dropped. When in 1933 Turkey celebrated the tenth anniversary of the republican regime, it was said in Varga's organ in Moscow that this was a holiday for the Soviet people, too, and that the Soviet Union stood for the promotion of friendly relations between the two countries. The young Turkish mercantile-industrial bourgeoisie was the main force behind Kemalism, but it was a progressive force because it had brought independence to Turkey and wanted to defend the economic independence of the country.[54] Karl Radek, in one of his last appearances in the Soviet press (in 1935), chose as a subject the economic assistance given to Turkey. The building of textile factories (in Kaisarie) was the symbol (he said) of Soviet aid and friendship for Turkey and all other economically backward countries. Anticipating the Soviet economic aid offensive in Asia twenty years later, he concluded: "Tomorrow or the day after we shall help other peoples to build their industries—not as conquerors but as friends who know that assistance creates conditions for mutual amicability . . ."[55]

Diplomatic relations between Turkey and the Soviet Union had been friendly even during the height of the "Third Period"; Tewfik Rustu, the Turkish Foreign Minister, was invited to Moscow in 1930, Litvinov came to Ankara in 1931, Voroshilov, Piatakov, and other Soviet dignitaries also visited Turkey in the early thirties. This demonstrated that the Soviet Union wanted to maintain good relations with Ankara, and the Comintern experts and the ideologists of the University of the Toilers of the East had to be told to muffle their criticism in order not to jeopardize these ties. Feridov's victory over Rotshtein and Osetrov in the ideological debate had been short-lived. Direct attacks on Kemalism ceased in 1934, and when Soviet experts dealt with Turkey's economy in the middle thirties they did not complain about the reactionary character of Kemalism, but about the inroads of the Germans, who had greatly increased their trade with Turkey.

14. Persia and Afghanistan

Soviet interest in Persia and Afghanistan declined during the "Third Period." Not a few Soviet observers in the early days had regarded these two countries as the "keys to the East." By 1930 nobody was likely to repeat that mistake, for the revolutionary movement had made no headway, and there was general stagnation. The "Second Persian debate" that took place in the early thirties was by no means a manifestation of interest in the country; it was an internal quarrel between Soviet experts, with Persia serving as a pretext for polemics.

Official relations between Russia and these two neighboring states continued to be normal, and trade relations were maintained, though on a somewhat reduced scale. Both Tehran and Kabul supported some of the Soviet foreign political initiatives made at the time, especially with regard to disarmament and the definition of aggression. Narkomindel's comment on Persia and Afghanistan was by no means unfriendly. Nothing of importance was expected to happen in either Persia or Afghanistan, and it was assumed that attention could safely and more profitably be devoted to the centers of world politics.

At the beginning of the "Third Period" the commentators still talked in terms of "the class struggle that was progressing with seven-league boots"[56] in Persia and there were alarming reports about military preparations by British imperialism in Persia. Both Persia and Afghanistan were denounced for "barbaric acts" in the service of British imperialism, e.g., the arrest of Communists and national revolutionary militants. But in later years Moscow observers tended to take less seriously both the dangers of Western military preparations and the potential of the revolutionary movement in these countries.

In 1932 Reza Shah quarreled with the British about Bahrain and the oil concessions, and it appeared for a while as if Moscow could profit from this conflict. But there were no great expectations in Moscow: Reza merely wanted a higher price for the oil, Madyar wrote. His government represented the semifeudal landowners and the big mercantile capitalists; it had not solved and could not solve the tasks of the bourgeois-national revolution.[57] The opportunity was used to re-examine the Soviet appraisal of Reza Shah's regime, and the conclusion reached was that the country had indeed become politically independent (up to a point)—in contrast to the predictions of the Bukharin-Radek-Rosa Luxemburg school. But economically—and this was believed to be the decisive criterion in Moscow—Persia had remained a semicolony of Britain.

In the middle thirties a new factor was introduced: German economic, cultural, and political infiltration. Soviet observers began to express some concern about the activities of Schacht, Baldur von Schirach, and other Nazi visitors to Tehran, and to Kabul, where the Germans also tried to gain a foothold. Even so, Soviet interest in these two countries remained quite moderate.

15. The End of the "Third Period"

With Hitler's advent to power in Germany and the emergence of the Rome-Berlin-Toyko Axis, Moscow was compelled to make a drastic revision of its policy throughout the world, and the sectarian and ultra-radical "Third Period" strategy had to be replaced by a "liberal" and popular-front line. This switch took place in Europe between the Thirteenth Plenum of the ECCI (in December, 1933) and the Seventh Congress of the Comintern in July, 1935. On the former occasion there were some hints of a change, though, by and large, the onslaught against "Social Fascism" continued with undiminished vigor. By the time the Comintern Congress took place, the popular-front policy was already an established fact. For meanwhile the Soviet-French pact had been concluded, Moscow had joined the League of Nations, Mr. Anthony Eden had visited Moscow, and generally speaking, a *rapprochement* between Russia and the West was under way.

The shift from a "radical" to a "liberal" line in the Middle East took place much more gradually. In Turkey the "Third Period" antics had been given up as early as 1933-34; in Syria and Iraq the change came in 1935; in Egypt, in 1936; and in Palestine, in an admittedly highly complicated situation from the Comintern point of view, only late in 1938. This change took a quite different form in the Middle East. In Europe and the United States the "Popular Front" meant an alliance with the socialist parties and other left-wing and liberal groups. In the Middle East, and in Asia in general, there were no strong socialist and left-wing parties, so the Communists favored a "national" rather than a "popular" front and sought for close collaboration with the national movement.

The appraisal of a given event or development *post factum* depends largely on the historical vantage point of the observer. The historian writing on the eve of World War II about the great debacle of Chinese Communism in 1927 would have regarded it as a decisive defeat in which irreparable harm had been done to the cause of Communism in China. The historian commenting on the same event in 1958, after the victory of Communism in China in the late forties, would merely regard the 1927 events as a temporary setback.

Similarly, ten or fifteen years ago most observers believed that the results of the "Third Period" policy in the Middle East were entirely negative. In 1958, following the great increase in Soviet and Communist influence throughout the Middle East after

World War II, they would be less certain that the "Third Period" had caused lasting harm to the cause of Communism in the area. It seems to be most likely that the "Third Period" policy did not have a great effect one way or the other, neither benefiting the Soviet Union and Communism nor greatly harming them. The upsurge in Communist and Soviet influence came during and after World War II as the result of two different processes: the internal crisis of the Middle East and the growth in Soviet international power and prestige throughout Asia. Even if the Communists had followed a "moderate" line in 1928-35 instead of their ultra-radical policy, even if they had collaborated with the national movement instead of dissociating themselves from it, they could not have made much headway. For the internal crisis in the Middle East had not yet sufficiently ripened, and Soviet power and prestige were by no means universally recognized during the early thirties. The radical wing of the national movement in the East, which was to become the main pillar of Soviet policy after World War II, was more fascinated and attracted by Hitler's Germany, Mussolini's Italy, and a militaristic Japan. The military defeat of the Axis powers was the prerequisite for Soviet collaboration with the radical nationalists in the East. Paraphrasing a famous (but apocryphal) dictum, it could be said that the way to Cairo and Damascus led via Rome and Berlin.

NOTES

1. D. Manuilskii in *Communist International,* May, 1931, p. 348.

2. Fully discussed in *Inprecorr,* 1928, pp. 1659-76 ("Theses on the Revolutionary Movement in the Colonies and Semicolonies Adopted at the Sixth Congress of the Comintern").

3. *Protokoll des 10. Plenums des Exekutiv Komittees der Kommunistischen Internationale, 3. Juli-19. Juli, 1929* (Moscow, 1929), p. 478.

4. *Inprecorr,* April 20, 1931, p. 405.

5. *Inprecorr,* September 1, 1933, p. 824.

6. *Compte Rendu Sténographique du VIe Congrès* . . . , p. 1188.

7. *Ibid.,* p. 1307.

8. *Ibid.,* p. 1272.

9. Pavel Mif: *Protokoll des 10. Plenums* . . . , p. 490.

10. *Compte Rendu Sténographique du VIe Congrès* . . . , p. 1485.

11. Other writings attacked were "Irandust": "Sushchnost Kemalizma" in *Za Partiiu*, No. 2, 1927; B. M. Dantsig: *Ocherki po Ekonomicheskoi Geografii Turtsii* (1930); A. Melnik: "Ekonomicheskii Krizis v Turtsii" in *Mezhdunarodnaia Zhizn*, No. 1, 1930.

12. See Feridov's articles in *R.V.*, Nos. 6, 7, 8, 9, 10, 1930, and Kysyl Khan's and A. Novichev's polemics in *R.V.* 9-10, 1930.

13. *R.V.* 1-2, 1932, p. 31.

14. See G. Ilinskii and Rendshbar in *R.V.* 1-2, 1932.

15. Rendshbar's articles about Sultan zade were published in *R.V.* 1 and 2, 1933, G. Ilinskii's reply in *R.V.* 2, 1934, and Rendshbar's admission of errors also in *R.V.* 2, 1934.

16. Kuusinen in *Compte Rendu Sténographique* . . . , p. 1630 *et seq.*

17. See *Diskussiia ob Aziatskom Sposobe Proizvodstva* (Moscow and Leningrad, 1931).

18. *R.V.* 1-2, 1932, p. 31.

19. See, for instance: *Istoriia Stran Zarubezhnogo Vostoka v Srednie Veka* (Moscow, 1957), p. 5.

20. *Ibid.*, p. 7.

21. *R.V.* 1-2, 1932, p. 30.

22. *R.V.* 29, 1935, p. 19 *et seq.*

23. The "Nadab"-"Shami" controversy in *R.V.* 8, 1930, and 9-10, 1930.

24. "Bit Yukhan's" review of S. Gecht's *The Steamer Goes to Jaffa and Back* in *R.V.* 5-6, 1936, p. 201.

25. *Compte Rendu Sténographique* . . . , p. 1141.

26. *Ibid.*, p. 1307-08.

27. *Inprecorr*, Nov. 15, 1929, p. 1372.

28. "Lam Alif" in *Inprecorr*, June 8, 1934, p. 871.

29. Enukidze in *M.Kh.M.P.*, Dec., 1934, p. 90 *et seq.*

30. *Compte Rendu Sténographique* . . . , p. 1309.

31. B. Dantsig in *M.Kh.M.P.*, April, 1931, p. 88 *et seq.*

32. "Avigdor" in *R.V.* 6, 1934, p. 65, p. 76.

33. "Avigdor" in *R.V.* 1-2, 1932, p. 102 *et seq.*

34. *Inprecorr*, 1932, p. 654 and "Avigdor" in *R. V.* 6, 1934, p. 65 *et seq.*

35. L. Madyar in *R.V.* 9-10, 1930, p. 61. He presumably had in mind A. Shami's little book *Kommunisticheskaia Partiia Egipta* (Moscow, 1930), in which it had been argued that the Wafd would not completely compromise with Britain, and which, generally speaking, was considered insufficiently hostile to the Wafd.

36. "Avigdor," *R.V.* 9-10, 1930, p. 71.

37. Seif el Din in *Inprecorr*, 1935, p. 1508, p. 1563.

38. "Ramsi" in *Inprecorr*, 1935, p. 1641.

39. "Mustafa Sadi" in *Inprecorr*, Sept. 4, 1930, p. 864.

40. "Mustafa Sadi" in *Communist International*, December, 1930, p. 303.

41. *Inprecorr*, Sept. 13, 1929, p. 1050 *et seq.*

42. *Ibid.*, Sept. 27, 1929, p. 1163.

112   *The Soviet Union and the Middle East*

43. *Ibid.*, Oct. 4, 1929, p. 1220.

44. Clark in *Kommunisticheskii Internatsional*, Nos. 46-47, 1929; also *K.I.* 36, 1929.

45. *R.V.* 8, 1930, p. 25 *et seq. R.V.* 9-10, 1930, pp. 130-59. See also "Abusiam": *Vosstanie v Palestine* (Moscow, 1930); Alexandrov's article "Palestina pod Britanskim Mandatom," in *Mezhdunarodnaia Zhizn* 11, 1929, and "Avigdor's" polemic against this article in *R.V.* 8, 1930, pp. 306-13; Bukshpan: "Britanskii Imperializm v Palestine" in *Blizhnii Vostok* (Baku, 1930)—attacked by "N." (Nadab?) in *R.V.* 1-2, 1932, pp. 363-66.

46. Leo Katz in *Inprecorr*, July 23, 1931, p. 724.

47. *Inprecorr*, April 21, 1933, p. 396.

48. "Letter from Berlin" in *Inprecorr*, September 15, 1933, p. 890.

49. K. Franz in *Inprecorr*, September 1, 1933, p. 824.

50. *R.V.* 7, 1930, p. 56 *et seq. R.V.* 8, pp. 72-84. See also B. F. (Ferdi?): "Kemalizm na Ushcherbe" in *Pravda*, November 26, 1929.

51. See the editorial note in *R.V.* 8, p. 53.

52. *Inprecorr*, March 5, 1934, p. 395.

53. Fakhri in *Inprecorr*, May 19, 1933, p. 496.

54. D. Enukidze in *M.Kh.M.P.*, October, 1933, p. 36 *et seq.*

55. K. Radek, "Abyssinia and Kaisarie," in *Inprecorr*, 1935, p. 1209.

56. Sultan zade in *Inprecorr*, May 13, 1931, p. 453.

57. L. Madyar in *Inprecorr*, 1932, p. 1239, and in *M.Kh.M.P.*, February, 1933, p. 55 *et seq.*

CHAPTER FOUR

THE LEAN YEARS

The decade between 1935 and 1945 is among the less eventful and exciting in Soviet relations with the Middle East. While Soviet attention was more and more focused on the Central European and Far Eastern danger zones, the Middle East became a backwater of international affairs. Only toward the very end of that period, in 1945-46, was a fresh attempt made to extend Soviet influence in the Middle East; pressure was exerted on Turkey to cede some territory, and Moscow also tried to gain a permanent foothold in Iran. The policy followed by the local Communists during most of that "fourth period" was one of "national front-ism" with one notable interlude, the twenty-one months between August, 1939, and Hitler's attack on the Soviet Union, during which somewhat different policies were followed. It would be wrong, nevertheless, to dismiss this decade as of no importance at all, from our present point of view, for it was during this period that the Middle Eastern Communists succeeded for the first time in establishing their organizations on a fairly broad basis—at least by Middle Eastern standards. It was also during these years, more specifically during the later stages of World War II, that Soviet prestige increased by leaps and bounds in the Arab world. Between 1935 and 1945 the groundwork was laid for the great Soviet and Communist successes of the middle fifties.

1. The New Strategy in the Middle East

In 1935 the Seventh Congress of the Comintern inaugurated the popular-front and national-front tactics. By that time the Comintern had ceased to be a body that could make important political decisions, but its discussions and resolutions are of a

113

certain interest, since they faithfully reflected the Soviet line in the East. Asia did not have so prominent a place in the debates as it had been accorded seven years before, which can undoubtedly be attributed to Hitler. When the "colonial world" occasionally cropped up in the discussion, it was China, and to a lesser extent Brazil, that attracted most of the attention. But there was some evidence of a change of line in the Middle East, too. "Ramsi," representing the Arab countries, put it in a nutshell when he declared, "We must make a radical turn with regard to the Arab bourgeoisie."[1] The main argument used by him, and by several other speakers, was that the Communists had underestimated during the "Third Period" the vigor and importance of the anti-imperialist struggle—as carried on by non-Communist groups. In Egypt, for instance, the local party(?) had been condemned to inactivity because it had persistently underrated the influence of the "national-reformist bourgeoisie" on the masses.[2] "National Reformism" was not, after all, as it had been thought for so many years, a mere maneuver on the part of those concerned, nor was it tantamount to a surrender to imperialism. In the future a united front was to be established with both national-revolutionary and national-reformist groups.[3] Even before the Seventh Congress, some such attempts had been made in the Middle East, but these had been "clumsy efforts" (such as in Syria) accompanied by the demand that whoever supported a national front had to join the Communist Party.[4] From then on, a more sophisticated approach was to be used: sweet reasonableness and friendly persuasion instead of steamroller tactics and unmitigated hostility. Instead of "destroying" the national reformists, they were now to be *forced* into the struggle against imperialism.[5] This was not considered an impossible task, for the "National Reformists" were said to have adopted a quasi-Communist phraseology, which made it easier to find common ground between them and the Communists.

For the mistakes of the "Third Period," scapegoats had to be found. In Egypt "police agents" who had infiltrated the party were said to be responsible for past mistakes. But above all, the Jewish element that had allegedly captured the leadership of the Palestinian party (and was removed only in 1933) had also infiltrated the Syrian and Egyptian parties in order to obstruct their work—"in the service of counterrevolution."[6]

By and large, the Seventh Congress revealed a much greater awareness of political realities than Comintern meetings for many years past. But there was still a strong tendency to exaggerate both Communist influence and Soviet prestige: one speaker came on record declaring that "Dimitrov and Thaelmann are quite popular among the Arab masses"; another voiced the opinion that the Arab masses regarded the Italian attack against Abyssinia as an attack against themselves. Nor was there much willingness to go all the way toward identification with the aims of radical Arab nationalism: a Palestinian representative stressed the necessity of fighting against *both* Zionist deviations *and* local Arab chauvinism.[7]

This national-front policy was propagated with varying success up to the outbreak of World War II. It was not discontinued after the German-Soviet agreement of August, 1939, nor were the local Communists advised to return to "Third Period" tactics. But one important change was introduced: up to 1939, opposition to the "fascist aggressors" had been the main plank of Communist policy in the Middle East, whereas after that date the Communists said that the main task was to fight British and French imperialism within the framework of a "national front," and to stay out of the imperialist war. After June, 1941, and up to 1945 the Communists again called for an all-out war effort against Nazism and Fascism, and while the rest of their program was not entirely jettisoned, it was subordinated to the overriding target of victory over Hitler and Mussolini.

2. The Experts and the Purge

If the decade that began in 1935 was not exciting on the political level, it was completely arid as far as the study of the contemporary East was concerned. With the exception of a few geographical and economic surveys (and a number of pamphlets about Axis activities during the war), not a single book was published in the Soviet Union between 1936 and 1948 on the recent political history or current affairs in the Middle East. The last issue of the *Revolutionary East* appeared in early 1937 and the "Association" (NIA) was dissolved the same year. The academic Orientalists continued to publish their studies but, with commendable and certainly not misplaced caution, refused to comment on current or recent events. With very few exceptions, which will be duly noted, Soviet comment on the Middle East during the period under review was on the daily newspaper level, and there was not much of that, either. Such comment as there was came to explain and justify Soviet activities in the East; there was no attempt to tackle Middle Eastern problems on the ideological level or to discuss problems of long-term political strategy. Nor was there any effort to analyze political, economic, and social conditions in the various Middle Eastern countries on the basis of Marxism-Leninism. One of the reasons (albeit not the only one) for this "great silence" that began in 1936 was the fact that most of the experts and advisers on Middle Eastern affairs disappeared during the big purge. Most of them had belonged either to the Soviet Foreign Ministry, the Comintern, the Communist Academy, or the University of the Toilers of the East. All of these institutions were hit severely by the purge, and the last two were in effect closed down. The only institution that, for reasons unknown, passed through the purge relatively unscathed was Varga's Institute for World Economics and World Politics, which fell victim to a later purge (in 1948). Not all of its collaborators were equally fortunate, but, while the physical survival-rate of purge victims elsewhere was extremely low, some of those purged in 1936-38 from Varga's Institute (such as the secretary of the Institute, Khmelnitskaia, or the Far Eastern expert Voitinskii) reappeared years later.

Of the Middle Eastern experts, about half a dozen survived, mainly those who had not taken a prominent part in the activities of the early thirties, junior personnel and non-party people like B. Dantsig, I. Genin, L. Vatolina, and V. B. Lutskii. The last two subsequently became the most prolific, if not perhaps the most influential, experts of the forties and early fifties. Vatolina, who specialized in Egyptian economy, had started her career at the Institute for Foreign Trade in the early thirties, had taught at several Moscow institutions that specialized in Eastern studies, and joined the Foreign Ministry during World War II.* V. B. Lutskii had been another of the Jewish pioneers who left the Southern Ukraine to do agricultural work in Palestine in the early twenties, but returned to Russia after a few years. He had not been a member of the Communist Party, which presumably saved his life at the time of the great purge. Like Vatolina, Lutskii belonged for some time to the Soviet Foreign Ministry staff, but was apparently ousted during the campaign against the "cosmopolitans" in 1949. He teaches at present at Moscow University. The few surviving Middle Eastern experts were, as already pointed out, only rarely given an opportunity to air their views. The few existing essays reveal competence, but none could be defined as of outstanding interest; indeed, it is hard to imagine how brilliance, or even the slightest measure of unconventional and independent thinking could have manifested itself. All the other experts disappeared into Moscow prisons or the labor camps of the North; several are said to have been posthumously rehabilitated after the Twentieth Party Congress in 1956, but their names and writings have not been mentioned again to this day.

It is doubtful whether the disappearance of the *Revolutionary East* in 1937 was a great loss to the study of the Middle East. For a number of years, especially since the end of 1934, it had been preoccupied with reprinting speeches by Stalin, Molotov, Beria, and other leaders on a great variety of subjects—but hardly ever on Asian affairs. In addition, there were editorials against the Trotskyite and right-wing traitors; for readers who had not read them elsewhere in the Soviet press, there were violent assertions that the struggle for democracy was impossible without fighting Trotskyism, that Spain could not be saved without defeating Trotskyism, that progressive mankind must realize that it could not support the Soviet cause without pursuing a relentless struggle against Trotskyism.[8] In addition to this, there were the mutual denunciations in print that became the fashion after 1934— declarations that the study of the contemporary East, like so many other disciplines in the Soviet Union, had been monopolized by "enemies of the people." It was an unedifying spectacle

* Her articles in *Kommunistischeskii Internatsional* in 1939-40 were published under the easily identifiable pen name of "Vatlain."

with fatal consequences for many individuals; sometimes it was a protracted process as well, and twelve or even eighteen months might pass between the first denunciation in print and the arrest. With the disappearance of the *Revolutionary East* the situation became somewhat less complicated; the responsibility for carrying out the purge of Orientalists passed to the police.

3. The Fight against Fascism in the Middle East

In 1936 German and Italian activities in the Middle East began to arouse concern in Moscow, but it was only late in 1937 that clear expression was given to these fears and apprehensions. In autumn of that year, attention was first drawn to the place accorded to the Pan-Arab movement in the plans of the Axis; the terrorist activities of Fascist-supported groups, such as the "Greenshirts" in Egypt; the translations of *Mein Kampf*; the preparations for a new "revolt in the desert," and the exploitation of all internal conflicts by Berlin and Rome.[9] It was then realized that many leaders of the nationalist movement were importing not only some of their political ideas but also more tangible means of support from the German and Italian capitals. Cairo was described as one of the centers of Italo-German Fascist agents, who were also said to be active in Syria, Palestine, and the Iraqi oil districts; who had formed clubs and political parties, and had enlisted "spies, dancers, governesses, and typists in their efforts to subvert the whole area."[10] With this sudden realization of a hitherto unsuspected danger, there came a reappraisal of the Arab revolt in Palestine, and its leader, the Mufti of Jerusalem. Up to the autumn of 1938, the Soviet attitude towards Haj Amin al Husseini had been one of qualified support. But then it suddenly appeared "beyond doubt that the Fascist agents were carrying on their agitation in order to force the Arab fight for freedom into a chauvinistic racial struggle against the Jewish people, that would be exploited by Fascism in its own imperialistic way."[11] Two months later this had become a certainty: "The reactionary elements among the Arabs constantly betray the interests of their country. The head of the insurrection, the Mufti ali Husain (sic) is a bought agent of German Fascism."[12] I. Renap, a British Communist, had become the main Comintern interpreter of Palestinian

and Arab affairs after the disappearance of the Soviet experts. He
was reliable enough as far as the exposition of the line was concerned, but not very astute in sensing impending changes. In
January, 1939, the very month that the *Communist International*
had finally reached the conclusion that the Mufti of Jerusalem
was a "bought agent of German Fascism," Renap described him
as belonging to the most extreme anti-imperialist wing of the
national movement, whereas the Mufti's enemies who stood for
moderation were "feudals and traitors."[13] Three months later,
Renap had caught up: the Arab people must wage an uncompromising struggle against the Mufti, he must be exposed as a
Fascist agent. The struggle in Palestine had ceased to be purely a
struggle of the Arab masses against British imperialism and Zionism. It had become complicated by the war aims of the Fascist
Axis directed against the democracies.[14] This was in April, 1939,
and the political lineup in the Middle East seemed clear at last;
all misunderstandings had been removed. But new complications
were ahead: as a result of the German-Soviet pact of August,
1939, "German agent" ceased to be a bad name. Renap, however,
was again caught napping when he continued to attack the Mufti
after August, 1939, as a tool of Germany. It took him several
months to digest the new line, but eventually (December, 1939)
he came out with a new theory that cannot be denied a certain
amount of originality: there had been a secret agreement between
the Mufti and the Nazis, but Haj Amin had changed his mind,
(as a result of the German-Soviet pact?) and had again become
a British agent, because he believed he could get more out of the
British.[15] It remains to be added that after Hitler's attack on the
Soviet Union in June, 1941, there was a fourth radical change in
the Soviet attitude toward the Jerusalem Mufti, who again became a "Fascist agent" and a "traitor."[16] After World War II,
however, his misdeeds were forgiven (or forgotten) and he was
restored to his position as a national leader.

The treatment accorded the Jerusalem Mufti was by no means
unique. As a result of changing Soviet foreign political alignments the attitude to most Middle Eastern problems was apt to
be radically modified on the shortest notice. These frequent
changes had, of course, no deep ideological significance, but

merely reflected the current fluctuations in Soviet foreign policy. There was no broad general conception of Asian affairs, as there had been, for instance, during the "Third Period." The Soviet Union was fighting for its existence, and most of the comment on secondary issues was of an *ad hoc* character.

Only the main lines of Soviet policy were clear. The imperialist war being waged by the Western Allies against Nazi Germany was unpopular throughout the Middle East (it was said in September, 1939), and all countries should stay out of it. The Middle Eastern leaders who had joined the war against the Axis were denounced as traitors; the peoples of the area did not want to be exploited as tools in the war, did not want to be sacrificed.[17] After June, 1941, the line changed, of course; those who refused to join the war against the Axis became traitors— at least for the duration of the war. Soviet comment on the Middle East had been sparse between 1936 and 1940; after that date it ceased altogether, with the exception of a few journalistic attacks against Turkey during the later part of the war. The Middle East interested Moscow only as a theater of war; Nazi activity in that part of the world was the only aspect of the region occasionally given some publicity.[18] It cannot really be argued that the Soviet Union missed many opportunities during these years, for sympathy with the Axis powers was widespread in the Arab countries, and to a lesser extent in Turkey and Persia. Even the Arab statesmen (such as Nahas, Ahmad Maher, or Nuri as Said) who supported the Allies, did so out of sympathy for England rather than friendship for Russia. But the younger generation, especially in the Arab world, was overwhelmingly in favor of the Axis, which, they thought, would bring them freedom and independence. German propaganda spoke in terms of "liberation from imperialism" and "Arab unity"; it praised the great courage of the Arab people and its historic cultural achievements; it promised the unselfish help of the Axis countries which (like the Arab countries) had until recently been victims of foreign plutocratic interests and imperialist intrigues.[19] The anti-Jewish motive was one of the many common ties that were stressed, and the emotional appeal of this propaganda could not possibly be matched by the Soviet Union.

For these and other reasons, Moscow did not even try to compete until victory over the Axis was in sight.

4. Egypt

One of the immediate results of the "national-front" policy in Egypt was a change in the Communist attitude toward the Wafd. During the "Third Period" this largest, and by far the most popular, of the Egyptian parties had been described as the Communists' chief enemy, but after 1936 most of these accusations were retracted. Soviet experts began to stress the achievements of the Wafd, noting the good work done in the field of agrarian reform, the attempts to wipe out illiteracy, etc.[20] The Egyptian treaty with Britain (in 1936) was not denounced as a national betrayal but welcomed as a step forward, and the Egyptian extremist groups who opposed this agreement were sternly admonished not to engage in infantile ultra-radicalism. This does not mean that this support was unqualified. From time to time the Wafd was criticized for its weakness, for not taking into account the "aspirations of the masses," for carrying out social and economic reforms only insofar as they corresponded to the interests of the bourgeoisie.[21] But by and large, the Soviet attitude between 1936 and 1939 was not unfriendly towards the Wafd—especially when it was in opposition.

There was one question that caused Soviet experts more than a little concern. This was the problem of defining the position of the radical anti-imperialist groups, such as the remnants of the old Nationalist Party and "Young Egypt," who outdid the Wafd in their animus against British imperialism and attacked it for its alleged weakness and lack of decision. What should the Soviet attitude be toward these groups? Traditionally, this opposition had been defined as left-wing,[22] but after 1937 the Soviet experts began to voice some doubts. It became obvious that these groups received political and financial support from the Axis, and Soviet observers had to modify their appraisal of a movement that was from then on called "pro-Fascist." The extremist student organizations were described as "mere provocators." Their struggle against the Wafd was "seemingly left-wing, but objectively reactionary."[23] These efforts to classify all movements in a country like Egypt as either "left-wing" or "rightist" were obligatory but frequently impractical—they did not make sense. One Soviet expert admitted as much in a fit of exasperation: "In the conditions of the political struggle in Egypt there is no sufficiently clear borderline between the right-wing and the leftist opposition,"[24] which was correct, though a somewhat risky observation from the Leninist point of view.

One of the main reasons for Soviet support of the Wafd between 1936 and 1939 was its stand against the Rome-Berlin axis, which, after August, 1939, became a cause of Soviet chagrin. The Wafdist influence on the masses, including many workers, was described as a major calamity, for it blunted their resistance to British military preparations and to the traitorous policy of the Egyptian government which supported the Allies against the Axis.[25] There were, however, certain encouraging trends as seen from Moscow: under the pressure of the masses the Wafd was forced to retreat from its pro-British position. The general mood was anti-Allied, and British officers and soldiers stationed in Egypt were frequently attacked by local patriots. "Even part of the Egyptian national bourgeoisie was hoping for the defeat of the British." One Soviet observer noted the anti-British ferment among the Egyptian officer corps, especially the subalterns, among whom the anti-British tradition could be traced back to Arabi Pasha. There were rumors (in 1940!) of a clandestine society or movement in the army ("Egyptian Independence Party") that was widely supported by the younger generation.[26] It took this movement twelve more years to come into its own.

As soon, however, as Hitler had attacked the Soviet Union, there was a radical reappraisal of the situation in Egypt. The Wafd, which had been scolded for being pro-Allied and too interventionist, was now criticized for trying to stay out of the war, despite the aggressive military actions of the Axis.[27] The "defeatist section" of the Egyptian bourgeoisie, and its prominent representatives, such as Ali Maher and Field Marshal Aziz al Masri,* were denounced in the strongest terms as despicable

* There was a sequel in lighter vein. In 1955, a Soviet historian innocently recalled the pro-Axis activities of Aziz al Masri, chief of staff of the Egyptian army during the early part of World War II, who tried in May,

foreign agents and traitors. These, however, were merely angry chance remarks; there was no systematic attempt to analyze the situation in the Middle East during the war years. The internal state of affairs in Egypt was of no interest to Moscow, though diplomatic relations between the two countries had at long last been established in August, 1943.

5. Iraq

Iraq first entered the Soviet field of vision in the middle thirties following a military *coup d'état* in which left-wing elements played a certain part. Previously, especially during the "Third Period," the revolutionary movement in Baghdad had not been considered very promising; its leadership was said to be in the hands of lower-middle-class students and artisans. The main danger in Iraq, as elsewhere, was of course "National Reformism."[28]

But in October, 1936, Bakr Sidqi staged his *coup d'état* in Baghdad, and his government (in which the "petty bourgeois students" of yesteryear took part) was undoubtedly a progressive one, with and without quotation marks, at least in the beginning. It came soon after the Seventh Congress of the Comintern and it was all Moscow could have desired: a "national front" par excellence, in which radical left-wing forces participated but did not take a conspicuous part. In their first enthusiasm Soviet experts greatly overrated the importance of this movement and ascribed to its leaders political aims and intentions they did not really possess. It was argued, for instance, that the Iraqi movement ("headed by the national army and supported by the broad masses") had put an end to the rule of feudalism in the country, a prediction that was wide of the mark.[29] Another observer even talked about the common struggle of the British and Iraqi peoples against the Fascist danger and for world peace.[30] But the leaders

---

1941, to escape to Rommel's army and took with him important military documents. The historian apparently overlooked the fact that by 1955 Aziz al Masri was back in favor as one of the protagonists of a pro-Soviet orientation in Egypt—and as a *persona grata ex officio,* being Egyptian ambassador in Moscow. This shows that even in the Soviet Union there is sometimes a lack of coordination.

of the "national army" had no inclination whatever to fight against the Fascist danger, as subsequent events were to show.

Soviet observers were equally optimistic about the domestic prospects of the group that headed the revolt, if only because all other parties had been dissolved (they added somewhat naïvely). The forces constituting it were said to be socialist in inspiration, some "scientific socialists," others "utopian." It was ridiculous (Moscow argued) to say that some of the new ministers were Communist, since the party continued to be illegal under the new regime. The regime's action program was highly commended for being progressive and yet not going too far; not to touch private property was said to be the only sensible course of action in the given conditions.[31]

But the progressive regime was overthrown after nine months, and a number of military coups followed, culminating in the pro-Axis coup of Rashid Ali in April, 1941. At the time, Rashid Ali and his backers were not viewed with disfavor in Moscow. The Soviet Union was the first country to give him diplomatic recognition, and the British attempts to oust him were decried. But a few weeks later Hitler attacked Russia, and in the realignment that followed, Rashid Ali became almost overnight a "Fascist hireling" whose policy had caused great dissatisfaction among the masses.[32] After 1941, Iraq, like the rest of the Arab world, again disappeared from the Soviet field of vision.

6. Rebellion in Palestine

In the summer of 1936 a new wave of unrest, by far the most violent and prolonged until then, spread through Palestine. The last rebellion, seven years before, had been the subject of much discussion in Moscow, and the Soviet position had been one of all-out support for the Arab insurgents. What would the Soviet attitude be this time? By 1937 it had become extremely difficult to talk about an authoritative Soviet position; most of the Middle Eastern experts had been purged, and those who remained did not want to touch the issue with a barge pole. Comment on events in Palestine was mainly left to non-Russian Comintern functionaries, and, though it can be taken for granted that their writings reflected, by and large, the Soviet line, it is doubtful whether

Moscow bothered to have a clear and detailed policy at every stage of the revolt.

The Soviet approach at the beginning of the rebellion was one of full support for the insurgents. This was somewhat surprising, for the "Third Period" had meanwhile given way to more moderate tactics, and Moscow wanted a reconciliation with the Western powers. But then it should be recalled that the Arab revolt, in its early stages at any rate, was mainly directed against the Jews, not the British. The Jews were an insignificant minority that did not count in Soviet political designs. In addition, the desire for closer relations with Britain did not imply that Moscow would disavow anti-imperialist and anticolonialist movements. Thus the Soviet attitude in 1936 closely followed the pattern established in 1929: the Arab rebellion had nothing in common with a pogrom, but was a war for national liberation. Biro Bidzhan was said to be the only real solution of the Jewish question. Hope was expressed that the revolt would spread to other Arab countries (such as Iraq) and the only visible effect of the "national front" tactics was the warning administered to the "left-wing" (Communist) sectarians, who maintained that there should be no negotiations with the imperialists until they decided to withdraw from the country.[33] Meanwhile the Comintern called for support for the "heroic insurrection" that was (almost) a revolution; the Leninist explanation supplied was that the Arab industries had been completely ruined by the Jews. In addition, German Jewish immigrants were accused of Hitlerism (two Syrian students had been refused a bath in Haifa), and the immediate stoppage of immigration from Nazi Germany and the preservation of the Arab character of Palestine were demanded.[34] Occasionally, however, the Zionists were applauded for the valuable work successfully undertaken by the immigrants: "Unstinted praise should be given to the young Jewish pioneers, the *halutzim*, for their hard work and splendid enthusiasm . . ."[35] This was a minority view, and quite untypical of the general tone. But that an opinion in such flagrant contradiction to the general line could be given publicity at all, tended to show that no decision on the line to be followed in Palestine had been taken at a very high level, and that the interpreters of the line had some latitude in their comments.

In 1937 Soviet and Communist supporters of the Arab struggle gradually had to face serious difficulties, for evidence of Axis support for the rebels became known. This problem was at first solved in a rather ingenious way. It was argued that there were two groups of insurgents in Palestine—the great camp of Arab fighters for national liberation, and a small group of "Fascist provocators and diversionists" who really had nothing to do with them.[36] One Arab Comintern commentator went further and absolved the Arab nationalists *in toto* of all guilt: they could not be blamed, for was it not British policy that was driving them into the arms of Hitler and Mussolini?[37] The question of the partition of Palestine was then first being debated, and Soviet opinion was set squarely against it. Partition meant, it was said, that the Arabs would lose their best land; the British intention was, of course, to deal a blow to the Arab national revolutionary movement by establishing a Jewish state. Nor would the Jews profit from such a venture, apart perhaps from a few Jewish bourgeois exploiters. For such a tiny state could do nothing for the solution of the Jewish problem in Europe.[38] Moscow did not have a solution of its own to offer, apart from advising Jews in Europe to wait for the victory of the forces of peace and progress over the camp of evil. During 1938 evidence of collaboration between the Arab insurgents and Rome (and Berlin) became overwhelming and made a gradual reorientation of the Communist line imperative. Official commentators began to argue that (unfortunately) there were Fascist elements in both the Arab *and* the Jewish camp, and that the progressive forces should rally in their struggle against them. Later on, the emphasis was shifted from support for the Arab rebellion to the necessity for Arab-Jewish cooperation and understanding.[39] While only eighteen months previously the insurrection had been hailed as heroic and progressive, it was now discovered that "the responsibility for the bloodshed lay on the pro-Fascist government of Chamberlain,"[40] which was quite a *volte-face*.

In the winter of 1938 the Mufti of Jerusalem was at last openly disavowed. But this did not mean that there had been a

Communist reconciliation with Zionism. When the famous "White Paper" of 1939 was published, the Comintern commented that British imperialism no longer had any use for Zionism; "In an ignominious fashion those lackeys are flung aside . . ."[41] But again there was no unanimity about the "reactionary character" of the Zionist movement. When the Zionist Congress convened on the eve of World War II in Switzerland, comment was for the first time almost friendly, and the Jews were lauded for their attempt to establish a "united front against Hitler, to defend democracy in every way, and to work for the military defeat of Fascism."[42] This friendly attitude was, however, of short duration, for that very week the non-aggression treaty between Russia and Germany was signed. Moscow radically modified its attitude toward Nazi Germany, and the Zionists' willingness to fight Fascism and Hitler ceased to be a virtue. The Zionists were now attacked as "warmongers" and Weizmann's activities as a "recruiting sergeant" in the war against Hitler were singled out for condemnation.[43] "The support which the Zionist leaders are giving to the war aims of British imperialism makes it abundantly clear that they want to repeat the first World War, and to drag one section of world Jewry into the vortex of conflicting imperialist power politics."[44] Instead, a policy of strict neutrality toward Hitler was advised. After June, 1941, all this was changed, of course. But Moscow was then preoccupied with more important problems, and nobody in the Soviet Union bothered during the war years to commit himself to any views or comments on the current situation in Palestine or to make suggestions for the future. Neither the Soviet Foreign Ministry, nor the Comintern (dissolved in 1943), nor even the general Soviet press, dealt with Palestine during the war. The only institution that could not possibly refrain from broaching the subject from time to time was the newly founded Jewish Anti-Fascist Solidarity Committee in Moscow. But this group, too, was not really interested in the Palestinian situation; its only task was to mobilize Jewish support and sympathies for the Soviet war effort. Its publications mentioned Palestine as one of many countries in which Jews happened to live. The Palestinian Arabs were even less fortunate; they received no publicity at all.

7. Turkey

Soviet-Turkish relations deteriorated during the late thirties. This, however, did not come as the result of some new Leninist analysis of the class character of the Kemalist regime, or of the poor prospect of the revolutionary movement in Turkey; it was the logical outcome of foreign political developments that pushed the two countries apart. Beginning in 1936, Soviet observers voiced serious misgivings about increased German activities in Turkey, about the exploits of the local agents of the Gestapo, the propaganda spread by General Franco's supporters, etc.[45] It was perhaps because of this incipient quarrel that Moscow did not support the Turks against Syria in the dispute over the Sanjak of Alexandretta. The growth of Nazi influence was explained by reference to the policy of Kemal, for though under his guidance the Turkish Republic had achieved much progress, he had also weakened the popular (i.e., left-wing) forces, strengthened the reactionary wing, and thus opened the door to infiltration by Fascist elements. Nevertheless, it was affirmed that the Turkish Communists would support all actions taken by the government against reactionary and Fascist elements.[46] By the middle of 1939, Soviet Middle Eastern experts were really concerned about developments in Ankara. The Turkish leaders wanted to continue a policy of neutrality between the democracies and the dictatorships, despite what Soviet sources called the obvious impossibility of being neutral in the struggle between two diametrically opposed systems. Relations between Turkey and the USSR had deteriorated since the Montreux conference, with historical materialism providing the following explanation: the leaders of the new "banking and mercantile bourgeoisie" (as represented by Celal Bayar) were hostile to the old Kemalist ideas of statism and were supporters of private capitalism. True enough, after Ismet Inonu had taken over, matters had improved somewhat. Nevertheless, Turkey had adopted a dangerous course of action in both its domestic and foreign policy. Most Turkish newspapers did not even condemn Fascist aggression.[47]

When Turkey signed a tripartite agreement for mutual assistance with Great Britain and France, Soviet reaction was not openly hostile at first, and on one occasion the pact was approved of, since it was argued that Soviet interests were not adversely affected.[48] This attitude, however, did not persist: following the reconciliation between Nazi Germany and the Soviet Union, Turkey was alternatively accused of not being neutral enough, and of trying to be friendly with both the Western allies and the Soviet Union. "Whatever phraseology the ruling circles may use to adorn this pact . . . they have concluded a mutual assistance pact with the belligerent imperialist powers and have thereby entered the path of war."[49] The Turkish press, which had been charged only yesterday with pro-Nazi sympathies, was now accused of "almost identical reproduction of the Anglo-French viewpoint."[50] England and France were hailed in Turkey as firm pillars of democracy—which was "unmitigated demagogy" and a serious threat to Turkish independence. In addition to praising the Anglo-French "warmongers," the Turks had launched an anti-Soviet campaign that would have been unthinkable in previous years, and there were even those who talked about Soviet expansionism.[51]

After June 21, 1941, the complaints about Turkey continued, but their substance changed. Turkey was again charged with being much too neutral, but for the opposite reasons. After 1943, in particular, there was persistent criticism in Moscow that Turkish neutrality really benefited Hitler, and strong pressure was brought to bear on Ankara to change its stand.[52] As for the internal situation in Turkey, it was said that although Inonu had carried out a number of progressive measures after coming to power, he had not followed up this promising beginning, for there had been no improvement in the situation of Turkish workers and peasants, nor had civil liberties been restored, or the Communist Party been made legal. The further "polarization" of the Turkish bourgeoisie was also noted. The great financiers and mercantile capitalists were, on the whole, against statism, while the industrial capitalists, the local merchants without foreign connections, and the "patriotic petty bourgeois intelligentsia" continued to defend the principles of Kemalism (and the independence of the country).[53] Such attempts at somewhat old-fashioned Marxist interpretation were the exception rather than the rule;

in general, Soviet comment dealt with such current events as the attempted assassination of von Papen (a "Nazi provocation"), or the activities of the Pan-Turanians, whose propaganda attracted considerable, probably exaggerated, attention in Moscow.[54] All in all, Soviet-Turkish relations reached a new low toward the end of World War II. The Soviet attitude was perhaps most dramatically illustrated in the open letter published by two Georgian historians (in December, 1945), in which they demanded the cession of Kars, Ardahan, and several other East Turkish districts, arguing that these regions had belonged to Georgia in the Middle Ages. There were also renewed Soviet demands for a revision of the international status of the Straits.

What caused this deterioration in the relations between the two countries? The Turks were certainly more fearful and distrustful of Soviet intentions in 1944 than they had been in the twenties or thirties. Nevertheless, their policy was not actively hostile to the Soviet Union. But Moscow expected apparently more than neutrality and assumed that Turkey would follow the Soviet lead in its foreign policy. It also seems to have expected some sacrifices from the Turks. It would be a mistake to look for hidden socio-economic explanations for these developments; they were really caused by the inner logic of foreign political processes. It is not excluded that Stalin's private dislike of all things Turkish also may have had its influence on Soviet policy toward Turkey.

The Soviet attitude toward Persia developed on very similar lines, but whatever we know about it is based on diplomatic exchanges and occasional comments in the daily press or on the radio. On the semiacademic or ideological level there was nothing at all on Persia, apart from occasional complaints about Nazi activities, up to August, 1939, and again after June, 1941.[55] After the Soviet occupation of Northern Iran the complaints also stopped, to be resumed only in late 1944 on very different grounds—the "reactionary character" of the Tehran government, the miserable living and working conditions of the population, and above all the regrettable reluctance of the Persian government to enter into an agreement with the Soviet Union for the common exploitation of Persian oil.[56] Middle East oil was the one subject in which Soviet students of the area displayed some interest during the final phase of the war, and the real, or alleged, competition between the Western Allies came in for occasional comment.[57]

But events and trends in the Arab world passed almost unnoticed.* It was only after the end of the war that Soviet experts tried to pass judgment on the efforts that had been made to pave the way for a greater measure of Arab unity. The Soviet reaction was not too friendly, claiming that the early Arab nationalist and Pan-Islamist groups had been used by the imperialists for their own purposes. A considerable number of leading Arab personalities (such as Haj Amin al Husseini, Rashid Ali, Aziz al Masri, Shakib Arslan, et al.) had been "unmasked as paid Fascist agents." Now, in 1945, the British believed that the Arab League would promote their interests in the Middle East. And the rightwing elements in the Arab League indeed wanted to make this organization a bulwark against "popular mass movements." It was also noted that though the Arab League had adopted a resolution against the presence of *French* troops in the Levant, the presence of *British* military forces had been ignored.[58] While openly critical of the Arab movement for unity, it was not denounced in principle, and the door was left open for collaboration with the "left wing" of the Arab League, if such a group should develop.

This lack of enthusiasm vis-à-vis Pan-Arab and Pan-Islamic movements was not due solely to the inroads made by Germany and Italy before and during World War II. The Soviet government was apparently not altogether sure of the loyalties of its own Moslems in the Caucasus and Central Asia. During the war it was thought necessary to combat the propaganda of the Nazis who attempted to "fan the flames of Pan-Islamism and Pan-Turkism," especially in the Caucasus and Crimea.[59] After this experience the cautious and rather negative approach of the Soviet rulers in the early postwar period can easily be understood.

* The only exception was perhaps the movement for Syrian and Lebanese independence, which was given political support, though not so as to offend Britain and France.

8. 1945—A Balance Sheet

The campaign against Turkey and Iran was stepped up as World War II drew to a close. But it is not certain in retrospect whether Stalin was ever willing to take much risk if his probings in the south were to meet resistance. Diplomatic relations had been established between Russia and most Arab countries between 1943 and 1945—but this had not resulted, for the time being, in any particular interest in Arab affairs. But any summary would be incomplete if it failed to mention the growth of pro-Soviet and pro-Communist sympathies in most Middle Eastern countries after 1943. It has been mentioned that the military defeat of the Rome-Berlin Axis was a precondition for the growth of Soviet influence, for many of the new converts to Communism had been Nazi or Fascist sympathizers. This fact is freely admitted by Communist historians, and one of them, tracing the early development of the Tudeh Party in Persia, says that "hundreds of intellectuals who had been enthusiastic supporters of Fascism for many years realized their errors and joined the Tudeh Party."[60] The situation in the Arab world was similar.

Soviet historians occasionally tend to exaggerate the inroads made during World War II when they say that pro-Soviet sympathies spread (as early as 1941) not only among the intelligentsia but also among the masses in the Arab world.[61] This is not quite correct, for the pro-Soviet movement was then restricted to certain circles in the intelligentsia. And yet this, too, was of some importance; for the first time the Communists had succeeded in gaining a firm foothold in Egypt, Syria, Iraq, and Persia. The main obstacle in the past had been their inability to win a hard core of a few thousand cadres that could transform the party into a mass movement in a time of "revolutionary crisis." Recent history in Asia has shown time and again that this second step has been comparatively easy; once the cadres exist, the masses rally around them. The Indian Communists had 2,000 members in 1942 in a country of over 400,000,000 inhabitants. Fifteen years later they emerged as the second largest party in the country. The Indonesian Communists had rather less than 2,000 members after the Madiun revolt in 1948; eight years later they counted 1,300,000 members and were the strongest party in Indonesia. The Syrian Communists probably emerged with little more than 1,000 militants when the Shishakli dictatorship was overthrown in early 1954; three years later they had become one of the strongest parties in the country.[62] The spectacular increase in Communist strength in Iraq in 1958 provides another illustration. Communism had failed in the East prior to World War II because it did not have the very minimum hard core that makes it possible to exploit a "revolutionary situation."

Of the many factors that helped to enhance Soviet prestige throughout the East during the latter part of World War II, two or three should be singled out. Germany had been thought invincible by many nationalists in Asia, the "wave of the future" par excellence, so that a country which proved stronger than Germany was bound to be highly esteemed. The Soviet Union became respectable during World War II, as the ally of the Western powers, whereas before 1941 all things Soviet had been suspect or downright taboo. But above all there was the beginning of what is called in Soviet parlance the "second stage of the crisis of the colonial system." World War II had given a strong impetus to the social and economic development of all Middle Eastern nations. Everywhere the movement for national independence emerged much stronger in 1945 than it had been in 1939. The Soviet Union was not yet considered to be an ally by the nationalist leaders, but it was certainly a potential source of support. It was not a "colonial power" in the traditional sense, it was not involved in Middle Eastern affairs—and it was not at all interested in the Arab world. Soviet attempts to intervene in Turkey and Persia in 1945-46 produced an anti-Soviet reaction. In the Arab world, on the other hand, (and in some other parts of Asia) Soviet prestige grew because the Russians did nothing at all.

Nobody in Russia paid much attention then to these developments in the Middle East, and it is certain that their full implications were not realized. According to the traditional Soviet view, Communism and the Soviet cause could make progress only as a result of hard work and patient efforts. The idea of unexpected gains to be made without investing any particular effort was not in accordance with Bolshevik ethics. It was to take the Russians ten more years to realize the extent and the potentialities of the "revolutionary situation" that had come into being in the Middle East.

NOTES

1. *Inprecorr,* 1935, p. 1541.
2. *Die Kommunistische Internationale vor dem VII. Weltkongress* (1935), p. 86 *et seq.*
3. Yussef (Palestine), *Inprecorr,* 1935, p. 1344.
4. *Die Kommunistische Internationale* . . . (1935), p. 103.
5. Naderi (Iran), *Inprecorr,* 1935, p. 1030.
6. Nadir, *Inprecorr,* 1935, p. 1299.
7. Yussef (Palestine), *loc. cit.* and p. 1029.
8. *R. V.* editorial 1, 1937, p. 17.
9. S. Ignatov, "The Pan-Arab Movement and the Plans of Fascism" *WNAV,* Oct. 1, 1938, p. 1096.
10. D. Davos in *Communist International,* June, 1939, p. 501.
11. *Communist International,* November, 1938, p. 1064.
12. "The Fighting in Palestine," in *Communist International,* January, 1939, p. 42.
13. *WNAV,* January 14, 1939, p. 37.
14. I. Renap in *WNAV,* April 1, 1939, p. 365.
15. *Ibid.,* December 16, 1939, p. 1151.
16. *Strany Blizhnego i Srednego Vostoka* (1944), p. 12.
17. N. Vasiliev in *M.Kh.M.P.,* October, 1940, p. 42 *et seq.* L. Vatlain in *Kommunisticheskii Internatsional* 9, 1940, p. 68 *et seq.*
18. See, for instance, V. Minaev: *Podryvnaia Deatelnost Germanskogo Fashizma na Blizhnem Vostoke* (Moscow, 1942).
19. See, for instance, Dr. Karl Graf von Meran, "Die Islamische Welt zwischen zwei Neuordnungen," in *Die Aktion,* September, 1942, p. 432 *et seq.*; A. Bolko von Hohenback, "Der Grossmufti als Kaempfer," *ibid.,* July, 1942, p. 384 *et seq.*; "Die Kampfziele der Araber" in *Wille und Macht,* August, 1942; Reinhard Huber, "Die Arabische Welt zwischen Furcht und Hoffnung," in *Volk und Reich,* June, 1941, p. 377 *et seq.*
20. R. Vitol in *R.V.* 5-6, 1936, p. 112 *et seq.*
21. L. Vatolina in *M.Kh.M.P.* 3, 1938, p. 92 *et seq.*
22. R. Vitol, *loc. cit.*
23. L. Vatolina, *loc. cit.,* p. 99.
24. *Ibid.*
25. L. Vatlain in *K.I.,* May, 1940, p. 65 *et seq.*
26. L. Vatlain in *K.I.,* September, 1940, pp. 68-71.
27. *Strany Blizhnego i Srednego Vostoka,* p. 188.

28. M. Kuperman in *R.V.* 6, 1934, p. 95.

29. R. Vitol in *R.V.* 1, 1937, p. 31 *et seq.*

30. S. Abud, *Inprecorr*, March 6, 1937, p. 267.

31. R. Vitol, *loc. cit.*; Salim Abud in *C.I.*, February, 1937, p. 151; S. Abud in *Inprecorr*, April 24, 1937, p. 442.

32. *Strany* . . . , p. 113.

33. R. Vitol in *R.V.* 4, 1936, pp. 85-97 *et seq.*

34. *Inprecorr*, June 27, 1936, p. 804; also Max Zimmering, *ibid.*, p. 884.

35. *Inprecorr*, June 6, 1936, p. 727.

36. A. Goodman, *Inprecorr*, 1937, p. 1156.

37. S. Abud, *Inprecorr*, 1937, p. 1183.

38. *M.Kh.M.P.* 10-11, 1937, p. 236.

39. I. Renap in *WNAV*, 1938, p. 901.

40. *C.I.*, January, 1939, p. 42.

41. I. Renap, *WNAV*, 1939, p. 617.

42. *Ibid.*, p. 978.

43. *Ibid.*, p. 1151.

44. *Ibid.*, p. 1152.

45. *WNAV*, February 18, 1939, p. 141.

46. I. Erdem in *WNAV*, November 26, 1938, p. 1281.

47. N. Vasiliev in *M.Kh.M.P.*, June, 1939, p. 40 *et seq.*

48. *WNAV*, November 4, 1939, p. 1064.

49. *Communist International*, December, 1939, p. 1175 *et seq.*

50. *Ibid.*

51. N. Vasiliev in *M.Kh.M.P.*, April-May, 1940, p. 141.

52. *Strany* . . . , p. 75.

53. *Ibid.*, p. 74.

54. V. Morozov in *V.I.R.K.*, No. 14, July 15, 1944, pp. 21-24.

55. V. Minaev in *Bolshevik*, October, 1941, p. 38.

56. I. Svetlov in *V.I.R.K.*, December 15, 1944, p. 13; M. Sergeev in *Novoe Vremia*, October 1, 1945, p. 23.

57. For instance, A. Manukian in *V.I.R.K.*, May 1, 1944, p. 11.

58. L. Vatolina in *M.Kh.M.P.*, June-July, 1945, p. 21 *et seq.*

59. A. Azizian in *Bolshevik*, August, 1942, p. 28 *et seq.*

60. Bozorg Alavi: *Kaempfendes Iran* (Berlin, 1955), p. 70.

61. *B.S.E.*, Vol. *XXIX*, p. 89 (entry on Lebanon).

62. V.A. Avarin: *Raspad Kolonialnoi Sistemy* (Moscow, 1957), pp. 219, 223.

CHAPTER FIVE

"THIRD PERIOD"—
SECOND EDITION: 1945-1954

1. Cold War in the East

Relations between the Soviet Union and the Western Allies rapidly deteriorated after the war in Europe and Asia had ended. The story of the gradual emergence of the East European "Popular Democracies" has frequently been described; so have the beginnings of the "cold war" in Europe. These events somewhat overshadowed the changes in Soviet policy in the East, which were complementary to the "hard line" preached by Zhdanov, and others, for Europe. Soviet political thinking after 1945 was in terms of a sharpening of the global conflict. Though considerable importance was accorded to the class struggle in the West and the fight for national liberation in the East, Stalin was convinced that lasting, decisive progress could be made only in territories under the direct control of the Soviet army. As most of Asia was outside the reach of the Soviet army, no spectacular progress was expected there, and the victory of the Chinese Communists came as a considerable surprise to the Kremlin.

The line adopted vis-à-vis the national movement in Asia resembled in some respects the "Third Period" policies. Considerable stress was put on the national liberation movement in Asia, but it was argued at the same time that this movement would succeed only under Communist leadership. Not only the national bourgeoisie but also the more radical petty bourgeois elements were said to be incapable of leading the nationalist movement; they were potential traitors, if they had not already betrayed the national interests of their countries. "The history of the national liberation movement in recent years has shown (one of the ideologists wrote) that the petty bourgeois nationalists are incapable of representing the interests of their countries. They are satisfied with formal independence."[1] The independence achieved by many Asian and African countries after World War II was described as "sham," not real, independence; Soviet experts argued that the mere fact of proclaiming India, Burma, Indonesia, Ceylon, or some Middle Eastern countries independent did not in the least affect their real colonial (or semicolonial) status. There were a few Soviet specialists who disagreed, and who (Varga, for example) ventured the opinion that Indian independence (for instance) would, after all, make a certain difference. They were sharply rebuked. According to the official Soviet version of 1949-50, such countries could not really follow an independent line in world politics; all the economic and military key positions in these states had remained in the hands of Western imperialism. Any other explanation would have been a justification of the old decolonization theory, which in 1950 was as yet quite unacceptable. In this world outlook there were two camps only: the camp of socialism headed by the Soviet Union, and the camp of imperialism and reaction under the leadership of the United States; a third possibility, a neutral camp, was not admitted. As the leaders of the national movement in Asia had not joined the "socialist camp," they were almost automatically classified as followers of the enemy camp. The idea of a neutral "zone of peace" was yet to be adopted. This extremely rigid concept was somewhat modified in 1952, but a radical change came only after Stalin's death. It is true that even at the height of the "cold war" the Soviet outlook on Asia was somewhat more malleable than during the "Third Period." Some efforts were made to collaborate with non-Communist movements and leaders (for instance, in the framework of the "Partisans for Peace"). But there was not too much determination behind this, and there certainly was no great enthusiasm to collaborate with the new "national governments" in Asia. All that can be said is that Soviet and Communist policies were not entirely consistent (even Zhdanov occasionally talked about peaceful coexistence!), and that there were inner contradictions. While warmly welcoming the struggle of the Egyptians against the British in 1951-52 (despite their non-Communist leadership), the Soviet Union as yet showed no willingness to come to their help.

Soviet writings about Asia in the late forties and early fifties were as yet full of complaints and denunciations of Gandhi and the Indian Congress, of Aung San, Thakin Nu and the Burmese AFPFL, of Nahas and the Wafd. They were equally bitter about the socialist, left-wing groups in the national movement. One expert on India, commenting on Nehru and Subhas Chandra Bose, conceded that "several experts, including the present writer, had adopted a mistaken position in appraising the 'leftist' leaders during the mid-thirties." They had been described as the real leaders of the revolutionary wing which had emerged at that time within the Congress party. This had been a most unfortunate mistake—who could possibly regard Nehru as anything but a reactionary in 1951?[2] Five years later, the same writer was to admit that he had been wrong in 1951, rather than in 1935, but it would be unwise to regard 1956 as the irrevocably last stage in a protracted development, full of surprises.[3] There was no real effort on the part of the Communists to collaborate with left-wing socialist groups in Asia or the Middle East; the latter were almost invariably denounced as hirelings of American imperialism. There were attempts to establish a "united front from below"—but this was not an innovation; it had been tried without success during the "Third Period," too.

Generally speaking, the Middle East was not accorded a prominent place in Soviet political thinking in the first decade after World War II. Several books and a few dozen articles were published during that period—a new beginning on an extremely narrow scale. Two (irregular) series of "Learned Communications" on the East were put out, but this could hardly be regarded as a systematic attempt to revive the study of the modern Orient; Eastern studies remained the Cinderella of the Soviet academic world. All this merely reflected the lack of political interest, for which a variety of good reasons could easily be found: In contrast to Western Europe (or China) there were no big Communist parties in the Middle East.* The ruling classes (or parties) were believed to be hostile to the Soviet Union; even if they professed sympathies, they were distrusted as potential traitors. The general crisis that was predicted for the imperialist system was to affect the Middle East, too—but it had not yet reached its climax. In these circumstances there was not much the Soviet Union could have done to enhance its position in the Middle East, apart, perhaps, from paying more attention to Middle Eastern events. This should have been seen already in 1946 as one of the more promising areas from Moscow's point of view—but it was not. What caused Moscow to underrate the importance and revolutionary potentialities of the Middle East? Years later the experts were willing to admit that they had underrated the contradictions between the "national bourgeoisie" and Western imperialism. Too strict adherence to the dogma of the twenties had temporarily blinded them to new facts and developments. But, as subsequent developments were to show, they had, at worst, lost several years—no lasting damage had been caused.

One of the reasons that acted as a barrier to Soviet activities in the Middle East (and a self-imposed one at that) was the "hard line" followed in the postwar years vis-à-vis both the Jewish and the Moslem minorities within the USSR. The official attitude toward the Jews in Stalin's last years has been the subject of much comment and need not be reviewed in detail; originally, only a group of "rootless cosmopolitans" was attacked in 1949. But it soon appeared that the great majority of those singled out were Jews; it was sometimes argued that the drive was directed not against Jews as such, but only against Zionists, yet the great majority of those victimized as "Zionists" (from Slansky and the Moscow Yiddish writers downward) had been active anti-Zionists all their life. These developments, it is needless to

* But even the existing working-class and Communist groups were not paid much attention. There were Russian translations of books about the situation of the peasants in Syria and Lebanon (Weulersse, 1952), in Egypt (Ayrout, 1954), and Iraq (Jafar Khayat, 1953), but not a single work on either trade unions or political parties in the Arab world during the first postwar decade.

stress, affected relations between the Soviet Union and the state of Israel. Relations with the Arab states, Turkey, and Persia, however, were also impaired, though perhaps in a less direct and dramatic way, following Soviet drives against the pan-movements (Pan-Islamism, Pan-Turanianism, Pan-Iranianism) in Soviet "Moslem" territories. Opposition to these "deviations" could be traced back to the twenties; but at that time it had been mainly confined to the political field, and the whole issue had been handled with caution. The drive for ideological purity in the forties went much further: it began as a critique of "bourgeois-nationalist historiography" in Central Asia and the Caucasus, but subsequently affected many other spheres as well.

This "bourgeois-nationalist deviation" was one of the concomitants of the theory of Soviet patriotism as developed in the middle thirties. It will be recalled that Soviet historiography underwent important changes at that time, and that many of the traditional Russian heroes, from Minin and Pozharskii to Suvorov and Kutuzov, who had all but disappeared from the textbooks during the first two decades of Soviet rule, were solemnly reinstated. Most historians of the minorities drew the seemingly logical conclusion that the national heroes of their peoples ought to be rehabilitated, too, regardless of whether they had been friends or enemies of Tsarist Russia. This, however, proved to be a mistake, for according to the new line in Soviet history writing, the positive character of Russian rule dated back not merely to 1917 but far beyond. Russian occupation of Central Asia and the Caucasus had not been a "lesser evil," but an act of great historic, positive significance. As a result, all the national leaders of the minorities who had resisted this historic process had not really been fighters for national liberation but reactionaries, or paid agents of British imperialism who had unsuccessfully tried to resist the wave of progress in Asia.

One of the first landmarks of the drive against these Eastern pan-movements was the official criticism of a history of the Kazakh Soviet Republic in 1945,[4] but the campaign reached its climax with the famous article published in *Bolshevik* in July, 1950, by the then first secretary of the Azerbaidzhan Republic, Bagirov, on the character of "Muridism" and Shamil, its leader.[5]

Very few native cadres in Central Asia escaped sharp criticism at the time; even Gafurov, who was to play a very prominent role in the renaissance of Soviet Orientalism after 1955, was sharply attacked at the time for having suggested in his *History of the Tadzhik People* that the Tadzhik revolts against Tsarism in 1898 and 1916 had been progressive in character.* Some of the more prominent Soviet academic Orientalists, too, got into trouble in connection with the campaign against the Eastern pan-movements. Historians like Krachkovskii, Bertels, or the late Bartold, who had weathered previous storms and purges, were attacked as "deviationists" between 1950 and 1953. This drive was not confined to the writing of history and a few allied fields: it permeated the whole political and cultural climate. Between 1947 and 1950 the general tendency had been to "annex" to the Soviet Union writers and thinkers who had been considered before that date as belonging to the culture of neighboring peoples. Alisher Navoi, who had lived in Afghanistan, thus became in retrospect an Uzbek poet; Firdaus, Hafiz, Sa'di, and others became Tadzhik writers, Nizami an Azerbaidzhani poet, etc.[6] After 1950, however, the line was to demonstrate that the cultural developments of the Soviet Eastern people had been completely autochthonous, that the Tadzhik had *not* been influenced by the Persian, that Azerbaidzhan had been free from either Turkish or Persian influence, etc.†

Among the noxious cultural (and political) influences condemned time and again by the party officials, Pan-Turanianism (or Pan-Turkism) was perhaps the one most frequently mentioned. O. Iusupov, first secretary of the Uzbek Communist party, declared, in a speech that was to be echoed by many others, "There are individuals among our historians and writers who deny the existence of a specific Uzbek culture. For them there is

* He subsequently rewrote his book, stressing the reactionary character of these anti-Tsarist uprisings, whereupon the revised edition was praised as a serious contribution to Soviet historiography (A. Yakubovskii in *Bolshevik* 1, 1953, p. 103).

† Which, in many instances, made an agonizing reappraisal necessary. Ghazali, who in 1949 had been called a great Tadzhik thinker by Gafurov in his *History*, became, in the *Great Soviet Encyclopedia* merely two years later, a reactionary and obscurantist Persian theologian (Vol. IX, p. 617).

only one culture: the Turkish."[7] According to the party line, this was a gross and harmful mistake—the Uzbeks had little, if anything, in common with the Turks; there was a superficial resemblance in language, perhaps, but nothing else. Pan-Turanianism was an invention of the enemies of the people who wanted to detach the Uzbeks from the Soviet Union, enslave them, and make them tools for the Anglo-American designs for a new war and world domination. For very similar reasons Pan-Iranianism was attacked—in connection with alleged attempts to draw Tadzhikistan into the Western orbit. Pan-Islamism was regarded as one of the ruses of the Western warmongers by which they wanted to establish a Moslem state (or bloc of states) reaching from Turkey to Pakistan. Not merely harmful in its foreign political implications, Pan-Islamism was said to be essentially wrong, for it wanted to substitute religious community for class contradictions, and it stood for the conservation of feudal relationships. It was a weapon of class oppression in the hands of both foreign imperialism and local reaction.[8] Pan-Arabism was thought to be a somewhat lesser danger, but only because there were very few Arabs in the Soviet Union. Basically, the movement for Arab unity was as emphatically rejected as the other Eastern pan-movements. According to the official formula, the idea of the formation of a united Arab nation could not be realized under imperialism and colonial division; in existing conditions it was merely used for the reactionary goals of American and British imperialism, which, under the flag of a "slapped-together union of Arab states," tried to create a basis for imperialist aggression in the Near East.[9] But Pan-Arabism was not only rejected as a "tool"; there were highly critical remarks about the excessive preoccupation of some people in the Soviet Union with Arabic language and literature, which, it was argued, could not really make any contribution to the Soviet cultural heritage.

After Stalin's death these attacks were toned down, though not altogether discontinued. While the campaign against the pan-movements continued, conditions were not propitious for a *rapprochement* between the Soviet Union and the Near Eastern peoples. Though the Arab nations had never evinced any great interest in the fate of the Moslem minorities of the USSR, public opinion in Turkey and Persia was more concerned about events in Azerbaidzhan and the Central Asian Soviet Republics. The drive against Pan-Islamism posed a serious problem to Soviet Eastern experts; it was somewhat difficult to engage in an intensive campaign against Islam in the USSR while professing friendship to Moslem believers abroad. There was no need (as subsequent experience has shown) to discontinue the anti-Islamic propaganda altogether, but more discretion became necessary after 1954 to coordinate Soviet Islamic policy at home and abroad.

2. Soviet-Turkish Relations

Direct Soviet pressure on Turkey abated somewhat after 1946, but the underlying hostility did not change. With the possible exception of the United States, Turkey was the country most bitterly and violently attacked by Moscow in the early postwar period. In the United States, Soviet writers found occasionally some redeeming feature ("progressive circles" and "partisans of peace"); in "Marshallized Turkey," however, even this was absent. There was no real difference between government and opposition in Ankara; both were described in Moscow as equally bad and reactionary.[10] There was some bitter irony in these attacks directed against a country that had once been Russia's closest ally. Nor were these attacks always consistent. It was argued, on the one hand, that Turkey had become a colony of Wall Street, a base for Western aggression, that Turkey had completely lost its national independence. Soviet writers were quite emphatic on that; Dantsig, in one of the very few books on the Middle East published during that era,[11] stated that while it had taken several decades (in the nineteenth century) to make Turkey a semi-colony, the process of turning Turkey into a full colony of Wall Street had been completed in only a few months.[12] But in the very same breath it was argued that it "would be wrong to assume that the present rulers of Turkey are merely blind tools in the hands of the American aggressors,"* which was somewhat

---

* Dantsig's anti-Turkish approach (of which this quotation is a fair illustration) was quite emphatic. But the spirit of the times called for even more violent language, and his work was, therefore, dismissed as "erroneous and harmful" (V. Tsybulskii in *V. E. 5*, 1950, p. 102).

surprising: a country with a foreign policy of its own was obviously not a colony. It is of some interest to compare the Soviet attitude vis-à-vis Persia during the same period; foreign (Western) influence in Persia was indeed much greater, and yet Persian governments were less harshly scolded by Moscow than the Turks; the Soviet assumption obviously was that there was no sense in blaming the Persians for things that were beyond their preventive powers. Soviet anger about the Turks stemmed not from the fact that they had lost their independence, but that they had voluntarily entered the alliance with the West.

Soviet comment on Turkey during the first postwar decade purported to show that grievous harm had been caused to Turkey's economy as the result of the country's "Marshallization," that its industry and agriculture were bankrupt, and that living conditions had deteriorated. Soviet writers at the time did not take account of the considerable progress achieved in the Turkish economy, especially between 1949 and 1953; these achievements were either ignored or dismissed as inventions of mendacious statisticians. More recently this progress has been duly registered, but it is argued that the progress has not benefited the masses, and that in agriculture, the situation has, if possible, grown worse.[13] In the political field, Soviet experts complained about the violent growth of militarism, the activities of Fascist, Pan-Turkish warmongers, the "chauvinistic psychosis instigated by the Turkish press, the suppression of the democratic elements," etc.[14] Turkish political and military alliances with Balkan powers (Greece and Yugoslavia) and certain Asian countries (Pakistan, Persia) provided fresh material for attacks.

The rational intention behind this campaign was not quite obvious. If the aim was to intimidate Turkey, hostile articles alone were hardly sufficient to do the trick. On the other hand, these attacks were hardly conducive to an improvement in the relations between the two countries. Their only effect was to make the Turks more apprehensive about Soviet designs and to drive them further into the Western alliance. This was realized in Moscow, at least partly, after Stalin's death, when for a time a more friendly approach prevailed.

The "standard" Soviet article on Turkey in the first postwar decade was likely to be called "The Turkish Reactionaries in the Service of Wall Street and the Pentagon." The typical essay on Persia was much more likely to be titled "The Predatory Policy of English and American Imperialism in Iran." The stress was more on the evil doings of Western oil companies than on the responsibility of the Persian "reactionaries," which of course did not mean that the ruling circles in Tehran were absolved from guilt. Prime Minister Hakimi, for instance, was described as an open enemy of the Soviet Union,[15] Qavam was called an "American agent,"[16] and even the most radical leader of the period, Mossadegh, was accused of being a tool of American imperialism.[17] This charge was retracted in subsequent years; Mossadegh had been inconsistent (it was argued) and had been afraid of mobilizing the popular democratic forces (e.g., the Communists) in the common struggle, but he had not, after all, been an imperialist agent.[18] Some Soviet observers were to compare unfavorably Mossadegh's course of action in 1951 with Nasser's in 1955-57; Nasser, it was said, had not hesitated to collaborate with the popular forces in the hour of decision. But Moscow was not altogether happy about the political efficiency (and especially about the quality) of the leadership of the "popular forces" in Persia—the Tudeh Party. The overthrow of the Azerbaijani regime in 1947, without even token resistance, had been a demoralizing factor. Subsequent developments in Tehran and the Persian Gulf area did not, apparently, strengthen Moscow's belief in the Tudeh Party—despite street demonstrations and the like. Internal divisions, lack of resolution, and other reasons made Tudeh the largest Communist movement in the Middle East, but apparently not the most reliable and promising one. Some fictional accounts apart, a sketchy survey published in 1948,[19] and a couple of articles in a general vein, Moscow preferred not to comment on the struggle of the "popular forces." It was surely a riddle to Moscow (as it is to the present writer) how the Tudeh could possibly fail to make more progress than it actually did; it is doubtful whether there have been, or are, more propitious "objective" conditions for the growth of Communism anywhere in the world.

3. *The Palestine Problem*

The full extent of the Jewish catastrophe in Europe became known only as World War II ended. At that time, and for five years to come, the Palestine problem overshadowed all other issues in the Middle East. The Soviet attitude toward Zionism had been hostile for a long time, and if the attacks against the Jewish national movement had become somewhat less violent after 1938, and had ceased during World War II, the basically negative approach had not changed. In a publication that appeared in 1946, the only one on the subject in the immediate postwar period, Soviet readers were told that Zionism really wanted not independence but the perpetuation of a foreign mandate, and that their thesis was "provocative" (namely, that there was no future for the Jews in Europe).[20] The Arab leadership in Palestine, on the other hand, was progressive in character, despite the fact that there were feudal, reactionary elements among them. The Zionists had "artificially linked" the Palestine issue with the Jewish problem in the capitalist West—in the socialist East, need less to mention, there was no such problem. And it was highly regrettable that "left-wing" circles in the West ("left-wing reactionaries," as Lutskii put it) supported these Zionist aspirations.[21]

In view of these well-known basic tenets of Soviet ideology, it came as a considerable surprise when Soviet spokesmen in the U.N. declared their support in 1947 for the idea of independent Jewish and Arab states in Palestine; they would have preferred, it was said, a united Jewish-Arab state, but they realized that this was impossible, at least for the time being. Various explanations have been offered for this about-face in the Soviet approach: disappointment with the Arab national movement that had preferred a German to a Russian orientation in the late thirties and early forties, and the belief that most Arab governments were pro-British, whereas the Zionists in 1947 were involved in a bitter struggle against the British. Nor is it impossible that the Soviet leadership shared the general belief that "something ought to be done for the Jews," in view of the terrible fate that had overtaken six million of their coreligionists in Europe. But it should be remembered that the Palestine problem was for the

Soviet Union a secondary issue to which nobody in Moscow paid much attention or attributed much importance. There is, in effect, some doubt whether the decision to support the establishment of a Jewish state was taken at top level; in view of subsequent developments it is at least possible that this course of action was recommended by some Foreign Ministry advisers and approved by Stalin in a fit of absent-mindedness.

Support for Israel did not mean sympathy with Zionism, the Soviet spokesmen pointed out (which was somewhat difficult to explain, for the Jewish state was Zionist in inspiration—no other movement had worked for it). Be that as it may, the criticism of "reactionary Zionism" continued, and the Palestine Communists were called to fight both the reactionary Zionists and the feudal Arab leaders.[22] However, Soviet comment on the Arab leadership by late 1947 was much more critical than it had been a year before. Their reactionary character had clearly emerged, it was said; they pretended to be in favor of equality for the Jews, but in fact they wanted to reduce the Jews to the status of a national minority in an Arab Palestine.[23]

On May 14, 1948, the British mandate ended, the Jewish state was declared, and the Arab League countries invaded Palestine. Official Soviet comment was indignant about this "act of aggression" against Israel, and called on the Arab governments to desist.[24] But the United States and Britain, too, had their share of blame; they had not been able to hide their role in the "organization of the aggression of Arab armies against the state of Israel."* The Soviet Union was described as the only true friend of Jewish

* *Novoe Vremia,* July 14, 1948 (editorial). The official Soviet attitude at the time (and until 1950) was that the Arab war against Israel had been an act of aggression, an unjust war by Marxist-Leninist standards. After 1950, when relations with Israel had deteriorated, a different version was adopted: the reactionary governments of both Israel and the Arab countries, instigated by Anglo-American imperialism, had been responsible for the 1948 war. (See, for instance, the article "Palestine" in *B.S.E.,* Vol. XXXI [1955] p. 602.) In 1957, following the Soviet *rapprochement* with Nasser's Egypt and other Arab states, yet another version was given currency: Israel had been the attacker in 1948, "taking advantage of the weakness" of the young Arab national movement. (See, for instance, K. Ivanov in *Mezhdunarodnaia Zhizn,* 12, 1957, p. 59.)

national independence; the United States, on the other hand, "merely pretended" to support the state of Israel.[25] The Americans were said to have done everything in their power to harm Israel: they had entered into a secret agreement with the British to truncate the Jewish state. In the spring of 1948 they had done their utmost to sabotage the execution of the U.N. resolution on Palestine; they had extended to Israel only *de facto* recognition—whereas the Soviet Union recognized the Jewish state *de jure*.[26] Soviet spokesmen sharply attacked the Bernadotte mission to Palestine and alleged that the intention behind the new mediation scheme was to thwart Israeli independence and to strengthen Jordan, the "British puppet." When Bernadotte was killed, the Soviet press suspected the British Intelligence Service of complicity.[27]

The friendly attitude toward Israel lasted, however, only for a few months; signs of a much cooler, even unfriendly, approach could be detected already in the autumn of 1948.[28] A progressive deterioration in the relation between the two countries set in after that date. It lasted four years and reached its climax with the preparations for the Moscow physicians' trial. Soviet charges against Israel were that it had not become the democratic and independent state whose creation the Soviet Union had supported.[29] Instead, it had turned out to be a tool of Wall Street, a reactionary, capitalist country, in which the national minority and the "popular masses" were oppressed and exploited.[30] These accusations became gradually very shrill until, in 1952-53, one might almost have gathered that Jews and Jewish organizations (not necessarily Zionist) were among the most dangerous enemies of the Soviet Union.

It would not be very rewarding to investigate these charges in detail; the close contact between Jews in Palestine and in the West was surely known in Moscow before 1948 and could not have come as a great and sudden surprise. What, then, were the real reasons for the change in attitude toward the Jewish state? The Soviet leaders had apparently underrated the response to the establishment of the state of Israel among Russian Jews, who, it was maintained in Moscow, had long ago lost interest in the Jewish national movement. But there was much evidence to the contrary in 1948-49. It seemed that the "Jewish question" in Russia was by no means solved, not, at any rate, to the degree believed by the Soviet leaders. Israel thus appeared (in contrast to the Armenian national movement) a centrifugal and disruptive force with regard to the Soviet Union. The frequent insistence by Zionist leaders on immigration from Russia was not conducive to putting the Soviet leaders in a more benevolent frame of mind. The campaign against the "rootless cosmopolitans," though not originally directed against the state of Israel, caused much natural indignation among Jews outside the Soviet bloc, including Israel, but the Soviet leaders regarded this reaction as a hostile, if indirect, interference in their domestic affairs. Though Israel followed a policy of "non-identification" with the big powers during the first years of its existence, its relations with the Western powers, especially the relations with Britain, which had been extremely tense in 1947-48, gradually became normal. With this disappeared an additional reason for Soviet support for Israel, for it was precisely the anti-British activities of Zionism that had induced the Soviet leaders to support the establishment of the Jewish state. In addition, there was a gradual improvement in relations between the Arab countries and the Soviet Union; the center of the anti-Western struggle in the Middle East shifted to Egypt in 1950-51 and it was only natural that the Soviet Union came to support the Arab states against Israel.

There has been no lack of comment on Palestine and Zionism at the journalistic level during the postwar period. But there is a curious reluctance to tackle this problem in a more substantial way; not a single book of non-fictional character on this subject has been published in Russian during the last quarter of a century.* If this were all, it would perhaps be explained as the result of lack of qualified experts. But this reluctance to comment on Jewish affairs in general extends now to the past, including the distant past. In the first edition of the *Great Soviet Encyclopedia* (1932), a survey of Jewish history, culture, and religion extended to more than fifty columns.† In a new edition of the same work

* See Appendix II, "Israel in the Soviet Mirror—1958."
† The fact that Marx was of Jewish origin—noted in the first edition of the *B.S.E.*—was not mentioned in the second edition.

of reference (1952) this entry has shrunk to exactly two pages.[31] In a similar way, references to the early history of the Jewish people in the standard history textbooks have been cut to the barest minimum, and are sometimes omitted altogether. The reluctance to deal with "Jewish affairs" thus extends far beyond their contemporary aspects. Perhaps this is because it continues to be an "unsolved question" on both the practical and the theoretical level, on which no authoritative ideological guidance has been given ever since Stalin wrote his essay on the National Question in 1913.

4. Arabs and Arab Unity

In the early postwar period, Soviet Eastern experts did not favor the movement for Arab unity as embodied at the time by the Arab League. But there was no outright rejection, either; the general consensus in 1946 was that the Soviet attitude would depend upon whether the Arab League followed a "reactionary" or a "progressive" course of action.* In 1947-48, with the intensification of the Cold War, the Soviet approach became much more critical; the Arab League was defined as a British agency, a "reactionary bloc," an "instrument in the struggle against the national liberation movement in the Middle East." It was said to have played an "ignominious role" in unleashing the Palestine war and in persecuting the progressive elements in the Arab world.[32] After 1950 considerable attention was devoted to the struggle for national liberation by the peoples of the Near East, but the emphasis was always on the activities of the "Partisans of Peace" and other front organizations; there was as yet no sympathetic approval of the policies of Arab governments or the movement for greater Arab unity.[33] The Arab League, originally described as a tool in the hands of *British* imperialism, was by 1950 generally

---

* V. B. Lutskii: *Liga Arabskikh Gosudarstv* (Moscow, 1946), p. 28. There were, however, minor differences of opinion. Lutskii argued, for instance, that the prospects were good for victory of the "progressive" elements in the Arab world, because the reactionaries were not very strong. P. V. Milogradov, on the other hand (*Arabski Vostok v Mezhdunarodnikh Otnosheniakh* [Moscow, 1946], p. 11), recalled the Fascist ties of some Arab leaders and was less optimistic about the Arab League.

characterized as a toy in the hands of the *American* imperialists.[34]

Egypt, the most important of the Arab countries, naturally attracted most attention. The approach was fairly conventional; Moscow supported Egypt in its struggle against Britain without necessarily endorsing the government of the day. Already in 1947, Soviet experts noted widespread anti-British feelings not only among the "popular masses" but also among the "mercantile bourgeoisie" and the big landowners.[35] Moscow approved of the Wafd left wing, but not of the rest of the party; its "inconsistency" and fear of a decisive struggle against the monarchy and the British were decried.[36] The "Nationalists" were forgiven their pro-Nazi escapades, whereas the attitude towards the Moslem Brotherhood was less friendly; this group was described as only outwardly an implacable enemy of Britain, whereas in effect it waged a relentless struggle against the "progressive forces" in Egypt.[37]

With the intensification of the anti-British struggle in the Suez Canal Zone, Soviet support for Egypt's national aspiration warmed, but the whole credit went to the Communists and allied front organizations; the Wafdist government had adopted an anti-imperialist line only under the pressure of these forces.[38] When the military junta headed by General Naguib and Colonel Nasser took over in July, 1952, Soviet comment for more than two years varied between an attitude of cautious reserve and bitter hostility; the junta was charged with meting out "cruel punishment to the workers' movement."[39] Following the army coup, reaction was said to have grown more intense. All democratic elements were reportedly persecuted by the madly reactionary regime. The Cairo junta lived in perpetual deadly fear of the Egyptian people, its cruelty being the best evidence.[40] The foreign policy of the new regime was denounced in equally bitter terms; the July, 1954, agreement on Suez with Britain was described as contrary to the national interests of Egypt and the Arab countries. The Egyptian workers were told that they would have to fight many more battles against their rulers before genuine democracy would prevail in Egypt.[41] There were complaints about the "antidemocratic structure" of the new government, the dissolution of the old political parties, the publication of anti-

Communist books and leaflets. The social and economic reforms carried out by Naguib and Nasser were subjected to equally harsh criticism. The law for agrarian reform was said to be insignificant—it was scheduled to save the big landowners from the inescapable revolution.*

By and large, the Soviet attitude toward the military regime in 1954 was more unfriendly than it had been vis-à-vis the Wafd government in 1950-51. The sweeping Soviet reappraisal of Colonel Nasser's regime came only in 1955, following Cairo's foreign political realignment.

5. Syria and the Arab Kingdoms

According to the general view in Moscow in the early postwar period, there was not much choice among the various Arab countries. But there always was a slight preference for Syria, presumably as the result of the relatively strong position gained by the Communist party and its front organizations in the Levant in the cultural and trade-union fields. There was not much sympathy, to be sure, for the various Syrian governments and dictatorships up to 1954. The democratic regime was blamed for persecuting the Communists in 1947;[42] Husni Zaim, the military dictator who overthrew the democratic government in 1949, was accused of representing American and French imperialism, of carrying out the "fascistization of the country," of repressing the popular forces, and of a great variety of additional misdeeds. Sami Hinnawi, another colonel, who overthrew Zaim, was described in Moscow as a British agent,[43] though the attitude toward him was, perhaps, slightly less hostile than to his predecessor. Hinnawi was followed by Adib Shishakli, and with regard to him, too, Soviet spokesmen preserved a measure of neutrality if

---

* M. F. Gataullin in his introduction to Abdel Razik Mohammed Hassan's *Krizis Ekonomiki Egipta* (Moscow, 1955), p. 11. There were, however, some dissenting voices already in 1954. According to one observer, "The land reform of 1952, although it did not solve the agrarian question, was a progressive step" (*V. I.*, 11, 1954, p. 152). This is also the current Soviet view: The agrarian reform cut away the basis of feudal landownership; "like any other bourgeois reform," it could not possibly accomplish more (*Araby v Borbe za Nezavisimost*, Moscow, 1957, p. 175).

not benevolence. It was only after Shishakli had been deposed in early 1954, that Soviet experts depicted the ex-dictator in an extremely unfavorable light.[44]

With the downfall of Shishakli, parliamentary democracy was restored, but, in the beginning, Moscow continued to be critical —particularly with regard to the policy followed by the Fariz al Khouri government, which was found deficient in anti-imperialist zeal.[45] Only after the elections in the autumn of 1954 (which were described in Moscow as a turning point) and the emergence of more radical forces in Damascus, was full satisfaction expressed.[46] On the Syrian domestic scene, Russia's sympathies were, needless to say, with the Communist party, whose prestige and authority had grown steadily and which had reportedly emerged as the strongest party in Syria.*

All other Syrian parties had been regarded during the Zhdanov period as dangerous enemies and rivals of the Communists; there was, however, a change in approach even before Shishakli was overthrown and a "national front" policy was once again adopted. Among the political parties regarded with favor in Moscow were the "National Party" headed (after a purge) by Sabri al Assali ("representing the national bourgeoisie and the landowners") and the Socialist Republican Ba'ath party ("representing the national bourgeoisie, the small entrepreneurs, some sections of artisans, and also having workers and peasants among its members"). Both these groups were described as favoring Syrian independence and opposing Western imperialism, while the People's party (Syria's biggest party up to 1955) was allegedly connected with monopolist capital and the upper sections of the national bourgeoisie, and, therefore, deficient in patriotic fervor and, generally speaking, an undesirable element.[47]

Iraq, Jordan, and Saudi Arabia always figured less prominently in Soviet thinking on the Middle East than either Egypt or Syria. All three had much in common as seen from Moscow; they could be defined in Leninist parlance (though not quite accurately) as

* *Ezhegodnik B.S.E.* (Moscow, 1957), p. 398. This Soviet statement is of some interest, for the general tendency in Moscow in recent years has been to play down, rather than magnify, Communist success in the Arab world.

"feudal monarchies." They were closely connected with Western imperialism and Western "monopolist companies" and served as bases for "Western military aggression." Nevertheless, there were considerable differences in the Soviet attitude toward each of them. The Iraqi governments up to July, 1958, whether headed by Nuri as Said or one of his colleagues, were considered beyond redemption. Iraq was described as a big prison, in which the masses were oppressed and exploited by a small clique of reactionary, feudal lords who had completely sold out to Western imperialism.[48] The attitude toward King Abdullah of Jordan was on similar lines, but after his assassination Moscow revealed more restraint toward his successors, Tallal, and, later, Hussein. There was not only support for the Jordan opposition, but also virtual abstention from any criticism of King Hussein (especially between 1955 and April, 1957), despite the young monarch's repeated anti-Communist statements.[49] It was then believed that Hussein did not actively oppose the Jordan "national liberation movement," which had received a strong impetus after 1953; the ouster of Glubb Pasha was, of course, applauded, and it was assumed that Hussein would follow Nasser's lead. Only in the summer of 1957, after Hussein's coup against the Nabulsi government and the suppression of the Communist and national socialist forces in Jordan, did Moscow change its line.

An even more lenient attitude was taken by the Soviet Union vis-à-vis Saudi Arabia. This country had always been regarded with some favor in Moscow; diplomatic relations had been established as early as 1926. The underlying assumption in Moscow in the twenties and thirties had been that in view of the great backwardness of the Arab peninsula, the national movement there should not be subjected to close inspection as far as its social and political content was concerned—provided Ibn Saud persevered in his anti-British course. In the late forties, however, the situation changed; the early hopes that had been put on Ibn Saud in Moscow (and elsewhere) as a potential Bismarck or Cavour of the Arab world had not been fulfilled. The country had moved into the American sphere of influence with the extension of the work of the oil companies and the establishment of the Dhahran air bases. Nevertheless, there were no such direct attacks against Ibn Saud, and his successor, as against Abdullah or Nuri as Said. Saudi Arabia and its rulers were described as *victims* of Western imperialism, the Americans and the British were made responsible for the prevalence of slavery on the peninsula, for the exploitation of the workers in the oil fields, for corruption, medieval justice, pre-medieval social practices, and the general backwardness.[50] Soviet publications never mentioned the luxury and the corruption in and around the royal court in Saudi Arabia, about which so much has been written in both the Western and the Arab press. The Saudi rulers were given credit for their stand against Western aggression, their struggle for independence and against imperialism, and they were supported in their conflict with Britain on the Buraimi oasis.[51]

This somewhat surprising Soviet benevolence was based, in all probability, on a mistaken assumption. There is much reason to believe that the extent of the Saudi rulers' independence in foreign politics, and especially their influence in the Arab world, was exaggerated. The Soviet attitude toward the Saudi rulers was apparently influenced by reminiscences from the twenties, when Ibn Saud had been considered the coming ruler of the Arab world. By 1950, or at any rate by 1955, it should have been obvious that Saudi Arabia had ceased to be decisive in the Arab World— if it ever had been. But Soviet, and some Western, experts were slow in accepting these new realities. It is quite possible, in addition, that Soviet experts assumed (wrongly) that any attack upon the Saudi rulers would be interpreted as an attack upon Islam—in view of their position as keepers of the holy places. They wanted to refrain from a head-on collision with Islam even during the height of the Zhdanov era—let alone during the general fraternization campaign and the spirit-of-Bandung period after 1955.*

* For similar reasons, Soviet comment on Yemen, the most reactionary kingdom of all, was never hostile, and since 1956 lavish praise has been bestowed on Imam Ahmad, its ruler (cf. *Sovremennyi Vostok* 6, 1958, p. 36). The Soviet assumption was that Yemen's foreign political orientation mattered, not its domestic policy or social structure, which were bound to change sooner or later.

6. 1954-55: The New Turn

The transition from an attitude of hostility toward collaboration with the national movement in the Middle East was a gradual one. There were some signs of a less rigid policy in 1952, but the real thaw came only after Stalin's death; in 1954, Communism in Syria was again squarely in favor of a national front. In Egypt the change came only in 1955. A Marxist-Leninist reappraisal accompanied these friendly overtures; the new rulers of Egypt and Syria were said to represent new, and more progressive, political and social forces. The struggle for national liberation and the revolutionary situation in the Middle East in general became the subject of much comment. The political implications of this change in line can hardly be exaggerated: it led to the great Soviet breakthrough in the middle fifties. To put this highly important reappraisal into proper perspective, two important reservations should, however, be made. The Soviet reorientation in the Middle East in 1954-55 did not come as the result of any startling new discovery made by Soviet Middle Eastern experts, nor did a new Marxist-Leninist analysis *precede* the change. The Middle East experts modified their approach after, not before, the politicians did. They continued to write in a critical vein on the Arab national movement for months after Shepilov had professed feelings of friendship for Colonel Nasser. If there had been a Leninist reappraisal of the Middle Eastern situation, it was carried out by the diplomats and the Presidium rather than by the experts —who followed a lead given from above. The second reservation concerns the extent of the reassessment of 1955. It did not affect, as is sometimes mistakenly believed, the entire Middle East. There was no radical change in approach to Turkey or Persia, and relations with Israel deteriorated. It was the Arab world that emerged in Soviet eyes as the great progressive force in the Middle East. Such a judgment was not quite inconsistent with the tradition of Marxism; Marx and Engels in their time had regarded some peoples (not merely their governments) in Eastern and Southeastern Europe as progressive, others as reactionary. It was, in a sense, only logical that peoples who opposed Soviet policies in the Middle East should be regarded as reactionary, whereas the Arabs who agreed to cooperate and professed sympathy with Moscow became the main pillar of Soviet policy in the Middle East.

NOTES

1. I. I. Potekhinin in *Sovetskaia Etnografia* 2, 1950, p. 26 *et seq.*
2. V. V. Balabushevich, *Zapiski*, Vol. X, pp. 46-47.
3. V. V. Balabushevich, *S. V.* 1, 1957, p. 174.
4. M. Morozov in *Bolshevik* 6, 1945. For a survey of the campaign against the "pan-movements," see Vincent Monteil: *Essai sur l'Islam en URSS* (Paris, 1953, Supplement: 1954), and Alexandre Bennigsen, "Les Peuples Musulmans de l'URSS et les Soviets," in *L'Afrique et l'Asie*, No. 20, 1952, and No. 21, 1953.
5. In *Bolshevik* 13, 1950. The most detailed survey of the Shamil controversy in English is Paul Henze, "The Shamil Problem," in W. Z. Laqueur (ed.): *The Middle East in Transition* (New York, 1958), pp. 415-43.
6. Sources quoted in Monteil, *Supplement*, p. 32.
7. *Kisil Osbekistan*, March 2, 1949, quoted in Monteil, *Essai . . . ,* p. 119.
8. *B.S.E.*, Vol. XVIII (1953), article on Islam, pp. 518-19.
9. *B.S.E.*, Vol. II (1950), article on Arabs and Arab League, p. 585.
10. Akopian in *Bolshevik* 7, 1948, p. 46.
11. B. Dantsig: *Turtsiia* (1949), p. 306.
12. *Ibid.*
13. *Narody Perednei Azii*, p. 331 (this chapter was written by A. D. Novichev).
14. Akopian, *loc. cit.*, pp. 42-43. See also I. Shatalov in *V. E.* 6, 1952, A. Valuiskii in *V. E.* 7, 1950, etc.
15. E. L. Steinberg: *Sovetsko-Iranskie Otnosheniia i Proiski Anglo-Amerikanskogo Imperializma v Irane* (Moscow, 1947).
16. M. S. Ivanov: *Ocherk Istorii Irana* (Moscow, 1952), p. 405.
17. *FLP*, August 17, 1951, p. 3. See also A. V. Bashkirov: *Ekspansiia Angliiskikh i Amerikanskikh Imperialistov v Irane* (Moscow, 1954).
18. See S. S. Abdullaev's review of Bashkirov's book in *V.I.* 11, 1956, p. 194. See also B. N. Zakhoder (ed.): *Sovremennyi Iran* (Moscow, 1957), p. 348.
19. A. V. Bashkirov: *Rabochee i Profsoiuznoe Dvizhenie Irana* (Moscow, 1948).
20. V. B. Lutskii: *Palestinskaia Problema* (Moscow, 1946), p. 28.
21. *Ibid.*, p. 28 *et seq.*
22. L. Vatolina in *M.Kh.M.P.* 12, 1947, p. 63 *et seq.*; S. Mikunis in *FLP*, April 15, 1948, p. 5.
23. L. Vatolina, *loc. cit.*

24. *Pravda, Izvestiia,* May 15-25, 1948, *passim.*

25. V. B. Lutskii: *Angliiskii i Amerikanskii Imperializm na Blizhnem Vostoke* (Moscow, 1948), p. 27.

26. *Ibid.*

27. *Novoe Vremia,* September 30, 1948.

28. See, for instance, Ilia Ehrenburg in *Pravda,* September 21, 1948.

29. *B.S.E.,* Vol. XVII (1952), p. 515.

30. L. Vatolina in *V.E.* 4, 1951, p. 94 *et seq.,* is a fairly typical illustration for comment on Israel in 1950-53.

31. See *B.S.E.* (first edition), Vol. XXIV, entry "Jews," and *B.S.E.* (second edition), Vol. XV.

32. V. B. Lutskii: *Angliiskii i Amerikanskii Imperializm . . . ,* p. 8.

33. L. Vatolina: *Borba Narodov Blizhnego Vostoka za Mir* (Moscow, 1952), p. 11 *et seq.*

34. L. Petrov in *Trud,* April 5, 1950.

35. L. Vatolina in *M.Kh.M.P.* 6, 1946, and L. Vatolina: *Sovremennyi Egipet* (Moscow, 1949), *passim.*

36. V. B. Lutskii: *Angliia i Egipet* (Moscow, 1947), p. 13.

37. *Ibid.*

38. L. Vatolina: *Borba Narodov . . . ,* p. 19.

39. *B.S.E.,* Vol. XV (1952), p. 460.

40. *Imperialisticheskaia Borba za Afriku i Osvoboditelnoe Dvizhenie Narodov* (Moscow, 1953), p. 126.

41. I. I. Potekhin and Olderogge (eds.): *Narody Afriki* (Moscow, 1954), p. 213.

42. *B.S.E.,* Vol. XXXIX (1956), p. 149.

43. *Sovremennaia Siriia* (ed. A. F. Sultanov) (Moscow, 1958), pp. 157-60; *FLP,* Jan. 13, 1950.

44. *Ibid.;* also M. F. Gataullin in *Araby v Borbe . . . ,* pp. 227-32.

45. M. F. Gataullin, *op. cit.,* pp. 239-40.

46. I. Tishin in *Kommunist* 16, 1954, p. 79 *et seq.*

47. *Zarubezhnie Strany* (Moscow, 1957), p. 504; M. Gataullin: *Siriia* (Moscow, 1956), pp. 18-19.

48. A. F. Fedchenko in *Araby v Borbe . . . ,* p. 373 *et seq.*

49. E. A. Lebedev: *Iordaniia v Borbe za Nezavisimost* (Moscow, 1956), pp. 95-120.

50. E. Primakov: *Strany Arabii i Kolonializm* (Moscow, 1956), *passim.*

51. Z. I. Levin, "Saudovskaia Arabiia," in *Araby v Borbe . . . ,* pp. 347-48.

CHAPTER SIX

EX ORIENTE LUX: 1959

1. *The Thaw in the East*

The thaw of 1953 could not fail to affect Soviet attitudes toward Asia. The fundamental axiom of Stalin's policy (as G. Lukacs put it) had been the inherent need for a constant sharpening of conflicts, which determined the internal affairs of the Soviet Union and involved the perspective of a third world war.[1] Stalin never went to the logical end in drawing conclusions from this doctrine; with a few exceptions, he acted after 1948 like a believer in "peaceful coexistence." But he did not do so gracefully; he never attempted to make the most of a policy that was in practice as peaceful as that of his successors. Nor was there any serious effort on his part to effect a *rapprochement* with the national movements (and the national governments) in Asia. He did not recognize a "zone of peace," a "third camp," or a neutral bloc, although the emergence of a group of neutral, unattached states, mainly in Asia, had been one of the most significant developments of the postwar period. Stalin at seventy was neither alert nor agile enough to take cognizance of these developments and to adjust his policy accordingly. This was left to his successors, who modified Soviet policy in Asia in a spectacular and most successful way after Stalin's death.

Important as the change was, it was neither a radical break nor an unprecedented development. The change was gradual: there had been some evidence of a growing appreciation of the importance of the national movement in the East back in 1951-52. Nor was there a sudden turn immediately after Stalin's death; in the books and pamphlets on Asian affairs published in Moscow in 1954-55 there is little evidence of a basic reappraisal; substantial modifications came only after the Twentieth Party Congress. Khrushchev and his colleagues took a more realistic view of the situation in Asia; they did not underrate the tensions and contradictions between these Asian countries and the West, and they thought it pointless to antagonize the non-Communist East by demanding acceptance of the Communist credo all along the line. They were in favor of assisting the movement toward neutralism in these countries—even if it involved substantial help for a political movement that was not Communist-controlled. For they were confident that in the long run, in a perspective of several decades, or perhaps even less, Communism would prevail anyway in the East, as the result of the inner momentum of social, economic and political developments, and of the incompetence of the present ("national") leadership of these countries, which had achieved national independence but would be unable to cope with the urgent social and economic tasks of independent government. The new Soviet rulers were sure of victory in view of the growing strength and prestige of the Soviet Union in Asia, and the increasing dependence of the neutral countries upon the Soviet bloc. In the twenties, Soviet support for the national movement in the East had always involved a big risk; to wit, that the nationalist allies would decide their own future (as had Kemal) or even turn against the Soviet Union (Chiang Kai-shek). But with the decisive shift in the balance of power, this risk had diminished and perhaps altogether disappeared. In the face of the overwhelming preponderance of the Soviet bloc it was extremely unlikely that a Sukarno or a Nasser would dare to turn against his allies; if he did, the outcome would hardly be in doubt.

There were no radical differences between Khrushchev and Stalin with regard to these long-term prospects of Communism in the East. But Khrushchev and the other Soviet leaders took account of developments in Asia after World War II, realized more astutely the potentialities of the "revolutionary situation" that had arisen; he and his colleagues were ready to make far greater concessions to assure the good will and collaboration of the national movement in Asia—and, as a result, they revolutionized the entire world situation in the middle fifties. Yet, such an about-face was not altogether unprecedented. There had been some attempts in the past, almost as far-reaching, to cooperate with the national movement in the East. That they were less successful had not been the fault of the Soviet leaders. Conditions in Asia had not then ripened for such an alliance; the Asian leaders had not been willing to seize the Soviets' outstretched hand. Only in the middle fifties was there a singularly happy concatenation of circumstances, when Soviet approaches coincided with revolutionary trends inside the Middle East and Southeast Asia and made the grand alliance possible. The broad outlines of Soviet reorientation in Asia after 1953 soon became obvious; the details, the ideological justification, were left to the experts. This involved a temporary retreat from the concept of the hegemony of the proletariat in the national movement in the East—and, in consequence, a rediscovery of the progressive role of the "national bourgeoisie." One Soviet Middle East expert, writing as late as 1955, noted that "only the proletariat can lead the national-liberation movement"; the national bourgeoisie had tried, at times, to put itself at the top of the movement, but, wavering and inclined to compromise with imperialism, had shown itself incapable of leadership. In addition, the Arab national bourgeoisie was relatively weak both politically and economically.[2] Less than two years later, however, the same expert went on record with the observation that the very active and broad participation of the national bourgeoisie in the national liberation struggle was a characteristic feature of the anti-imperialist struggle in the Arab world; that the national bourgeoisie had grown much stronger of late, and that the proletariat (the "leading force" of 1955!) was only *beginning* to play the role of the *avant garde* in the national liberation struggle in 1957.[3] This revaluation is highly illuminating; it was not, of course, based on any new statistical knowledge of the relative strength of the social classes in the Middle East. Similar interesting changes in attitude emerge from a comparison of the two discussions of Soviet Orientalists (in the spring of 1955 and the autumn of 1956) about economic developments in Asia and the role of the

national bourgeoisie.* Some Asian experts argued that certain
basic tenets ought to be revised in the light of *new* facts that had
recently emerged. Others, such as the late I. M. Reisner, maintained that the "new facts" were not really of recent date and
that the study of the contemporary East in the Soviet Union had
merely been impeded by the compulsory adherence to the dogmatic *obiter dicta* of the late Josef Stalin. One illustration provided was the description of Gandhi as an imperialist agent and
the assumption (by Stalin) that there had been a decisive split
in India in 1925 between those within the national bourgeoisie
who wanted a compromise and the others who wanted to resist
Western imperialism.[4]

These discussions were scheduled to deal with the national
movement in Asia in general, but soon turned into a debate about
the character of the "national bourgeoisie." Let us look a little
more closely at the dilemma facing Soviet Asian experts at this
juncture. The great new insight gained by 1956 was that, though
the capitalist system in the world in general was in a state of
general crisis and decomposition, the bourgeoisie of certain (Eastern) countries, such as India, Indonesia, or Egypt, could still play
a progressive role. The Soviet experts did not think in terms of
economic growth; it would have been absurd to argue that such
countries as Indonesia or Egypt had made, or could in the near
future achieve, greater economic progress than the United States,
Western Europe, or Japan. It was the social and political aspects
of the problem that the Soviet Orientalists had in mind. In the
West, they argued, the bourgeoisie had exhausted its usefulness
and the limits of its potentialities as far as the organization of
production was concerned. But in the economy of the East there
were still remnants of feudalism, and the struggle against them
was the "progressive task" of the national bourgeoisie; as in
nineteenth-century Europe this class was to act, albeit uncon-

* See *S. V.* 4, 1955, pp. 138-146 for the 1955 discussion based on a
report by V. A. Maslennikov, then the editor of *S. V. (S. V.* 4, 1955, pp.
31-42). A shortened version of the 1956 discussion, which lasted several
months, is given in *S. V.* 1, 1957, pp. 174-184. The 1956 discussion was
opened by V. V. Balabushevich, an expert on India.

sciously, as the midwife of new social forces and the gravedigger of the old order.[5]

These various assumptions led the Soviet experts to conclude that the national bourgeoisie in the East (including even the "monopolist bourgeoisie"!) was progressive in character, and therefore a potential ally of the Soviet Union, whereas no such alliance could possibly be envisaged with the bourgeoisie in the West. It was a neat scheme, but open to serious objections, even from purely Marxist-Leninist premises. All the arguments about the prevalence of feudal elements in the East, and the struggle against them, had already been known to the ideologists of the "Third Period," who had, nevertheless, reached very different political conclusions, namely, that the national bourgeoisie was incapable and unwilling to eradicate these feudal remnants, and that they were more afraid of the native proletariat than of foreign imperialism. If this appraisal was mistaken, they had erred by underrating the political, rather than the economic, conflicts between the middle-class-led national movement in Asia—and the West. If the later experts took a more favorable view of the national bourgeoisie, it was the result of taking cognizance of political, rather than startlingly new economic, trends. Some of their current assumptions could, of course, be well founded, such as, for instance, the expectation that a policy of statism would gradually pave the way toward a non-capitalist social order by swelling the ranks of the industrial working class and giving a strong impetus to the class struggle while inhibiting the further growth of the "national bourgeoisie." (True, this had not happened in Turkey, but it might lead to different and, from the Communist point of view, more desirable results in other Asian countries.) All participants in the 1956 discussion maintained that in the current phase of development the interests of the national bourgeoisie coincided with the economic and political interests of the people, their social and economic progress. But it was also argued that this coincidence could never be complete —nor would it last forever. No answers were provided to two important questions: What independent action should be taken by the "progressive forces" against the national bourgeoisie if the harmony of interests was not complete? And when, under what conditions, would the national bourgeoisie cease to fulfill its "progressive function"?

These considerations apart, it was not certain whether the new conception of the national bourgeoisie and its historic role could really be applied in this form to the Middle East. The national bourgeoisie, to recall the traditional definition, are the local industrialists, the merchants and bankers who want to promote capitalist development. But it could hardly be argued that such a class was in power in the United Arab Republic or that, to any important degree, it influenced the policy of its government. Some Soviet experts have realized this difficulty and have used such *ad hoc* terms as "military intelligentsia," of which Karl Marx would hardly have approved. If the rulers of the United Arab Republic represent any specific social class, it is, of course, the lower middle class rather than the national bourgeoisie.* This, in its turn, poses another serious problem: The "military intelligentsia" (or petty bourgeoisie) fulfilled a progressive role by doing away with the "feudal remnants." But by doing so, did it not exhaust its own usefulness according to the Leninist scheme? For the bourgeoisie, by definition, can fulfill a progressive role only so long as it is engaged in a struggle against a more antiquated social order and form of production (i.e., the "feudal remnants"). Once it has achieved this task, it ceases to be progressive. But the United Arab Republic and its rulers obviously retain their progressive character for the time being, and the reason, again, is to be found outside the domestic economic setup. For the struggle of the United Arab Republic against the West continues, not because of any direct economic clash between "Western imperialism" and the plans of the national bourgeoisie of Egypt and Syria for the development of their economy—but for

* Most Soviet observers differentiate between the lower middle class and the "lower national bourgeoisie." The members of the latter are defined as exploiting hired labor, thus absorbing part of the surplus value, whereas the former are independent producers, mainly artisans or (comparatively) well-to-do peasants who do not employ outside labor. The former class is believed to be both more progressive and more reactionary than the latter: the element of exploitation is absent—but then the traditional lower middle class is mostly rooted in a precapitalist mode of production (A. I. Levkovskii in the 1956 discussion. *S. V.* 1, 1957, p. 182).

very different reasons. This clearly shows the limitations of the attempts to explain current developments in the Middle East on strictly orthodox Leninist terms—even in the revised version of 1956.

2. The National Movement—Revisited

The spring of 1955, the spring of Bandung, was the great divide in the Soviet attitude toward the national movement in the East. Up to that date the struggle for national liberation had been supported in Moscow but in the traditional terms of "proletarian hegemony," agrarian unrest, and, at best, a national anti-imperialist front that developed *in opposition* to the government. Some of the hostility against the ruling "bourgeois nationalists" had gradually disappeared after 1953; "Western imperialism," rather than the native reactionaries, was regarded in Moscow as the main enemy. But cooperation with the national movement and its leaders on a wide scale was certainly not yet envisaged; the national bourgeoisie had its quarrels with the West, to be sure, but its opposition to imperialism was thought to be inconsistent; in view of its very class character, it could not be regarded as a reliable ally.[6]

Soviet foreign policy and diplomacy were not, however, unduly affected by these traditional ideological considerations, when they faced new and highly promising realities in the East. The spring of 1955 brought not only the Bandung conference but also Khrushchev's and Bulganin's trip to India and the arms deal with Egypt. As a result, a distinct hiatus developed between the Soviet government's efforts to improve relations with Asian and African political leaders and the tone of writing favored by the more or less scholarly journals in the USSR. It can hardly be supposed that the Soviet Eastern experts were blind to what was occurring in the political field, and yet these same writers continued to subject the Soviet government's Asian and African interlocutors to criticism in the approved orthodox manner— possibly from a belief that the political changes were merely tactical and did not require any doctrinal modification. There was apparently a tacit assumption for a while that one could very well cooperate with Nehru (in 1955) without necessarily retreat-

ing from the stand taken vis-à-vis the Indian national movement
in the past. But this proved to be a mistaken assumption; collaboration with the national movement in the East became a
matter of long-term strategy in 1955; the ideological justification
had to be provided not only for current policies; past history,
too, had to be rewritten. It was clearly impossible to embrace the
slogans of the national movement in Asia and at the same time to
vilify the past leaders of this movement and their ideas. One
month after Bandung, an unsigned editorial in *Kommunist*, the
official party organ, first stated that Soviet writers had been
guilty of exaggeration in denouncing movements such as Kemalism in Turkey and Gandhism in India.[7]

There was a regrettable, but perhaps unavoidable, time-lag in
compliance with the new line. Throughout 1955 and up to early
1956, books and pamphlets continued to appear that were permeated with the old "militant" spirit. The second volume of a
standard textbook on the *Most Recent History of the Peoples
of the East,* published by Moscow University in the spring of
1956, was a typical illustration.[8] Covering the decade prior to
World War II, the authors still continued to describe the national
movement in the East in terms of "national reformism," "betrayal," and "agents of imperialism." Almost immediately after its
publication, this work was, however, subjected to acid criticism
for being out of touch with the new spirit. Concentrating on the
treatment of Gandhi, A. Guber, then director of the Institute for
Oriental Studies in the Soviet Academy of Sciences, stated that
though the late Indian leader's philosophical ideas did not at all
coincide with Marxist-Leninist ideology, it was wrong to over-
look the positive aspects of his life work and political struggle.[9]
These and similar admonitions sufficed to put an end to the
public expression of old-fashioned, quasi-revolutionary views in
the field of Eastern studies. On some occasions the "Third
Period" approach was even described as downright harmful, for
impairing the relations between the Soviet Union and the national
movements in the East. It would be wrong, however, to exaggerate the damage done as the result of this time-lag in 1955-56.
The writings of the Soviet Eastern experts had never been followed with great attention in such countries as India or Egypt;

they were, and remained in effect, largely unknown outside the Soviet Union. As far as Cairo and New Delhi were concerned, the sympathetic declarations and friendly actions of Khrushchev, Bulganin, and Shepilov mattered far more than the tenor of books or articles published in Moscow.

It was easy enough for the Eastern experts to adhere to the new line, but considerably more difficult to provide an explanation for it in Marxist-Leninist terms. Part of the ideological justification had been provided in the discussions on the economic role of the national bourgeoisie in the East. But this debate had left some of the more important political problems unsolved. Above all, there was the issue of future perspectives in the Middle East and other parts of Asia. For all the friendship and sympathy, Moscow obviously did not regard the present state of affairs in Asia as the final stage of development. However desirable the trend toward state capitalism, and the present foreign policy of the "national bourgeoisie," these processes were regarded only as transitional phenomena on the way toward a "Popular Democracy," Asian style, and, eventually, toward Communism.* In other words, the present leadership of the national movement (the national bourgeoisie) would have to give way, sooner or later, to a leadership more representative of the "popular masses." At present, the interests of this leadership and the masses coincide, but they will not continue to coincide forever. On these admittedly ticklish issues, little if any guidance has been offered to Soviet Eastern experts. Only very infrequently is comment made on these lines—by hints and implications rather than direct reference and plain speaking. One writer has drawn an interesting

---

* State capitalism, though preferable to "monopoly capitalism," was not necessarily regarded as a step in the peaceful and gradual transition toward socialism. Gafurov, the main party spokesman in the field of Eastern studies since 1956, complained in the summer of 1957 that some Soviet scholars had misinterpreted the instructions of the Twentieth Party Congress by regarding the growth of the state sector in the economy of certain Asian countries as the starting point for a socialist transformation of the economy. It was quite wrong to assume (according to Gafurov) that socialism might possibly be built under the leadership of the bourgeoisie—in Asia or elsewhere (B. G. Gafurov on the "Immediate Tasks of Soviet Oriental Studies" in *Vestnik Akademii Nauk*, 9, 1957).

parallel between the national movement in Asia and Russian populism of the nineteenth century; Soviet experts should not be deterred (he argued) by certain strange features of this new nationalism which ought to be explained in the context of the general backwardness in the East. In good time the progressive kernel only would remain, whereas the secondary ("non-progressive") features would gradually disappear.[10] Another authority, in a more outspoken vein, admitted that at the present time the anti-imperialist movement in Asia and the Middle East was led by parties and groups very far removed from Communism. These parties and groups might set themselves very limited aims. But for the Marxist-Leninist, "what matters is not so much the subjective tendency as the objective consequences of those actions and their real historic importance."[11] In other words, no Communist should be put off by the insistence of national leaders that their movements were "integral nationalist," and that they would follow their own independent way. The Communist assumption was that the logic of events would gradually propel these national movements toward "Popular Democracy," though their leaders did not want it and had never envisaged such a development. Such attempts to anticipate future developments were infrequent, however; on the whole, they were not encouraged—for publication, at any rate. The slogan of Soviet policy under Khrushchev was, as it had been under both Lenin and Napoleon, "*On s'engage, puis on verra.*" Which did not preclude a large measure of confidence about what there would be to see in ten or fifteen years' time.

3. Revival of Oriental Studies

The new interest in Asia was reflected, not quite surprisingly, in the publication of new periodicals and books, in the establishment of new organizations scheduled to study the contemporary East, in meetings and conventions, public speeches, editorials in *Pravda* and *Kommunist,* and in many other ways. Oriental studies, for so many years the Cinderella of Soviet scholarship, again became, almost overnight, a respectable discipline of great importance. Some modest beginnings had been made in 1950 when Oriental Institutes were established at the Soviet Academy of

Sciences in Moscow, and the Uzbek Academy of Science in Tashkent. But these new institutions apparently lacked both the essential means and the specialists needed, nor was there any visible
intention to tackle the problems of the contemporary East. The
almost total neglect of Near and Middle Eastern problems continued, and was noted by Soviet as well as foreign observers. At
a meeting of historians and economists in Moscow in 1954 a
participant drew attention to the fact that in the Far East the
national liberation movement had been much more successful
than in the Middle East because it had been headed by the "working class" rather than the "national bourgeoisie," which perhaps
explained the greater interest shown by Soviet experts in Far
Eastern and Southeast Asian affairs.[12] A real impetus was given to
Soviet Eastern studies only in the spring of 1955 with the publication of the new central organ of Soviet Orientalists, *Sovetskoe
Vostokovedenie* (the first number appeared in April, 1955—the
month of Bandung). At the same time, there were public and
very emphatic appeals in the Soviet press for an intensification of
the work of Eastern experts. These appeals for a new beginning
started, as a rule, with a reference to the great achievements of
Russian Orientalism in the Tsarist era and in the early Soviet days,
and ended with the complaint that the work done recently was
quite insufficient in the light of new exigencies. Nobody mentioned what had caused the eclipse in Soviet Eastern studies after
the middle thirties.[13] Soviet Orientalists were criticized on many
counts: for neglecting Eastern languages and committing ideological mistakes, for a low scientific level, and leaving out of their
purview entire areas of the East (such as the Arab countries and
Africa), for not training enough "cadres" and not establishing
research and training centers in the Central Asian and Transcaucasian republics. Mikoyan had this to say on the subject at the
Twentieth Party Congress: ". . . another institute at the Academy
of Sciences studies the problems of the East. Yet all that can be
said of it is that, while the entire East has awakened in our time,
the institute goes on dozing contentedly. It is about time that it
should lift itself to the standard required in our day."[14] Mikoyan
also noted with astonishment and regret that the 139-year-old
Moscow Institute of Eastern Studies (the former Lazarev Insti-

tute) had been closed at a time when Soviet ties with the East were increasing, and when economic, cultural, and political ties were rapidly developing.*

Following this intervention on the very highest level, the study of the contemporary Middle East received a strong impetus.[15] Within less than eighteen months, Soviet orientalists were convened at an All-Union Conference in Tashkent, a new monthly and many books and booklets had appeared, new research centers had been created. It was obviously a case of "accelerated growth," and if the quality was sometimes deficient, the very fact that so many activities could be carried out in a very short time was in itself a triumph of improvisation. This upsurge of interest in Asian studies was reflected in the personal fortunes of some of the leading scholars in the field: A. A. Guber, an expert on Southeast Asian affairs, became head of the national committee of Soviet historians, E. M. Zhukov was appointed secretary of the history department of the Academy of Sciences, and B. G. Gafurov, who

---

* An Institute of Eastern Languages was opened at Moscow State University in September, 1956. In its second year the Institute had eighty students. Eastern languages are also taught at the Eastern faculty of Leningrad State University, the Central Asian State University in Tashkent, the Aberbaidzhan State University, Baku, at Kazan State University, Kazan, the Soviet Ministry of Foreign Affairs' Institute of International Relations, the Soviet Army Institute of Foreign Languages, etc. The current trend is away from the traditional historico-philological emphasis toward a stress on the spoken language combined with an interdisciplinary approach to contemporary problems; ". . . the aim is to prepare specialists who are actively in command of the languages of the appropriate countries and know profoundly all aspects of their economics, history, and culture" (*Vestnik Moskovskogo Universiteta*, Historical-Philological Series, No. 1, 1956, p. 156). In addition, attempts have been made since 1956 to teach Eastern languages in Soviet schools beginning in the second grade (from the age of eight years). Among the schools which took part in this program were the Boarding School No. 23 in Moscow (Hindi or Urdu), two boarding schools in Leningrad, five schools in Tashkent (Hindi, Urdu, Chinese, or Arabic), two schools in Stalinabad (Persian and Arabic). Several schools in Baku teach Persian and Arabic; three schools in Samarkand and Bukhara provide courses in Persian and Urdu, and Persian only is taught at School No. 70 in Ashkhabad. Such initial difficulties as the absence of textbooks have apparently been overcome, and a future expansion of the program seems likely (*Inostrannye Iazyka v Shkole*, 1957-1958, *passim*).

is now in charge of Eastern studies, became, at the death of Anna Pankratova, the only Soviet historian to be a member of the Central Committee of the party, thus attaining a position of undisputed authority among his colleagues. Some of the leading figures in this Orientalist revival had started their careers in the late twenties (for instance, A. A. Guber and I. Potekhin, the expert on African affairs), but most of the junior personnel had entered the field only in the postwar period. Of considerable interest is the attempt to use specialists of Central Asian origin in leading positions. The case of Bobodzhan Gafurovitch Gafurov is of some significance. Born in a little village near Leninabad in 1909, this young Tadzhik journalist became a university teacher, specialized in the history of his own people, subsequently chose a party career, and for several years held the post of first secretary of the Communist party in the Tadzhik Republic. His transfer to become head of, and to supervise from Moscow, the reorganization of Eastern studies was a further promotion. His collection of Orders of Lenin (five) is surpassed only by that of the geneticist Lysenko. Another party dignitary of Central Asian origin, Mukhitdinov, was made to deliver the central address at the Soviet Orientalists Congress in Tashkent in June, 1957.* The appearance of this first generation of leading cadres of Central Asian origin who were completely "Sovietized" was undoubtedly a great achievement. There had been a similar attempt in the early twenties to promote Communists or fellow travelers to key positions in the field of Soviet Eastern studies (and Eastern politics),

---

* N. A. Mukhitdinov (born 1917) is now the youngest member of the Soviet Presidium, and the first Communist of Moslem background ever to have attained such a position. He was active in consumers' cooperatives before World War II, worked his way through the party hierarchy, and became first secretary of the Uzbek party Central Committee in 1955. Mukhitdinov's meteoric rise to the party's top leadership (he joined the Communist party only during World War II) is probably unique in the recent history of the Soviet Union. He was apparently favored on more than one occasion during his career by a singularly fortunate set of circumstances. His speech at the first All-Union Conference of Eastern experts was subsequently published as a booklet: *K Novym Uspekham Sovetskogo Vostokovedeniia* (Moscow, 1957). He visited Cairo in September, 1958, as Colonel Nasser's guest

but it had not been a success. The Narimanovs, Sultan Galievs, and Ryskulovs had been less reliable politically and were not free of "nationalist deviations"; their Communism had been based on feelings of sympathy rather than a firm schooling in Leninist ideology. The Gafurovs and Mukhitdinovs were not, perhaps, great ideologists with original ideas of their own, nor were such thinkers needed, for all the great ideas were already present (as far as Moscow was concerned) and the main problem was to apply them in the East. But they were competent and apparently quite reliable; if anybody complained about the comparatively low level of the new leadership, it could rightly be argued that this was the first generation of Soviet native cadres, and that neither Rome nor Tashkent had been built in a day.*

The reorganization of Soviet Eastern Studies ("in the light of the instructions of the Twentieth Party Congress") got under way in the summer of 1956, but it was only in the subsequent year that the first results could be seen; the number of scientific personnel at the Institute for Eastern Studies in Moscow rose from 185 to 338 between January and December, 1957 (450, if we include those preparing themselves at the Institute for the Soviet equivalent of a Ph.D. dissertation). Nevertheless, complaints about "lagging behind" continued for some time; Mukhitdinov and Gafurov, in their speeches at the All-Union Conference in Tashkent in 1957, noted that contemporary events were as yet neglected by Soviet Orientalists. Gafurov pointed out that there still was undue emphasis on the distant past, and that, at the Tashkent Conference itself, only two papers (out of a dozen) had dealt with the current stage of the national liberation struggle in the

* It is difficult to pass judgment on Gafurov's qualities as a party boss and as an Orientalist in his specialized field. But the single fact that the very same man could be both first party secretary in the Tadzhik Republic and present a paper at an international Orientalist Congress (in Munich, 1957, on the Samanide state in the ninth and tenth centuries) is an impressive achievement that attests the versatility of the new Soviet leading functionaries. It was, in addition, extremely important to have the Soviet Union be represented by experts who were themselves of Asian, rather than Great Russian or Jewish, origin. A. F. Sultanov, head of the Middle Eastern department of the Oriental Institute (of the Academy of Sciences), is another leading expert of apparently "Moslem" origin.

East.[16] Maiskii, the former Soviet diplomat and now an Academician, said in a similar vein at a meeting in Moscow in 1958 that Soviet Orientalists had less reason than anybody else to rest on past laurels—in view of the stormy developments in the countries of the East.[17]

Like so many other projects in the Soviet Union, the reorganization of Eastern studies was carried out in the form of a five-year plan. Among the newly founded or revived establishments were a new Oriental Institute in Tashkent (September, 1957) and one in Baku (March, 1958), with presumably more to follow. There was no clear division of labor between these various centers, but Tashkent concentrated more on Persian and Afghan studies, while the Baku center was to give much attention to the recent history (and current affairs) of the Arab world. Preparations were also made for the opening of similar institutes in Tiflis and the capitals of the smaller Central Asian republics. In many of these places there had been branches of the VNAV in the twenties, but they and the leading local experts had disappeared; in 1957 one had to start again from the beginning.

Sovetskoe Vostokovedenie, a bimonthly published since 1955, has remained the main scientific organ of Soviet Orientalists, dealing with both current issues and various historical, linguistic, and economic topics. Between 1955 and 1957 it was edited by V. A. Maslennikov, an economist; in the summer of 1957 I. S. Braginskii, a historian, took over. In July, 1957, an illustrated monthly, *Sovremennyi Vostok* ("Contemporary East"), edited by Gafurov, began to appear, dealing almost exclusively with current topics—with the stress on politics. Both in form and in content the contributions to this new magazine were quite different from the old-style Leninist essays published in *Novyi Vostok* or *Revoliutsionnyi Vostok* thirty years ago: the new-style articles were only a fraction of the length of their predecessors and also in a somewhat lighter vein. Instead of internal polemics and discussions, there were interviews with Asian and African political leaders, travelogues, etc. At the same time, the two series of learned papers continued to appear under the auspices of the Oriental Institute of the Academy of Sciences, and the newly

founded publishing house for Eastern literature put out such
highly specialized studies as *The National Revolutionary Movement in Iraq in 1920-21* or *The Situation of the Egyptian Peasants on the Eve of the Revolutionary Upheaval of 1952.* Some of
the work done in 1954-55 (such as that of Vatolina on Egypt and
of Belaev on the Arab League) apparently had to be shelved in
view of the change in line, but this hardly mattered in view of
the steady growth in the number of publications each year.
Among the more noteworthy contributions were such country
surveys as *Contemporary Persia* and *Contemporary Syria,*
providing political, historical, and economic source material.
There was not yet, however, any authoritative modern history
of the countries or of the national movement in the East, for the
first two volumes of the *Noveishaia Istoriia*[18] published by
Moscow University had been written before the change of line
in 1955-56 and were, therefore, unusable. Some countries (and
subjects) benefited more than others from this revival of Soviet
Eastern studies: new branches in the central research institute
included departments for Africa and Southeast Asia and one for
the analysis of current economic trends in the countries of the
East. (Africa, as the result of some administrative quirk, had been
the monopoly of the Institute of Ethnography at the Academy of
Sciences up to 1957.) There were many new books on the Arab
countries after 1955, but comparatively little has been published
on Turkey and Persia, and only one pamphlet on Israel. This new
interest in the Arab world was not reflected solely on the political-
economic level; beginning in the autumn of 1955, translations of
Egyptian and other Arab writers (mostly of "progressive" persuasion) were published.

The great increase in quantitative output is undoubted; it is
more difficult to pass judgment on the quality of this new literature. Ideological limitations quite apart, many of these new books
were somewhat deficient in competence; they were frequently
based on secondary, and not always relevant, sources. The impression they give is that the authors had not yet altogether
mastered their new subjects. (There were some exceptions, such
as the competent little book by E. A. Lebedev on Jordan pub-

lished in 1956.)* Frequently it appears that, given the traditional
and current limitations of the Leninist approach, more sophisticated and better-informed articles and books could have been
written. A steady improvement has been noted, however, since
1955. Nor did the level of political and social analysis of the
Soviet experts compare unfavorably with the work done outside
the Soviet Union. They were more interested in politics, economics, and social affairs than many of the Western experts, and
their Marxist-Leninist ideological equipment was perhaps better
suited occasionally to cope with the revolutionary situation in
the Middle East than the empirical approach of many Western
students of the Middle East. While their Western colleagues debated hopes and fears, and the intentions of Colonel Nasser and
his colleagues, the Soviet experts occupied themselves, with
varying success, with the political, social, and economic realities
of the Middle East.

4. Islamic Problems

The *rapprochement* with Arab nationalism opened a wide
vista to Soviet policy in the Middle East but also created certain
problems of a rather delicate nature. The attitude toward Islam
was one of these questions to which no easy answer could be
found. According to the official version there were still capitalist
(or "feudal") Islamic remnants in the Soviet Union that had to
be combatted. But some of the Soviets' new allies in the Middle
East were believing Moslems who might be antagonized by a
pronounced anti-Islamic propaganda campaign, even if it were
destined only for Soviet home consumption. It has been impossible, so far, to find a satisfactory solution for this problem; the
Soviet leaders have toned down the anti-Islamic propaganda and
stressed on many occasions that, while there is freedom of anti-

* Another exception is A. N. Kotlov's book (1958) on the revolt in Iraq
in 1920. It is based on a very thorough study of both Western and Arab
source material—from a Leninist vantage point, needless to mention. The
abundance of footnotes is in the German (or neo-American) tradition. I. P.
Belaev (*American Imperialism in Saudi Arabia*, 1957) and M. F. Gataullin
(*Agrarian Relations in Syria*, 1957) also combine an orthodox outlook with
the extensive use of Arab and Western source material.

religious propaganda in the Soviet Union, there is also freedom of religious worship. Visiting delegations of Moslem dignitaries from the Arab world, Indonesia, and elsewhere were permitted to tour mosques in the Soviet Union and to meet Soviet mullahs and imams; not a few of these visitors have accepted the official version, namely, that there is full religious freedom in the Soviet Union and that the malevolent rumors about anti-Islamic persecutions have been spread by Western imperialists to sow dissension between the Soviet Union and their friends in the Middle East.

The Soviet dilemma with regard to Islam, though a real one, has been overemphasized by some Western observers, and its political implications have been exaggerated. While it is certainly true that Soviet propaganda speaks in different voices to Moslem believers in the Soviet Union and those abroad, there is some doubt whether the whole issue continues to be a very important one. For Islam in the Soviet Union appears to be very much "under control"; large sections of the population in the former "Moslem" republics have lost their religious consciousness. Of all the great world religions, Islam is perhaps the least dangerous rival from the Soviet point of view. The Soviet leaders have no reason for apprehension with regard to the new contacts between their allies in the Middle East and Soviet Moslems.* They do not anticipate a religious or nationalist revival, for the Central Asian republics and Azerbaidzhan have made so much economic progress in comparison with most Middle Eastern countries that they

* The friendly Soviet attitude toward the national bourgeoisie in the Arab world and elsewhere in Asia, however, induced some historians in Soviet Central Asia and the Caucasus after the Twentieth Congress to rehabilitate the liberal-democratic movement (Jadidism) among Russian Moslems in the two decades prior to 1917. These historians were sharply rebuked by Gafurov, who argued that Jadidism had been reactionary in character since 1905 and that no "false analogies" with the Middle East ought to be drawn. The Jadidists, he said, fought against the revolution, were in favor of Pan-Turanianism and their slogans were "pseudo-nationalist." The policy of the (bourgeois) nationalists in the Middle East and in Asia, on the other hand, is progressive, inasmuch as it is anti-imperialist (*Kommunist*, 11, 1958 pp. 18-19). This official reaction was not unexpected; it remains to be seen whether the explanation given will be accepted, or whether the party leadership will have to cope with further "nationalist deviations" at home as the result of their new policy in Asia.

are hardly likely to be influenced by what must appear to them to be the ideas and customs of backward cousins. Arab interest in the fate of Islam in the Soviet Union, moreover, has been strictly limited, contrary to the belief of some Western observers. The new regimes in the Arab world are mainly secularist in outlook and tend to welcome (rather than condemn) any similar tendency elsewhere.

For all these reasons, there has not been a stringent necessity for any such dramatic about-face in the Soviet attitude toward Islam as there was vis-à-vis nationalism. After Stalin's death and throughout 1954, the anti-Islamic propaganda continued. Klimovich, who has probably written more books and articles against Islam than any man since the Middle Ages, went on record in October, 1954, reiterating the traditional definition of Islam: "an antiscientific, reactionary world concept, alien and inimical to Marxism-Leninism. Islam is in opposition to the optimistic and life-affirming materialistic teaching, it is incompatible with the fundamental interests of the Soviet peoples."[19] During the summer months of 1954, anti-Islamic propaganda was stepped up;[20] there were frequent appeals to "raise the level of scientific, atheistic propaganda"; hundreds of meetings were convened, in which the harmfulness of Islam in general and such specific obligations as the fast, in particular, were denounced. Occasionally, some of the international ramifications were mentioned, too: the "reactionary role" of Pan-Islamism, Pan-Turkism, and even Pan-Arabism in world affairs; was it not typical that the main protagonist of the Pan-Islamic idea* had been for many years an employee of the British embassy in Constantinople?[21] N. A. Smirnov, whose *Outline of Islamic Studies in the USSR* was pub-

---

* Jamal al Din al Afghani has not been restored to favor to this day. In a recent essay on the "Characteristics of the Arab Enlightenment in the 19th Century," Z. I. Levin praises Nasif al Yasidji, Butrus al Bustani (who "preached patriotism and religious tolerance"), Tahtawi and Kawakebi (who were "fighters against feudalism"), Francis Fathalla Marrash (introduced as a "utopian reformer" but also a "fighter for freedom"), and even Mohammed Abdo (who stood for progress and "undermined official Islam"). But Afghani, who was their teacher, is not even mentioned (*Voprosy Filosofi*, 6, 1958, pp. 91-99). Afghani's main work is *Refutation of the Materialists*—which may provide one of the keys to this riddle.

lished in 1954,[22] wrote in a very similar vein about the duty of
Soviet historians to unmask the imperialists' ideological helpers
who wanted to "cover up under the slogan of defense of religion
the class character and the exploitative nature of contemporary
religion."* Despite a highly tendentious preface and occasional
lapses (not to mention the obligatory quotations from Stalin and
Malenkov and many significant omissions), Smirnov's book is a
serious study that deservedly received considerable attention in
the West.

After 1954, the tenor of anti-Islamic propaganda became
milder; there seemed to be a desire, as one Western observer has
put it, to distinguish between what the Soviet mind regarded as
the essential fallacy and harmful effect of Islamic dogma and
practice, and the achievements of Moslem peoples throughout
the ages.[23] It was conceded that many Moslem religious dignitaries outside the Soviet Union were playing a "progressive" role
in the struggle against imperialism; a limited number of Soviet
pilgrims went to Mecca and the visits of Middle Eastern delegations to Tashkent and Bukhara continued. But the indefatigable
Klimovich and his assistants continued their work, too. In a booklet published in October, 1956,[24] he talked about Mohammed in
terms of the "cult of the individual," and in a broadcast in May,
1958, he decried not merely circumcision, the celebration of the
Kurban Bairam holiday, and the Moslem attitude toward women, but also the attempt to interpret the Koran in a democratic
and proletarian light.[25] Similar opinions were echoed in the Soviet
provincial press.[26] At the same time, all Islamic experts were
urged to realize the very complex character of the problem; while
the "aggressive Baghdad Pact" exploited the slogan of "unity of
Islam," there were still many people strongly influenced by

---

* Four years later a French Orientalist was criticized for having quoted
at a lecture in Damascus from Smirnov's book (and other Soviet specialists
such as Klimovich and E. A. Belaev). While the correctness of the quotations was not disputed, it was argued that the French Orientalist had omitted
facts that gave evidence of the appreciation of the Soviet government, even
in the very early days, of the religious feelings of the Moslem believers.
Had not the Petrograd Sovnarkom decided in 1918 to restore to the local
Moslem committee the *Holy Koran of Osman* that had been brought from
Samarkand? (*Sovremennyi Vostok* 4, 1958, p. 59).

religious sentiments in the Arab countries—who played, nevertheless, a progressive role in the fight for independence. All these
different facets of one and the same problem should be considered (an authoritative source stated); "great political insight
and a profound grasp of the contemporary social processes are
needed in order to carry on a proper fight against Islam."[27]

This anti-Islamic "information campaign," strictly limited to
the Soviet Union, was not very virulent in tenor and probably not
very extensive in comparison with past performances. At the
same time, some measure of freedom of worship for Moslem
believers did indeed exist in the Soviet Union. Islam even enjoyed certain privileges that were not extended to all other religions; as early as 1955 a small group of Soviet Moslem students
of theology (or of atheism) enrolled at Al Azhar university in
Cairo. There is no good reason to assume that the Soviet attitude
toward Islam inside the Union will ever again become an issue of
paramount importance; Islam in Russia may continue to be an
administrative problem, but it has ceased to be, according to most
evidence, a major political issue. The Soviet attitude toward (domestic) Islam may yet cause minor complications on the international scene, but it is unlikely that it will constitute a major
obstacle in Soviet relations with the Middle East and the Moslem
world in general.

5. The Middle East in 1959: Gathering the Harvest

The Middle Eastern scene as viewed from Moscow in late
1958 provided much cause for optimism. Relations with Afghanistan could not be better; there has been an attempt to use
Afghanistan as a model for demonstrating the benefits of peaceful coexistence and the advantages of neutralism—just as the
example of Finland is frequently cited in Europe. The attempt
has not been too successful, for political, social, and economic
conditions in Afghanistan are not attractive enough to arouse
much interest, let alone emulation. On Persia there has been for
the past year or two a curious silence. The Shah and his governments have not been attacked with the same bitterness as Menderes and Nuri as Said; on the other hand, Soviet experts did not
find much to praise in contemporary Persia, the writings of some

"progressive" Persian poets apart. On Turkey, Soviet expert opinion has been blowing alternately hot and cold, following the practice of Soviet diplomacy vis-à-vis that country: complaints and bitter criticism continued about the Turkish alliance with the West and its allegedly ruinous consequences for Turkey's economy, security, and political position in the Middle East.[28] On the other hand, there were frequent offers to let bygones be bygones; Khrushchev himself had said in a speech in December, 1955, that Turkey had not been solely responsible for the deterioration in the relations between the two countries over the past fifteen years. But the Turks did not respond to these overtures, and the quarrel continued about how and why the deterioration had occurred.[29] Moscow urged that a new beginning could be made, if only the Turks would again adhere to the political principles of Kemal Ataturk in both their foreign and domestic policy; but the international situation was not what it had been in the early twenties, and the Turks, mindful of more recent events, remained distrustful. No important change in the relations between the two countries has taken place, or seems likely.

The hostile attitude toward Israel did not change. While on occasion the very existence of the state was put into question, more frequently a return to the frontiers decided upon by the United Nations in November, 1947, was demanded, in addition to the resettlement of Arab refugees in Israel. The country itself was described as an American colony, an outpost of Western imperialism. Not only was the country's foreign policy condemned (for example, the acts of retaliation, the Suez campaign, etc.) but also its domestic policies: the alleged exploitation of new immigrants and workers in general, and the discrimination against the Arab minority.[30] All this despite the fact that Israel was ruled by an all-Labor coalition, some of whose members were long-standing supporters of Soviet policies. What mattered in Soviet eyes, however, was not the measure of socialist progress *inside* a country like Israel but its foreign political alignment; in view of the specific position and geographic distribution of the Jewish people, it was most unlikely that Israel would turn against the West in the same way as the Arabs. The Arab world was incomparably more promising ground for the Soviet Union, and the choice all too obvious. A Communist Israel would have been a constant embarrassment for Soviet policy in the Middle East; support for Arab nationalism offered far greater prospects. The whole issue was complicated by the problem of Soviet Jewry; the situation of Jews in Russia had improved somewhat since the winter of 1952-53 but they still remained unequal to others, in a country where all are said to be equal. Soviet sources denied the existence of any connection between the Russian stand on Israel and the problem of Soviet Jewry; there was, however, little doubt that such a connection did in effect exist. It would have been difficult, otherwise, to explain the publication of a series of articles throughout 1957-58 in both the Soviet central and provincial press in which living conditions in Israel were described in the worst possible way. The obvious intention was to discourage potential emigrants and Zionist sympathizers in general.

The approach to the Arab world became, or remained, cordial. Continuous, unreserved praise was bestowed on the new leaders in the Arab world, and the Arab peoples in general: their courage, their love of freedom, their perseverance in the struggle for independence, their burning desire to create a better world, their steadfast participation in the struggle for world peace, their industry and diligence in economic development, their tremendous cultural achievements past and present. All books, articles, and speeches since 1957 were written in that spirit; specific illustrations seem unnecessary. As elsewhere in Asia, the state capitalist policy of the leaders of the UAR and Iraq was welcomed, not merely because it served the interests of the national bourgeoisie against foreign capital but because it coincided with the "general interests of the people."[31] At the same time, there was an unavoidable measure of ambiguity as to the "next phase" in the Arab world. Some Soviet experts argued that Russia had no intention whatsoever of "Sovietizing" the Middle East and establishing Communist regimes in the Arab countries.*

* I. Belaev in a polemic against Professor Bernard Lewis and the *Middle East Journal* (*Sovremennyi Vostok*, 5, 1957, p. 44). Stalin had been the first to argue (in the Roy Howard interview) that it was a tragicomic misunderstanding of the West to believe that revolution was for export.

Such declarations were probably correct as far as they went, but they did not tell the whole story. The underlying Soviet assumption was that, given the necessary conditions, these countries would move toward some form of "Popular Democracy" by their own momentum, without any foreign intervention. Khrushchev presumably had this perspective in mind when he talked in July, 1958 (after his meetings with Nasser), about the Arab national liberation movement as the "first stage."

The panorama of 1959, however fascinating, is neither a starting point nor the final phase as far as the Soviet image of the Middle East is concerned. The authoritative views of 1959 are subject to modification and change; they may be entirely discarded a few years hence. The basic pattern of 1959 seems firmly enough established: the alliance with Arab nationalism, the opposition to Israel, the cautious approach to Islam, the ambivalent attitude toward Turkey and Persia. An early change in this general picture may appear inconceivable to many. The temptation to regard the present pattern as static should, however, be resisted, at a time of social and political transformation in the Middle East. The Soviet position toward the various Middle Eastern problems is bound to change with, and as a result of, internal developments in that area. Much will depend upon the future course of Arab nationalism. If it should veer closer toward the East in both its foreign orientation and its domestic policies, it will undoubtedly retain Soviet support. If, on the other hand, it should show signs of real independence in its foreign policy and at home, the Soviet approach may become less friendly. All this may appear obvious, but it ought to be stated, for there is a strong inclination at present to regard the current state of affairs as likely to continue forever. Nor is it certain that the Soviet Union will retain its present interest in the Middle East. The current upsurge of interest in the Arab world is a natural reaction against the almost total neglect that lasted from the late thirties to the early fifties. This revival was more than timely and it will probably continue for some time to come; this interest is bound to persist as long as the Middle East figures so prominently in the global struggle. But in the long run a certain decline in interest is a distinct possibility; it should be remembered that the Middle

East has gained its present prominence in world affairs not as the result of a sudden growth in its own strength but as a consequence of the clash between the Western and Eastern camps. Even if the Middle Eastern nations (or, at any rate, all the Arab peoples) should unite and pool their resources, even if they should somehow succeed in modernizing their economies and social structures in a very short time, their numbers and material resources are limited and they could not aspire to great power status in a world in which the number of such powers has become extremely restricted. Some Middle Eastern nations have profited in recent years from a highly fortunate constellation: the atomic stalemate, which provided a large measure of independence of action and freedom to maneuver. One day the favorable constellation is bound to disappear; on that day these nations will be judged on the basis of their own strength and achievements, and their passive bargaining power in the competition between East and West will disappear. In such circumstances, Soviet interest, too, would palpably decrease. Like other great powers, the Soviet Union is more interested in key areas than in backwaters of history. Despite outward appearances and a current boom, the Middle East in an industrial age is not favorable ground for the creation of a new world power.

6. Problems and Prospects

Since 1918, the pendulum has swung back and forth more than once in Soviet thinking about the Middle East: from close preoccupation with the area toward neglect (and back), from attaching great importance to the Middle East to almost ignoring it, from giving unqualified support to the national movement to calling for its destruction and vice versa. These changes in approach are likely to continue—but on a different level and background. For by 1959 the great process predicted and impatiently expected in 1918 has at last taken place: the awakening of Asia, its gradual emancipation from Western domination. In 1918, the Russians had to deal with an Asia that was for the most part either hostile or apathetic and certainly not independent. In 1959 one part of Asia is under Communist rule, while other countries have gained independence under the leadership of a non-Communist national movement. The relationship with the new Communist regimes, possible tendencies toward "national Communism" (in whatever guise) will be the main issue at stake in Soviet relations with such countries as China, Viet Minh, or North Korea. As for India and most of the Arab countries, the main problem for Russia is to smooth the way and remove complications for a gradual transition to Communism via national socialism and national Communism. (Soviet ideologists differentiate between national Communism in Europe and Asia. National Communism in Poland and Yugoslavia would be a retreat in their eyes; in Asia or the Middle East it could be a form of progress toward the final goal. There are, in addition, certain anti-Soviet overtones in European national Communism which are notably absent in the Asian species of the movement.)

Many of the problems of the twenties and thirties have either been solved or have lost their relevance. No new debate about decolonization is to be expected, nor is a discussion of the historical roots of Kemalism likely to produce violent emotions nowadays, for Kemalism is a stage that has been passed in Soviet relations with the Arab world. Some of the old issues are still likely to come up in one form or another: Pan-Islamism and, of course, the attitude toward the national bourgeoisie. The national bourgeoisie or, to be more precise, the non-Communist leadership of the national movement, is not to hold power forever; the problem for the Communists will be to gain control over the national movement, to remove the elements opposed to a close alliance with Communism and the Soviet Union, and to neutralize or win over the rest. Whether this is to be effected according to what Rakosi termed the "salami tactics" or in some more gradual and peaceful way, nobody can say for sure at present; the Soviet Union seems willing enough to experiment, to proceed by trial and error, rather than establish a preconceived pattern to be rigidly adhered to in the whole area. It could be a very gradual, long-drawn-out process in which no pressure whatever will be exerted by the Soviet Union. If there should be, however, a change in the international balance of power, if the position of the West should be further weakened, it is possible that the Soviet Union would become somewhat less patient with a slow rate of progress in the Middle East. There is, after all, a very close connection between the future of the Middle East and the international balance of power. Soviet political observers would be the last to deny it.

NOTES

1. G. Lukacs quoted in *Soviet Survey*, November, 1956, p. 15.
2. L. Vatolina in *S. V.* 2, 1955, p. 66.
3. L. Vatolina in *Araby v Borbe* . . . (1957), p. 14, p. 18.
4. *S. V.* 1, 1957, p. 179.
5. *Ibid.*, p. 183; see also A. Levkovskii, "Gosudarstvennyi Kapitalizm v Indii," in *Sovremennyi Vostok* 5, 1958, pp. 10-16.
6. I. Tishin, *Kommunist* 16, 1954, p. 69 *et seq.*
7. *Kommunist* 8, 1955, p. 74 *et seq.*
8. *Noveishaia Istoriia Stran Zarubezhnogo Vostoka*, Vol. II (Moscow, 1955).
9. A. A. Guber in *M. Zh.* 3, 1956, p. 61.
10. V. Mikheev, *Kommunist* 12, 1955, pp. 80-94.
11. E. M. Zhukov, *M.Zh.* 9, 1957, pp. 39-43.
12. *V. I.* 9, 1954, p. 173.
13. *Kommunist* 8, 1955, p. 74 *et seq.*
14. *Pravda*, February 18, 1956.
15. *S. V.* 1, 1956, comments in its editorial on the decisions of the Twentieth Party Congress as affecting Soviet Orientalists. This number of *S. V.* appeared with almost five months delay.
16. *Pravda Vostoka*, June 11, 1957.
17. *V. I.* 5, 1958, p. 187.
18. See note 8.
19. *Zariia Vostoka*, October 10, 1954.
20. Cf. *Bakinskii Rabochii*, June 20, 1954; *Pravda Vostoka*, June 18, 1954.
21. *Kazakhstanskaia Pravda*, June 3, 1954.
22. N. A. Smirnov: *Ocherki Izucheniia Islama v SSSR* (Moscow, 1954), p. 8.
23. G. E. Wheeler, "Recent Soviet Attitudes to Islam," in *Soviet Survey* 16-17, 1957, p. 15.
24. *Islam, ego Proiskhozdenie i Sotsialnaia Sushchnost* (Moscow, 1956).
25. Moscow Radio, Home Service, May 22, 1958.
26. Cf. *Kazakhstanskaia Pravda*, July 30, 1957; *Turkmenskaia Iskra*, April 16, 1957.
27. *Voprosy Filosofii* 5, 1957, p. 224.

28. Cf. B. Potskhveriia in *Sovremennyi Vostok* 5, 1957, pp. 23-24.

29. Cf. the polemic of A. Miller against Ahmad Shukru Esmer in *M.Zh.* 2, 1958, p. 103 *et seq.*

30. A. Leonidov, "Behind the Curtain of Zionism," in *Sovremennyi Vostok* 5, 1957, pp. 17-19, and 6, 1957, pp. 7-9.

31. L. Vatolina in *Sovremennyi Vostok* 6, 1958, p. 12.

PART TWO

THE GREAT BREAKTHROUGH

CHAPTER ONE

ON THE EVE: 1954

It is tempting to attribute Soviet successes in the Middle East, the "great breakthrough" of the middle fifties, solely to the radical changes in Soviet foreign policy after Stalin's death. Under Stalin, and especially during his last years, the Middle East was not one of the main fields of Soviet foreign political activity; in fact, it was largely ignored. Only after Stalin's death was it discovered or rediscovered, as one of the most promising areas for the extension of Soviet and Communist influence. Under Stalin, the general attitude toward the national movement in Asia was hostile. Stalin did not trust even Asian Communists, how could he rely on the Nehrus, Sukarnos, and Nassers, all "national reformists" (in the jargon of 1930) and potential traitors.

Stalin suffered from what one school of psychoanalysis has defined as a "parataxic distortion"[1] of real situations and persons. He interpreted and met current situations almost entirely in terms of past ones: he was unable to understand what was novel in each new situation. The new leaders of the national movement in Asia became "eidetic personalities," Stalin treating them as if they were people who had been significant in his past political life. In other words, Nasser, Nehru, and Sukarno were all potential or real Chiang Kai-sheks preparing the great betrayal of 1927.

Up to 1953, a close alliance with the "national bourgeoisie" in Asia and the Middle East appeared out of the question. After Stalin's death, the Soviet leaders re-examined the situation and gradually reached the conclusion that such an alliance would be very desirable. Soviet successes in the area became possible only as a result of the adoption of this new, less orthodox, and more elastic approach. But one should not overemphasize the impor-

189

tance of this change. Soviet and Communist policy in Asia had not always been so rigid as it had been during the five or six years before Stalin's death. There had been national- and popular-front policies before, and though the attempts to make friends and influence people in Asia after 1954 went further than any earlier efforts, these moves were not altogether new in inspiration.

Soviet successes in the Arab world in the middle fifties cannot be explained by any single trend. It is doubtful whether, among the several factors involved, this change in the Soviet attitude was really the most important one. For even if the Soviet attitude became more elastic, it did not yet display any Machiavellian political acumen in its dealing with the area, nor, in the beginning, any intense, relentless endeavor to gain a foothold in the Middle East. It will be shown that the initiative for Soviet involvement in the Middle East came from Cairo and Damascus as much as from Moscow. At first, there was evidence of certain Soviet doubts and a reluctance to get too entangled, whereas there was no such reluctance on the part of Cairo and Damascus, which regarded Soviet involvement as prerequisite for playing off East against West. There is some reason to believe that only subsequently, after this involvement had become an established fact, did the Soviet leaders realize how promising their chances really were.

All this points to the fact that the change in Soviet tactics after 1953, important as it was, would not have reaped such a political harvest if there had not been a parallel trend in the Middle East, i.e., the emergence of a revolutionary situation in the Arab world that had not been created by any Soviet or Communist influence, the emergence of new social and political forces that were replacing the old ruling classes, and the deepening of the clash between Arab nationalism and the West. The disintegration of the old order, of the established beliefs and values, had created a spiritual and ideological void that was probably more important than the strategic vacuum that existed there. A new force in the area had tried to fill that void: radical Arab national socialism as exemplified by Colonel Nasser and his colleagues, and the Ba'ath. This was a movement with a tremendous emotional appeal throughout the Arab world, but it did not possess any distinctive political, social, or economic philosophy of its own. It stood for Arab unity, but did not clarify the conditions in which unity would, or in any case should, take place. A close observer of the Egyptian scene has given a vivid description of the decision taken by the Egyptian *progressistes* to cultivate the military junta after 1952 in view of its lack of ideology and technical cadres, and its inexperience in practically all fields. "The junta is a coming force," they said. "But where is it headed? They do not know themselves, so let us provide the necessary guidance."[2]

The previous Soviet drive in the Near East, immediately after World War II, had been a three-pronged offensive against Greece, Turkey, and Persia. By 1947, the Communist regime in Persian Azerbaijan had been overthrown after the evacuation of Soviet forces, partisan warfare in Greece had come to an end shortly after Yugoslavia's defection from the Cominform in the summer of 1948, and the Truman Doctrine had convinced the Turks that they did not have to give in to Soviet pressure. By late 1948, the Soviet offensive was over, and during the subsequent six or seven years Moscow showed only a limited interest in the Middle East. Most of its political moves came as a response to Western attempts to organize the military defense of the area. During the winter of 1949-50 the United States and Britain had resumed arms supplies to several Arab countries (such as Egypt, Iraq, and Jordan), Greece and Turkey joined NATO in the autumn of 1951, an agreement about American military aid to Persia had been signed a year before, and a similar pact with Saudi Arabia giving the U.S. the Dhahran air bases was signed in June, 1951. Throughout 1950, and even more so during 1951, Western efforts to establish an Allied Middle Eastern Command continued. In October, 1951, the Egyptian government was officially invited by the Western powers and Turkey to take part in this defense organization.

These Western efforts were doomed to failure for a variety of reasons. They ignored the fact that popular opinion in the Arab countries was anti-Western, or, at best, neutralist. When a British military delegation had negotiated shortly before with Mustafa Nahas, Prime Minister of Egypt, and had tried to impress upon him the necessity of keeping the Suez bases in a state of readiness in the case of Soviet attack, it encountered incredulity. "But why should we care about Russia?" Nahas is reported to have answered. "Russia is four thousand miles away." A look at the map would have shown that this was a considerable exaggeration, but psychologically, this incident was very revealing. For Arab public opinion, Russia was perhaps much farther than four thousand miles away, and the West was still very much there.

The Western suggestions were emphatically rejected by Egypt, and further negotiations became impossible for the time being in view of the aggravation of the British-Egyptian conflict. When Mr. Dulles, the Secretary of State of the new Republican administration, returned from a fact-finding trip through the Middle East in the early summer of 1953, his report of the chances of a regional defense organization was far from optimistic, and he did not regard it as an immediate possibility. The Mutual Security Act of 1953 again put the stress on economic and technical help, and it was only in the spring of the subsequent year that attempts for a defense alliance were renewed with the conclusion of an agreement between Ankara and Karachi that was subsequently to become the cornerstone of the "Northern Tier"—the Baghdad Pact.

The Soviet leaders, needless to say, regarded an extension of NATO to the Middle East with grave misgivings. Turkey was warned against joining the "aggressive Atlantic Pact" in a number of diplomatic notes (November 3, November 30, 1951, etc.), whereas the other Middle Eastern countries and the Western powers were told by Mr. Gromyko that nobody threatened peace in the Middle East and that the projected Middle East Command would therefore be regarded as an openly hostile act by the Soviet Union (November 21 and 24, 1951).

After Stalin's death, Soviet notes became somewhat more conciliatory, and for a time there was a definite attempt to improve Soviet relations with Turkey and Persia. The Turkish ambassador in Moscow was told by Mr. Molotov in June, 1953, that the misunderstandings of 1945-46 ought to be cleared up, that the Georgian and Armenian republics had renounced their territorial demands on Turkey, and that an agreement acceptable and favorable to both sides should be reached about the Straits.[3] To this and to similar moves (such as Mr. Malenkov's speech before the Supreme Soviet on August 8, 1953), the Turkish government and press reaction was lukewarm.

The war of notes was again intensified later in 1953, when news of the Ankara-Karachi axis became known.[4] It was pointed out in Moscow that these treaties would aggravate the general situation just when the Soviet Union was making considerable efforts to lessen international tension.

Soviet press and radio propaganda stressed not only the danger to the Soviet Union but also dealt with the "new menace" to Pakistan's neighbors, such as India and Afghanistan, and the Arab countries.[5] At the same time, the peaceful character of Soviet Middle Eastern policy was juxtaposed to "aggressive American policy"; "We shall prove with actions that we want peace," Pravda announced.[6]

It remains to be noted that similar Soviet protests followed the Iraqi-Turkish pact in January, 1955, and Persia's adherence to the Baghdad Pact in October of that year. However, these Soviet moves did not make much impression: Iraq had cut off diplomatic ties with the Soviet Union a few months before, and the Persian government, being the last to join the Pact, had obviously anticipated the Soviet reaction.

At first it seemed that these Soviet protests would not have any greater impact on the state of affairs in the Middle East than similar ones five, ten, or twenty years previously. But in 1954 it so happened that Soviet interests in the Middle East coincided for the first time with the policies of a number of Arab countries, above all Egypt and Syria. The Turko-Pakistani pact and the subsequent agreements leading toward the Baghdad Pact had been attacked with growing violence in Cairo and Damascus.[7] This hostile reaction was not confined to Egypt and Syria. In Lebanon, Jordan, and even Iraq (a member state of the new defense link) a majority of newspapers opposed the Baghdad Pact; they undoubtedly reflected public opinion.

It has been argued that the Egyptian leaders were offended by the suggestion that they would have to play second fiddle to

Turkey in the projected Western defense organization, and that they might have agreed to participate if they had been given the leading role in Turkey's place. Such a view disregards the deep hostility in the Arab world toward an alliance with the West. "Positive neutralism" was not born in 1954—it had been the attitude of the Arab intelligentsia, the officer corps, and public opinion in general, during World War II and much earlier. This hostility was not the result of the Western attempts to "organize" the area—it merely found its expression in opposition to the Baghdad Pact. India had more reason to feel offended and endangered by the Baghdad Pact than Egypt, for it meant that India's main enemy, Pakistan, would be militarily strengthened. For Egypt, the Baghdad Pact was not a military threat—some of its members had hitherto maintained friendly relations with Egypt (Pakistan, Persia), and the ties with the others had at least been normal. And yet there was no such sudden and far-reaching deterioration in India's relations with the West as there was in Egypt, nor did the Baghdad Pact push New Delhi to so close a *rapprochement* with Moscow as that of Cairo and Damascus. This tends to show that, however important (and perhaps misguided) Western attempts to "organize" the area may have been, they do not suffice to explain Soviet successes in the Middle East in reference to the Baghdad Pact. The sources of the Egyptian and Syrian *rapprochement* with the Soviet Union were considerably deeper and more complex.

At this point a more detailed analysis of Soviet policies toward the various Middle Eastern countries in the early fifties seems called for. Such a review would not fulfill its aim if it were to concentrate on one particular aspect—such as regular diplomatic activities. With several Middle Eastern countries Moscow did not have diplomatic ties during the period under review; nevertheless, economic or cultural relations and the activities of local Communist parties and pro-Soviet organizations had a political impact almost everywhere in the Middle East.

1. Egypt

The rise to power of new political forces in Egypt in July, 1952, did not produce a great stir in Moscow at the time. During

1953, too, Soviet comments about the situation in Egypt were few and far between, and there was no diplomatic activity worth mentioning. Soviet Middle Eastern experts were obviously none too happy about Naguib and Gamal Abdel Nasser,[8] and the Egyptian Communists fought the military junta as a collective reincarnation of Hitler, Mussolini, and Hirohito. Official Soviet policy was more cautious and oscillated like a fever chart between 1953 and 1955: whenever the Egyptian government took up a firm anti-Western position, the Soviet attitude became friendly for a while, whereas any sign of willingness on Egypt's part to compromise with the West produced unfriendly noises in the Soviet capital. It would be tedious to retrace these almost weekly changes in the political barometer; a few illustrations will have to suffice.

During the winter of 1953-54, tension between Egypt and and Britain rose, incidents occurred almost daily in the Suez Canal area, and Soviet-Egyptian relations became friendly for a while. An Egyptian trade delegation (significantly headed by the Deputy Minister of War) visited Moscow, and a first trade agreement was signed in Cairo in March, 1954. Hassan Raghib subsequently related that he had been greatly impressed by what he saw in Moscow, while Aziz al Masri, the Egyptian Minister in Moscow, warmly praised the Soviet stand "in favor of the peoples fighting for national independence"—while on home leave in Egypt. Meanwhile, Mr. Daniel Solod, the Soviet Ambassador and probably the main architect of the Russo-Egyptian alliance in 1955, became a frequent visitor to the Egyptian Foreign Ministry and promised full support for the Arab national cause against military collaboration with the Western powers. On the international scene this first honeymoon was reflected, *inter alia*, in a Soviet veto of the New Zealand proposal in the U.N. Security Council in favor of the freedom of navigation through the Suez Canal. (This was mainly directed against Egypt's refusal to let Israeli ships pass through the canal. In a similar debate three years before, the Soviet representative had abstained from voting.) Following this and similar evidence for a general improvement, the Egyptian press expressed much satisfaction with the *rapprochement* in April, 1954.[9] These amicable exchanges continued during the early summer of 1954. Egypt started to import Russian wheat and fuel in sizeable quantities and extended its commercial relations with such other Eastern European countries as Hungary, Czechoslovakia, and East Germany. Soviet films were shown regularly from then on in the Egyptian capital, and Soviet athletes competed for the first time in Cairo in April, 1954. On the political level there was similar friendliness: the Egyptian press announced the impending recognition of Communist China,[10] an event that was to take place only two years later. Abdel Hakim Amer, commander in chief of the Egyptian army, was quoted by *Izvestiia*[11] as having said that the only danger to the Arab world came from the West, not the Soviet bloc, and the Soviet press reciprocated by scrupulously abstaining from commenting on internal developments in Egypt. When the first great conflict broke out between General Naguib and Colonel Nasser in May, 1954, the Soviet press refused to take sides[12] and did not bother to reply to the many attacks against Communism published at that time in Egypt. The various Communist factions in Egypt, it should be recalled, continued to attack the Naguib-Nasser regime and, in view of the chaotic organizational situation, it is difficult to ascertain whether this was a prearranged division of labor or simply a breakdown in the political instruction transmission belt.

But the idyll, alas, was interrupted. The Anglo-Egyptian agreement of July, 1954, on the future of Suez was viewed with extreme disfavor in Moscow and interpreted as a victory of American diplomacy, a reconciliation between Egypt and the Western camp. Suez became the preoccupation of Soviet foreign policy, the Soviet press bitterly reproached the Egyptian leaders for having jumped on the American bandwagon, for their short-sightedness and weakness.[13] While official Soviet comment was still comparatively restrained, expressed more in sorrow than in anger, and putting the main blame on the Americans who had ensnared the Egyptian leaders, some subsidiary Soviet propaganda organs such as the "Voice of National Independence and Peace," an Arabic radio station in Budapest, became far more outspoken, accusing the Egyptian leaders of high treason and calling upon the Egyptian people to revolt against them. As the months passed, Soviet leaders became more and more convinced that the

Suez agreement had merely been the "first step toward the inclusion of Egypt in the Western bloc."[14] The former reticence about Egypt's internal affairs was given up, and in its propaganda Moscow supported the Moslem Brotherhood against the junta, General Naguib against Colonel Nasser—the Wafd against the new regime.[15] TASS protested against the shameful treatment of Communists, "Partisans of Peace," and fellow travelers in general: "The whole nation dissociates itself from a government that has been utterly dishonored."[16] And the leadership of the DMNL, the main group in Egyptian Communism, in a manifesto published in Turah concentration camp, said, "We here in Egypt face a military dictatorship as brutal as Shishakli's in Syria."[17]

Arrests and political trials of potential and real enemies of the regime continued throughout the winter of 1954: the Moslem Brotherhood was destroyed, and large groups of Communists were given lengthy prison terms. Soviet sources made no secret of their sympathies with the more progressive and democratic elements that were persecuted. (At that time, the "progressive and democratic elements" included not only the Partisans of Peace, but also the Moslem Brotherhood, General Naguib, and the remnants of the Wafd.) However, critical as the Soviet approach was, Moscow took great care not to burn all its bridges. For even if Nasser's Egypt had taken a step toward reconciliation with the West, it had not joined the Western camp. And since in the winter of 1954 tension between Egypt and certain Western powers (above all Turkey) again became pronounced, a more friendly Soviet attitude followed almost automatically: Soviet comment on internal events in Egypt disappeared again.

2. Syria

Colonel Shishakli's military dictatorship was overthrown in February, 1954, and the parliamentary democratic regime reestablished, though the army command had the last say on all important issues. Though they had been suppressed under Shishakli like other groups, within three years the Communists became one of the strongest political groups in the country.[18] Soviet influence was, however, by no means restricted to the growth of the local CP—its impact on political life in general was spectacular.

It should be recalled that, though Moscow had no particular reason to like Colonel Shishakli, the official Soviet attitude toward his regime had by no means been unfriendly; when Shishakli was overthrown, the Soviet press and radio refrained from commenting on the event, though the local Communists had opposed him. The charges that Shishakli had been a "Western agent" and that the "great popular democratic movement" began with his downfall, were only made long afterwards. Soviet good will toward the Shishakli regime was reflected, for instance, in Mr. Vyshinskii's vote in the Security Council in January, 1954, when the Soviet Union gave Syria full support in its quarrel with Israel over the use of the Jordan waters.

Subsequently, Soviet support for Syria became more consistent and pronounced. Cultural and commercial relations were developed; a first Syrian student delegation visited Russia, and a Soviet film festival took place in Damascus. When the Syrian government decided to ban the Soviet film *The Fall of Berlin*, Moscow put the blame not on Damascus but rather on the pressure allegedly exerted by Bonn and Washington.[19] One of the main topics of Soviet press and radio propaganda was the alleged Turkish threat; the Turks, it was said, wanted to annex Aleppo and other regions in North Syria.[20] These and similar alarmist rumors would always fall on fertile ground, as expected.

While Soviet amity with Egypt suffered a temporary eclipse in the summer and autumn of 1954, relations with Syria continued to improve. This was reflected in cultural exchanges, such as the visit to Russia of Syrian physicians, agricultural experts, and student groups. The Soviet representatives at the Damascus fair (August–September, 1954) stole the limelight, and the Soviet pavilion, being the largest and most lavish, attracted general attention. A group of Syrian scientists touring the Soviet Union in November and December, 1954, was warmly received and this event, like Soviet participation in the Damascus fair, provided material for the editorial columns of Syrian newspapers for many weeks.[21] Moslem dignitaries back from Moscow testified about the "absolute freedom" enjoyed by Soviet Moslems and advised the Syrian people to emulate the Soviet experience.[22]

Additional impetus was given to the general pro-Soviet feeling by the Syrian Communist Party's participation in the election campaign of September, 1954, in which Khaled Bakdash, the party's general secretary, was elected to parliament. Both Soviet and Communist propaganda continued to warn the Syrian people against sinister and mostly unspecified Western (and Turkish) plots to deprive Syria of its independence, to restore a military dictatorship, and so on.[23] However imaginary these specters were, the conjuring trick worked, and there can be little doubt that this line of propaganda was extremely effective. But it does not explain why Syrian public opinion was so receptive—more receptive, in fact, than public opinion elsewhere in the Arab world. The reasons for the general spread of pro-Soviet feelings will be studied in a different context. It should be remarked in passing, however, that this process can certainly not be explained by reference to economic crises and social unrest; Syria experienced an unprecedented boom in the postwar period (until 1955) which was reflected in a yearly investment rate of 12 to 14%. The fact that economic prosperity did not result in political stability should dispel illusions about an easy and direct correlation between economic progress and the growth of democracy.

3. Sudan

Official diplomatic relations between the Soviet bloc and the Sudan did not yet exist in 1954, and trade relations developed slowly. When the Sudanese Minister of Commerce visited the Leipzig fair in September, 1954, he was given an official welcome. The Soviet attitude toward the Sudan during that period was largely influenced by Soviet relations with Egypt. During the first half of 1954, when Soviet relations with Egypt were improving, the pro-Egyptian line followed by Ismail al Azhari in Khartum was supported by Moscow. The idea of a union with Egypt was favored and "British intrigues" to divide the Sudan and join the southern part of the country to Uganda and Kenya were denounced.[24] This did not prevent occasional criticism of the "reactionary character" of the Sudanese government evidenced by the persecution of Communist organizations in the country.[25]

The Soviet approach changed after the agreement between Cairo and London on the evacuation of Suez strained relations between Moscow and Cairo for a while. During that time Moscow displayed no interest whatsoever in a Sudanese-Egyptian Union. The Azhari government was attacked for not permitting Sudanese students to demonstrate *against* Colonel Nasser[26] and the anti-Egyptian propaganda of the Sudanese Communists became extremely violent for a while.[27] General Soviet comment on the domestic situation stressed the hard lot of the Sudanese workers in considerable detail; it was declared to be "growing worse" daily.[28]

In the winter of 1954-55 Soviet relations with Egypt improved again and there was a corresponding reaction in Soviet policy toward the Sudan: the unity of the Nile Valley again became a desirable solution.[29] The Sudanese Communists, on the other hand, continued to attack Egypt, to favor Sudanese independence, and to charge the Azhari government with perfidious betrayal for "selling out the Sudan to Gamal Abdel Nasser."[30] This apparent contradiction between Soviet and local Communist propaganda was the rule rather than the exception in both the Sudan and Egypt during 1954-55. It took the various Communist groups in these countries more than a year to rally to the Soviet thesis of support for Nasser, and even afterwards there were occasional deviations from the general line of Soviet policy in that part of the world.

4. Jordan

There were no diplomatic ties between the Soviet Union and Jordan in 1954, nor economic or cultural exchanges worth mentioning. Nevertheless, Soviet policies occasionally had an indirect impact on Jordan; the most outstanding event in this context probably being Vyshinskii's support of Jordan in the UN Security Council in April, 1954, in a particular phase of Jordan's long-standing conflict with Israel (the Nahalin incident). Vyshinskii's stand was much appreciated in Amman, and the Jordan parliament voted him a message of thanks. Such incidents did not have any palpable influence on official Jordan policy; the cabinet headed by Fawzi al Mulki, who had favored a cautious *rapprochement* with the Soviet Union, resigned shortly thereafter and was replaced by one headed by Tawfiq Abul Huda, who had been a leading protagonist of a Western orientation for many years. But it did influence public opinion in Jordan, which, (as in Syria) then began to show pronounced pro-Soviet leanings. It would be mistaken to explain this interesting ferment solely as the result of what Moscow did at the time or refrained from doing. Ultimately, this upsurge of radical ideas combined with a general pro-Soviet orientation in world affairs has to be explained by internal political developments in Jordan and Syria. But there can be no doubt that Soviet foreign policy did everything it could to expedite this ferment and thus contributed to the process.

The general tenor of the Soviet press and radio was one of benevolent, sympathetic interest: Jordan was defined as the present victim of British, and a future target of American, imperialism.[31] The formation of a semiofficial Communist-front organization with a journal of its own was warmly welcomed in Moscow,[32] and the Jordanian people was described as fighting in the forefront of the struggle for national independence and peace. The political program of this movement was given unreserved support, and its achievements during the first months of its existence were warmly applauded.[33]

This official benevolence did not at first extend to the "ruling circles" and the king. At a later date (in 1956, to be precise), Soviet spokesmen refrained for a while from criticizing anybody at all in the Hashemite kingdom of Jordan. In 1954, however, the official Soviet attitude was more outspoken. The Jordan regime was characterized as feudal, reactionary, and one of colonial dependence,[34] and the elections of October, 1954, were said to have taken place in a climate of police terror.[35]

It may be of some interest to note that one propaganda motive that was subsequently to become of considerable importance throughout the Arab world was given its first tryout in Jordan. The Soviet Union is stronger than the West (this argument ran), and will prevail in the contest for world power. For that reason,

if for no other, it was in the interest of the Arab peoples to establish a firm alliance with Moscow.[36]

5. Lebanon

Soviet foreign policy has devoted considerable attention to
Lebanon in the last fifteen years, with less success than in the
other Arab countries. This could be explained by Lebanon's
comparatively strong ties with the West, and the fact that in
Lebanon Communism has had to compete with a more sophisticated public opinion, politically speaking, than elsewhere in the
Arab world. During 1954 Lebanon was subjected to the same
treatment as Egypt and Syria: cultural exchanges, an economic
treaty,[37] friendly political comment in the Soviet press and radio.
A Lebanese cabinet minister was invited, and went, to the Budapest meeting of the "Partisans of Peace." Vyshinskii's stand in the
United Nations in favor of the Arab cause and against Israel
provoked some favorable comment in Beirut.[38] But, by and large,
all these activities had much less impact on Lebanese public
opinion than in neighboring Syria or Jordan.

Soviet advice to Lebanon during that time included the usual
warnings against a political or military involvement with the
West. American economic and technical assistance to Lebanon
(Point Four—the Litani irrigation project) particularly drew
Soviet fire.[39] Acceptance of such assistance, Moscow announced,
was really tantamount to becoming subject to enslavement by
American imperialism. On the whole, Soviet political observers
abstained from commenting on internal Lebanese developments.
Not, however, on the course to be taken by the Lebanon in world
affairs. On the anniversary of Lebanese independence, the necessity of strengthening ties with the Soviet Union was pointed out,
for it was the "friend of the Arabs, who had always supported
that country's national aspirations, and who had been one of the
first to establish diplomatic contacts with Beirut." Such selfless
friendship was undoubtedly preferable to closer ties with the
United States; for the Americans only wanted to replace the
French as the colonial power in Lebanon, and to make the country a military base.[40]

6. Iraq

Iraqi official circles, though not Iraqi public opinion, had been pro-West on the whole. Moscow's main efforts during 1954 were directed toward a prevention of Iraqi involvement in a Middle Eastern defense organization. A. Denisenko, the Soviet chargé d'affaires in Baghdad, delivered a note in March, 1954, in which the establishment of a Western-sponsored Middle Eastern defense organization was defined as a "hostile act toward the Soviet Union." However, Fadhil Jamali, then the prime minister, was not *persona grata* in Moscow—at that time he was the only Arab statesman actually to come in for a full vituperative blast because of his pro-Western orientation.[41] There were no illusions in Moscow about his policy and the possibility of influencing him, and Soviet propaganda was thus mainly directed to opposition groups and public opinion in general. Did Iraq really want to become a second Turkey, an American colony, exploited by foreigners, a springboard for Western imperialist ambitions?[42] Fortunately, resistance to the Western alliance was crystallizing around the "National Front," or so Moscow believed. Nuri as Said, who followed Fadhil Jamali as Prime Minister, fared no better than his predecessor; his trip to Turkey in October, 1954, was called another step toward Iraq's inclusion in the Western defense system.[43] Other subjects of Soviet criticism were the exploitation of the country by Western oil companies, the miserable lot of the Iraqi worker, and kindred topics.

Official relations between the two countries, which had never been particularly close or cordial, came to an abrupt end when Iraq closed its legation in November, 1954, to be followed by a decision to sever diplomatic relations altogether on January 3, 1955. Direct Soviet political action became impossible after that date, and the Russians had recourse to the strategy of indirect approach, via the illegal local Communist party, its various front organizations, and political allies.

7. Israel

Diplomatic relations with Israel had been broken off by the Soviet Union following a bomb incident near the Soviet legation in Tel Aviv in January, 1953. However, shortly after Stalin's death, diplomatic ties were renewed and for a time became as close as before, if not more so. A trade agreement concluded in December, 1953, provided for the import of Soviet fuel oil in sizeable quantities; Israeli imports from the USSR in 1954 were forty times higher than they had been in 1950-51.[44] In June, 1954, the Soviet Legation in Tel Aviv and the Israeli Legation in Moscow were raised to embassy level. The Soviet ambassador in Tel Aviv, Abramov, used this opportunity to present his credentials in Jerusalem, the capital, an action that was widely commended in Israel because of the unwillingness shown by most other powers to recognize Jerusalem as the country's capital. In many meetings and visits, the Soviet ambassador stressed the necessity of developing closer relations, and, generally speaking, made considerable efforts to win friends and influence people. Cultural exchanges became more intensive than before: delegations of Israeli farmers, and women's and other organizations toured the Soviet Union, while a delegation of Soviet women came to visit Israel. The "Friendship League" and the "Friendship Congress" (the former without Communist participation) held many meetings during the period under review and did what they could for the development of close relations between the two countries. Israeli relations with the "Popular Democracies" improved, too, with the exception of Czechoslovakia and Rumania, where arrests and trials of Jewish and Zionist leaders continued in 1954. An Israeli governmental delegation toured China in early 1955; it was expected at the time that this move would be followed by more tangible results, such as political and economic agreements. These expectations were not fulfilled.

However, the general picture of Israeli-Soviet relations was not as rosy as appeared at first glance. On a number of occasions in 1954, Soviet representatives in the United Nations supported the Arab side against Israel (over the Nahalin incident, the Lake Huleh conflict, the question of free passage through the Suez Canal), which made an extremely unfavorable impression in Israel, though it was really only a very mild foretaste of things to come. Nor did cultural exchanges proceed in a very satisfactory way from the Israeli point of view; they were curiously one-sided and amounted in effect to Soviet cultural propaganda in Israel without any corresponding willingness to have Israeli writers and artists visit the Soviet Union. When official Israeli insistence on a basis of reciprocity in cultural exchanges met with Soviet disapproval, the Israeli government refused to grant visas to a Soviet delegation that was to participate in a Communist-sponsored Congress in Tel Aviv. This incident produced a minor crisis in Soviet-Israeli relations at the time.[45]

While, on the whole, Soviet observers refrained from commenting on internal developments in Israel, attacks on Zionism and on Israel continued in the broadcasts of Radio Warsaw (in Yiddish) which was then the main propaganda outlet aimed at Jews outside the Soviet bloc. Nor were the hopes for mass emigration from Russia and the other Soviet bloc countries fulfilled; there was a small trickle of such immigrants,[46] all of them very old people or "compassionate cases."

8. Turkey

The Soviet approach to Turkey underwent several important changes during 1954. Under Stalin it had been one of open hostility for many years, and there was no real improvement until about a year after his death. In the early summer of 1954 there were some signs of Soviet willingness to normalize relations with Turkey, but the anti-Turkish campaign was soon resumed when it appeared that both Turkish official circles and public opinion strongly distrusted these Soviet moves. Farther-reaching and more determined Soviet attempts to establish closer relations came in the autumn of 1954 but were again discontinued after Turkey had joined both the Balkan and Baghdad Pacts.

According to the Soviet view, Turkey had become a Western dependency, had ruined its national economy, betrayed the Arabs, and assumed the role of an American military springboard and a West German economic colony.[47] Such purely negative propaganda, or the Soviet note of March 18, 1954, protesting the Ankara-Karachi pact, was perhaps intended to intimidate Turkey or isolate it in the Middle East, but was hardly likely to gain good will in the country. A more friendly line was taken by Malenkov in a speech made on April 26, 1954, in which he stressed the desirability of better relations between the two countries. This new approach was coupled with a series of other moves in a similar vein, such as the visit of a Soviet commercial mission, an announcement that the Soviet Union would participate in the annual Izmir Fair, etc. These feelers were not very well received in Turkey[48] and the Soviet line again hardened in the late summer—partly, perhaps, as a protest against Turkey's new ties with Yugoslavia and Greece in the framework of the Balkan Pact.

The Soviet press asked, "Why does Turkey need so much armament?"[49] and, generally speaking, expressed strong criticism of Turkey's foreign policy.

In late October, 1954, this campaign was temporarily discontinued, and fresh attempts were made for a time (in connection with the thirty-first anniversary of the foundation of the Turkish Republic) to influence the Turkish government by means of a more friendly approach. The Soviet press and radio recalled the good-neighborly relations that had prevailed between the two countries in the twenties under Kemal Ataturk. On one occasion, *Pravda* even defended Mustafa Kemal against Western denigrators (the American news magazine *Time*).[50] It was pointed out that the Soviet Union had been the only power to help Republican Turkey in its war of independence, and reference was made to statements by Ataturk in favor of Soviet-Turkish cooperation. Some Turkish newspapers welcomed these declarations,[51] but, by and large, the reaction of the Turkish government and public opinion was again extremely reserved: "The acrobatics of Soviet policy, the continual oscillation between friendship and hostility, do not inspire much confidence," commented one editorial.[52] Soviet professions of friendship did not altogether cease as the winter of 1954-55 drew to its end, but Soviet criticism again became more pronounced as the Baghdad Pact assumed more definite and tangible form. Molotov, in a speech before the Supreme Soviet (in February, 1955), declared that Russia wanted good neighborly relations with Turkey, but that the policy followed by the Ankara government made the restoration of the traditional friendship impossible. This again provoked angry recriminations in Turkey, where the opportunity was used to remind Moscow of its unfriendly policy between 1940 and 1953. Fuad Koprulu, the

Turkish Foreign Minister, emphasized in one of his speeches (January 25, 1955) that relations with the Soviet Union were normal, but this statement made a "strange impression" on official Soviet circles, who thought it incompatible with Turkey's military pacts, which were defined as "prejudicial to Turkey's national interests and its future."[53] Changes in the Soviet attitude toward the Arab world were in sight, but the cold war against Turkey was to continue.

9. Persia

As far as Soviet-Persian relations were concerned, 1954 began auspiciously. Despite the fact that Tudeh was violently opposed to General Zahedi's rule and did everything it could to overthrow his regime, Soviet policy tried in various ways to improve relations with Tehran. The meeting between Lavrentiev and General Zahedi in early March was widely interpreted as the sign of a new beginning.[54] Even before that date, an important trade agreement had been signed in Tehran (on December 29, 1953), and another agreement was reached in June, 1954. Negotiations were begun on some of the outstanding differences between the two countries, such as the question of fishing in the Caspian Sea, border revisions, the problem of Persian gold retained in the USSR, and the "Iran Sovneft" oil company. A group of Soviet physicians visited Persia, Soviet films were again shown in Tehran, and the Avicenna millenary became a starting point of closer cultural relations.[55] A Persian agricultural delegation and a sports team toured the Soviet Union, and for a time it appeared as if relations between the two countries would become closer. There was some adverse comment in the Soviet press about American activities in Persia but it was not astringent, since Persia was described as an innocent victim of Western intrigues.

The Soviet attitude again hardened after agreement was reached in midsummer between the Persian government, the United States, and Britain about the establishment of an international cartel for the exploitation of Persian oil. The agreement was described as prejudicial to Persia's interests,[56] and Persia was charged with straying from the path of neutrality.[57] A number of other snags had occurred meanwhile; an agreement on fishing in the Caspian Sea had been reached, but there was no progress in the negotiations about border rectifications. On the contrary, a number of fresh border incidents had taken place.

The Persian press reported that the Soviet military attaché, General Rodionov, was implicated in the big Tudeh conspiracy in the Persian army and air force that was uncovered in August and September, 1954, and that led to the arrest of several hundred officers. Previously, a leading member of Tudeh had been arrested in the car of another Soviet diplomatic representative. Moscow viewed Persia's *rapprochement* with Turkey and Pakistan with extreme disfavor and an official Soviet note of protest was sent on July 8, 1954.[58] Nevertheless, the Soviet reaction was less violent than that toward Turkey, and the mounting tension did not prevent the conclusion of an agreement on the rectification of the border in the Azerbaijan and Khorasan area, which was coupled with a number of economic treaties. This agreement, which involved certain Soviet concessions, was not given much publicity in Moscow[59] but was hailed in Tehran as a great step forward that indeed signified a new beginning in Soviet foreign policy after Stalin's death.[60]

As time went on, and Persia's adherence to the Baghdad Pact became first a virtual certainty and then an established fact, Soviet comments again became bitter: *Pravda* reminded the Persian government that it did not have the right to join any "anti-Soviet" pact according to the treaties of 1921 and 1927.[61] Soviet charges and Persian countercharges lasted through the spring of 1955. Despite these mutual recriminations, there was an impression that Moscow believed Tehran more open to friendly persuasion or pressure than Ankara: Soviet attacks on Zahedi were considerably less virulent than those directed then and afterwards against the Turkish government.

NOTES

1. See Harry Stack Sullivan: *Conceptions of Modern Psychiatry* (Washington, 1947).
2. Jean and Simonne Lacouture: *L'Egypte en Mouvement* (Paris, 1956), p. 269. It is interesting to note an almost literal coincidence in the relationship of the Argentine Communists vis-à-vis a regime not radically different

from Colonel Nasser's: ". . . Perón is an empiricist with no particular theory of his own. They believed that if they worked closely with Perón they could provide the philosophical and ideological basis for his regime." Robert J. Alexander: *Communism in Latin America* (Rutgers Univ. Press, 1957), p. 173.

3. See *State Department Bulletin*, Dec. 21, 1953, p. 863.

4. The text of the Soviet note to Pakistan was published in *Pravda*, December 1, 1951, the text of the note to Turkey *ibid.*, March 20, 1954.

5. For instance, *Izvestiia*, February 27, 1954.

6. *Pravda*, January 29, 1954.

7. See the interview with Abdel Latif Boghdadi, then Minister of War, in *Al Ahram*, February 22, 1954, and Salah Salem, Minister of National Guidance at the time, in *Al Gumhuriya* of the same date, as well as Gamal Abdel Nasser's declaration on April 14, 1954: "The Turko-Pakistani Pact is contrary to our interests."

8. See *Imperialisticheskaia Borba za Afriku i Osvobozhditelnoe Dvizhenie Narodov* (Moscow, 1954), p. 97 *et seq.*, and *Narody Afriki* (Moscow, 1954), p. 213.

9. *Al Musawwar*, April 22, 1954, and *Journal d'Egypte*, April 23, 1954.

10. *Al Gumhuriya*, May 22, 1954.

11. *Izvestiia*, May 18, 1954.

12. *Pravda*, June 2, 1954.

13. Kudriavtsev in *Izvestiia*, August 8, 1954.

14. Radio Moscow, November 16, 1954.

15. Radio Moscow, November 16-17, 1954.

16. *TASS*, November 25 and 28, 1954.

17. This (illegal) pamphlet was published in November, 1954; it congratulated Khaled Bakdash on his election to the Syrian parliament.

18. *1957—Ezhegodnik Bolshoi Sovetskoi Entsiklopedii*, article on Syria, p. 398.

19. *Izvestiia*, April 4, 1954.

20. Radio Moscow in Arabic, May 8, 1954.

21. *Al Alam*, September 9, 1954, and *Al Jabal*, September 10, 1954.

22. Interview of Shaikh Mohammed al Bitar in *Al Talia*, December 12, 1954.

23. Radio Moscow in Arabic, December 11, 24, 1954.

24. *TASS* in English, February 19, 1954.

25. Radio Moscow in Arabic, March 8, 1954.

26. *Al Maidan* (Khartum), October 9, 1954.

27. *Sudanese Review*, June 3, 1954. *Al Maidan*, September 2, 1954, described the situation in Egypt as "unprecedented governmental terror."

28. *FLP*, July 16, 1954.

29. Radio Erivan in Armenian, January 21, 1955.

30. *Revue Soudanaise*, November, 1954.

31. Radio Moscow, January 27, February 16, 1954.

32. *TASS*, July 17, 1954.

33. *Kommunist* 22, 1954 (November, 1954).

34. *Pravda*, November 5, 1954, quoting an "open letter" by a group of Jordanian "Partisans of Peace."

35. Radio Moscow, October 18, 1954.

36. *Hawl al Alam*, March 20, 1954. This statement referred to a declaration by Field Marshal von Paulus, the German army commander, shortly after his release from a Soviet POW camp.

37. The communiqué at the conclusion of the treaty was published in *Pravda* of May 1, 1954.

38. *Telegraf, Le Matin*, May 7, 1954.

39. Radio Moscow, December 15, 1954.

40. Radio Moscow in Arabic, November 22, 1954.

41. Radio Moscow in Arabic, March 13, 1954.

42. Radio Moscow, March 20, 1954.

43. Radio Moscow in Arabic, October 11, 1954.

44. Moshe Sharett in a Knesset foreign policy debate, September 1, 1954.

45. *Jerusalem Post*, October 17, 1954.

46. *Ha'aretz*, November 3, December 17, 1954.

47. Radio Moscow in English, February 20, 1954; *Trud*, April 5, 1954.

48. *Milliyet*, May 2, 1954; *Hurriyet*, May 3, 1954; *Cumhuriyet*, April 27, 1954.

49. *Krasnaia Zvezda*, July 16, 1954.

50. *Pravda*, September 17, 1954.

51. *Dunya*, October 31, 1954.

52. *Halkci*, November 1, 1954.

53. *Krasnaia Zvezda*, April 1, 1955.

54. *Ettela'at*, March 5, 1954.

55. *Pravda*, April 13, 1954.

56. *TASS*, July 6, 1954; *Komsomolskaia Pravda*, July 9, 1954.

57. *Pravda*, July 2, 1954.

58. Text in *Pravda* of July 10, 1954, and *Keyhan* of the same date.

59. A brief official communiqué was published in *Pravda* of December 4, 1954.

60. *Sedaye Mardom*, December 1, 1954.

61. *Pravda*, March 16, 1955.

CHAPTER TWO

1955: THE ARMS DEAL

The Soviet-Egyptian arms deal in September, 1955, was regarded at the time as the great turning point in the Middle East, the end of one era and the beginning of another. There is no need to revise that view in retrospect; the arms deal was, indeed, the great divide. That is how it appeared to both the Western and Eastern blocs, with only the Egyptian leaders taking exception. The latter argued that Egypt was an independent country and thus entitled to get weapons wherever it wished. Had not the Turks accepted Soviet arms in the early twenties? And had not the Western powers themselves been partners in a military alliance with Russia in World War II? Anyway, the arms agreement was a purely commercial transaction; Egypt was only to import weapons and ammunition from the Soviet bloc, not political ideas.

These were the arguments of the Egyptian leaders, and they were no doubt sincere. The fears of the West (and the hopes of the East) were less concerned with the good intentions than with the objective results of Colonel Nasser's actions. There was nothing morally reprehensible about a policy of playing the two great world blocs against each other, especially since it might have appeared to be in the best interests of the Egyptian people. However, to make neutralism a paying proposition, some prerequisites were required; it had been comparatively easy to take the first and second steps, but then a political chain reaction followed. When Naguib and Nasser took over in July, 1952, they solemnly (and sincerely) declared that they merely wanted to purge the country of traitors, and then step down again in three weeks or as many months. But the political situation made this intention illusory and, having accepted responsibility, they had to go on

211

ruling the country. It could also be shown that Nasser's road to the eminently respectable Bandung Conference in 1955 eventually led to the 1957 meeting in Cairo (the "solidarity conference" of the Afro-Asian peoples) which was anything but neutralist. The danger, from the Western point of view, was not in the Soviet arms deal itself (which was relatively unimportant), but in Egypt's growing dependence on the Soviet Union. Egypt's neutrality, it was feared, would give way to positive neutralism (positive toward the Soviet Union) and this, in turn, would gradually lead toward open hostility to the West and a close alliance with the Soviet bloc.

From the Soviet point of view there were no scruples or hesitations about the arms deal[1] once it had been discovered how attractive such offers were in Arab eyes, and how much sympathy could be gained in the Middle East by such relatively inexpensive outlays. Moral or ideological scruples did not come into the picture; many years had passed since the Soviets had decried the fiendish activities of the "merchants of death." The only risks were practical. Would Nasser take the arms but try to preserve his independence? What if he used his new military equipment in a local Middle Eastern war? What if he were defeated and the Soviet arms fell into other hands? And if he were victorious— would he become too strong to be manipulated?

These questions were apparently given careful study in Moscow, but the conclusion reached was that the risks involved were small. It was undoubtedly anticipated that Nasser would try to preserve his independence, but then Egypt's internal and external situation would make the continuation and strengthening of the Soviet alliance imperative for him.

If he used the arms in a Middle Eastern war and was defeated —*tant pis*, it would mean that he needed new arms and these would again come from the Soviet Union. If he won a war, he would have Soviet military assistance to thank, and Russian prestige would increase enormously. Either way Moscow could not lose.

There has been some evidence that there were some differences of opinion in Moscow regarding the new Egyptian alliance. Shepilov used to call this alliance his brainchild, but the preparations for the *rapprochement* had been made before Shepilov ever came into contact with Nasser. Khrushchev subsequently accepted the Shepilov view about the importance of the Cairo alliance, whatever his other disagreements with the former editor of *Pravda*. Molotov, on the other hand, and perhaps Malenkov in his wake were apparently more skeptical about the advantages of the alliance with Nasser. In any case, Khrushchev prevailed, and there is no reason to exaggerate the importance of these differences of opinion. If there was such a dispute, it was on a tactical level and could not be compared with the big clash between Stalin and the left-wing opposition in 1927 about the line to be taken on Chiang Kai-shek.

What induced Colonel Nasser to sign the arms agreement which subsequently became a full-fledged alliance? The Baghdad Pact, the Israeli attack in the Gaza region in February, 1955, and the Bandung Conference have been mentioned in this context. There is a grain of truth in each of these arguments, but no one in isolation, nor all of them together, offers a satisfactory explanation.

The Baghdad Pact was unquestionably a calamity from Nasser's point of view. He and his colleagues opposed a defensive alliance with the West because they thought it contrary to the national interest of the Arab world. In addition, such an alliance would split the camp, make it impossible for Nasser to carry out his plans for the unification of the Arab world. The Baghdad Pact did not directly endanger Egyptian interests and Colonel Nasser's rule, but it certainly made it more difficult for him to carry out his plans for the Arab world. It aroused Cairo's bitter enmity and inclined Nasser to a progressive *rapprochement* with the Soviet Union in the summer of 1955.

Another reason prominently featured in this context is the Israeli attack on Gaza in February, 1955. It was claimed that this full-scale military attack demonstrated Egypt's weakness. Colonel Nasser simply had to get arms and since the Western powers had refused them, or had supplied them in insufficient quantities, or had made the supply dependent on unacceptable conditions, he was driven into the Soviet embrace. Previously, his military weakness had not been felt, but in view of the general clamor that he hit back—and his inability to do so—the Soviet arms deal became inevitable. This version has frequently been given by Egyptian spokesmen (including Nasser himself) and has been accepted by many Western observers. This is magnifying one particular incident out of proportion to its actual significance, as if one were to explain the causes of the American Civil War by reference to Fort Sumter, or the origins of World War I by pointing to Sarajevo. The Israeli attack was only one link in a long and protracted border war; it followed Egypt's announcement that a new partisan army, the "Fedayeen," had been created and stationed in Gaza for infiltration into "Jewish-occupied Palestine." Gaza may have been the turning point, but it was hardly the deeper cause of the new policy. A change in Egypt's foreign political orientation was in the air; in these circumstances even a comparatively unimportant incident was bound to have far-reaching effects. Arms were needed by Egypt for a more independent and activist foreign policy.

The Bandung Conference was Nasser's first trip abroad and a great personal success. He dominated the Conference, together with Nehru and Chou En-lai. It certainly strengthened his neutralist convictions. But most of the countries represented at Bandung did not subsequently develop such close ties with the Soviet bloc.

For a real explanation of the dramatic events that took place in the Middle East in 1955, one ought to go back at least a number of years, perhaps several decades. One would have to take into account mounting anti-Western feeling and the growing radicalization of the Arab intelligentsia from the late thirties onwards. The idea of an alliance with Russia, even of an arms deal, was not at all new; it had been mentioned before as a very desirable possibility. The Wafd had played with the idea in 1950-52 and the Syrian government had reportedly concluded a pilot agreement in 1954. There was an overwhelming desire to defy the West, to put an end once and for all to dependence on the Western powers, after so many years of direct and indirect Western rule and humiliation. Such an open, ultimate act of defiance could only be made with Soviet assistance. Most important of all was the Egyptian shift in primacy from domestic problems to foreign policy. This does not mean that prior to the spring of 1955 Colonel Nasser did not care about foreign affairs, or that domestic reforms were altogether discontinued after that date. But there can be no doubt that the emphasis passed from one field to the other at about that time. A full description and explanation of the process would involve a review of recent Egyptian history. What should be emphasized here is that the Cairo junta came to power first and foremost on a platform of domestic reform. The fight for Egypt's national aspirations was, of course, also envisaged, but the immediate aim was to "put the house in order," to establish an economic and social basis for this struggle. During 1953 and 1954 several domestic reform projects were launched in various fields—the agrarian reform, to mention only one. By early 1955 the immediate aims had been attained: the political parties had been dissolved and their former leaders purged, and the new order had more or less taken shape.

But the basic problems on the home front had not yet been tackled; neither the "population explosion," nor the fact that income per capita had been falling for many years and was continuing to decrease, while the great majority of the population was vegetating at subsistence level. It could be argued that Colonel Nasser and his colleagues had to choose between long and protracted development schemes that would bear fruit only after many years, or a "primacy of foreign policy" that would harvest quick, easy successes. It could also be argued (and the present writer has gradually come to accept this view) that such a dilemma did not in fact exist for the simple reason that Egypt's economic problems were insoluble in the given framework. It is doubtful whether any regime could have succeeded in these conditions, even the most purposeful and ruthless dictatorship. In contrast to the Russia of 1917 or the China of 1949, Egypt did not have plenty of unused land or considerable natural resources; the conditions of "primitive accumulation" to provide the basis for a policy of speedy industrialization did not exist. Colonel Nasser's regime was neither very purposeful nor very ruthless as dictatorships go, but it was "dynamic," of necessity. If any ruler was ever driven by the sheer force of circumstances to seek salvation in an "activist" foreign policy, Colonel Nasser was.

The Soviet Union and the Middle East

These conditions are mentioned here not to condemn, nor as extenuating circumstances, but as political facts that decisively shaped the subsequent course of events.[2] They led straight to an alliance with the Soviet Union. Since a full-fledged grand alliance in the eighteenth-century style had gone out of fashion by the middle of our century, this assumed the pattern of a series of agreements and understandings in the military, economic, and, ultimately, in the political sphere.

The year of the great breakthrough did not start at all promisingly from the Soviet point of view. The early months of 1955 witnessed a series of purges, arrests, and mass trials in Egypt—mainly directed against the leadership of the Moslem Brotherhood, and to a lesser degree against the various Communist factions. Soviet spokesmen refrained from commenting directly on these events, but there was no doubt that they were following them with considerable misgivings.[3] Normal trade relations between Egypt and the Soviet Union continued—and new commercial agreements were reached with Poland and Hungary. Czechoslovakia held an industrial exhibition in Cairo in March, and the Soviet Red Cross offered Egypt money to help the flood victims in the Kina district.

Such minor events apart, the picture, as seen from Moscow, was not too rosy, for Nasser was still considered a "reactionary" following the Western lead. However, once Colonel Nasser's regime had emerged intact from its trials and internal reshuffles, it had to pay more attention to foreign political problems. The Baghdad Pact scheme had made threatening progress, and Cairo launched a violent propaganda campaign against Turkey, Iraq, and the West in general. The Soviet government, for reasons of its own, also decided in the spring of 1955 that something should be done to arrest the progress of the Baghdad Pact. In an official statement published by the Soviet Ministry of Foreign Affairs on April 16, 1955,[4] it was said that the general situation in the Middle East had been aggravated in recent months as a result of the Western powers' attempt to draw the Arab countries into mili-

tary alliances. Particular mention was made of pressure brought
to bear on Syria and Egypt to join these alliances and it was
stressed that the Soviet Union would not remain indifferent to
these Western machinations. Such an attitude on the part of the
Soviet Union (it was added) was only comprehensible, for the
Soviet Union, after all, was a state adjacent to the Middle Eastern
countries, in contrast to the United States.

Notice was thus given that Soviet Middle Eastern policy was
to be activated, but very few observers in the West paid sufficient
attention.[5] But what practical form would this intensified Soviet
activity assume? Since February, 1955, Soviet envoys in the Middle Eastern capitals had made unofficial offers of Soviet economic
and technical help "without any strings attached." In March,
Hassan Ibrahim, a member of the Cairo junta, visited several East
European countries and had talks with Communist leaders in
East Berlin. In May, Daniel Solod met Gamal Abdel Nasser and
discussed the question of Egypt's diplomatic recognition of Communist China.[6] And in the same month (as he subsequently told
an Egyptian weekly) Nasser was approached by Solod at a diplomatic reception: "He led me into a corner and asked me whether
my government would be disposed to buy arms from the Soviet
Union. In the case of an affirmative reply, he would inform
Moscow . . . I replied, in the same tenor, that this suggestion
appeared very interesting indeed and that I was ready to enter
negotiations in this spirit . . ."[7] The talks that ensued were held in
strict secrecy; for once there was no leak. Even *Al Gumhuriya*,
the semiofficial organ of the junta, was slightly out of step when
it said (in late April, 1955) that the peoples of the Middle East
were not veering towards the Soviet Union, and that such pro-
Soviet feelings as were to be found in the Arab world were really
the consequence of anti-Arab Western policy.[8] Unknown even
to an official editorial writer, matters had already progressed far
beyond that point.* The stage had been set for the big arms deal.

* According to another version, published in the Egyptian press in
December, 1958, Chou En-lai (who had met Nasser in Bandung) mediated
between Cairo and Moscow, and transmitted Nasser's request for arms to
the Soviet Presidium.

Meanwhile a spectacular though somewhat platonic *rapprochement* had taken place between Cairo and Peking. At the Bandung Conference Nasser had met Chou En-lai and had been greatly impressed by him and by what he was told about the situation in Communist China. Nasser was persuaded that Islam was not persecuted in China, that the Chinese revolution, in contrast to the Russian revolution of 1917, had been a popular uprising, not really a "Communist" revolution,[9] that the two countries should collaborate economically and cooperate in defense of world peace. In general, Nasser discovered that Egypt and China had a great many things in common, and the willingness to apply "Chinese solutions" to all kinds of Egyptian problems became more and more pronounced after 1955.[10]

In April, 1955, when Cairo was desperately looking for new buyers, the Egyptian press announced that China would purchase a great quantity of Egyptian cotton.[11] Cultural exchange negotiations between China and Egypt were led by Shaikh Hassan al Baqouri, Minister of Waqfs, who toured China during the month of May and returned tremendously impressed and rich in new ideas, as he declared in an interview.[12] Meanwhile, official Chinese circles gave much publicity to these new ties with Egypt: it was pointed out in the Chinese press that both Egypt and China were countries of very ancient culture, that the ties between them went back not merely to Ibn Battuta but to the Sung dynasty,[13] that Egypt was pursuing an independent foreign policy, that the Chinese people had nothing but feelings of friendship for Egypt, and that the two countries would collaborate on the basis of the Bandung resolutions.[14] If there was competition between the Soviet Union and China in Egypt, there was certainly no overt evidence to that effect at the time.

On July 21, 1955, Shepilov, editor of *Pravda* and head of the Foreign Affairs Commission of the Supreme Soviet of the USSR, arrived in Egypt for a one-week visit to take part in the celebrations of the third anniversary of the Egyptian revolution. He met all the leading personalities of the regime from President Nasser on down and made a great number of statements, all in a very

friendly spirit. To one correspondent he said that if the program
of the Egyptian government were fulfilled, Egypt would undoubtedly become the strongest country in the Mediterranean.[15]
On another occasion he warmly approved of the fact that Egypt's
policy was socialist in aspiration, "the best thing that could possibly happen to a country fighting for reform and progress."[16]
And on the eve of his departure there was again much praise,
though in a more discreet way, with the stress on the Egyptian
people, its industry, its love for freedom and independence. "One
says the pyramids are always mute, but the Egyptian people is not
mute. It has demonstrated its great energy in its struggle against
the imperialist oppressors . . . The sympathy of the Soviet people
is all with the aspirations of the Egyptian people."

Shepilov's visit had overshadowed the celebrations, and his
meetings with the Egyptian leaders attracted much interest and
aroused speculation. At the time, nothing was known about the
negotiations for the supply of arms, but several other agreements
were made public during Shepilov's stay, or shortly afterwards.
In early September a VOKS mission (the Soviet association for
cultural relations with foreign countries) arrived to inaugurate
the new Soviet Cultural Center in Cairo. Delegations of Egyptian
physicians and journalists were invited to Russia and on September 6, 1955, a barter deal exchanging Egyptian rice for Soviet
petrol was announced.

A group of Soviet Moslem pilgrims stopped over in Cairo in
mid-August on its way to Mecca and declared, in a much-pub-
licized press conference, that religion was completely free in the
Soviet Union. A similar pronouncement was made by Christo-
foros II, Greek Orthodox patriarch of Alexandria, upon his
return from the Soviet Union in the same month. Earlier, August
10, the Soviet ambassador in Cairo had handed Nasser an invitation to visit the Soviet Union, and the Egyptian president announced that he would come to Moscow in the spring of 1956.[17]
In an interview with a Lebanese newspaper, Colonel Nasser made
it clear that this visit did not contradict "our anti-Communist
principles." Anyway, the Soviet ambassador had assured him that
his government had nothing whatever to do with the Egyptian
Communists. "Nothing prevents us from strengthening our eco-

nomic ties with Russia even if we arrest the Communists at home and put them on trial."[18]

President Nasser's activities evoked much enthusiasm among the Soviet pilgrims back from Mecca: "As far as our coreligionists in the USSR are concerned," it was said, "Nasser had made Egypt the greatest Moslem country." Inside Egypt the impending trip of the chief of state became a matter of much favorable comment. It demonstrated the "new course" in Egyptian foreign policy: not to come out in favor of one camp or the other, but to show willingness to collaborate with everybody. The Egyptian government and people might oppose Communism, but "Communism is one thing and cooperation with the Soviet state such as it is—another."[19]

Only in September did the news about an arms deal with the Soviet bloc begin to leak out gradually. Official confirmation was given by Colonel Nasser himself on September 27, 1955, in a speech at an arms exhibition at Gezira. He retraced the story of his attempts to strengthen the Egyptian army: for the last three years he had tried to get arms wherever possible, but the Americans and the French put forth demands that were incompatible with Egypt's dignity and independence. The British sent something—but by no means enough. Only Czechoslovakia had responded favorably: "This transaction will have a purely commercial character like any other commercial operation." Nasser had accepted a new barter agreement: Egyptian cotton and rice against Czechoslovakian heavy arms. In order to forestall Western critics, Nasser added that this agreement did not indicate Soviet hegemony in the Middle East—on the contrary, its only intention was to put an end to foreign domination.[20]

Three days later Nasser offered several additional explanations. The arms deal did not signify a reorientation of Egyptian foreign policy. Nor did he want any foreign technicians in the Egyptian army ("This is more important for me than any other thing"). Why should the West be so outraged? After all, he had told the British and American diplomats back in June that he would have to buy arms from the Soviet Union if he could not get them from the West.[21] As he spoke, Hassan Raghib, Deputy Minister of War, was already on his way to Prague to supervise the delivery of the arms. If President Nasser was moderate in his explanations, semiofficial comments were less restrained. He had represented the arms deal as an *ultima ratio*, whereas the Egyptian press was more outspoken: Egypt had broken the chains of imperialism; from now on it was clear who were Egypt's real friends, and who its enemies.[22]

The exact details of the arms deal have never been made public; subsequently it became known that there were provisions for the delivery of guns, heavy tanks, submarines, modern jet planes, etc. And it proved to be quite incorrect (as some Western observers had predicted) that Russia would merely use the pact to dump antiquated war material on Egypt. Was it true that Egypt could not receive the arms it wanted from the Western powers? By and large, Nasser's description of Egypt's applications and requests was in accordance with the facts: Washington, London, and Paris had wanted to prevent a Middle Eastern arms race that could only have led to a new war. Nasser was not quite correct in charging the West with giving Israel preferential treatment. If America had not given Egypt the war material it had required, neither had any been given to Israel. Britain supplied Egypt with Vampire and Meteor jets and with heavy Centurion tanks, of which Israel had none. As far as can be established, France had given Israel only small quantities prior to September, 1955. Substantial French arms shipments to Israel only came considerably later—after the Egyptian-Soviet arms deal.

But what did Nasser want the heavy equipment for? The official explanation was that he needed it for the defense of Egypt against Israel. If this version had been believed in Western capitals, he would presumably have received the arms he needed. But at the time the general view, rightly or wrongly, was that Nasser needed these weapons not only, and perhaps not mainly, against Israel, but to establish an Egyptian "co-prosperity sphere" throughout the Middle East and North Africa. He would have clashed with Turkey, with Iraq, with the West over Aden and North Africa, and possibly with Sudan, Jordan, and other neighboring countries. Such a development was clearly not in the Western interest. The Soviet Union, on the other hand, had no qualms in this respect. No direct Soviet interests were involved in the Middle East, and in whatever direction Colonel Nasser tried to make headway he would clash with the West.

Would Western arms supplied in spring or summer of 1955 have forestalled Nasser's *rapprochement* with the Soviet Union? This is a hypothetical question that could be debated endlessly. In the opinion of the present writer, the West could have prevented the Soviet-Egyptian alliance at the time only if it had (in addition to shipping arms) given up the Baghdad Pact and its remaining positions in the Middle East and North Africa, reached an understanding about the future of Arab oil, and delivered Israel to its fate. Whether such a course of action of the part of the West would have prevented a more gradual and less dramatic *rapprochement* between Egypt and the Soviet Union is doubtful; this long-term process was motivated by inner social and political tensions that could not possibly have been affected by the supply of Western arms. The decision to ask for arms from the Soviet bloc was dictated by political necessities. The main thing for Colonel Nasser was not to obtain more and better arms, important as this was. Above all, he wanted to be free to use the arms as he wished. This aim could not be achieved so long as the "Western arms monopoly" still existed.

These developments in the late summer and autumn of 1955 were probably a source of considerable gratification in Moscow. But there were no shouts of triumph; on the contrary, there was a virtual Soviet embargo on news and comment from the Middle East for quite a while. The reasons for this reticence are not too difficult to divine. The arms deal with Egypt coincided with the Geneva Conference, and undue publicity given to Soviet successes in the Middle East would not have contributed to the success of that meeting. In addition, Moscow anticipated that the supply of arms to a military dictatorship would not be too well received by left-wing opinion outside the Soviet bloc, where some of the more "soft-headed liberals" and socialists might have regarded it as impairing the prospects of peace in the Middle East. The Soviet Union had appeared as the champion of peace for many years, and did not want to give up the role. For these and other reasons, the importance of the arms deal was systematically played down. There was a short official communiqué on October 2 to the effect that Moscow had informed the Western capitals that every country in the world was free to buy arms where it wanted, and that Western pressure on Egypt had been quite impermissible.[23] There was a noticeable reluctance to discuss the political effects of the arms deal. Though Colonel Nasser's speeches and interviews were otherwise reported in full, the sentences in which he attacked Israel and elaborated on the eventual use of the arms were omitted altogether, and when Colonel Anwar al Sadat wrote about "Western raving madmen"— in the Soviet press this became "people who are not in their right minds." Czechoslovakia, the country ostensibly involved in the commercial transaction, was somewhat more outspoken. Egypt was praised by the organ of the Czechoslovak army high command as a nation that had been increasingly active in supporting a policy of "international cooperation and world peace,"[24] Israel was blamed for the tension and unrest on the Egyptian border,[25] and *Obrana Lidu* called the assertion of Moshe Sharett, the Israeli Foreign Minister (that the arms deal had caused a deterioration of the Middle Eastern situation), "audacious and ridiculous."

The Soviet silence was broken on November 1 with an attack on Israel and further explanations of the arms deal. Israel, it was said, had no reason to complain about a shortage of arms: "its aggressive appeals did not reflect any shortage of arms."[26] Another official commentator said that the 1950 Three-Power Declaration (guaranteeing the existing Middle Eastern borders) was null and void: for the Arab states, that document possessed no more legal force than a certificate granting right of possession to the moon (this was two years before the Sputniks). The logic of events made it imperative for Moscow to take sides openly in the Egyptian-Israeli conflict, which it had previously refrained from doing. For the first time, the attention of the Soviet reader was drawn to the community of interests between Russia and Egypt: "Both Egypt and the Soviet Union stand squarely on a platform of peace and oppose the policy of aggression."[27] A survey of the Israeli-Egyptian conflict put all the blame on the former: if the U.N. Truce Supervision Observers had found the

Egyptians guilty of a number of attacks, this should not be given too much importance, "for the Egyptian embassy in London had denied General Burns's assertions." In any case, there had been negotiations between Egyptian and Israeli army officers during the summer, and the Israelis had broken off these talks—undoubtedly under American influence—as the Americans wanted to exert pressure on the Arab countries.[28]

These explanations, stressing Egyptian love of peace and Israeli bellicosity, became more frequent and more strident. There is some reason to believe that in the beginning the Soviet leaders had wanted to keep out of the internal Middle Eastern conflicts; it might even be correct (as Soviet diplomats asserted privately at the time) that, as far as they were concerned, the arms deal had nothing to do with the Arab-Israeli conflict. For Moscow, Israel was a minor issue—the main intent was anti-Western. But the arms shipment did directly affect the political situation in the area, with growing tension and the gradual Soviet involvement in the Arab-Israeli conflict.

There is no need here to discuss the Western reaction to the arms deal, which was both precipitate and ineffective. It was the reaction in the Arab world which proved to the Russians that they were on to a good thing. The arms deal was received enthusiastically not merely by radical public opinion in the Middle East but by every public figure in the Arab world. The Saudi ambassador in Cairo said that Nasser had the full support of all other Arabs, and even Nuri as Said, Nasser's archenemy, had to pledge his full and unreserved support.[29] In all the Arab countries Nasser had suddenly become the great liberator who had broken the Western yoke, and the Soviet Union became the only true and selfless friend of the Arab peoples. Nasser had declared that he was dealing with the Soviet Union as a state—not with Communism; that he was importing arms—not political ideas. But it proved to be extremely difficult to draw a dividing line. Where did Communism end, and the "Soviet state" start? Thus, only a month after Nasser's speech, one of his cabinet ministers appeared in print with an article that expressed considerable enthusiasm for something more than "the Soviet State."[30] It was the harbinger of a new spirit.

In this general wave of popular enthusiasm there was one group that took no part in the general rejoicing—the Egyptian Communists. For many years the Communist movement in Egypt had been divided into several factions. One group, consisting mainly of writers and journalists, had jumped on the Nasser bandwagon fairly early but the two main sections, the Democratic Movement for National Liberation (DMNL) and the Egyptian Communist Party (ECP), continued their violent opposition to the Nasser regime.[31]

At the time of the mass trials in early 1955, the Communists not only protested against the persecution of their own comrades but attacked the sentences imposed on other political groups with equal vehemence, especially the Moslem Brotherhood.[32] Throughout the year a stream of illegal pamphlets denounced the treatment of political prisoners in Egypt,[33] and many appeals were made to international "front" organizations, drawing attention to these persecutions and containing requests for help.[34] In one of these publications, the number of political prisoners was given as 26,000, and there were allegations of torture to extract confessions, reports of hunger strikes, and even of killings by the concentration camp authorities.[35] Yussef Hilmi, secretary general of the Egyptian "Partisans of Peace," denounced the junta as traitors and called upon the people to resist the "illegal and criminal government."[36] This was in the beginning of 1955, but the basic attitude of the two Communist factions did not change during the subsequent summer and autumn—despite Bandung, the arms deal, and the general *rapprochement* with the Soviet Union. True enough, the Communists welcomed both Bandung and the arms deal, and said so in a number of manifestoes. But they did not support the government that had carried out this policy; Nasser and his colleagues remained potential traitors, reactionaries, and even "Fascists." An illegal leaflet published in December, 1955, said that the popular democratic revolution of July, 1952, had been usurped by a group of military dictators who had established a despotic rule based on all-pervasive, mendacious propaganda. The promises made had been broken, and during the preceding forty months the working class had been subject to persecutions such as they had never experienced before. The agrarian reform was a fraud, the intellectuals were reduced to silence, all freedom had been abolished, a climate of naked terror prevailed. The only law was the order of the dictators; the prestige of the Egyptian people abroad was zero, because it was believed to be a people resigned to its fate, without dignity, having submitted to a gang of extravagant degenerates.[37] The appeal ended with a demand to overthrow the military dictatorship.

As relations with the Soviet Union became closer, these Communist factions had to modify their stand. After long and heated internal discussions, both the DMNL and the ECP came around and gave their support wholeheartedly to Nasser in the spring of 1956. Many individual Communists became part of the Egyptian "establishment" and reached key positions in the propaganda apparatus, press, and radio. Some Communist groups persevered in their opposition, or in any case had important reservations about the character of the regime. One does not know whether, and in what direction, the Soviet Union tried to influence the Egyptian Communists. On one occasion there was a curious reference in the Soviet press to "provocateurs" in Egypt who called themselves Communists and who dared to come out against Nasser's regime.[38] As the months went by, a peculiar situation developed: there were really two Communist parties; one, part of the regime, the other in opposition to it. It was a remarkable situation but not an altogether unique one—a similar state of affairs had existed in Argentina under Perón, in Venezuela in the mid-forties, and in Cuba in the early fifties. It is unlikely that this split developed according to a preconceived division of labor, for it seems to have been spontaneous. But such a situation had its advantages. The Soviet Union could freely disavow the Communists who opposed Nasser, while keeping an iron in the fire for future developments.

Aside from this discordant note, 1955 was a veritable *annus mirabilis* as far as Soviet-Egyptian relations were concerned. The alliance had developed faster and more dramatically, had become closer than anybody had anticipated—perhaps including those who were most directly concerned. For Moscow a certain risk was involved—what if Nasser should take the arms but otherwise remain impervious to Soviet influence? What if he would turn "traitor" like other "national reformists" in years past, from Kemal Ataturk to Chiang Kai-shek? But the risk involved was quite small compared to the situation in Turkey in 1920 and in China in 1926. It was a gamble in which the Soviet Union could hardly lose. In the following two years, which brought the Suez conflict and the Syrian crisis, it appeared that the Soviet calculation had been essentially correct.

NOTES

1. Originally it was announced that the arms deal had been concluded with the Czechoslovak government. At the time, many observers believed that Prague was merely acting as an agent for Moscow. This was subsequently confirmed by Colonel Nasser (in a series of speeches and interviews in July and August, 1956) when he explained that Czechoslovakia had been brought into the deal merely as a matter of convenience.

2. For a more detailed discussion of the facts of economic life in Egypt, the reader is referred to Charles Issawi: *Egypt at Mid-Century* (Oxford University Press, 1954); for a general account by an eyewitness of the situation in the Egyptian village and the effects of the land reform, cf. Jean and Simonne Lacouture: *L'Egypte en Mouvement* (Paris: Editions du Seuil, 1956), pp. 293-343. Also Gabriel Baer, in *The Middle East in Transition*, (W. Z. Laqueur ed., New York, 1958), pp. 80-99.

3. Cf. the *TASS* communiqué about the arrests of left-wingers and Communists in Egypt on February 9, 1955.

4. The text was published in *Pravda* of that date.

5. *Le Jour* (Beirut), April 18, 1955.

6. *ANA* (Arab News Agency), May 21, 1955.

7. Quoted in Lacouture, *op. cit.*, p. 214.

8. *Al Gumhuriya*, April 27, 1955.

9. This thesis has since been repeated in countless Egyptian books and articles. Occasionally members of the junta have quoted Mao Tse-tung in defense against the criticism of the Egyptian Communists. Cf. Anwar al Sadat: *Kasat ath Thawrat kamelat* (Cairo, 1956), pp. 28-30.

10. The "China pattern" was noted, for instance, by Edouard Sablier in a series of articles on his impressions of Egypt (*Le Monde*, February 7, 1958). But it had been in existence for at least three years.

11. *Akhbar al Yom*, April 16, 1955.

12. *La Bourse Egyptienne*, July 2, 1955, and *Akhbar al Yom* of the same date.

13. *Kuan Ming Jih Pao*, May 20, 1955.

14. *Jen Min Jih Pao*, June 2, 1955.

15. In an interview with *Agence France Presse*, July 24, 1955.

16. It is of some interest to note that both these declarations were published in the Egyptian, but not the Soviet, press.

17. The visit was subsequently postponed to 1958.

18. *Al Jarida* (Beirut), August 16, 1955.

19. *Al Akhbar*, August 10, 1955.

20. *La Bourse Egyptienne*, September 28, 1955.

21. In an interview with T. R. Little, at that time director of the Arab News Agency in Cairo, September 30, 1955. In this interview the Israeli attack at Gaza was mentioned for the first time as the main immediate reason for concluding the Soviet arms deal. "Until that moment I had been willing to be patient . . ."

22. *Al Gumhuriya*, September 29, 1955.

23. *TASS*, October 2, 1955.

24. *Obrana Lidu*, October 1, 1955.

25. Jiri Hronek, editor of *Prace*, on Prague radio, October 4, 1955.

26. *TASS*, November 1, 1955, quoting a statement by the Egyptian Embassy in Washington.

27. *Mezhdunarodnaia Zhizn*, November, 1955.

28. *Ibid.*, October, 1955.

29. Nuri as Said in the Iraqi Parliament. Radio Baghdad, March 29, 1956.

30. Fathi Radwan in *Akhbar al Yom*, October 1, 1955.

31. For a more detailed discussion of the various factions in Egyptian Communism prior to 1955 see W. Z. Laqueur: *Communism and Nationalism in the Middle East* (New York, 1956) pp. 42-51, and Lacouture *op. cit.*, pp. 242-52.

32. Cf. "La Persécution des Frères Musulmans" in *Nouvelles d'Egypte* (December, 1954), published by the DMNL.

33. "Help the Political Prisoners in Turah Camp," *ibid.*, which is the translation of an illegal leaflet in Arabic. Another such leaflet about the situation in Cairo Central Prison was reprinted in *Al Itihad* (Haifa), May 20, 1955.

34. "Appeal of Egyptian Women," published on August 25, 1955, in *Nouvelles Brèves*, the organ of Fédération Démocratique Internationale des Femmes. Cf. also the report (also circulated as an illegal leaflet) of the "National Democratic Front" to the Congress of Asian Lawyers in January, 1955.

35. "Appeal of Egyptian Women," *loc. cit.*

36. Hilmi had escaped from Egypt earlier that year and was given a prison sentence in Cairo *in contumaciam.*

37. "Appeal of the National Democratic Front" distributed in Cairo in December, 1955.

38. I. Bochkarev, "The New Spirit in Egypt," in *New Times* (Moscow) No. 3, 1957.

CHAPTER THREE

THE YEAR OF SUEZ

The arms deal laid the cornerstone of the Soviet-Egyptian alliance, and the Suez crisis provided the solid foundation. The present survey is an attempt to analyze how this alliance affected, and was affected by, the events of 1956. It does not purport to be an account of the Suez crisis as such.

The declared policy of the Egyptian government after 1955 was one of "positive neutralism," meaning that Egypt neither belonged, nor wanted to belong, to either the Western or the Eastern military pact system. This was technically correct, but it was no secret that Egypt's ties with the Eastern bloc had become very close, and its relations with the West rather strained. There was a certain automatic tit-for-tat in this trend. The arms deal aroused enthusiasm in Egypt, and distrust and ill will in the West. Consequently, the Egyptian leaders and press began to denounce the West in even stronger terms, which in turn led to a further deterioration in relations with the West. Comparisons between the Soviet Union and the United States became the fashion: "United States democracy leaves the capitalists free to rule the country while the masses chase dollars and watch baseball. The USSR, on the other hand, is a true democracy with rulers taken from the people through the Communist Party."[1] As for Britain, well, "Goebbels was right in everything he said about that cursed country. Every Egyptian is a new Goebbels nowadays. Great Britain was able to defeat one Goebbels, but can it prevail over the innumerable Goebbels that have now emerged in the Nile Valley?"[2] These two quotations are fairly typical of the anti-Western campaign that went on throughout 1956 and that presumably did not cause much displeasure in Moscow.

It could be argued that too much attention should not be paid to such crudities, for Egyptian editorials had been pitched in a shrill key for two generations. But they were hardly conducive to good relations with the West even after the necessary discount had been made.

Meanwhile, cultural and economic exchanges between Russia and Egypt continued at a merry pace. Colonel Nasser's government eventually recognized Peking in April, 1956. The Soviet press denounced Israeli "war hysteria" and the Israeli allegations that the Czechoslovak arms had somehow lessened the chances of peace in the Middle East;[3] the Western powers certainly had no right to complain, because they were continuing to ship arms to the Middle East themselves.[4] Khaled Bakdash, head of the Syrian Communists and the outstanding Communist leader in the Arab world, was officially invited to Cairo, interviewed by the Egyptian press, and widely lionized. In March, 1956, an "Arab Workers Federation" was founded on Egyptian initiative; from the beginning it opposed the Democratic Socialist ICFTU; later it began to collaborate with the Communist WFTU.[5]

The spring of 1956 also witnessed a minor peace offensive in the Middle East that deserves to be recalled in this context because it was apparently Soviet-sponsored. On the eve of the visit of Khrushchev and Bulganin to Britain, the Soviet Union published a surprisingly conciliatory statement about the situation in the Middle East[6] in which it urged "a peaceful solution in accordance with the national interests of all countries concerned." At an Israeli independence day meeting in New York, the chief Soviet UN delegate, Arkadii Sobolev, suggested to the Israeli ambassador, Abba Eban, that his country had some interesting proposals for the solution of the Arab-Israeli conflict.[7] The nature of these proposals was never fully disclosed, but there were certain definite hints in the European and Egyptian left-wing press. In a French periodical, Yussef Hilmi, a leading exponent of Egyptian Communism who has already been mentioned in these pages, came out in favor of an Israeli-Arab settlement, calling for a just peace, asking that extremists and fanatics on both sides be curbed, since war would be a disaster for all concerned, and so on.[8] The very same week, *Rose al*

Yussef, the main organ of the Egyptian fellow travelers, carried an appeal in the same vein;[9] apart from routine concessions to anti-Israeli propaganda, it also pushed the Middle Eastern Geneva theme. Again the same week, the London *Daily Worker* ran a series on "Hopes for Peace in the Middle East" by the *éminence grise* of British Communism, R. Palme Dutt, revealing a surprisingly objective approach in which the desirability of peace negotiations was stressed at great length.

All these peace feelers were soon forgotten in the wake of the Suez crisis. But at the time it made some observers believe that it might not be too difficult to reach agreement with the Soviet leaders on the future of the Middle East, since, it was argued, their main aim had been to gain a foothold in the Middle East. Once this foothold was established and their right to have a say in the area had been recognized, they were perfectly willing to sit down and participate in a general peace settlement. It is conceivable, on the other hand, that there were some second thoughts then in Moscow about giving unqualified support to Nasser. The original Soviet intention had been to counteract the Baghdad Pact, and in this they had succeeded. But what if Colonel Nasser should use his newly acquired arms against Israel, and what if this should lead to a war involving the big powers? Soviet support of Egypt and Syria against Israel had not made a favorable impression in some circles in the West—particularly among Socialists, and even within Western Communist parties, which had been infected by a new spirit of criticism. (The news of the Khrushchev speech at the Twentieth Party Congress was circulating just then.) Since they were entertaining popular-front ideas at the time, the Soviet leaders were more sensitive to public opinion in the West.

It is difficult even now to establish which of these causes made the Soviet leaders put out peace feelers in the spring of 1956. Most likely it was a combination of several motives and considerations.

On July 19, 1956, the United States government informed Cairo that it was "not feasible in present circumstances" to take part in financing the Aswan High Dam, and this was followed by similar statements on the part of the British government and the World Bank. A week later, President Nasser announced the nationalization of the Suez Canal, the revenues obtained from Canal tolls to be used to build the dam. The Suez crisis was on. The wisdom of the American decision has since become a subject of heated dispute. In retrospect, it would appear that Nasser intended to nationalize the Canal anyway—in 1957 or in 1958, if not in 1956—and this, at any rate, is what he subsequently revealed. It may well be, on the other hand, that the somewhat brusque and unexpected way in which the American decision was made known both precipitated and aggravated a crisis that might otherwise not have assumed such dangerous proportions. There had been rumors throughout the early summer of 1956, presumably from Egyptian sources, that if America did not finance the Canal, Russia would be only too glad to oblige. These rumors might have had a certain value in bringing pressure to bear on the United States and the World Bank, but the Soviet government was not very enthusiastic about the High Dam scheme. When Shepilov (by then Foreign Minister) visited Egypt in June, 1956, he was reported to have told Nasser that, though the Soviet Union would make a great contribution towards Egypt's industrial development, it could not commit itself with regard to the Aswan Dam.

When America refused its backing, many observers expected Russia to use the opportunity to step in, but Moscow did nothing of the sort, merely declaring that the High Dam project was not the most urgent task facing Egypt. In a Soviet survey of the Aswan problem, published three weeks after the American refusal, Soviet interest in the project was not mentioned at all and Soviet participation not even intimated.[10] Only two years later, in the light of fresh political developments, did Moscow decide to make a major contribution toward the construction of the High Dam. (See Appendix III.)

Whether or not the Soviet Foreign Ministry felt embarrassed during that last week of July, we do not know; after a few days the whole matter was forgotten, for the ensuing open conflict between Egypt and the West overshadowed everything else. Soviet comment on the nationalization was, of course, favorable. The Soviet press congratulated Egypt on having at last become master of the Canal,[11] and said that it rightfully belonged to Egypt.[12] Khrushchev, in a speech in the new Moscow Central Stadium, said that Egypt had been perfectly within its rights, no violation of international law had taken place, and anyway, the nationalization did not touch the interests of the West regarding free passage through the Canal.[13]

Meanwhile, the three Western foreign ministers had met in London and decided to convene a conference to draw up an international commission for the administration of the Suez Canal. The Soviet government did not reject the idea of a conference, but it opposed everything else contained in the Western proposals. It wanted the conference to be held in Cairo rather than in London, submitted a list of participants very different from that suggested by the Western foreign ministers (Moscow wanted to include all East European states, all Arab countries, and Communist China), and did not want the conference to deal with the internationalization of the Canal.[14] In addition, the Soviet Union sharply condemned Western attempts to put pressure on Egypt and the campaign "scheduled to create a hostile mood towards independent Egypt." However, with all these reservations, the Soviet Union accepted the Western invitation.

The first Suez conference opened in Lancaster House in London on August 16 (with Egypt boycotting the meeting), and the first notable event was Shepilov's speech on the following day. Repeating the Soviet arguments, he protested against the composition of the conference, and in particular against the exclusion of certain countries, and stressed that the Soviet Union did not have any specific interest in the Middle East apart from the overriding one of making it a zone of peace, progress, and international collaboration. At the same time he warned against Western military preparations that could precipitate a large conflict which "could cover the area of the Near and Middle East and possibly go outside these limits."[15] Shepilov thought that Egypt was perfectly entitled to nationalize the Canal; other countries (including Britain) had taken similar measures on their own territory. As for the question of freedom of passage, this was no real problem either, because Egypt did not want to close the Canal. In any case, the imposition of an "international regime" as envisaged by the Western powers was altogether impermissible, a violation of international law and the United Nations charter, and practically an act of war.[16] In a subsequent session Shepilov came forward with a Soviet plan for the solution of the crisis according to which the administration of the Canal would be in Egyptian hands, an international committee would advise the Egyption administration on the questions of tariffs and the issue of freedom of shipping, and all disputes would be forwarded to the United Nations. This Soviet plan was almost identical with the one tabled by Krishna Menon on behalf of India, and the Indian plan in turn was largely identical with a project suggested by Colonel Nasser on August 12.

These various suggestions were debated for several days, four countries, including the Soviet Union, being in favor of the Menon plan, while eighteen supported a somewhat modified version of the project worked out by Mr. Dulles.

The only practical result of the conference was a resolution to delegate representatives of five powers (the "Menzies mission") to meet Colonel Nasser and present the eighteen proposals to him. In a press conference held after the end of the conference, Mr. Shepilov made it quite clear that the Soviet Union opposed this mission.[17] This ended the first phase of the Suez meetings, for the Soviet Union did not participate in the second London conference convened on September 21, 1956, by what later came to be known as SCUA (Suez Canal Users' Association). For Moscow, the talks continued only on October 5, when the Security Council met in New York to discuss the Suez situation.

While the first London conference was still going on, Soviet commentators made it quite clear that Egypt had Russia's wholehearted support. Revolutionary changes, it was said, had taken place in Egypt, and Nasser understood the interests and potentialities of his people. Thanks to the self-sacrificing spirit of the Egyptian people, the British had been forced to give up their base in Suez. The Egyptian government had given sufficient proof of good will, and did not have to make more concessions.[18] It enjoyed the sympathy of world public opinion, whereas the Western powers were acting against the principles of the United

Nations charter. Mr. Dulles' "anticolonial" speech had admittedly caused some confusion in the colonialist camp, but his real intention was, of course, to make the United States the master of Suez.[19] Meanwhile, Israel was playing with fire, stepping up its military preparations, which were completely unnecessary because nobody threatened it, anyway.[20] These were the main themes constantly repeated during the months of August and September. Politically, this period was not very eventful, the only notable occurrences being Bulganin's suggestion that another conference was needed, since the first London conference had been prepared in haste,[21] and a declaration by the Soviet government on September 16, expressing concern about the military preparations being made by France and Great Britain. The statement dealt at some length with the nature of these activities and accused the United States of not protesting against these preparations, thus indirectly encouraging Britain and France.[22] In addition there were professions of sympathy with Egypt by such organizations as the World Peace Committee, the Soviet trade unions, Soviet women and youth organizations, and so forth.

Soviet attempts to enlist support for Egypt were generally successful in Asia, where pro-Nasser sympathies existed anyway. His defiance of the Western powers could not fail to strike deep emotional chords in these countries. In Western Europe there was less sympathy even on the extreme left wing. The London *Daily Worker* published readers' letters highly critical of Soviet policy in the Middle East ("we here in Stepney do not share your admiration of Colonel Nasser; it would not be surprising if a few buckets of whitewash will next be poured on gallant General Franco . . ."), the Paris pro-Communist daily *Libération* called the Soviet exclusion of Israel from the proposed conference "opportunistic," and the Communists' chief ally in Italy, Pietro Nenni, wrote in his newspaper *Avanti* that "we oppose as socialists and democrats the Pan-Arabic program of Nasser, which is aggressive and basically imperialist." It is difficult to know what people in the East European "Popular Democracies" thought about Soviet support for Nasser's Egypt. The general impression is that there was no spontaneous popular support for it, nor was there any strong opposition.[23] Most of these countries, Poland and Hungary above all, were then preoccupied with domestic problems and regarded Egypt as a relatively unimportant side show.

Soviet support for Egypt did not remain purely rhetorical. The arms shipments were stepped up and there was a fairly big influx of Soviet and East European diplomats and technicians. Their number, at the end of October, 1956, was estimated by some observers at two thousand.[24] At the same time, several hundred Egyptian military and technical experts were receiving their training in various Eastern European countries, mostly in Czechoslovakia and Poland. The staff of the Soviet satellite embassies doubled and trebled throughout 1955-56. Close relations were established between the official Egyptian Middle East News Agency and the TASS and Chinese news agencies, and the Egyptian press and radio began to lean heavily on these sources. In early September it was announced that several Soviet pilots had left Russia on their way to Egypt to take over from the Western Suez Canal pilots who had been ordered home by their governments.[25] When the Soviet pilots arrived at Cairo airport, there were highly emotional scenes: "Soviet-Egyptian kisses, tears in everybody's eyes," reported the local press.[26] Other new arrivals in Cairo included a small group of Moslem "theological students" from the Soviet Union who were to study at Al Azhar university. This was the first time Soviet citizens had been permitted to study at a foreign theological seminar.

On October 5, 1956, the Security Council met in New York for a debate on the Suez situation, and Shepilov made the Soviet attitude known again in two speeches. This attitude, needless to say, had not changed: it condemned Western pressure on Egypt and called upon the West to negotiate on the basis of Colonel Nasser's proposals. Shepilov saw an encouraging sign in the fact that unofficial contacts between Britain, France, and Egypt had been established.[27] When the Anglo-French proposals for a Suez Canal Users' Association were put to a vote, Russia used the veto, and the Council broke up on October 13 without taking any decision. Shepilov did not expect an armed conflict to break out at the time; in an interview with an Egyptian newspaper he declared, "There will be no resort to force."[28] During the rest of the month Soviet declarations continued in more or less the same vein. A constructive approach was needed, the Western policy of saber-rattling and economic aggression was bankrupt.[29] Egypt was lauded for "not stopping halfway in her struggle for independence,"[30] while Turkey and Iran were charged with playing a double game. Israel came in for more attacks ("playing with fire—dangerous consequences"), but on the whole Moscow apparently anticipated that "negotiations would win."[31] Only on October 18, following Prime Minister Eden's sudden trip to Paris, were new fears expressed in the Soviet press: the Western governments had apparently not given up the idea of an imposed solution. Between that date and the outbreak of hostilities later in October, no other initiative was taken by the Soviet government.

Meanwhile, however, unknown to all but a handful of people, an exchange of letters had taken place between Bulganin and the Prime Ministers of England and France.[33] These letters were published in Moscow only six months later, and though their content does not greatly add to our knowledge of the issues involved in the Suez conflict and its prehistory, they do provide some interesting insights. It appears that at one time, in September, the Soviet leadership was seriously concerned about a possible war in the Middle East, and in his letters to Eden and Mollet, Bulganin pointed, more in sorrow than in anger, to the potentially fatal consequences of military action. He indignantly rejected the allegation that the Soviet Union had incited Colonel Nasser against the West and said that "we learned about the nationalization of the Canal only from the radio." The last letter, written on October 23, tends to show that by that time Bulganin was somewhat reassured, apparently thinking that the immediate danger of an armed conflict was over.

The insistence in these letters (and earlier in 1956, during Khrushchev and Bulganin's visit to London) that the Soviet Union took account of legitimate Western interests in the Middle East ought to be taken cum grano salis. The Soviet leadership above all considered its own interests, namely, that the West be ousted from that part of the world. However, there is much reason to believe that the Soviet leaders wanted an orderly Western exodus, brought about by mutual agreement under the combined pressure of the Arabs, the Bandung bloc, the Soviet bloc, and perhaps sections of Western public opinion. They did not want to gamble when time seemed to be working for them anyway. An armed conflict would have been a gamble, for nobody could be certain that such a conflict would remain localized. The Israeli invasion of the Suez peninsula, followed by the unsuccessful Anglo-French "Musketeer" operation took Moscow apparently by surprise—despite the many warnings about Western military preparations in previous months. The first Soviet reaction was a fairly routine announcement in which the attack against Egypt was sharply denounced, and the Security Council was called upon to take measures against this aggression.[34] Only several days later, after the American attitude had become somewhat clearer, did the Soviet government decide to take a strong stand.

On November 5, Bulganin sent out a number of letters addressed to Washington, London, Paris, and Tel Aviv. President Eisenhower was asked to give the American Mediterranean fleet instructions to collaborate with the Soviet navy and air force to stop the aggressors.[35] Eden and Mollet were told that the Port Said expedition could turn into a third world war and that the Soviet Union was firmly resolved to use force to destroy the aggressors and restore peace in the Middle East. In addition, there was a broad hint about the vulnerability of England and France vis-à-vis Russia: the possibility of attacking these countries with ballistic missiles was mentioned ("You would, of course, call that a barbaric action").[36] The sharpest letter of all went to Ben-Gurion, who was told that the very existence of Israel had been put into question.[37]

For a short time it appeared as if the Soviet government considered moving into the area in force, but soon it became clear that if any action were undertaken, "volunteers" would be delegated. On November 6, the Egyptian government had officially asked for volunteers, and the Chinese government had expressed readiness to oblige even before that date.[38] On November 11, the Soviet government repeated the threat to send volunteers to fight in Egypt—a possibility that had first been mentioned by Khrushchev back in September.[39] This announcement was made in terms somewhat reminiscent of those used by the Chinese government before Chinese volunteers had been sent to the aid of the North Koreans; even the names of some of the "volunteers" were mentioned in the Soviet press and it was said that many of them were World War II veterans with considerable combat experience.

The Suez war coincided with the Hungarian revolution, and both sides claimed for a time that there was a close connection between the two events. It was argued in Moscow that the West had "staged" the Hungarian revolution in order to cause difficulties for the Russians, and to be free to act against Egypt.[40] It is hardly necessary to refute this line of argument in detail, for when the Sinai campaign and the Port Said expedition were being prepared, nobody could possibly have known about the dramatic events soon to occur in Hungary, which took everybody by surprise. Nor could it be seriously argued that the Hungarian revolution was started and led by outside agents. Many Western opponents of Eden and Mollet argued, on the other hand, that Soviet intervention in Hungary only became possible because Moscow could use the Western aggression in Egypt as a pretext ("They would not have dared, otherwise . . ."). Subsequent developments have made this argument appear unconvincing, for all the available evidence indicates that Soviet forces would have invaded Hungary in any case, once power in Budapest had passed into "enemy" hands.

But was Moscow really willing to send "volunteers" to fight in Egypt, was the world indeed close to a world war in that first week of November? There is no certain answer, but Soviet timing makes it appear as if the threats were made only after it was virtually certain that there would be no need to follow them up with military actions. The threatening letters to Eden, Mollet, and Ben-Gurion were sent only after it became clear that the United States would not intervene, and the official Soviet statement about the dispatch of "volunteers" came only after the armistice in Egypt had already come into force. The risk, from the Soviet view, had been small, as usual, but most of the credit for stopping the aggression subsequently accrued to Moscow. It was argued at the time that the Anglo-French-Israeli action had served to throw a Soviet master plan out of gear, that Russian forces would have been at Suez a few months later if the Western powers had not forestalled them. The considerable amount of war material found during the Israeli offensive in the Sinai peninsula was adduced as evidence, since it far exceeded what the West had anticipated—and also exceeded, it was believed, what the Egyptian army could possibly need. While no satisfactory explanation has so far been found for the presence of some of this material, neither is there any convincing evidence of a Soviet plan to establish a military base at Suez at that time.

On November 2, a "Hands Off Egypt" campaign was started in the Soviet Union, mainly, it would appear, for the benefit of the Asian countries but also for domestic consumption. Was not the Anglo-French-Israeli aggression against Egypt a striking proof that the Soviet policy had been correct all along? Bulganin wrote Nehru, suggesting that the Bandung powers convene and deliberate on a common course of action. Voroshilov wrote to Sukarno in the same vein. Meanwhile there were "spontaneous demonstrations by the youth and students of the capital" in front of the embassies of the aggressor countries in Moscow.[41] A campaign was started to collect wheat, medical supplies, and other material for Egypt, and, according to the Soviet chronicler, great quantities were handed over to the Egyptians as a gift of the Soviet people.[42] The religious leadership of the Moslems of Soviet Central Asia announced that it had learned with pain of this breach of the peace,[43] and public figures of Jewish descent were also mobilized to express their disgust and horror of the action of the Israeli government.[44] It was the first time in over ten years that Soviet Jews had been permitted to appear in the Soviet press in a collective appeal.

There is reason to doubt whether there was any popular enthusiasm comparable to the "*No pasarán*" days of the Spanish Civil War. One reason, no doubt, was the fact that the campaign lasted only a few days, another the news of the Soviet action in Hungary, which had a somewhat disturbing effect, and above all, of course, the fact that the issues in the Middle East were more complicated than the struggle of democracy against Fascism in 1937. Be that as it may, the Soviet action made a very favorable impression in the Arab world, where the events in Hungary passed unnoticed, or were regarded as another Western imperialist intrigue. The president of Syria was among the first to thank Bulganin and to express the delight of the Arab nations about the Soviet stand.[45] "We owe a debt to the Russian workers and peasants who have enlisted to fight on our side," wrote the Egyptian press,[46] and Gamal Abdel Nasser, in a talk with Soviet journalists, officially thanked the Soviet people and government: "The help that we received reflected Soviet-Egyptian friendship, and I want this friendship to become even stronger and to grow further."[47] The impression in the Arab world was that it had been Soviet threats rather than American warnings that had caused Britain, France, and Israel to stop their military offensive. This was a sobering thought, for had not the Egyptian press announced that Egypt alone had succeeded in defeating the aggressors? However, the impression was not altogether incorrect, for among the various considerations that induced Britain, France, and Israel to accept the armistice, the Soviet threats were undoubtedly quite prominent.

The aftermath of the Suez campaign was of decisive importance from the Soviet point of view. Moscow had demonstrated its support for Egypt and the Arab cause in general, and this had been warmly appreciated. But the United States had supported Nasser, too, and there was a danger that America would be given credit, too, and that the blame would be put only on Britain, France, and Israel. This would have been very undesirable as far as Soviet interests were concerned, for in the great global struggle that was going on, Britain and France were only secondary factors, and Israel less than that. The main task was to prove to the Arabs that Dulles, and American foreign policy, had been the real culprits.

To achieve that aim, an intensive propaganda campaign was started soon after the fighting had stopped, and the Soviet Union continued to give full support to Nasser in the subsequent negotiations with the United Nations about the armistice provisions. The degree of tension still prevailing in the Middle East was deliberately exaggerated in the Soviet press: "The struggle is far from over," a report from Cairo read in mid-December.[48] America was trying to pose as the friend of the Arabs, but actually only wanted to oust the British and replace them.[49] A harsh line was adopted toward Israel, the Soviet ambassador in Tel Aviv having been recalled earlier, and the Soviet-Israeli commercial agreement providing for Soviet supply of fuel being canceled by Moscow. When the United States accepted the Israeli viewpoint on freedom of shipping in the Gulf of Aqaba, the Soviet Foreign Ministry was not slow to make political capital of it.[50]

There was a parallel change, more gradual but no less palpable, in the Egyptian attitude towards the United States; perhaps it was part of the debt owed to the "Russian workers and peasants." From the day of the Israeli invasion to the end of December, 1956, no word critical of America was permitted to appear in the Egyptian press. But in the very last days of 1956 two ominous articles appeared in *Pravda* and *Izvestiia,* written by Abdel Rahman as Sharqawi and Abdel Rahman al Khamisi. Both were prominent Egyptian journalists, and both had been in trouble with Colonel Nasser's police two years before because of pro-Communist activities.[51] Now they said quite openly that the struggle against Britain and France was only the beginning and that every Arab knew that in the coming phase the United States would be the main enemy. Both imperialist actions—the Western attacks on Egypt and Hungary—had the same aim: "to strike a blow against freedom and to endanger world peace."[52] The closed season on America was over.

For the Soviet Foreign Ministry, the great opportunity for successful propaganda in the Middle East campaign against the United States came with the announcement of the Eisenhower Doctrine in early January, 1957. It has been criticized in the West as being exceedingly vague, and it can hardly be doubted, in retrospect, that its importance was almost exclusively demonstrative. It was no mean achievement of Soviet foreign policymakers to create the impression that this harmless (and indeed meaningless) manifesto constituted a deadly threat to the whole Arab world. In this, however, they were greatly assisted by the general climate of opinion in these countries, which was one of hypersensitivity and of extreme suspicion of the West.

President Eisenhower's message to Congress on January 5, 1957, was immediately followed by a wave of Soviet protests. The United States (it was said) was trying to present its policy as anticolonialist, but this was clearly intended to dull the vigilance of the peoples of the East.[53] The Eisenhower Doctrine wanted to turn the Middle East into an American colony; the authors of the Doctrine had unmasked themselves; behind their backs the real sponsors were visible, the Rockefellers and Mellons, Texas oilmen, and New York bankers.[54] Even in the history of American foreign policy, full of examples of oppression, such an openly aggressive doctrine could not be found.[55] It was in conflict with the United Nations charter and the Bandung resolutions; it was a veritable doctrine of atomic war.[56] "In President Eisenhower's message he sounds the voice of war, not the voice of peace."[57]

Soviet propaganda did not fail to concentrate on what was undoubtedly one of the weakest psychological points in the message: the issue of the "vacuum." The Doctrine stressed that a military vacuum had been created in the Middle East, and the Soviet leaders astutely realized that nothing could possibly offend the Arabs more than drawing attention to their military weakness, their inability to defend the area against big-power aggression. The American reference to the "vacuum" became the chief motif in Soviet propaganda. It should be noted in passing that this was not a unique incident, but highlighted an important difference in the American and Soviet approach. The American attitude toward Egypt had been matter of fact, similar to that taken to a mature West European country such as Holland or Sweden. Soviet foreign policy makers, on the other hand, realized from the very beginning of the *rapprochement* in 1955 that a Middle Eastern country that had gained its independence only recently obviously had to be treated differently. They understood that an appeal to such emotional factors as pride was of immense importance, and that a little flattery would go a long way in making friends in that part of the world. Thus, Soviet propaganda dwelt incessantly on the great industriousness of the Egyptian people, the farsightedness of the Egyptian leadership, the heroism of the Egyptian army, etc. Not many such compliments came from Western diplomats.

Inside Egypt, the American Embassy was permitted to circulate the text of the Eisenhower Doctrine, but the Soviet counterarguments received far more publicity and were unanimously approved in the press and in a number of semiofficial books and pamphlets published by the Egyptian government.[58] The Egyptian "Partisans of Peace" were mobilized and declared in a special manifesto that the Eisenhower Doctrine was not really different in purpose from the Anglo-French aggression.[59] The Soviet theses about the Doctrine were accepted in Egypt without reservation. Intensive Soviet diplomatic activity followed the announcement of the Doctrine: Khrushchev speeches,[60] TASS statements,[61] and two official Soviet notes to the Western powers calling for non-intervention in the Middle East.[62] The only point of interest in these notes was perhaps the Soviet suggestion of a mutual embargo on arms shipments to the Middle East. But the real battle of propaganda had already been won by Russia: public opinion in the Arab world had rejected the Eisenhower Doctrine.

NOTES

1. Cairo Radio, October 11, 1955.

2. *Al Tahrir*, April 10, 1956. Also quoted in *Bourse Egyptienne*, April 13, 1956.

3. *Izvestiia*, March 22, 1956, and April 8, 1956.

4. *Izvestiia*, January 5, 1956.

5. Hans Tütsch in *Neue Zürcher Zeitung*, June 3, 1956. Mr. Tütsch's articles subsequently appeared in book form: *Die Arabischen Voelker am Kreuzweg* (Zurich, 1956).

6. *Pravda*, April 18, 1956.

7. W. Z. Laqueur, "Prospects for a Mideast Geneva," in *New Leader*, May 21, 1956.

8. *L'Observateur*, April 25, 1956.

9. By Mahmoud Amin al Alem.

10. G. Skorov in *Izvestiia*, August 12, 1956.

11. *Izvestiia*, July 28, 1956.

12. *Pravda*, July 29, 1956.

13. *Pravda*, August 1, 1956.

14. "Note of the Soviet Ministry of Foreign Affairs to the Embassy of Great Britain on the Question of the Suez Canal," and "Declaration of the Soviet Government on the Question of the Suez Canal," both in D. T. Shepilov: *Suetskii Vopros* (The Suez Question) (Moscow, 1956), pp. 111-20.

15. Shepilov, *ibid.*, pp. 20-37.

16. *Ibid.*

17. *Ibid.*, pp. 65-75.

18. *Krasnaia Zvezda*, September 13, 1956; *Izvestiia*, September 18, 1956.

19. *Krasnaia Zvezda*, October 3, 1956.

20. *Izvestiia*, September 21, 1956.

21. In an interview with an INS correspondent on September 20, 1956.

22. Shepilov, *op. cit.*, pp. 127-36.

23. An East European diplomat told the present writer at the time that he did not entirely agree with Soviet policy in the Middle East. However, "my country has no specific Middle Eastern policy of its own, we are a small country and follow the Soviet lead."

24. *New York Times*, October 29, 1956.

25. *Pravda*, September 7, 1956.

26. *Al Gumhuriya*, September 25; *Bourse Egyptienne*, September 25, 1956.

27. Shepilov, *op. cit.*, pp. 78-104.

28. *Al Gumhuriya*, October 9, 1956.

29. *Izvestiia*, October 10, 1956.

30. Nikitina in *New Times*, No. 42, 1956.

31. *Pravda*, October 16, 1956.

32. Ratiani reporting from Paris: *Pravda*, October 18, 1956.

33. The Bulganin letters, published in *Izvestiia*, April 23, 1957, were dated Sochi, September 11, Sochi, September 28, and Moscow, October 23.

34. Shepilov, *op. cit.*, p. 142.

35. *Ibid.*, pp. 146-48.

36. *Ibid.*, pp. 149-54.

37. *Ibid.*, pp. 155-56.

38. NCNA (New China News Agency) announced on November 7 the ardent desire of a quarter of a million Chinese workers, peasants, women, and students to volunteer on the side of the Egyptians.

39. *TASS*, November 11, 1956.

40. E. Primakov, R. Arutiunov: *Pouchitelnii Urok* (A Salutary Lesson) (Moscow, 1957), pp. 44-46.

41. *Ibid.*, p. 39.

42. *Ibid.*

43. *Izvestiia*, November 4, 1956.

44. A group of Jewish public figures published an open letter in *Pravda* on November 6, 1956. Other groups, such as the Bukharan Jewish Community, followed suit (*Izvestiia*, November 28, 1956).

45. *Pravda*, November 9, 1956.

46. *Al Ahram*, December 15, 1956.

47. On December 27, 1956, quoted in L. Vatolina (ed.): *Araby v Borbe za Nezavisimost* (The Arabs in the Struggle for Independence) (Moscow, 1957), p. 194.

48. *Izvestiia*, December 15, 1956.

49. *Pravda*, December 19; *Izvestiia*, December 20, 1956.

50. *Pravda*, February 25, 1956.

51. Al Khamisi was one of the defendants in the trial of a group of 44 Communists in February, 1954. Many of the journalistic pillars of the regime of 1956-57, such as Yussef Idris, Ismail Abdallah, Hamdi al Aila or Ali Shalakani, had been out of prison for less than a year.

52. See in particular al Khamisi's article in *Pravda*, December 31, 1956.

53. *TASS*, January 12, 1957.

54. D. Kraminov in *Pravda*, January 9, 1957.

55. A. Kunina: *Doktrina Eizenkhovera* (Moscow, 1957), p. 47.

56. *Ibid.*, pp. 48-52.

57. *TASS*, January 13, 1957.

58. Mohammed Abbas Said Ahmad: *Mashrou Eisenhower—Udwan Jadid* (The Eisenhower Doctrine—A New Aggression) (Cairo, 1957), and Abdel Rahman al Khamisi and Fat'hi Kamil: *La-ya* Eisenhower (No—Eisenhower!) (Cairo, 1957).

59. Quoted in Kunina, *op. cit.*, p. 67.

60. In Tashkent, on January 13, 1957.

61. *TASS*, January 13 and 24, 1957.

62. On February 11, 1957, and again on April 19, 1957.

CHAPTER FOUR

1957: THE SYRIAN CRISIS

The sudden Western panic over Syria in August, 1957, underlined the vacillations of American policy in the Middle East. There had been a creeping crisis in Syria for several years, but these developments had not been sufficiently noticed in the Western capitals. When the events that had taken place during a number of years were telescoped into a number of days, the sudden realization came as a shock. If Soviet and Communist influence in Syria had been vastly underrated before, there was a tendency afterwards to exaggerate these influences, and to expect the full and early satellization of the country.

By midsummer of 1957, Syria was the Arab state that had moved closest to the Soviet Union—and also the country in which the Communist Party had become the strongest, single political force. All this had not happened suddenly: these developments could be traced back to the days of the French mandate, the upsurge of left-wing groups during World War II, and the postwar period. It is comparatively easy to state what factors were not involved, but more difficult to find a satisfactory explanation for the origins and causes of this trend.

Not directly involved, to begin with, were economic factors. It has already been mentioned that from 1945 to 1955, Syria, in contrast to many other Asian and Arab countries, had made astonishing economic progress. It could not be argued that Syria was stagnating economically—on the contrary, the country experienced a major boom. Nor could the Syrian crisis be explained by reference to an immediate conflict with the West. Most Syrians felt bitter about Israel and suspicious about Turkey. But there was no direct clash with the West; the West did not continue to occupy part of Syria's territory (as it did in Egypt until 1955), nor were there any Western bases on Syrian soil—as in Saudia, Jordan, Iraq, or Libya. Nor could one fairly regard Soviet policy or Soviet propaganda as the main cause of these developments. If the Soviet Union influenced happenings in Syria prior to 1956, it was only in a roundabout way, by means of the "anticolonialist" ideas that had been absorbed by Arab nationalism and, of course, by way of the Communist party. The process of radicalization in Syria was both spontaneous and homegrown. It had much to do with conditions inside the country; outside factors were secondary.

Developments in Syria may be explained in terms of national character—an unrewarding field of investigation, for it is limitless in time, depth, and speculation. All that can be done in the present study is to present the facts, namely, that Syrian politicians and Syrian public opinion had in 1957 become more hostile and suspicious of the West than those of any other Arab nation. They were, perhaps, also more dissatisfied with their own political record at home: the incompetence of the old-style politicians and traditional political parties, the frequent military dictatorships. They were less experienced and sophisticated in world affairs than some of their neighbors—the Lebanese, or the politically conscious section of the Egyptian nation. On the basis of many discussions with young Syrians, a Swiss observer drew the following picture of the Syrian situation in midsummer of 1956: "A Soviet official whom I met in Cairo told me openly that 'our serious magazines cannot possibly compete with the West European and American trash.' In other words, people in Cairo and Alexandria want to see pictures of American movie stars and Parisian pin-up girls, not pictures of combine harvesters in the Ukraine, coupled with a virtuous story by Gorky. The Syrian people appear somewhat less peace-loving and jovial than the Egyptians. The Syrian laughs but seldom, he is always conscious of his dignity. Conversations are frequently held in a very loud voice. The system of government is one of organized chaos . . . Communism owes much to a certain predisposition in the Syrian mentality. The Syrian loves to play with fire. This notion of courage is boasting of daredevil exploits. If such action has no chance of success, if it is virtually certain that it will fail, then its romantic appeal is even greater. Communism in Syria profits by the fascination of danger. 'We cannot bear life as it is. Let us risk a big adventure; we shall either perish or gain everything.' The particular effect of Communist propaganda is in the fascination of the dangerous which flatters the Syrian, who is dimly conscious of his own inferiority. From this he expects gains for which there is otherwise no reasonable hope of fulfillment in the world as it is."[1] These observations certainly contain more than a grain of truth. Without reference to a certain predisposition of the Syrian mentality, Soviet and Communist successes in Syria remain incomprehensible. As events in Iraq during the second half of 1958 were to show, this predisposition was, however, by no means limited to Syria, and it is quite likely that Jordan public opinion, given the opportunity to express itself, will react one day in a similar way.

The story of the most recent, and most important, phase of Soviet gains in Syria starts with the overthrow of the Shishakli military dictatorship in early 1954. All major political parties had been suppressed under Shishakli, but the Communists emerged stronger than before, because they alone had been able to preserve their cadres and activities in conditions of illegality. Political power first passed into the hands of the traditional parties and the veteran politicians. Shukri al Quwatli, the former president was brought back from his Egyptian exile. Subsequently, the Soviets were to praise him as an outstanding patriot,[2] but at the time, the Communists took a very dim view of the attempts to restore him to a position of authority.[3]

The results of the elections in September, 1954, already tended to show that the traditional parties would not have things the way they wanted: a new force, the Ba'ath, obtained twenty-two seats in the new parliament; a fairly big group of "Independents" was headed by Khaled al Azm, who came increasingly to be identified with the Communists; Khaled Bakdash, the Communist leader, also was elected. The meaning of these elections was correctly appraised in the headlines of a leading Egyptian newspaper: "Syrian public opinion turns its back to the West and opposes an alliance with the West."[4] A Communist journal predicted the early overthrow of "feudalism" and its political supporters in Syria.[5] The Conservatives still had a majority in parliament, but many of their supporters had been elected in what were practically rotten boroughs, whereas the radical forces had gained their victories in the main urban centers. The election of only one Communist representative was likewise misleading, for in some places, such as Homs and al Gezira, they had polled more votes than all other candidates, and only after being subjected to considerable pressure did the Communist candidates withdraw, or accept defeat by a coalition of all non-Communist groups.

During 1955 and 1956 political power gradually passed into the hands of a new coalition which included the Ba'ath, the bloc of Independents headed by Khaled al Azm, and a group of "Nationalists" headed by Sabri al Assali and Fakher al Kayali. The army officers' corps, which was mainly under Ba'ath and partly under Communist influence, also exerted considerable influence. The conservative and pro-Western forces were gradually eliminated in "cold purges" and treason trials; in March, 1956, all the major political parties signed the so-called "National Pact," in which they agreed on "democratic reforms" and "a neutralist policy."[6] None of these groups could be called extreme left wing, and even the domestic programs of the Ba'ath or the Communists were moderate by Western standards. This did not prevent these groups from taking up a consistently anti-Western stand in foreign affairs and favoring a close *rapprochement* with the Soviet Union. Little need be said about the Syrian Communists, since their attachment to the Soviet Union was only to be expected.[7] The Ba'ath had been in existence for only a few years and had come into being as a result of the merger of two smaller groups. Some of its leaders had originally been Communists, others had belonged to the semi-Fascist PPS. Most of them were young intellectuals, of middle-class origin, or young army officers. The Ba'ath symbolized both the intensity of feeling and the vagueness of program of the radical intelligentsia in the Arab countries. Its influence was soon to spread to Jordan, Iraq, and other Arab countries. It stood for a radical brand of national socialism in the Arab world, violently opposed the traditional forces ("feudals" and clergy) and, of course, the

West, which was believed to be responsible for most of what had gone wrong with the Arab world. There was nothing in the program of the Ba'ath that would have made a pro-Soviet orientation in world affairs inevitable,[8] but in practice the extreme anti-Westernism of the party brought it, temporarily, at any rate, into the Soviet orbit. According to the Soviet view, the "Ba'ath" represented the interests of the "national bourgeoisie," the small entrepreneurs, and part of the artisans, though many of its rank and file members were peasants and workers.[9]

Few if any ideological motives were involved, as far as the other protagonists of the Soviet alliance in Syria were concerned. Khaled al Azm, a multimillionaire and erstwhile "collaborator" with the French (he had been Prime Minister back in 1939), became the closest ally of the Communists and the most trusted confidant of the Soviet Union, out of a mixture of resentment and shrewd business sense. He had been greatly offended at not having been elected President (or Prime Minister) in 1954-55, as he had hoped, and wanted to get even with his political enemies; he also held a number of highly profitable agencies as Damascus representative of several Soviet trusts. Other supporters of the Soviet alliance, such as the Nationalists Sabri al Assali and Fakher al Kayali or the "populist" Marouf al Dawalibi, had reached the conclusion that the Soviet Union was going to win the global struggle and thought it preferable to back the right horse. Some had been bitterly anti-Western for many years, and the gradual shift from a pro-Axis to a pro-Soviet orientation appeared to them neither illogical nor in any way reprehensible. The same applied, *mutatis mutandis*, to the young majors and lieutenant colonels who were again to play a decisive part in Syrian politics in 1956-57; they, too, were ardent and impatient patriots who wanted to get things done. Western democracy, or democratic socialism, had little attraction for them, and they preferred dynamic movements and powers to cumbersome democratic and parliamentary processes.

Throughout 1956 the *rapprochement* between Damascus and Moscow continued. Shepilov visited Damascus in June and met the leading public figures. On August 20 a cultural agreement was signed, providing for the exchange of delegations, the sending of Syrians to study in the Soviet Union, the appearance of Soviet artists in Damascus, and the showing of Soviet films. There was great enthusiasm for all things Soviet in Damascus, much greater than in Cairo, and Russian visitors were most favorably impressed by the general climate of friendship and admiration they encountered. "We fell in love with you, dear Syrians," reported the minister for culture of the Soviet Azerbaidzhan Republic.[10] A Soviet journalist who had accompanied the delegation of the Supreme Soviet on a visit to Syria in the autumn of 1956 and who subsequently recorded his impressions in a little book, stated that everybody in authority in Damascus told him that Syria would never have come into existence were it not for the USSR.[11]

The first Syrian crisis coincided with the Suez war. President Quwatli had left on a state visit to the Soviet Union on the eve of the outbreak of hostilities. A few days later a communiqué was signed in Moscow which stressed Soviet-Syrian friendship;[12] more important, perhaps, was the Soviet arms supply to Syria. It was not publicized, but according to all accounts it was greatly stepped up during the months of November and December, 1956. These arms were brought to Latakia in Soviet ships, and to Syrian airports by Soviet aircraft. The Syrian government put a news blackout on all these operations, so that general interest in the West was even more strongly focused on these transactions. There was talk—not only in the West, but also in the Arab world—of Syria having become a Soviet military base and of an "on-the-eve-of-revolution atmosphere in Damascus."[13] What had really happened was that the army high command had taken over, in cooperation with some of the civilian cabinet ministers. A state of siege was imposed which remained in force for several months, and Foreign Minister Salah al Bitar declared on November 29: "The matter of the Russian arms shipments to Syria is not within the purview of everyone's knowledge." Some Western observers exaggerated the direct political importance of the Soviet arms supplies. Since Syria was not adjacent to the Soviet Union, and since Soviet officers were not put in key positions in the Syrian army and police force, it was not correct, strictly speaking, to talk about the complete satellization of the country. As for the installation of Soviet military bases, the situation was more complex; the details about the Syrian-Soviet agreements were not made known, but there was much suggestive talk, from President Shukri al Quwatli downward, to the effect that "the Soviet Union will march with us" and that "our army will stand by the side of the Soviet army in defense against aggression, whenever the two armies are required to defend peace and freedom in the world."[14] The Syrian ambassador in Moscow declared, "The Soviet Union is Syria's best friend."[15] Obviously one did have obligations towards one's best friends.

More important than the arms supplies was the internal shift of power in Syria. The purge of conservative and pro-Western leaders was intensified, and on January 8, 1957, a mass trial of 47 members of these groups was opened. The main charge was that they had tried to overthrow the government and to replace it by pro-Western elements. The last party to be *gleichgeschaltet* was the People's Party. In June, 1957, thirty-six of its parliamentary deputies resigned in protest against a speech by Khaled Bakdash, the Communist leader. The Communists remained discreetly in the background all these months, their strength being revealed in incidents like this, when one of their members could bring about the resignation of thirty-six opponents.

Early in 1957 the situation calmed down for a while. Though trials and purges continued, Syria had, for the moment, managed to settle its disputes with its Arab neighbors, and the Western powers tended to take a less panicky view of the Syrian situation. During this lull, between one crisis and another, Soviet influence continued to grow at a rapid rate. Unfriendly or critical remarks about the Soviet Union or Soviet policies had long been banned.[16] Soviet cultural activities in Syria became too numerous for listing. Economic relations were very close, for the Syrian government had made a determined effort to strengthen economic ties with the Soviet bloc for political reasons. When a Czechoslovak offer to build an oil refinery near Homs was accepted in March, 1957, the Ba'ath leader Akram Hourani declared in parliament that the offer had been accepted mainly for political reasons. The fact that it was also the lowest offer was only incidental. Similarly, a loan by the World Bank was refused by Syria on the grounds that the rate of interest was too high, and that it was afraid of political pressure.[17] This fear of political pressure from an international organization did not prevent Syria from asking the Soviet Union for the loan instead.[18]

Meanwhile tension was maintained somewhat artificially by alarmist news put out by the Syrian government; since officially there was still a state of national emergency, it seemed necessary to justify it. "The danger of a Western invasion has not diminished," declared Khaled al Azm in March, and there were many similar statements made about internal and foreign conspiracies, Turkish and Israeli plans of aggression, Iraqi and Jordanian intrigues, and so forth.

Russia's aims in Syria were obvious—they were to make Syria an ally (or a client state) rather than a satellite. It was an unprecedented situation, for never before had a non-Communist regime moved so close to the Soviet Union voluntarily, without war or civil war. The European "Popular Democracies" had become part of the Soviet sphere of interest as a result of occupation by the Soviet Army; the voluntary element was, and presumably still is, notably absent. In Syria, both government and public opinion were, with negligible exceptions, in favor of the Soviet alliance; there was no need, as in the East European countries, for the stationing of large Soviet army units as a guarantee of lasting friendship. This cordial relationship was admittedly based mainly on common foreign political interests, rather than on the Syrian wish to emulate Soviet experience in the economic and social field. However, in the Soviet view, foreign policy was all that mattered; in the Middle East, as in the rest of Asia, the cold war and anti-Westernism had become, at least for the time being, the main criteria of the progressive character of a given country. Internal reform, or revolution, on the Soviet or Chinese pattern, it was confidently expected, would almost automatically follow in due time. This was very gratifying from the Soviet point of view, but it also created a number of problems. Perhaps the main problem was that the Syrians tended to move too fast; they did not realize (as Moscow undoubtedly did) that if Soviet and Communist influence in Syria were made too obvious, if it made headway too dramatically, other Arab countries might be deterred and reconsider their attitude towards the Soviet Union. The Soviet leaders would no doubt have preferred to make gradual progress on a broad front in the Middle East, rather than engage in spectacular exploits that would only create unnecessary complications. In this endeavor they did not have assistance, though the local Communist Party (despite its rapid growth) apparently had strict orders to move cautiously and inconspicuously.[19] But the other Syrian leaders were strongly tempted to pick quarrels with both the West and their immediate neighbors and thus did create (from the Soviet point of view) needless complications. The spectacular progress of Soviet influences was coupled with indignant denials of Western allegations by Syrian leaders. Such allegations, it was argued, were malevolent "smears" of political opponents, "McCarthyism." Marouf al Dawalibi declared, "There is no such thing as a Communist problem in Syria."[20] Akram Hourani maintained that "the Communist Party is the weakest political party in this country."[21] Sabri al Assali said, "I am not a Communist. This Moslem country cannot become a Communist country. If I thought that these people were working for Communism, I would not remain Premier for one moment."[22] Khaled al Azm, who had repeatedly declared that he was a very rich man and would not allow his property to be nationalized, expressed a slightly unorthodox view. When asked by a foreign correspondent whether Syria might not gradually be transformed into a Soviet bloc country, he replied, "If this were to happen, I would see no harm in it, either for Syria or for the world."[23]

By and large, however, everybody in authority agreed that there was a great difference "between Communism as a doctrine and the Soviet Union as a state" (Sabri al Assali). There can be no doubt that most (though perhaps not all) of those who made these declarations did so in good faith. There is no doubt, either, that they did not have any clear idea about the direction in which they were moving; for them, Communism was what it had been thirty or forty years previously, namely, a movement that wanted above all to fight Islam, that opposed Arab nationalism, and that saw its main task as the pursuit of the class struggle. But this early "extremist" Communism had disappeared long ago, and they saw no reason, therefore, to worry about what seemed to them to be imaginary dangers. They did not realize the tremendous changes that had taken place in Communist tactics, especially in Asia and the Middle East. They were neither pro- nor anti-Communist, but pre-Communist and thus quite incapable of recognizing Communism in its more modern guise.

The second Syrian crisis broke out in mid-August, 1957, after a sudden deterioration in Syrian-American relations, a less sudden intensification in Syrian-Soviet collaboration, and a new purge affecting the Syrian army high command and the civil service. It began in July, when Khaled al Azm (by now closer to the Communists than the Ba'ath) went on leave to Europe. It was generally believed that al Azm was in disgrace, and that he had been sent away to appease King Saud, whom he had offended in a speech made a few weeks earlier. However, during the last week of July, Khaled al Azm, at the head of an official Syrian delegation, appeared in Moscow and started talks with Soviet leaders. Little was made known about the contents of the talks and there were the usual announcements about economic help for Syria.[24] However, the fact that high army officers had taken part in the negotiations (Sokolovskii and Rokossovskii on the part of the Soviets), tended to suggest that military issues had been prominent. On August 6, an official communiqué announced the successful conclusion of the Moscow talks. On August 9, the chief of the Syrian army, Tawfiq Nizam ad-Din, a "moderate," was forced to resign, and was replaced by Colonel Afif al Bizri, a Communist sympathizer.[25] Three days later, on the twelfth, the Syrian government announced the discovery of an American conspiracy in the Syrian capital, allegedly aimed at overthrowing the present regime. The recall of four American diplomats was demanded. Washington retaliated by declaring the Syrian ambassador to the United States *persona non grata*. The crisis was on again.

It is doubtful whether Moscow had anything to do with this crisis, or whether it knew about it beforehand. As far as the Soviet Union was concerned, the crisis was entirely unnecessary and perhaps harmful, for reasons already discussed. It is not even certain whether the Syrian government had planned the crisis, for it would appear that it more or less stumbled into it. The conclusion of the new Moscow treaty had been hailed as the end of one era (cooperation with the West), and the beginning of another ("cooperating with the honorable rulers of the Soviet Union to limit the oppression of imperialism").[26] The new purge was desirable for domestic reasons, and the discovery of the plot was bound to keep public opinion in a state of excitement. It is doubtful whether the Syrian government anticipated such a sharp American reaction. But once the State Department reacted as it did, Damascus could not retreat, and the crisis became acute.

The first Soviet reaction to the new Middle Eastern eruption was comparatively restrained, and the events were not featured prominently in the Soviet press and radio. The discovery of the plot was announced, but then what could one expect from the Americans but scheming of this sort to establish reactionary regimes in the Middle East?[27] They had tried it before, with varying success, in Jordan and Egypt. Anyway, the vigilance of the Arab peoples would frustrate all these Western conspiracies.[28] The first Syrian reaction was one of pained surprise: Eisenhower had again been misled by the Zionists; all the talk about Syria's being controlled by international Communism was utter nonsense. But meanwhile Radio Damascus broadcast little but Soviet military marches and TASS communiqués and the Communist *Al Nur* was considered by some *cognoscenti* to be equivalent to an official gazette. On August 18, the dispatch of Mr. Loy Henderson to the Middle East was announced, and comment in both Damascus and Moscow became shriller.[29] (Mr. Henderson, to be sure, had never been a Soviet favorite.) "Dangerous Moves," proclaimed *Pravda*,[30] "America is using blackmail and pressure—this is the Eisenhower Doctrine in action, America has learned nothing from Britain's experience." Again, a few days later, a "Hands Off Syria" campaign was started, similar to the "Hands Off Egypt" drive the year before.[31] "The United States prepares aggression; the American aggressive conspiracy should be suppressed at once,"[32] became the new slogans.

Thus the propaganda campaign and the political activities of the Soviet Union entered a new phase. From early September, the Soviet press began to report in great detail the military preparations allegedly made by Turkey and Iraq to invade Syria.[33] Turkey was said to be scheduled to move first, and Iraq was to intervene later—to save Syria from Turkish aggression. Israel, too, was mentioned in the beginning as preparing to attack Syria; after two weeks, however, the "Israeli theme" was dropped by Moscow and the propaganda offensive was concentrated on Turkey.[34] On September 9, the U.S. Sixth Fleet was reported to have been sighted off the Syrian coast, and TASS reported that the "hysterical hullabaloo" in the United States had reached a new climax.

If the importance of the August events in Damascus had been somewhat magnified in the West, Moscow was soon to show that the old slogan of "catching up with and overtaking America" could make sense in the field of political warfare as well. A systematic campaign was launched against the Western powers and Turkey that was to last, off and on, for three months. It began with the customary notes handed to the three Western diplomatic envoys in Moscow and with a Gromyko press conference. The notes did not contain any startling new material. There were accusations of trying to subvert the independence and sovereignty of the Arab countries, and a proposal for a new four-power declaration on the Middle East.[35] A new element was introduced with a stern warning sent by Bulganin to Menderes[36] in which a Soviet invasion of Turkey was virtually promised in the event of Turkey's undertaking any anti-Syrian activities. Marshal Rokossovskii was appointed commander of the Caucasus military district at the same time.

In contrast to the rest of the world, the Turkish public, out of phlegm or heroism, or both, was not greatly impressed by these and similar threats. Turkey was then in the midst of a hotly contested election campaign, and the Soviet threats did not even attract much attention. The Soviet press, on the other hand, echoed by the Syrians and Egyptians, tried to create the impression that the situation was rapidly deteriorating, and that the world was on the brink of an abyss as a result of Turkish military provocation.[37]

On October 19, TASS published extensive excerpts from an alleged Turkish plan to attack Syria, but only a few days later the sun of peace was shining again; Khrushchev himself took part in a reception at the Turkish embassy and made most reassuring statements.[38] One does not know with certainty what went on in the Kremlin during those days, and how the sudden anticlimax came about, but the Zhukov affair probably had something to do with it. In the very same reassuring statement in which Khrushchev announced that there would be no war with Turkey after all, there was also a cryptic allusion to an adventurous line that had allegedly been followed by the Soviet Defense Minister, who had just been deposed and ousted from the Politburo. Whether this was indeed the case we do not know. It is equally possible that Khrushchev used the time-honored technique of creating or magnifying an international crisis when it was required for domestic purposes, for obviously, at a time of crisis, all have to rally around the supreme leadership and accept its orders. The news about Turkish troop concentrations went on for some time, but the campaign slowly petered out. There was one more Bulganin note to Menderes, already more conciliatory in tone: it was not true that Russia had turned Syria into an arsenal—Turkey itself was such an arsenal, but in any case the Soviet Union wanted friendship with Turkey, and if Turkey would only reciprocate, everything would be settled.[39] By the end of 1957 the anti-Turkish campaign was over.

The last phase of the Syrian crisis was the shortest; it ended somewhat abruptly with the disappearance of Syria as a separate state. As a result of the merger with Egypt, Syria became part of the United Arab Republic on February 1, 1958. It was an unexpected development, and the initiative for once came neither from the Soviet Government nor from Colonel Nasser. A federal union between Syria and Egypt had been envisaged for many months and when Khaled al Azm was in Moscow on one of his regular trips in mid-December, 1957, he spoke with great certainty about the "federal union with Egypt which we are going to establish soon."[40] But the Ba'ath leaders suddenly wanted a much closer tie with Egypt, and after two weeks of negotiations in Cairo, they and their supporters in the Syrian army (Abdel Hamid al Sarraj, et al.) succeeded in winning over Colonel Nasser, who had been somewhat lukewarm in the beginning.

Nasser certainly would have preferred a looser form of union, for there were practical reasons militating against a complete merger, and there was the danger that a fusion of the two countries would impede rather than expedite the all-Arab union that Nasser and most of his followers wanted. Such a merger set a pattern to which all other Arab countries would have to adhere in the future, and it could be anticipated that some Arab countries which might have been willing to join a federation would be more reluctant to become part of a complete union. The Communists, for different reasons, would also have preferred a federation; in Syria, Communism had full freedom of action, whereas conditions in the United Arab Republic were less ideal. Be that as it may, the Ba'ath leaders apparently felt they had good reasons to press for complete unity. According to some reports, they felt their hold slipping. They had argued for a long time that the Communists were a small and uninfluential group in Syria, but the real balance of power was apparently very different. Several important by-elections were to be contested in the spring of 1958, and the Ba'ath leaders apparently did not feel confident of victory. In addition, there was the danger that they would be politically outmaneuvered by a coalition between Khaled al Azm and the Communists; in the army command, too, some key positions were no longer in the hands of Ba'ath sympathizers.[41] Perhaps the Ba'ath leaders exaggerated these dangers, but then there was a Syrian tradition of magnifying both internal and external dangers which had become something of a conditioned reflex. Union with Egypt must have seemed the easiest way out of all these dilemmas.

The union came as a surprise to Moscow, and there was no official Soviet comment for some time.[42] Prior to 1957, the Soviet Union had given no support to the concept of the Arab nation; instead, "Arab nationalism" had been advocated.[43] Arab unity was still somewhat suspect, in view of its affinity with Pan-Arabism and Pan-Islamism and because of a lingering prejudice against the Arab League. In the early thirties some Arab Communist parties had for a while favored an "Arab Federation," but this was forgotten, and if in 1957 Arab unity was given more friendly treatment in a number of essays,[44] it was apparently assumed that this unity would come about at a later date, perhaps already under Communist auspices. From the Soviet point of view questions of principle were not involved; it might have been easier for Moscow to deal with separate Arab countries, but even a united republic with some thirty or even forty million inhabitants was not really a potential threat to Moscow. To criticize the new union would have been tantamount to losing much of the prestige and good will the Soviet Union had earned in the Arab world in previous years, and so the new republic eventually received Soviet blessings given with good grace.[45] Opinions in the West were divided. Some observers saw the emergence of the United Arab Republic as a setback for Soviet and Communist influence, while others viewed it as a step further toward drawing the Arab East into the Soviet sphere of influence.

NOTES

1. A.H., "Die Kommunistische Infiltration in Syrien and Aegypten," in *Neue Zürcher Zeitung*, July 21, 1957.

2. M. Gataullin: *Siriia* (Moscow, 1956), p. 18.

3. *Al Sarkha*, April 12, 1954.

4. *Al Ahram*, September 25, 1954.

5. *Al Sarkha*, September 27, 1954.

6. Both slogans are put in quotation marks because they had a very specific meaning in the prevailing conditions.

7. For the history of the Syrian Communist Party, cf. Walter Z. Laqueur: *Communism and Nationalism in the Middle East* (New York, 1956), pp. 137-70.

8. For the attitude of the Ba'ath to the great powers, cf. its program, (minhaj) paragraph 24, and its statutes, section III, paragraph 1.

9. *Zarubezhnye Strany* (Moscow, 1957), p. 504.

10. *Sovetskaia Kultura*, November 20, 1956.

11. S. Sikov: *V Solnechnoi Sirii* (In Sunny Syria) (Moscow, 1957), p. 13.

12. M. Gataullin, *op. cit.*, pp. 38-39.

13. Cf. *Al Sha'ab* (Baghdad), December 3, 1956. There were also broad hints to this effect in the Beirut press, though both news coverage and editorials were then heavily censored in Lebanon. For a Soviet description of this crisis, see also P. Demchenko: *Siriiskaia Respublika na Strazhe svoei Nezavisimosti* (Moscow, 1957), p. 17 *et seq.*

14. Khaled al Azm in *Al Rai al Am*, August 8, 1957.

15. Jamil Farrah, Syrian ambassador in Moscow, April 18, 1957, as reported by Radio Moscow; see note 16 below.

16. As early as September 18, 1956, at a press conference he gave, Sabri al Assali asked journalists to refrain from criticizing Russia and the "Popular Democracies" and to describe the Soviet Union as the Arabs' best friend. He did this (he explained) despite his opposition to Communism as a creed and dogma, because the national interest necessitated this attitude.

17. The Soviet Union offered a loan at a lower rate of interest (2½%) than the World Bank. On the other hand, no prices were mentioned for the merchandise that Syria was to buy in the Soviet Union, nor was there any guarantee that Russia would not dump Syrian cotton and wheat on Syria's old customers at cheaper prices, thus causing a fall in prices, to the detriment of the producer.

18. This comprehensive agreement for economic and technical cooperation between Syria and the USSR was signed on October 28, 1957.

19. This was in stark contrast to their activities in 1949-52, when they tried to produce as much "sound and fury" (in Bakdash's words) as humanly possible.

20. Interview with *Al Nasr*, February 6, 1957.

21. *Al Akhbar*, September 2, 1957.

22. *Ibid.*

23. *La Nuova Stampa*, September 16, 1957. Subsequently, al Azm denied having made this declaration.

24. *Pravda*, July 26, 1957, and August 6, 1957.

25. His official party affiliations were not established at the time. He apparently joined the Communist Party while in training in France. At a press conference he declared that if the Syrian people wanted to embrace Communism or Fascism (*sic*), this was their own affair and foreigners had no right to interfere.

26. *Al Barada*, August 13, 1957.

27. Radio Moscow, August 15, 1957.

28. *Pravda*, August 15, 1957.

29. Radio Damascus, August 21, 1957.

30. *Pravda*, August 24, 1957.

31. *Izvestiia*, August 27, 1957.

32. *Jen Min Ji Pao*, September 5; *Pravda*, September 8, 1957.

33. *Krasnaia Zvezda* (on September 10) published a most detailed report indicating how Turkey, Iraq, and Israel, in a five-stage plan, would attack Syria. This was published on the authority of an obscure Indian newspaper.

34. Another incident in Soviet-Israeli relations was caused in September 1957, as a result of the arrest by Soviet authorities of an Israeli diplomat in Odessa. D. Zaslavskii in *Pravda*, September 22, 1957.

35. *TASS*, September 4, 1957.

36. *Pravda*, September 14, 1957.

37. *Sovetskaia Rossiia*, October 12; *Pravda*, October 11, 1957.

38. The reception at the Turkish Embassy took place on October 30, 1957.

39. *Pravda*, November 27, 1957.

40. *Sovremennyi Vostok* 1, 1958, p. 19.

41. President Nasser forced General Afif al Bizri to resign seven weeks after the armed forces of the two countries had been merged.

42. The Soviet press merely reported the resolutions adopted by the Egyptian and Syrian parliaments. *Pravda*, February 7, 1958.

43. "A New Pattern in Soviet Middle Eastern Studies," in *The World Today*, February, 1958, p. 74.

44. Cf. V. B. Lutskii in *Sovetskaia Etnografia* 1, 1957.

45. *Pravda*, February 23, 1958.

CHAPTER FIVE

SOVIET TRADE AND ECONOMIC AID: 1954-1958

The timing of the Soviet trade drive and the loan and technical assistance offers in the Middle East makes it obvious that their motivation was mainly political. Up to 1954, trade between the Middle Eastern countries and Communist China was insignificant; trade with the Soviet Union and the East European countries ranged between 5 and 10% of the total volume after World War II. Many of these imports and exports came from, and went to, Turkey and Iran, Russia's traditional trade partners, rather than the Arab countries. After 1954, the proportion of the exports from the area to the Soviet Union increased rapidly; by 1956, it had trebled, whereas imports from the Soviet bloc had doubled. During 1957 and 1958, this sharp increase continued, and the rise affected most of the Middle East.[1] But as Soviet trade with some countries (Iraq, Jordan, Saudi Arabia) was almost nonexistent, and with others (e.g., Israel) insignificant, the trade reorientation of Egypt seemed even more striking. More than half of Egypt's exports were going to the Soviet bloc by 1957. The political motivation of the Soviet aid program is also clearly revealed by the preference given to Egypt and Syria in the Soviet economic aid schemes: the two components of the United Arab Republic were given 760 million dollars credit—more than any other non-Communist country in the world, three times as much as India.[2]

If the motivation was mainly political, one must still discover the Soviet government's object in undertaking this trade offensive, and to what extent its aim was achieved. Soviet foreign trade has been authoritatively defined as both an organic part of the

Socialist economic system and an integral element of Soviet foreign policy.[3] The pattern of Soviet foreign trade, loans, and technical assistance has been fairly consistent since 1955 throughout Asia and Africa. The interest is 2½% on the average, and the loans are repayable in ten to fifteen years. Deferred payment may be made for these long-term, low-interest loans in local currencies; very frequently they are based on barter deals or similar arrangements.[4] The principal device used to foster trade was some form of bilateral commercial agreement; by July, 1957, no less than 297 such agreements between Middle Eastern and Soviet-bloc countries were in force.[5]

The political objective of Soviet foreign trade in Asia and Africa is said to be the development and strengthening of friendly ties and close collaboration with the receiving countries and also the facilitation of their development in a direction corresponding to their interest and to that of the Soviet Union.[6] The emphasis is invariably on the disinterested and businesslike character of these loans and exchanges. Western aid is always described as selfish in character, an extension of nineteenth-century colonialism, an attempt to gain political domination by way of "economic imperialism," and above all as involving various conditions (such as military bases), whereas Soviet aid is depicted as free from any such strings and selfish motives.

Other characteristics of the Soviet trade and aid program are the virtual exclusion of any gift and "charity" schemes, in contrast to Western practices. This approach has been highly successful for it has not provoked suspicions in the countries concerned (as Western gifts had done); it took into account the great touchiness and sensitivity characteristic of the inhabitants of the area. Trade agreements and loans were obviously much more acceptable than presents and did not affect national self-esteem. The Russians usually pictured their aid program as a joint enterprise, a comprehensive expansion of normal economic links based on equality and mutual benefit.[7] This emphasis on equality was psychologically important, as the objective result of the "mutual benefit."

The Soviet Union does possess several important advantages in this competition with the West. Soviet planned economy and the state monopoly of foreign trade make it far easier to plan ahead and coordinate an over-all government policy. It makes it possible to disregard occasionally ordinary commercial considerations—e.g., to undercut the West in aid offers or tenders. It makes it possible to absorb gluts of produce from certain countries (rice from Burma, cotton from Egypt). Primary producers who found it increasingly difficult to dispose of their commodities in normal cash markets have been increasingly drawn toward the Soviet bloc. For in the Soviet Union and the other countries of the bloc, expanded capital goods production and the demand for food and raw materials provide an economic basis for trade with the underdeveloped countries. These practical Soviet advantages apart, the Soviet pattern of economic development has attracted Asian and Middle Eastern economic planners (and the public in general) much more than Western schemes. Western thinking on economic development in underdeveloped countries has been almost entirely on the lines of balanced growth between the various sectors of the national economy and has been critical of the mystique of accelerated industrialization. Soviet thinking has been extremely critical of these Western views,[8] and public opinion in the backward countries has usually followed the Soviet lead in regarding rapid industrialization as a panacea for economic stagnation, poverty, and the absorption of overpopulation.

Accelerated industrialization may well be the best solution for the economic problems of some backward countries, though not for others. According to the Soviet view, which is widely approved in the Arab countries and elsewhere throughout Asia, industrialization is the only solution. Western economists have pointed out that the higher level of real income in more industrialized countries was not necessarily the result of a higher degree of industrialization, and that the presence of surplus population on the land was not conclusive evidence in favor of industrialization rather than the extension of agriculture.[9] The acceptance of Soviet views on accelerated industrialization in the underdeveloped countries cannot, therefore, be explained on the level of economic arguments alone. Political and psychological considerations were in some cases perhaps more important than the wish to attain a higher level of real income.

The Soviet pattern of development promised growing economic independence, an increase in political and military power as a result of the concentration on heavy industry, and spectacular rates of progress. The expected gain in political and military power more than counterbalanced the possible advantages of balanced growth and diversification. Consequently, the Soviet offers of machine tools and industrial equipment (and the lack of interest in agricultural development projects) coincided with the ideas held by many in the underdeveloped countries.

Certain ulterior motives were undoubtedly involved, apart from those already mentioned and widely propagated, as far as Soviet interest in the trade offensive was concerned. There were, to begin with, the simultaneous intentions of reaping economic benefits and weakening the West as a result of the further shrinking of the "capitalist world market." (The fact that the Soviet trade campaign in Asia and the Middle East was mainly political in inspiration did not mean that it would necessarily have to be pursued at a loss to the Soviet bloc.) Secondly, it could be assumed that accelerated industrialization would make a strict system of central planning imperative and would give fresh impetus to the working-class movements in the countries concerned. Both these trends were expected to have political consequences that corresponded to Soviet long-range policies in Asia and the Middle East. But the Soviet Union also gained a certain measure of political leverage in a more immediate way: massive Soviet bloc and Chinese purchases from countries such as Egypt became a major stabilizing factor in the economy of the selling country. This in turn had direct political implications. It could (and in effect did) happen in various ways. The countries concerned became increasingly dependent on these purchases in order to maintain the internal market price for their staple products. In addition, there was a tendency for such a country to run up great positive trade balances with the Soviet bloc, which made the stability of its economy dependent on the increase of purchases from that bloc. It is true that Soviet trade and aid has no ostensible strings attached, but elsewhere (e.g., in

Yugoslavia, in Australia after the Petrov affair, in Finland, and in Israel) the Soviet government canceled trade agreements to bring political pressure on the countries concerned. Soviet trade had been a minor factor in the Australian and Israeli economies, but in countries where Soviet imports and exports had assumed much greater proportions, the governments concerned were subject to much greater pressure, and would undoubtedly think twice before risking Soviet displeasure. The state of affairs was in some respects similar to the situation in the Balkans on the eve of World War II, where certain countries had become largely dependent on German trade. The only mitigating circumstance was the very backwardness of the countries concerned; the less industrially developed a country, the less subject it was to economic pressure. Or, as some observers had put it rather irreverently, countries that were already bankrupt could not be made more bankrupt by withholding aid from them and boycotting their produce. This had been Britain's experience, in any case, with Dr. Mossadegh in 1950-51.

Another secondary aspect that should not be overlooked was the dispatch of fairly large contingents of Soviet technical personnel to the underdeveloped countries, and the training of a growing number of such technicians from Egypt, Syria, etc., in Soviet bloc countries. The political implications of this exchange should not be underrated, and the impact of these exchanges was certainly more strongly felt in the Middle East than it would have been in Europe or America, where Communism had no great attraction as an ideology.

The ability of the Soviet bloc to provide extensive loans, credits, and technical assistance was undoubtedly somewhat impaired by a number of circumstances, such as Soviet internal needs (the "second technological revolution") and the necessity to help China in its industrialization. The East European "Popular Democracies" had been indiscriminately exploited under Stalin; under his successors a change was necessary, and some of them became economic liabilities rather than assets from the Soviet point of view. This meant that some of the credits and technical assistance that could previously have been used in Asia and the Middle East now had to be diverted. On the other hand, the means needed in the Middle East were not so very extensive, and the continuing rapid growth in Soviet industrial development, and the consequent growing ability to absorb certain increases in imports from the Middle East, made the continuation of the trade campaign perfectly possible.

According to Soviet sources, trade relations between the Soviet bloc and the Middle Eastern countries were insignificant up to 1953.[10] This is a somewhat inaccurate statement, for, to give but two samples, 17% of Egypt's exports went to the Soviet bloc in 1952, and in the same year 27% of Iran's imports came from Russia. It is true, however, that a concentrated attempt to step up trade was made only after 1953. While it is impossible to enumerate all the stages in this drive, some of the major landmarks will be listed below.

Trade agreements between the Soviet Union and Egypt (March, 1954), Lebanon (April, 1954), and Syria (November, 1955), paved the way for the promotion of Soviet bloc trade with the Arab world. At the same time, the East European "Popular Democracies" intensified their trade relations with these countries, and with a trade agreement between Communist China and Egypt (August, 1955) this Eastern power made its first appearance on the Middle Eastern commercial scene. These trends began to attract general attention in the West following the Egyptian arms deal with Czechoslovakia (i.e., the Soviet Union) in 1955 and the parallel agreements between Moscow, Syria, and Yemen. Three major loans were extended by the Soviet Union: Afghanistan received 100 million dollars in December, 1955; according to a twelve-year economic and technical aid pact with Syria (in October, 1957) the Moscow and Damascus governments were to engage in several large-scale development projects estimated to cost 400 million dollars;[11] in January, 1958, the Soviet Union granted Egypt a twelve-year loan of about 175 million dollars and agreed to provide technical assistance for the development of several major industrial projects. It should be noted in this context that Middle Eastern statistics, and especially those relating to Middle Eastern-Soviet bloc commercial relations, have to be regarded as indicative of certain trends rather than as accurate figures: some of the transactions were barter deals that were not reported, and in many cases it has been impossible to determine the terms of Soviet trade relative to the terms of trade of the Middle East in free markets. The figures specified in the trade and credit agreements are regarded as mere targets, and experience between 1954 and 1958 has shown that Middle Eastern trade with the Soviet Union, Communist China, and Eastern Europe has frequently fallen far short of the amounts specified in these agreements. "The failure to fulfill these targets is further amplified if one takes into account the fact that some of the actual trade is not part of the trade agreements. Both imports to and exports from the Middle East fail to meet the targets."[12] These reservations about the accuracy of trade statistics do not, however, affect the main trend, namely, the spectacular growth of Soviet bloc-Middle Eastern trade.

Conditions varied considerably from country to country, and it is impossible to generalize about Soviet bloc trade relations with the Middle East as a whole. More detailed analysis may be called for at this point. Turkish exports to the Soviet bloc went up from 5% (of all Turkish exports) to about 20% in 1957, which would imply a very considerable increase. It should be recalled, however, that Turkey and Persia had been traditional, and in a sense natural, trade partners of Russia, that 1952 was the nadir of Soviet bloc trade relations with the outside world, and that before World War II about 15% of Turkey's exports had gone to the Soviet Union. (Turkish imports from the Soviet bloc went up from 4% in 1952 to 17% in 1957.)*

Persian trade with the Soviet Union has been rather erratic during the last decade, and it is difficult to establish any consistent pattern. (Persian exports to the Soviet bloc, less than 1% in 1948, went up to 22% in 1952, but fell again to 9% in the following year.) In 1956 about 17% of Persia's exports went to the Soviet bloc, and the country received about 10% of its imports from the same source. Trade between Israel and the Soviet Union was mainly limited to a barter deal (Israeli citrus products for Soviet fuel oil). Israeli-Soviet trade fell from 11.5 million dollars in 1954 to 8.5 million dollars in 1956 and came to a standstill in

* *Directory of International Trade*, March, 1958.

1957 as a result of the Soviet abrogation of the trade agreement with Israel during the Suez war.[13]

Figures on Iraqi exports to the Soviet bloc are not available; Iraqi imports from the bloc (mainly Czechoslovakia and Hungary) amounted to only about 2% of total Iraqi imports before the overthrow of the old regime in July, 1958. After that date, Iraqi trade became mainly orientated toward the Soviet bloc. There was no trade between Jordan and the Soviet bloc.

Considerable efforts were made by Soviet and East European planners to increase their purchases and sales in the Lebanese and Sudanese markets. Lebanon was offered aid for the Litani River project, assistance in the construction of dams and highways, the establishment of cement and textile factories, a metallurgical plant, etc.[14] The Sudan was offered assistance in the construction of water works, and the Soviet Union hinted at its readiness to purchase large quantities of Sudanese products (mainly cotton) when the Sudan was having difficulties in disposing of its main crop on the world markets (1957). These efforts were not, however, crowned with great success. About 4% of Lebanon's total exports went to the Soviet Union in 1956, and the country's imports from the bloc were even smaller. Sudanese imports from the Soviet bloc were about 6% in 1956 (and fell to 3% in 1957); its exports to the bloc (mainly China) were 4% in 1957.* Neither the Lebanese nor the Sudanese government has shown much inclination to receive bloc offers of credits and technical aid.

Precise details about Soviet trade with Saudi Arabia and Yemen are not known. A first Soviet trade delegation toured Yemen in January, 1956, and, according to a first trade agreement concluded between that country and the Soviet Union in March, 1956, Yemen was to export coffee, hides, and dried fruit in exchange for Soviet industrial and agricultural machinery. Two more trade agreements were signed with Czechoslovakia and East Germany, while Saudi Arabia made a commercial deal with Poland in the winter of 1955. There is sufficient reason to assume that the total value of the trade involved was very small.

* *Directory of International Trade*, May, 1958.

Egypt and Syria became the main Middle Eastern commercial partners of the Soviet bloc and China. In 1956, Egypt alone accounted for half of the Soviet bloc trade with the Middle East, and the share of Egypt and Syria in 1957 was nearly two-thirds of the total. Big Soviet aid offers were made to Egypt after the arms deal in 1955. These contracts included agreements on a great number of industrial projects (including a nuclear laboratory in Cairo), and culminated in the big 700-million-ruble loan in November, 1957. Exports of Egyptian cotton to the Soviet bloc area and to China increased from 35 million dollars in 1953 to 95 million dollars in 1956. N. Menshikov, head of the Soviet foreign trade agency, came to Cairo in 1956, and the foreign trade chiefs of other East European countries visited the Egyptian capital in 1956 and 1957.

The increase in Syrian trade with the Soviet bloc began later than in Egypt, the main reason undoubtedly being the fact that Damascus was not so hard-pressed for outside aid as Cairo. Syria's economy was less dependent on the sale of one particular product, and, generally speaking, was in much better shape than the Egyptian economy. A first significant increase occurred only in 1956, when Syrian exports to the Soviet bloc were 7%, and Syrian imports 4% of the country's total foreign trade. By 1957 Syrian exports to the bloc exceeded 10% of the total and continued to rise, while Syrian imports from the bloc lagged behind. The comprehensive trade and aid agreement of October, 1957, initiated a further considerable increase in Syria's economic relations with the Soviet bloc.

In this list of Soviet bloc economic activities, the main commodity exported to the Middle East has been notably absent. It is assumed that the Soviet bloc shipped arms and ammunition valued at between 400 and 500 million dollars to Egypt, Syria, and Yemen between 1955 and 1958, making armaments the most important single item by a considerable margin (out of total economic and military aid estimated between 750 and 800 million dollars).[15] The first Soviet arms deal was originally said to have involved 80 million dollars,[16] but as time passed and arms shipments continued, the value of the deliveries was considered to be much higher (250-400 million dollars). The original Soviet arms deal with Syria (Spring, 1956) was reported to have been for 30 million dollars. But Soviet bloc arms shipments were much more extensive than anticipated in 1957, and estimates varied between 50 and 100 million dollars by the end of 1957. Yemen was said to have received smaller quantities—between 15 and 20 million dollars. Neither the precise amount of the arms shipments, nor the price to be paid by Egypt, Syria, and Yemen, nor the conditions of payment were published. It is known, however, that these transactions were very substantial, and Colonel Nasser repeatedly stressed that Egypt had become the strongest military power in the Middle East and had acquired the strongest air force. It is known, in addition, that Egypt and Syria received several hundred MIG-15, MIG-17 and MIG-19 aircraft as well as a quantity of IL-28 medium jet bombers. In addition, both countries received several hundred T-34 heavy tanks and self-propelled guns, several submarines, torpedo boats, minesweepers, and other naval craft. It was frequently suggested in 1955 that the arms supplied by the Soviet bloc would be obsolete and would therefore be sold at a fraction of their original or "real" value. It subsequently appeared, however, that the arms delivered were by no means obsolete, but included the very latest models of Soviet military equipment. The Soviet Union agreed to take cotton in payment for arms, to charge only a small rate of interest (2 to 3%) and to allow payment to be made over a period of seven to ten years. However cheaply priced these arms, the deal probably ran into several hundred million dollars, and a large part of the Egyptian cotton crop had to be mortgaged for a number of years. Arab statesmen and commentators argued that they had no alternative but to accept the Soviet bloc offers, for the West had refused to supply similar military equipment. But it also seems to be true that from a purely commercial point of view the arms were acquired at bargain prices. One observer reached the conclusion that it is possible, "assuming low prices for arms and high prices for cotton, that the Middle East has obtained a quantity of arms in the arms transaction which it would not have obtained in an equivalent transaction with the Western countries."[17]

The men who negotiated these deals on behalf of the Soviet

bloc were experts, who were able to take quick decisions, and who conducted themselves impeccably, treating the Arab representatives as equals worthy of respect. After the deals had been concluded, the Soviet bloc countries did their best to carry out their obligations fully and on time. Nevertheless, there were unavoidable difficulties and complaints. Some of the commodities delivered did not meet expectations in quality and specifications. Others, ordered at a time of shortage, arrived after the emergency was over. Kerosene delivered by the Soviet Union to Egypt had to be refined again before it could be used. And above all there were suspicions that the Russians had dumped some of their large quantities of Egyptian cotton on West European markets at a discount of 20 to 30%.[18] Some of these conflicts and misunderstandings were undoubtedly real; others were probably magnified in the Western press. They did not deter the Egyptians from continuing and extending their trade relations with the Soviet bloc. After some four years of experience, Aziz Sidqi, head of an Egyptian trade delegation to Moscow, declared, "We found real understanding by the Soviets of our aspirations, and sincere help for the realization of our hopes . . ."[19] It would be very wrong to regard Soviet-Arab trade relations as a one-sided affair in which all the initiative came from the Soviet side. "It must, of course, be admitted," wrote an Arab observer, "that Soviet generosity is not entirely altruistic. Whose is? But it is quite wrong to picture the Arab world as a Little Red Riding Hood who doesn't know what Granny's nightcap is hiding. Such innocence no longer exists in the twentieth century, either among children or among states."[20] Whether such innocence was to be found among certain states in the mid-twentieth century is a more uncertain proposition than this observer believed. But, while we do not know whether these people knew what they were doing, at any rate, they thought they were striking a very good bargain.

What were the economic and political consequences of the Soviet economic campaign in the Middle East? The non-Arab countries were not greatly affected by it; if there was an increase in trade, it had no political repercussions. In the United Arab Republic and Iraq, the situation was quite different. It is difficult to comment on Syria, because massive Soviet economic involvement in that country started only after 1956. Syria had experienced a boom between the end of World War II and 1954; between 1949 and 1953 alone the national income had increased by 28%. By 1955, this boom had spent itself, and a mission of the International Bank that toured Syria in that year reached the conclusion that it was unlikely that private enterprise would be able to maintain the past rate of expansion unaided. Large-scale public investment was needed for improved communications, irrigation projects, and the establishment of power plants. In these conditions the Soviet credits could have given a welcome impetus to Syrian economic development, provided they were really to be used mainly for economic development projects rather than for military equipment, and provided that Damascus was able to make the most rational use of the credits—two somewhat uncertain prerequisities. The merger of Syria and Egypt makes it impossible to deal separately with the Syrian economy after February, 1958.

The economic consequences for Egypt were, perhaps, not what Colonel Nasser's government had anticipated. After four years of intensive trade with the Soviet bloc, a financial and trading situation had developed that was not very promising for the long-term development of the country. Egypt did export too much to the East, and imported too much from the West. "Behind that formula lies a Muscovite lesson in elementary political economy in which President Nasser's dream of independence of the West has been neatly converted into the fact of strangulation by the East."[21] In addition to trade and financial difficulties, per capita income in Egypt continued to fall under Colonel Nasser (as it has been doing for many years previously), and the Egyptian pound lost one-third of its value.

Such an appraisal, while factually correct, could perhaps be described as lacking in fairness; were not Egypt's economic difficulties insoluble anyway under the circumstances—with a population increase of 500,000 a year, a lack of land, general poverty, and the absence of major natural resources? Be that as it may, there can be no doubt that the political high life led by Egypt in 1956-57, which was largely based on Soviet offers and promises, accelerated the downward movement. It made the Egyptian economy far more dependent on the East than it had ever been on the West. Cotton accounts for about 80% of Egypt's exports. Soviet bloc purchases of Egyptian cotton had reached 60 to 70% of the total in 1958, and bulk buying at prices above world levels killed competitive interest in Egyptian cotton in the West. The Egyptian government tried by various means (offering premiums and juggling with price mechanisms) to regain some of its lost markets, but these attempts were fruitless, since the Soviet bloc had established its hegemony over the Egyptian cotton market.* "As Egypt's hard currency withers, the Eastern bloc can name its own terms, making up for the higher prices it pays for Egyptian cotton (in depreciated Egyptian pounds) by adding to the cost of its own exports to Egypt."[22]

At the same time there was a large trading surplus on Egypt's side, for her imports from the Soviet bloc had risen much less than her exports. Egypt gained a sizeable favorable trade balance, a fact that proved to be only of abstract interest, for military supplies were not listed in the trade figures. Hidden military imports accounted for the fact that, though Egypt theoretically had a great trading surplus, its *balance of payment surplus* was virtually nonexistent.

The net result was that Egypt again had to look to the West for many of its ordinary imports. Despite severe restrictions on the import of consumer goods (which began to affect not only the middle classes but also the broad masses of the people) there was a great payment gap in trade with the West. Further cuts in imports, it was feared, would affect Egypt's economic development detrimentally. Foreign observers estimated in 1958 that Egypt could not maintain its economic and political high life for more than about another three years, for it would then have reached the end of its foreign trade tether.[23] All this was accompanied by much talk about the necessity for planning—and the absence of any real over-all plan to coordinate the various, frequently conflicting projects. Up to 1955, Soviet observers took a dim view of the economic policy of the Naguib-Nasser regime.

* Cf. *Vneshniaia Torgovlia SSSR so Stranami Azii, Afriki i Latinskoi Ameriki* (Moscow, 1958), p. 163.

The economic and social reforms were said to have been carried out merely to prop up the tottering social system and to save the big feudal landowners from their unavoidable doom.[24] After 1955, the approach of Soviet commentators became much more conciliatory and some very favorable essays on Colonel Nasser's economic policy appeared in Soviet periodicals in 1956-57. Even so, there is no reason to assume that many illusions were entertained about the real state of affairs in Egypt. The professions of friendship and sympathy did not prevent Soviet observers from occasionally saying what they really thought about the agrarian reform: "Like every bourgeois reform, the agrarian reform in Egypt cannot solve the agrarian problem as far as the big masses of peasants are concerned . . ."[25] If the Soviet Union gave Colonel Nasser economic assistance, it was undoubtedly because he worked for close cooperation between the two countries. In ideological terms, this could be easily justified, for Colonel Nasser's economic policy led toward the strengthening of the state capitalist sector, which, from the Communist point of view, was a progressive trend. And lastly, there was perhaps the same motive that had led Mao Tse-tung to approve, for a while, the distribution of land to the Chinese peasants, rather than procceeding to collectivization—the intention to demonstrate, in other words, that things could not possibly work that way, that a radically different, scientific Communist approach was needed. After only four years, it is difficult to assess how politically decisive Soviet economic dominance in Egypt has become. Yugoslavia had managed to survive economically after 1948, despite the fact that its economy had until then been closely geared to the Soviet Union. (Following that experience, Marshal Tito is said to have advised President Nasser in 1956 that the ideal solution for Egypt would be to have one-third of its foreign trade with the East, one-third with the West, and the rest with neutral countries. President Nasser did not pay much attention, or perhaps was not in a sufficiently strong bargaining position to make use of the advice.) This example tends to show that economic domination, even by a totalitarian state, is not necessarily an irreversible process. On the other hand, it should be kept in mind that for a variety of reasons, both political and economic, President Nasser was in a weaker position in 1958 than Tito had been a decade earlier. The only sure shock absorber was, as already mentioned, the very poverty of Egypt, the fact that about 90% of its inhabitants existed at subsistence level, which made Egypt less vulnerable, and less open to pressure than a highly developed industrial country. Egypt's poverty guaranteed its rulers a somewhat greater freedom of maneuver, but it did not provide a long-term solution for any regime committed to rapid economic development and a rise in the standard of living.

The Soviet pattern of economic development and industrialization has retained, and will presumably continue to retain, its great force of attraction, despite its political and economic drawbacks. Capitalism in the Middle East is a synonym of exploitation and imperialism. It has never been really tried, and the prospects for private enterprise as a basis of economic development in the Middle East are far from ideal. Public opinion in the Middle East, not only in the United Arab Republic, agrees that the initiative should come from the state, that a planned economy and some form of socialist regime are needed. Unfortunately, these ideas have not yet been developed anywhere systematically and in detail; they have been set forth only in the vaguest and most general way as the expression of an anticapitalist mentality that is not a novel phenomenon in history, and which may even betray inspirations far removed from socialism. The appeal of a planned economy was irresistible in these circumstances, and the Soviet Union, in contrast to the West, stood for a planned economy. One may speculate whether Western Democratic Socialist governments—if they had been in power instead of the government based on more orthodox capitalist lines that prevailed in most Western countries in the middle fifties—would have been more attractive to Middle Eastern public opinion. There is no certain answer to this question, but neither is there much room for optimism. Regimes such as Colonel Nasser's had also declared themselves in favor of democratic socialism, but the similarity of terms by no means indicated that they had the same thing in mind. Political rather than economic considerations were ultimately decisive; the desire to attain a position of political and military strength, rather than the wish to engage in welfare-state economics, to pursue gradual reform and balanced development. In these circumstances the appeal of quasi-Communist solutions was bound to be powerful.

NOTES

1. R. L. Allen: *Middle Eastern Economic Relations with the Soviet Union, Eastern Europe, and Mainland China* (Univ. of Virginia, 1958), p. 14 *et seq.* Joseph S. Berliner: *Soviet Economic Aid* (New York, 1958), pp. 94-95 *et seq.* In this chapter I have also referred on several occasions to an unpublished paper ("The Soviet Union in the Middle East: Foreign Aid Policy since 1955") prepared by Miss Louise Lander for a course given by the present writer at the University of Chicago in the spring of 1958.

2. Estimates based on a study prepared by the U. S. State Department on Soviet economic aid. *New York Times*, January 4, 1958.

3. *Vneshniaia Torgovlia*, November, 1954, p. 1.

4. *Soviet Technical Assistance*, Staff Study No. 7, Committee on Foreign Relations, Subcommittee on Technical Assistance Programs (Washington, 1956), p. 4 *et seq.*

5. Allen, *op. cit.*, p. 29.

6. V. E. Motylev, quoted in S. Yakobson: "Soviet Concept of Point Four," *The Annals of the American Academy of Political and Social Science*, March, 1950, p. 134.

7. A.Z., "The Soviet Bloc and Underdeveloped Countries," *The World Today*, XII (June, 1956), pp. 224-26.

8. Cf. V. Kollontai, "Burzhuasnaia Politekonomiia o Problemakh Ekonomicheskogo Razvitiia Slaborazvitikh Stran" (Bourgeois Political Economy in the Economic Development of Underdeveloped Countries) in *Voprosy Ekonomiki* 3, 1956, pp. 125-40.

9. Cf. W. Arthur Lewis: *The Theory of Economic Growth* (London, 1955); H. G. Aubrey, "Deliberate Industrialization," *Social Research*, XVI, pp. 158-82; S. H. Frankel, "United Nations Primer for Development," *Quarterly Journal of Economics*, LXVI, pp. 301-26; Peter T. Bauer and Basil S. Yamey: *The Economics of Underdeveloped Countries*, (Cambridge University Press, 1957).

10. V. Poliakov in *Vneshinaia Torgovlia* 3, 1957, p. 2.

11. A Syrian spokesman mentioned a much lower sum, 170 million dollars. The discrepancy may perhaps be explained as a result of the well-known difficulty in establishing a realistic exchange rate between Soviet and Western currencies.

12. Allen, *op. cit.*, p. 33.

13. These and the following figures are based on *Directory of International Trade*, Vols. VI and VII.

14. *Le Commerce du Levant* (Beirut), March 31, 1956.

15. *New York Times*, February 8, 1958.

16. *Middle East Journal*, Summer, 1956, p. 295.

17. Allen, *op. cit.*, p. 53.

18. The *Economic Bulletin of the National Bank of Egypt* reported that "strong rumors are circulating that Egyptian cotton was being re-exported to some countries with a discount of 20 to 30%." (Volume X, No. 1, p. 29.) There were reports about the dumping of Egyptian raw cotton in Western Germany. It is difficult to ascertain whether this was some cunning Soviet maneuver or a mere misunderstanding (faulty cost accounting and price determination).

19. Quoted in *Pravda*, January 31, 1958.

20. Burhan Dajani in *Middle East Forum*, December, 1957, p. 39.

21. "Colonel Nasser's Egypt: Communist Trade Stranglehold," *The Times* (London), February 12, 1958.

22. *Ibid.*

23. *Ibid.*

24. See M. F. Gataullin's introduction to Abdel Razik Mohammed Hassan: *Krizis Ekonomiki Egipta* (Moscow, 1955), pp. 6-13.

25. L. Vatolina in *Araby v Borbe* . . . , p. 175.

CHAPTER SIX

SOVIET CULTURAL POLICY AND THE INTELLECTUAL CLIMATE IN THE ARAB WORLD

There has been an unending procession of Soviet writers, journalists, painters, musicians, historians, ballet dancers, weight-lifters, and other cultural representatives to the capitals of the Middle East, mainly Cairo, Damascus, and Baghdad. These visits attracted a good deal of attention in the West and were duly catalogued.[1] The mere listing of Soviet cultural activities is of only limited value in understanding the aims, scope, and success of this campaign. There was nothing startling in the resumption of Russian cultural contacts with the Arab world. Between the two world wars these ties had been virtually nonexistent. But Russian cultural influence in the Middle East antedates the revolution; there were Russian schools in Palestine and Syria prior to World War I, and not a few of the leading Arab poets and critics of the time had been graduates of these institutes and had lived part of their lives in Russia. Neither was there anything sensational in the visits of Soviet writers and artists, and if most Cairo movie houses showed Hollywood products, one could not well protest against the showing of two or three Soviet films. There was no reason for particular concern in the West about the effects of "socialist realism," since it had not attracted much interest in the West itself. Its influence had been strictly limited to the party faithful, and even among these, strayers from the true path of regimentation and oversimplification were not lacking. An overdose of Soviet art in Eastern Europe (and not only in Poland and Hungary) had resulted in a wholesale, and perhaps even exaggerated, rejection of Soviet culture in general. Why worry, then, about patently innocuous Soviet cultural exports to the Middle East?

While Soviet cultural activities did not have a very great direct impact on the Middle East, "socialist realism," nevertheless, became quite fashionable in Cairo, Damascus, and Baghdad (and to a lesser degree in Amman and Beirut) in the early and middle fifties. As one close and sympathetic observer of the Egyptian literary scene has put it: "The Egyptian reading public was about as exposed to a diet of 'socialist realism' as the public in Warsaw and Belgrade" (in 1954).[2] This apparent contradiction can be explained by reference to internal developments in the Arab world rather than to the Arab intellectuals' fascination with Soviet cultural activities.

It is one of the basic facts of international life that the Soviet political, social, and economic system has attracted more sympathizers and imitators in the backward countries than in the more developed ones. It presented a blueprint for the rapid modernization of backward societies, while to those that had already reached a higher stage of development it did not have much to offer. Similarly, Soviet culture has found admirers in the backward, rather than the developed, areas of the world. In Western Europe, even leading Communist writers and artists (from Picasso to Louis Aragon) shy away from "socialist realism," whereas in Latin America or Asia and the Middle East, Soviet cultural fashions have also exerted influence outside the local Communist parties. Certainly the most sincere Communist writings of the past decade or two have come from Chile, India, or Turkey rather than Paris, London, or Rome. In Egypt and Syria, literary and artistic influences had long been mainly of English or French origin, while the political, social, and economic realities facing the Arab intellectual were quite unlike those prevailing in Western Europe. This unilateral cultural orientation toward Western Europe was somewhat artificial and came to an end when Colonel Nasser took over. The military *coup d'état* was followed by revolutionary changes in the cultural field, and there were similar trends in other Arab countries in the wake of the general radicalization of public opinion during and after World War II.

The leading figures in Egyptian (and Arab) cultural life between the two world wars were men like Taha Hussein, Tewfik al Hakim and the brothers Mohammed and Mahmoud Taimour, who had been regarded as innovators, "Westerners" (by and large) who had tried to lay the foundation for a new, national, and distinctly Egyptian, literature. They were the *avant garde*, but after 1945 their influence decreased; whether they had indeed lost contact with life (as some critics argued) or only contact with the younger writers, is irrelevant in the present context. By 1953 they were somewhat out of touch with the *Zeitgeist*.

After World War II, two other groups had moved into the foreground. A foreign visitor could assume that the cultural scene in Cairo was dominated by a group of cosmopolitan literates "who were always up-to-date on what was going on in the world, read *Foreign Affairs*, and the polylingual Roman review *Botteghe Oscure*, had digested authors as dissimilar as Marx, Heidegger, and Stirner, who went abroad every year to renew their contacts with such illustrious Western figures as Jaspers, Abellio, or Papini." In their journals they tried to combine Communism with surrealism, dedicated special issues to anniversaries of Kierkegaard, Nietzsche, and Kafka. "Published by a very restricted group and intended for a happy few, the magazine fulfilled no real need, was not addressed to any specific public, and pretended, not without a certain presumption, to teach the West about its own thinkers . . . These publishers-intellectuals were unaware of the situation of their class and that it was in its death throes." In the middle of a great crisis and social reforms, they went on collecting paintings of the Paris school, old rugs, and the gewgaws of Fabergé. They thought they were the heirs, at a distance of twenty centuries, of the ancient Alexandrian élites. "They did not seem to grasp that their preoccupation with metaphysics, dandyism, Julian the Apostate, and the Sephirot—in a nation 80% illiterate—was not only paradoxical but scandalous."[3]

Another group, consisting mainly of Communist fellow travelers, came to dominate the Egyptian cultural scene after

1953, in the wake of the military coup. They had been present in Cairo, less conspicuously, for quite some time, and in other parts of the Arab world (Beirut) their influence dated back a further ten to fifteen years. These were, *inter alia*, the members of the "Al Tali'a" group, a left-wing Wafdist faction that came under Communist influence in the late forties, the writers and journalists who had contributed to *Al Jamaheer*, a Communist periodical, and after its suppression found a refuge on the staff of *Rose al Yussef* and other daily papers and weekly magazines. After 1954 these men came to control "almost all the cultural sections of the Egyptian press." Everyone had to write like Gorky, or, to be more precise, "like the boys who wrote like Gorky."[4] Similar fashions were to be found all over the world, but what made the Egyptian situations somewhat disconcerting was the fact that "the local preceptors of socialist realism had all the key positions, and that it was a very brave act indeed *not* to follow the line . . ."[5]

The most prominent representatives of this group were Abdel Rahman as Sharqawi (author of *Al Ardh*, a novel translated into several European languages), Abdel Rahman al Khamisi (b. 1920, the son of a Port Said worker), Yussef Idris (b. 1927, a physican by profession, and perhaps the most gifted member of the group, author of *Arkhas Layali*), Naguib Mahfouz (author of a trilogy on life in prerevolutionary Egypt), Yussef Jawhar (*Samira Hanem*), the poet Ibrahim Abdel Halim, the novelists Rushdi Saleh and Mahmoud al Badawi.[6] Many members of this group were arrested and sentenced to prison terms for Communist activities in the early years of the Naguib-Nasser regime (1952-54) but subsequently became quite respectable and received a virtual monopoly on literary life in Egypt. And it should be recalled that in Arab society the influence of writers and poets on public opinion has been traditionally much greater than that of their colleagues in the West.

It is not within the scope of the present survey to provide literary criticism, and we confine our investigation to the political and social background of these writers and the ideological content of their writings. Their aesthetics are undoubtedly "socialist

realist," and much of their writing is openly propagandistic.
"The new literature is a popular literature, a literature for the
workers to whom it shows life, its struggles, and hopes; this
literature sets out to open the eyes of all to the horrible realities
in which they live, and wants to show them the way out, to guide
them toward a transformation of this reality," as one of this
group, the critic Murad, described its aims. Marx and European
Marxism are largely unknown in the Arab world, and the main
inspiration is derived from Lenin, Stalin, and recent Soviet
literature. There are also, not unnaturally, pronounced populist
elements in this literature and a strong dose of sentimentality of
which the Soviet literary authorities would probably not approve.
The absence of culture has been defined as the "outstanding
characteristic of these new intellectuals."[7] "Unlike their predecessors, they are very rarely polylingual. They have read very little,
mostly bad translations of Dostoyevski and Sartre. To read a lot,
you need leisure and money, because foreign books cost two or
three times as much in Cairo as in their countries of origin. They
have very little leisure and almost no money. Almost all of them
write for the newspapers, and some write film scripts for the
movies. Culture is the province of the rich and exhausted classes,
of those 'who do not belong.' Almost all of them come from the
villages of Egypt. They have been hungry because they are
the sons of peasants or of impoverished petty officials, and this
explains their attitude to the people who would go to Europe
to overload their stomachs, and who were the exploiters of their
fathers . . . Their lack of money is almost a metaphysical state;
as Cossery puts it, they are 'eternal beggars in the best of all
possible worlds.' "[8] The implications of poverty and the widespread academic unemployment cannot possibly be exaggerated
in this context; if the "saturated" (but alienated) intellectuals in
the West are regarded as the gravediggers of their society, how
much more room for dissatisfaction and radical slogans can be
found in societies in which the majority of students find it impossible to obtain work in their profession? Another distinct
feature of this new intelligentsia is its atheism, which makes
communication between its members and the older generation

(who were either religious believers or tolerant of Islam) rather difficult. And yet, this new intelligentsia, however radical, lacks the intensity and seriousness that was so characteristic of successive generations of the Russian intelligentsia in the nineteenth and early twentieth centuries. The curious mixture of "socialist realism," radical nationalist slogans, and society gossip in which the Egyptian weekly *Rose al Yussef* has specialized for many years and which has made it the rallying ground of the radical forces throughout the Arab world is something without parallel in the history of socialist or populist movements. This combination of Gorky and *Reveille* (England), of Sholokhov with *Confidential* (United States) is an original, though not very edifying, contribution to the history of socialist belles-lettres.

Similar trends could be observed in other Arab countries. *Al Tareek*, published in Beirut after 1942 by the local "Anti-Fascist League," originally edited by Omar Fakhuri (d. 1945), served for many years as the mouthpiece of the pro-Communist intelligentsia in the Levant; it eventually received a Stalin prize for its services. But culturally as well as politically, Communism has never been quite so successful in Lebanon as in Syria, and after 1954 the center of Communist cultural activities shifted from Beirut to Damascus. On the initiative of the "Association of Syrian Writers," the "First Arab Writers' Congress" was convened in the Syrian capital in September, 1954. This subsequently became a highly efficient front organization, extremely active in shaping Syrian cultural life and public opinion. In view of the ban on open Communist activities in Iraq and Jordan there were no open manifestations of sympathy in these countries; it is known, however, that the books and periodicals edited in Cairo and Damascus reached a sympathetic public in Iraq (even before July, 1958) and in Jordan. The situation in Turkey and Israel was different. In these countries there were intellectual fellow travelers, too, but they constituted the opposition (and not a very strong opposition at that) rather than the mainstream in public opinion. The state of affairs in these two countries resembled the situation in the West, and is, therefore, not of particular interest in the present context.

A cursory analysis of the intellectual climate in the Arab world in the early and middle fifties was required in order to put the Soviet cultural offensive into perspective and to explain its success. The Soviet Union exported the very same films to the Middle East and to Western Europe, and the Moiseev Ballet danced in both Cairo and New York. The basic difference was that in the West these cultural exports were judged on their merits: if they were good, they were applauded; if found wanting, they were criticized. In Baghdad or Damascus they were frequently viewed as political demonstrations and, therefore, were enthusiastically welcomed, regardless of quality or content.

Opposition to Western culture had been part of the general "anti-imperialist campaign" long before the Suez war, but it was given fresh impetus by the Anglo-French attack. "Teachers must aim to obliterate all traces of English and French cultural domination from our children's minds," Kamal al Din Hussein, the Egyptian minister of education, directed.[9] Even earlier, a Soviet deputy minister for cultural affairs who toured the Middle East in the summer of 1956 reported "tremendous sympathy for the Soviet Union. The appearance of a Russian in the street evokes friendly smiles. The passers-by wave their hands whenever they see a car with a red Soviet flag. The interest in all things Soviet is very great."[10] A leading Egyptian writer visiting the Soviet Union declared that the literature and art of Uzbekistan should serve as a lodestar for Egypt, and concluded, paraphrasing Maiakovskii, "I would like to live and to die in Russia if there were no Egypt . . ."[11] A leading Egyptian composer said in Moscow that Egyptian music was at the crossroads: it had to decide between the camp of the West, jazz and atonal music ("in my opinion the most dangerous enemy"), and the camp of Soviet and Russian classical music; he was going to opt for the East.[12]

Western observers found it difficult to understand these attitudes. However shining the cultural achievements of the Soviet Republic of Uzbekistan, there were also other places in the world that could serve as an example and a source of inspiration. However "ugly" Western jazz and however "cacophonic" atonal music might be, there were undoubtedly several other "camps" between this curious amalgam and the "camp" of Soviet music;

the alternatives were somewhat artificial ones. But then the decision to opt for Soviet culture was a political, not a cultural, one and a result of the internal crisis in the Arab world and of opposition to the West. It should be noted, however, that though Soviet cultural imports had official blessing in Egypt, Syria, and Iraq, the Egyptian public developed a certain sales resistance, and both Soviet movies and literature were not so successful as had been expected. The reason was, presumably, that the Egyptian public had been exposed too long to harmful Western influences. In the other, less-sophisticated Arab countries (notably Syria and Iraq), Soviet books and films received a more enthusiastic welcome.[13]

Soviet cultural activities in the Middle East came into full swing in 1954. Groups of Soviet movie technicians came to Syria and Egypt in that year, Uzbek and Armenian circus ensembles performed in Beirut and Damascus, cinema festivals were arranged in various Middle Eastern cities, the distribution of Soviet magazines and books was undertaken. Soviet sports teams began to participate in open competitions in Egypt, Syria, and Lebanon. These delegations were frequently accompanied by some Soviet deputy minister from one of the "Eastern" republics (Azerbaidzhan, Armenia, Uzbekistan); they were received as honored guests by Presidents and Prime Ministers in Cairo, Beirut, Baghdad, and Damascus, and local orders and medals were bestowed on them. In Moscow and Cairo, societies for cultural collaboration between the two countries were established, and the Egyptian branch soon began to publish a special journal to popularize Soviet culture (*Al Sharq*, "The East"). Addressing a meeting in Moscow dedicated to the strengthening of cultural ties between the two countries, the Egyptian ambassador declared: "Soviet culture has become an object of love in Egypt because it is based on the principles of democracy and love of humanity that are characteristic of the Soviet Union."[14]

Sergei Kaftanov, the Soviet Deputy Minister for Cultural Affairs who set out to negotiate agreements with the Arab countries in the autumn of 1956, did not find everywhere an equal willingness to collaborate. The Syrians were the most enthusiastic and at once concluded an agreement with Moscow. Cairo was somewhat less sanguine and took two years to give its assent. The Lebanese were even more reluctant and merely appointed a study group to examine the various proposals.

Among the various cultural exchanges, the impact of books was traditionally the most important. Gorky had been a widely read author in the Arab world ever since 1905.[15] More recent Soviet literature had been translated only sporadically, but after 1955 the number of translations increased greatly. They included not only Sholokhov, Fadeev, Ehrenburg, and other present-day writers, but also such precursors of Eastern Marxist thought as Plekhanov (on literary criticism) and even the Bulgarian Christo Botev.[16] Somehow or other, these books did not greatly fascinate the Egyptian reader, for the reality described by the Soviet writers was after all a very remote (but not an exotic) one, and the main result of the Soviet cultural campaign was perhaps an increased interest in the Russian writers of the nineteenth, rather than the twentieth, century, from Pushkin to Chekhov. Several collections of Egyptian and Arab belles-lettres were published in Moscow after 1955, and two Egyptian movies were shown (*Fight in the Valley* and *Meeting with Happiness*). The Egyptian and Syrian writers who were translated into Russian undoubtedly felt quite flattered (since most of them had been ignored by the West). In addition there was the element of "material interest," never quite absent in Soviet policy, for Moscow began to compete with King Saud as a Maecenas of Arab journalism, literature, and the arts by way of various grants-in-aid, free trips to the Soviet Union, soliciting articles and books, etc.

Soviet movies shown in the Arab capitals included all the main films produced after 1953—and some products of former periods in the history of the Soviet cinema (*Potemkin, Chapaev, How the Steel Was Forged*). At a cinema festival in Damascus in 1956 the Soviet film *Othello* was given the first prize. Cairo, as usual, was somewhat more discriminating, and a film version of Gorky's *The Mother* was even banned by Colonel Nasser for a few days for fear of revolutionary propaganda. Other exchanges included Soviet exhibitions and the appearance of Soviet artists, both collectively and individually, representing many fields of entertainment and artistic endeavor.

Radio Moscow also increased considerably its Arabic language broadcasts after 1955. The importance of the Soviet radio
has frequently been overrated, since Middle Eastern listeners were
not, as a rule, greatly excited by talks on cotton-growing in
Tadzhikistan, by songs in Uzbek, and detailed comments on the
Soviet constitution. They were more interested in wholesome
praise for the Arab nation, its great cultural achievements, its
tremendous courage, its undaunted stand in the struggle for
national independence, its progressive fight against reactionary
imperialism and aggressive Zionism—topics that were treated
with increasing frequency by Soviet broadcasters. However, even
in that field, Radio Moscow could not quite compete with the
highly emotional flavor of the "Voice of the Arabs"—and their
singers could not compete with Um Kulthum and Abdel Wahab.
Large youth delegations went from Egypt, Syria, Lebanon, and
even Jordan and Iraq, to the various youth festivals in East European capitals—such as the Moscow festival (the sixth) in the
summer of 1957. (The Syrian delegation alone came to 450
members.) The Egyptian press was very impressed by the enthusiastic reception accorded to the Egyptian delegation in Moscow.[17] Some young Egyptians and Syrians came to Russia and
other East European countries on a more permanent basis. There
were twenty-one Egyptian students, for instance, enrolled in the
faculty of physics at Moscow University in the winter of
1957-58.[18] All in all, the number of Egyptian students at Soviet
and East European universities was still small in comparison with
the many hundreds studying in the West. But the balance was
changing rapidly in 1958 as a result of financial difficulties and
political considerations.

This catalogue of Soviet cultural activities could be prolonged; the intention, however, is to point to some of the main
trends after 1955, not to give an exhaustive list. The Middle East,
more specifically the Arab world, was rediscovered by the Soviet
Union as a highly promising recipient of cultural exports in the
wake of the political 1955 *rapprochement*. Previously, no one
in Moscow had paid much attention to the area, and one of the
leading pro-Soviet spokesmen in Lebanon had even charged the
Soviet Union with neglect. "The Soviet Union," wrote Dr.

Georges Hanna, "did not reveal a sufficiently serious attitude. It confined itself to the sending of some Soviet films to the local branch of VOKS in Lebanon, and the mailing of a certain quantity of Soviet literature to a small group of people. This was the result, perhaps, of the policy of sectarianism that prevailed up to the Twentieth Party Congress."[19]

There is a close parallel between the Soviet cultural and political impact on the Arab world. The Soviet Union made a concerted effort to gain influence in the Middle East after 1954. The direct impact was not very great. Neither Fadeev nor Ehrenburg, neither the "Beryozka" dancing ensemble nor the Soviet weight-lifters that toured Egypt made many converts to the ideology of Marxism-Leninism; they only helped to strengthen somewhat the latent pro-Soviet feelings. If the general intellectual climate became palpably pro-Soviet and even pro-Communist, the cause was internal rather than external and the operative factor was the social and intellectual ferment within the Arab world. What appealed to the Arab intelligentsia was not straight Leninist ideology but the local adaptations, the potent mixture of populist, nationalist, and Communist elements that permeated the speeches and writings of the Egyptian and Syrian leaders of the radical "lower intelligentsia." (The differentiation between higher and lower intelligentsia was first introduced by Mao Tse-tung for China—and has much to recommend it in the Middle East.)

Various explanations have been offered by local observers in the Arab world for the emergence of this pronounced pro-Soviet cultural climate, but none is really convincing. Some argue that it was the natural reaction to the Arab's exposure to a Western materialism that was decisively rejected. But shifting one's sympathies to Soviet ideology would be a curious way of opposing materialism. Others said that it came as a protest against the "cultural imperialism" of the West, the activities of the Christian missions, etc. But the Christian missionaries have never really been regarded as a major threat in the Moslem world and it is well known that they never made many converts there. Soviet culture, far from being "anti-Western" in original inspiration, was the radical and uncompromising development of certain specifically Western theories of the nineteenth century. It was "anti-Western" only in the immediate political context of the fifties.

The Soviet-Arab cultural *rapprochement* was partly the result of a misunderstanding. A French historian already noticed in the early twenties in Asia "a veritable horror of European civilization. The Soviets are hailed and loved less for what they bring than for what they destroy."[20] Quite a number of people in the Arab world concluded that if Arabs and Russians had a common enemy, their positive interests would also coincide. Such misunderstandings are not really new; in the East, Napoleon had been hailed for a while as a great liberator because of his opposition to the Catholic Church.

But it was not a complete misunderstanding, for Soviet civilization is in some respects closer than Western culture to the feelings and aspirations of the intelligentsia in backward countries, as Soviet economic planning is preferred to Western capitalism—or a mixed economy. It was, or in any case professed to be, "closer to the people" than a rarefied, highbrow, Western culture accessible only to the happy few. "Socialist realism" may not be taken seriously in the West, but it did make more sense than *l'art pour l'art* in countries like Egypt, Syria, or Iraq. The neo-classicism of Soviet painting and music was more attractive, and in any case easier to understand and master, than Western modernism. If Soviet cultural propaganda had any serious competition in the Arab world, it was not from Henry James, Joyce, Valéry, or Proust but from American "mass culture."

Soviet progress in the natural sciences has been the source of much admiration (and concern) in the non-Communist world. Few people in the West have been overwhelmed by Soviet achievements in the social sciences, art, and literature. With a few notable exceptions, the work done in these disciplines has been dismissed as fairly crude and rather primitive. The very qualities that antagonized the West were the key to success among wide sections of the intelligentsia in the backward countries.

NOTES

1. See N. N. Kulikovich, "Ekspansiia Sovetskoi Kultury i Iskustva v Stranakh Arabskogo Vostoka" (The Expansion of Soviet Culture and Arts in the Countries of the Arab East), in *Vestnik Instituta po izucheniiu SSSR,* (Munich), March, 1957, pp. 99-109, and Ivar Spector, "Soviet Cultural Propaganda in the Near and Middle East" in *Soviet Survey* No. 16-17, 1957, pp. 16-22.

2. Jean and Simonne Lacouture: *L'Egypte en Mouvement* (Paris, 1957), p. 256.

3. Georges Ketman, "The Egyptian Intelligentsia," in *The Middle East in Transition,* (W. Z. Laqueur ed., New York, 1958), p. 481.

4. Lacouture, *op. cit.,* p. 402.

5. *Ibid.*

6. Most of these writers have not yet been published in Western languages. Soviet publishing houses began translating them in 1954. See *Egiptskie Novelli* (A. Goldman ed., Moscow, 1956), and *Rasskazy Arabskikh Pisatelei* (Stories by Arab Writers) (O. Konstantinov ed., Moscow, 1955).

7. Ketman, *op. cit.,* p. 482.

8. *Ibid.*

9. "Egypt Spurns Culture of 'Aggressor' States," *The Times* (London), May 17, 1957.

10. S. Kaftanov in *Sovetskaia Kultura,* October 25, 1956.

11. Abdel Rahman as Sharqawi in *Sovetskaia Kultura,* November 3, 1956.

12. Aziz al Shawan in *Sovetskaia Kultura,* October 28, 1956.

13. See A. H. in *Neue Zürcher Zeitung,* July 21, 1957.

14. *Sovetskaia Kultura,* December 21, 1956.

15. S. G. Areshian, "Gorky i Literatura Vostoka," in *Sovetskoe Vostokovedenie* (Moscow, 1945), pp. 177-182.

16. *Inostrannaia Literatura* 1, 1958, p. 281.

17. *Sovetskaia Kultura,* July 30, 1957.

18. *Sovremennyi Vostok* (Interview with Fathi Ridwan) 1, 1958, p. 35.

19. Georges Hanna in *Sovremennyi Vostok* 6, 1957, p. 12.

20. Sylvain Lévy in *Actes de la Société de Géographie,* May, 1924.

CHAPTER SEVEN

COMMUNISM IN THE MIDDLE EAST: 1955-1958

The great changes in Soviet policy in the Middle East after 1954 obliged the Arab Communists to adjust their line. For several years, especially during the era of Zhdanovism, their policy had been one of intransigence and self-imposed isolation. They had attacked not only the "feudal" elements at home but also left-wing, "reformist" forces and had proclaimed that only the victory of the Communist Party, the "vanguard of the working class," would bring salvation.[1] Their foreign political aims already coincided at that time with the views of other groups, but because of their unwillingness to compromise and to undertake political alliances with other groups, the Communists had no real influence on the course of events. After 1954 this began to change, the ideological justification being as follows: Lenin had argued that in the bourgeois national movement of oppressed countries there is a progressive nucleus which should be supported without reservation. The bourgeois national movement in the Afro-Asian countries fought for the liquidation of colonialism, and the defeat of "Western imperialism" was the main aim of the Soviet Union and the Communist movement as well, so there was a community of interest which could be the basis of an alliance. In this struggle the Communist Party should be the most extreme and *avant garde* group. "In this fight of Arab nationalism against imperialism, we cannot pursue any other aims, apart from the liberation of our fatherland and the victory of our people . . . ," one of the leaders of Arab Communism stated.[2] There had been alliances and "fronts" before, but this time it

294

was different; while in the past these alliances had been defined as "temporary" and "partial," this time they were to be "lasting" and "all-embracing." This did not mean that the Communists surrendered their final aim, namely, the victory of Communism, but anticipated that the struggle against the West would go on for a fairly long time, and the alliance with the national bourgeoisie would retain its usefulness for many years to come—possibly, until the country in question was firmly integrated into the Soviet sphere of influence. But would the national bourgeoisie be willing to go along with the Communists all the way? There was no certainty about that, but prospects were much better than in the West. In Western Europe and in America the Communists had to compete, when working with a national or popular front, with socialist and other left-wing parties, and had no monopoly on political organization or a distinct party program. In addition, Communism in the Arab world was assisted by the greatly increased prestige of the Soviet Union; the change in the international balance of power likewise tended to make the position of the Communists less complicated than in the thirties. Up to 1955, the general Communist view had been that the national bourgeoisie was weak[3] and that its interests were not identical with those of the Communists, both reasons obviating the necessity for any close collaboration. After 1955, a revision was made on both counts. The middle-class nationalists were not so weak, after all. On the contrary, "the national bourgeoisie has been considerably strengthened of late,"[4] whereas the industrial proletariat, which years before had been reported as "heading the struggle for freedom," was now said to be only at the *beginning* of its progress. Only the working class headed by its vanguard, the CP, (it had previously been said) could achieve national independence, for the class interests of the national bourgeoisie compelled it to compromise with its Western patrons. Now it was stated that the interests of the national bourgeoisie were essentially identical with popular interests, and the claims of the bourgeois national leaders in their dealing with the colonial powers were the objective reflection of the whole people united in the struggle for liberation.[5]

All this had become possible because Khrushchev and the

other Soviet leaders divided the world into three camps, the Soviet bloc, the hostile Western camp, and the neutral zone, (which should be a "zone of peace"), whereas for Stalin there had been only two camps, black and white. This Communist strategy, successful as it was, left two important questions open. The new alliance would be highly effective in creating that neutral zone of peace, (which was the Soviet minimum program), but would it be of any help at a later stage to make the zone of peace a Communist zone? Presumably not, but the Communist leaders preferred not to worry about developments that lay years ahead; by that time, they confidently expected, the leaders of the national bourgeoisie would have demonstrated their inability to solve their domestic problems and would be discredited. The Communists would be firmly entrenched and able to take over, and the Soviet Union, with the international balance of power tilted in its favor, would be in a position to exert pressure, if the leaders of the national bourgeoisie should prove uncooperative. In other words, they might try to turn against the Communists at a given stage, but they would not stand a much greater chance than Beneš and Jan Masaryk in Prague in 1948.

The other difficulty was merely a short-range one. If the Communist parties in the Arab world dropped so much of their Marxist-Leninist "ballast"; if they appeared as staunch nationalists, and almost nothing else; if they did not pursue (as they declared) any separatist, partisan aims, why should anybody care to join them rather than another nationalist Arab party? This could be a real obstacle, and the Communists had some difficulty in striking the right balance between respectability and subscription to the nationalist program in its entirety—and still retaining a sufficient measure of independence. Their main asset in this dilemma was affirmation that they were like everybody else in the national movement, only more so—namely, more radical in the fight against "Western imperialism" and in the struggle against the "feudal remnants" at home. Perhaps they did not unduly stress the fact that they were the only party to have a consistent theory of economic and social development, but the fact could not remain unknown to a generation of young Arab nationalists looking for solutions to the various problems besetting their countries. Hence, the great attraction of Communism, especially for the intelligentsia.

1. Egypt

The Communist movement in Egypt had been split into several factions ever since the early twenties. In the winter of 1947-48 an attempt to restore unity proved abortive, but in the autumn of 1955 some of the many existing groups were merged into one larger unit. Several important sections did not join it because of personal quarrels between the leaders of these groups as well as differences of opinion about organizational issues and the attitude to be taken to the military regime. One section of Communists and most of the fellow travelers had joined Colonel Nasser's movement; many of the key positions in newspapers, magazines, publishing houses, and the radio were in their hands. Colonel Nasser apparently did not mind the activities of the Communist intellectuals very much, whereas Communist trade-union organizers were regarded with considerably less trust and sympathy. Some of the influential dailies and weeklies such as *Al Massa* and *Rose al Yussef* were in "progressive" hands, and it was sometimes difficult even for initiates to differentiate accurately between Communist party-liners and President Nasser's spokesmen.

While the Communist Party continued to be suppressed (as were all other political parties), some of its front organizations, such as the "Partisans of Peace," were legal. The head of the "Partisans," Yussef Hilmi, who fled Egypt in 1953 and became a political émigré, returned to Cairo in late 1957 and was allowed to resume his activities.

The efforts to restore unity in the Communist camp in Egypt continued throughout 1956, and in September of that year a new central committee of the majority faction was elected at a meeting in Rome. The Italian Communist Party, and especially Velio Spano, its expert on foreign affairs, played the role of conciliator and mediator and apparently took a leading part in the negotiations between the various groups.[6]

However, even then three of the main factions preferred not to join the "Rome" Central Committee; only in June of 1957 did one of these groups declare its readiness to join. On this occasion a manifesto was addressed to the Egyptian people that reflected fairly accurately the party line regarding the regime. On the whole, the party was optimistic, since the Arab nation was growing and winning many victories. Egypt was at the threshold of a new kind of parliamentary life and had taken a step toward strengthening democracy and granting political and trade union liberties.[7] Colonel Nasser's government was wholeheartedly supported; "for the first time in its history contemporary Egypt rejoices in a national government." There was another reference to valiant President Nasser, and one of the slogans at the end of the manifesto read, "Long live our National Government headed by Gamal Abdel Nasser." If all was well, and was going to be even better, who needed a Communist Party? The reply to this question was provided, not very convincingly, in another manifesto published by the secretariat of the Egyptian United Communist Party at about the same time.[8] "We support the general orientation of President Nasser's policy; we are not in agreement with him, however, on certain questions of internal policy—such as his attitude to political parties in general, and to the existence of a legal Communist Party in particular." Further on, the Communists made it clear that they were not so much concerned with the principle of political freedom in general ("Because all political parties are *not* in the same category") as with their own group. However, here they were obviously on weak ground; if they were indeed, as they had defined themselves, "the best defenders of our national government led by valiant President Gamal Abdel Nasser,"[9] and if Nasser said he did not need a legal Communist Party, the Communists were obviously not in a position to challenge his opinion. It was a natural development, in a sense, for the Communists had given up so much of their own distinctive program, and the "national government" had borrowed from them so heavily in its propaganda, that the dividing line had become increasingly blurred.

One Communist group, the Egyptian "Communist Party of Workers and Peasants" (formerly the "Vanguard of the Workers"), still remained outside the new, unified party and great efforts were made to include them, too. Negotiations and ideological discussions continued for about ten months, and on January 8, 1958, the first session of the new Central Committee of the united party was convened in Cairo both to celebrate the newly achieved unity and to adopt a new program.[10] A new secretariat and Politburo were also elected at that Cairo convention. For the first time in 35 years, it was said, a unified Communist Party of Egypt was again in existence.*

These developments within Egyptian Communism did not adversely affect the relations between Egypt and the Soviet Union. Some observers had assumed that Moscow would have to choose between the friendship of Colonel Nasser's government and support of Communism in Egypt—just as it had had to choose between Kemal Ataturk and Communism in Turkey in the twenties. If events in Egypt did not follow the same course, the causes are not too difficult to divine: the Soviet Union in the twenties was isolated and much weaker; the Bolsheviks needed Kemal at least as much as he needed them. In addition, the alliance with Turkey had a mystique and national ideology of its own, and was not greatly influenced (and not even much interested) in Soviet and Communist ideas. Nasser's Egypt was much more exposed to foreign ideological influences.

2. Syria

Communism in Syria had emerged from the Shishakli dictatorship as "the only organized force on the field of battle,"[11] the following years being described by a Soviet observer as a period of the "irresistible growth of the authority of the Syrian Communist party."[12] The main political aim of the party was to establish a "national front" through which it could operate;[13] such a front came into being in 1956. This national front has been described as the "union of all the forces of the country

---

* It should be mentioned, however, that even after January, 1958, one faction remained in opposition to the new united party. This was the "Egyptian Communist Party" (Bolsheviks) that had come into existence as the result of the merger (also in January, 1958) of two smaller groups, the "Democratic Vanguard" and the "Communist Union." It was anti-Nasser and was denounced in a leaflet of the new united party as comprising "deserters from the national movement" (see Appendix III).

against imperialism, and for the cooperation of the Arab states in the field of economic development."[14] With the exception of a few flunkeys of imperialism who were beyond redemption, everybody could join this national front and was in effect invited to do so.

To make the position of the Communist Party within the National Front easier, Khaled Bakdash appeared in the Syrian parliament with rather sweeping statements that his country was, and would remain, "Arab nationalist and nothing else in addition." In an interview with an Egyptian weekly he went on record as saying that he was "above all an Arab nationalist." Communism and Arab nationalism could exist side by side very nicely, and in any case, his party would not get entangled in partisan strife until Syria was altogether liberated from imperialism."[15]

This did not depend only on the Communists, and the decision of the Ba'ath in January, 1958, to opt for union with Egypt no doubt came as an unpleasant surprise. No Communist Party had ever voluntarily dissolved itself, Khaled Bakdash said when asked about the fate of his movement in the United Arab Republic. But it was not at all clear whether and to what extent Colonel Nasser would want to force the Communists to discontinue their activities; the Communist newspapers, in any case, continued to appear in Syria after the merger.

If a period of new trials was ahead, the Syrian Communists certainly could face it with considerable confidence. Their prestige and influence were higher than ever before, for they held commanding positions in all three Syrian trade-union confederations and in various intellectual popular-front organizations that had been founded by them (such as the Arab Writers' Congress, the Lawyers' Association, etc.), and among the youth, student, and teacher groups their position was almost unassailable. In addition, there was the submerged but very important section of the party: the members in the army command, the internal security forces, and those who had been won over from, or had infiltrated into, other political parties.

In the past, anti-Communist groups had thought they possessed two effective sticks for belaboring the Communists. Communist atheism, the struggle of the party against religion, had been one of the main propaganda assets of the Communists' political enemies. But for a long time prior to 1958 the Communists had abstained from any antireligious activity; on the contrary, they had tried hard, and successfully, to win over a number of leading religious dignitaries to their front organizations. Similarly, the Syrian Communist leadership had taken care that there should be no room for accusations of "weakness" in their stand on Palestine. Previously, they had been accused of being "soft" towards Israel, of favoring the 1947 partition plan rather than the "liberation of Palestine." Since 1955, however, they had taken great care to be second to none in their extremist slogans.

All in all, the Syrian Communists had become respectable patriots;[16] they had little to fear from political rivals whose aims and intentions coincided with their own short-range political program. Their open activities would probably be restricted in the future, but they would continue to exist and be active, as they had in similar circumstances before. Khaled Bakdash, in any case, was optimistic about the prospects of his party when interviewed by a Czechoslovak newspaper after the union had taken place.*

3. Lebanon

Beirut had long been the political and organizational center of Communism in the Arab world. But Communism had never been able to make great headway in Lebanon, and if the Lebanese Communist Party figured prominently in the news between 194? and 1952 as the result of a concentrated effort to attract general attention through demonstrations, rallies, and the publication of countless leaflets and appeals, there came an inevitable anticlimax to this hectic but artificial activity. After 1953, Communist demonstrations in Beirut and other Lebanese cities began to attract fewer and fewer people and soon ceased altogether.

A short revival in 1955 produced the usual May Day manifestoes and demonstrations[17] and some national-front activities, such as Communist participation in the "Day of the Martyrs,"[18]

* *Rude Pravo,* February 27, 1958.

as well as protests against the Baghdad Pact on the occasion of
Mr. Menderes' visit to the country, but nothing more important.
The reasons for this relative failure are manifold. One was the
all-pervasive influence of the *esprit de clan* in the country, the
fact that many citizens still felt a primary loyalty to their ethnic
minority or religious group rather than to the country or the
nation. In these conditions, political groups that tried to base
themselves on a nation-wide organization faced considerable
difficulties. In addition, some Lebanese political leaders who had
followed Communist activities in previous years with little interest and less concern became alarmed as the result of the
growth of Communism in neighboring Syria. Thus, certain re-
pressive measures were adopted to curb Communist activities in
the country.

The only achievements of the Communists were in the "popular-front" field, the collection of 230,000 signatures for the
Vienna manifesto of the "Partisans of Peace." The split that occurred inside the Lebanese left in October, 1956 (when some of
the pro-Nasser elements left the Progressive Socialist Party of
Kamil, Jumblat), did not apparently involve the local Communists.

Lebanon was a source of disappointment to the Communists,
and the Syrians tried to so something about it in January, 1958.
Shortly after Khaled Bakdash's return from a visit to Moscow,
the Central Committee of the Communist Party of Lebanon and
Syria was convened and decided to launch a new and more
militant campaign against the Lebanese government, which, it
was said, "had become a hotbed of imperialist conspiracies against
Syria and Egypt"; "Lebanese enmity to all Socialist countries,
among them the Soviet Union, the best friend of Lebanon," was
strongly condemned. However, soon afterwards the Syro-Egyp-
tian union took place, with the subsequent curb on Communist
activities in Damascus. The Communists participated with other
opposition groups in the struggle against the Chamoun government from May to July, 1958, without, however, greatly en-
hancing the influence of the party.*

* Some of the party's manifestoes were extremely violent in tenor: "Let
us fight the greedy invaders and exterminate its fifth column with every

4. Jordan

The Jordan Communist Party, acting through the "National Front" established in May, 1954,[19] reached its apogee of success in 1956. The party had several deputies in parliament, and one of its representatives was a cabinet minister. Through its alliance with the Ba'ath and Sulaiman Nabulsi's National Socialists it had considerable political influence, particularly among youth and student organizations. Dr. Abdel Rahman al Shukair, who emerged as the party chief in Amman, was one of the leaders of the mass demonstrations against General Templer during his visit to the Jordan capital in December, 1955, and in January, 1956. All in all, the situation strongly resembled the state of affairs in Syria. King Hussein and the conservative elements were put increasingly on the defensive and had to give in to the demands of Nasserite and Communist leaders step by step.

When King Hussein decided to make a last stand against his cabinet and parliament, he chose the issue of Communist propaganda in Jordan. In late January, 1957, a new Communist newspaper[20] had begun to appear, and in a note to his prime minister, Hussein demanded its suppression, as well as a ban on all other Communist and pro-Soviet propaganda.[21] The Nabulsi government ignored this order, and the king took this and an alleged military conspiracy against him (in April of that year) as a pretext for deposing the government, dissolving parliament, and carrying out a purge in the Arab Legion command. Part of the officer corps of the Arab Legion (the Jordan army) had been won over by the opposition, which tended to orient itself, however, toward Cairo rather than Moscow before the Iraqi revolution in July, 1958.

This coup from above was successful; all the opposition groups were dissolved, the Communist leaders had to flee to Syria or were caught and imprisoned, and a period of strong

---

weapon in your possession. Kill them wherever you find them with the bullets of your guns and machine guns. Aim your bombs at them, attack them with everything that comes to your hands, tear them with your teeth," etc., etc. (Statement of the Lebanese CP, July 21, 1958). The political effect was apparently in inverse ratio to the violence of the language.

repression of the party began. It was assumed at the time that King Hussein and his entourage would not be successful in this struggle, even temporarily, for public opinion was overwhelmingly against them. As subsequently appeared, however, public opinion was not too strong either, being restricted in effect to the small middle class and the intelligentsia of the major cities of the kingdom. Whether in the long run the support of the Bedouin and the officer corps would be enough to prop up the regime appeared less certain.

5. Iraq

The Communist Party of Iraq had been illegal in 1958 for the previous ten years.[22] In addition, the party had been weakened following the arrest of successive party politburos—the last in mid-April, 1953,[23] and also as a result of internal splits. A semiofficial report in 1955 enumerated three active Communist sections,[24] and on several occasions the internal conflicts came out into the open in public accusations and counteraccusations.

Communist activities continued, nevertheless. The party concentrated its efforts on propaganda among secondary-school and university students, among whom it had held a commanding position since 1949. Communist sources claimed that, in 1954, 85% of all students of secondary and higher institutions of learning belonged to the General Association of Iraqi Students (dominated by the Communists), which had continued functioning even after the government had suppressed it.[25] Among the peasants, too, Communists were more active than before: the "Association for the Liberation of the Peasants" was banned by the government, but according to Communist sources it succeeded in establishing a minor Soviet republic in the Kut el Hai area in November, 1956, which lasted for several weeks.[26] Subsequently, the Communist Party organized the submission of petitions to the government under the general slogan of "land and freedom," with, however, less spectacular results. It is difficult to judge whether the Communist Party merely tried to exploit the existing discontent in the countryside, or whether more ambitious schemes for the establishment of the nucleus of a partisan army were involved. The main aim remained, needless to add, the struggle against the Baghdad Pact, and the party repeatedly declared its willingness to collaborate with all other opposition groups against Nuri as Said and Fadhil Jamali. Meanwhile, among the opposition, the new Ba'ath group grew stronger, while the influence of the traditional oppositionists, such as Kamel al Jadirji, somewhat decreased. Many Western observers expected the financial boom of the middle fifties to work wonders. But it should be remembered that the boom did not affect everybody in the country, and certainly not all people to the same extent. Moreover, economic development schemes, however desirable in themselves, could not possibly solve the social and political conflicts that were at the bottom of the Iraqi malaise.*

6. Sudan

There has been a curious disproportion between the strong position gained by the Communist Party in the Sudan in the trade-union movement, and also in sections of the urban intelligentsia and among the peasants in the northern region—and the comparatively light impact of the party on the political life of the country ever since the Sudan gained independence. The Federation of Sudanese trade unions has been under Communist control since the very beginning (1950) and has faithfully followed the Communist lead ever since in its adherence to the WFTU, and in its activities on behalf of the "Partisans of Peace" and other front organizations.[27] Communist activities in the Khartum schools and colleges, and among the peasants of the Al Gezira region go back even further. It was expected that these strong footholds would gradually be reflected in terms of political influence, such as successful pressure on the government or the assumption of a leading role in the organization of the opposition, and, of course, in election results. All that happened, however, was that the Communists established an "Anti-Imperialist Front" which collaborated with the "National Unity" party and other groups in forming a united opposition—but which by no means dominated the opposition.[28] In terms of election results,

* See Appendix III, "Iraq, Nasser, and the Communists," for a short survey of developments after July, 1958.

too, the Communists were unsuccessful. While Communist control of the trade unions remained a great political asset of the party, a number of other factors apparently inhibited its growth, above all the fact that, for historical reasons, anti-Westernism was less acutely felt in the Sudan than in other parts of the Arab world. Sudan's interests did not clash directly with the West, and Israel was far away, while relations with Egypt tended to be less than cordial at times. Nor was there the same desperate urgency as in Egypt with regard to economic and social problems: more land and water, and less population pressure make the Sudan more promising ground for economic development and progress than Egypt.

7. Israel

Communism in Israel had stagnated since 1955, which in itself was no mean achievement. For Soviet policy since 1954 had been one of clear and unequivocal support for the Arab countries, whereas the attitude toward Israel could hardly have been more unfriendly. The Israeli Communists had to support Soviet foreign policy, and had, in addition, to justify the policy of Russia's allies in the Middle East, Egypt, and Syria. This meant that the Israeli Communist Party had to favor a return to the partition program of November, 1947, as the basis of a solution; it had to attack the "aggressive and bellicose" policy followed by the Ben-Gurion government and to contrast it starkly with the peaceful attitude displayed by Colonel Nasser and the Syrians. It had to oppose the Suez war, and to support the Arab governments, whatever the occasion and the reason for their current conflicts with Israel. It was not surprising that the party did not win any new sympathizers in these circumstances, that most of its front organizations were paralyzed, and that part of its "periphery" was estranged in the process. The hard core of Jewish party members, nevertheless, remained faithful, and for the Arab Communists (about a third of the total, or slightly more), Soviet support for Nasser and Iraq was certainly no reason for great dejection. At one time, in the winter of 1957-58, the feasibility of an "Algerian development was discussed in party circles—the establishment of a nucleus of an anti-Israeli guerrilla army on Israel soil. Practical considerations were, however, against it, and the idea was dropped—at least for the time being.

Another factor that strictly limited the appeal of Communism among the Jews to the true believers was Russian policy on what is commonly defined as "the Jewish question" inside the Soviet Union.

8. The Anticolonial International

Whatever its ultimate place in history, the Afro-Asian Solidarity Conference in Cairo (December 26, 1957, to January 1, 1958) provided a most interesting illustration of Communist tactics and policies in the Middle East. The meeting stressed the common struggle against the West and was attended by official delegations from the Soviet bloc, Egypt, Syria, Yemen, and the Sudan, by unofficial representatives drawn largely from Communist-front groups by most other African and Asian nations, and by exiles from Jordan, Iraq, and other places who were self-appointed delegates from their native lands. The conference established a permanent council and a secretariat with its seat in Cairo—the nucleus of a new International.

The idea of holding this Afro-Asian Solidarity Conference was first proposed by R. Chandra, a member of the central committee of the Indian Communist Party, at the Stockholm meeting (November, 1954) of the "Partisans of Peace." The first conference of this new body took place in New Delhi in April, 1955, but was not an outstanding success. It was overshadowed by the Bandung Conference; Nehru and other Asian leaders did not view it with much favor, and the Soviet and Communist inspiration behind the new organization was still too obvious to make it of real value as a "front." Only two and a half years later had conditions ripened for a more successful conference. In view of the close *rapprochement* that had meanwhile taken place with some of the countries concerned, the Soviet and Communist organizers could take a back seat and leave their politically less obviously committed colleagues in the limelight—which had been the original intention.

Parallels have been drawn between the Cairo conference in 1957, the famous Baku conference in 1920 and the Amsterdam congress arranged by the "League Against Imperialism and Colonial Oppression" in February, 1927. There are, however, important differences that should not be overlooked. In both these congresses (which remained isolated incidents and were not followed up) "Westerners" had taken the initiative, whereas at the Cairo meeting Europeans were not invited at all, not even "anti-imperialist," "anti-Western" Europeans. Even the considerable percentage of natives of Asian Russia tried to remain in the background. (An interesting parallel between the Amsterdam and the Cairo conferences was provided by the fact that, though both were organized and controlled by the Communists, in both cases indignant Communist protests were made against such slanders: did not the majority of delegates belong to other political groups?)[29]

No mention was made in Cairo of the man who many years earlier had originated the idea and worked out the strategy for a Colonial International. Mir Sayid Sultan Oglu, Sultan Galiev as he was known in Russian, was born in Kazan around 1890. As a young man he joined the Socialist Revolutionaries, then the Mensheviks, and finally, in the autumn of 1917, the Bolsheviks. In 1918 he became one of Stalin's chief lieutenants in the Commissariat of Nationalities. One of his main tasks was editing the Commissariat's organ, *Zhizn Natsionalnostei*. Before long, Sultan Galiev was accused of "nationalist deviations" and in 1923 he was arrested. After his release from prison he did not return to Soviet politics, and in the purges of the thirties he disappeared.[30]

Sultan Galiev's ideas about colonial revolution, subsequently developed further by some of his friends and disciples, were first set forth in a series of articles in October and November, 1919, in *Zhizn Natsionalnostei*. Forty years later these articles make extremely interesting reading. The following were his basic arguments:

1. Classical Marxists are making a mistake by concentrating their attention and hopes on the industrially developed West. The backward countries of the East provide a far more fertile territory for Communism.

2. The backward nations of the East are more truly progressive than the working class in the West; they are the real pro-

letarian nations. It is extremely doubtful whether any community of interest exists between the Eastern countries and the Western working class.

3. The establishment of a dictatorship of the proletariat in the West would not be tantamount to world revolution; it would only mean the perpetuation of Western rule over the rest of the world. Real change could only be brought about by a dictatorship of the colonial peoples over the metropolitan nations.

4. Since all classes in the Eastern countries have been subjected to Western rule and exploitation, there is no room for a class struggle. Communist policy should be based on an alliance between all classes, including the upper and middle classes.

5. A new International of colonial peoples should be created. It should be independent of the Comintern, though Russia should participate in it. The leading roles in this new International must be taken by the ex-colonial peoples themselves, above all by Moslem representatives. In the Soviet Union of 1919 these views were anathema. Less than forty years later almost all of Sultan Galiev's basic tenets had been accepted in such countries as Egypt, Syria, Iraq, and Indonesia. They were also adopted (on the tactical level, in any case) by the Soviet Union, and thus formed the basis of an understanding between Moscow and the "progressive" countries of Asia and the Middle East.

By 1957 it had become one of the basic assumptions of Soviet foreign policy that the opportunities for expanding Soviet influence were much more promising in the Middle East and Asia than in the industrial West. Similarly, radical nationalist leaders in the Arab world and North Africa contended that their peoples were, on the whole, more progressive than those belonging to left-wing movements (even the Communists) in the West. Thus, *Al Mujahid*, organ of the Algerian FLN, declared in December, 1957, that there was no link between its followers and the French Left because the French worker was also participating in the exploitation of Algerians.[31]

Sultan Galiev's strictures against class war have been accepted in the United Arab Republic and tacitly approved by Moscow for the time being. Cairo regards this as a permanent condition, though Moscow evidently considers it only as a transient stage in the development of Middle Eastern Communism.

Finally, Sultan Galiev's outline for the new Colonial International was followed quite closely. The Soviet Union and the Communist parties of the respective countries prepared the Cairo conference but did not take a leading role at the meeting. They conducted themselves like "guest artists," as one friendly observer put it, even though "they were organized with an efficiency which in guests was almost tactless."[32]

The resolutions adopted by the Cairo conference were not of outstanding interest. They included the routine appeals for the preservation of world peace, the cessation of atomic bomb tests, condemnations of the United States, France, Britain, and Israel, denunciation of imperialism in general, as well as certain recommendations for economic, technical, and cultural cooperation between Asian and African countries.[33] It was, however, of considerable interest to note that though the words "Communism" and even "Socialism" were not once mentioned in these long documents, the resolutions faithfully reflected the Communist line (down to small details, such as the condemnation of the European Common Market). Dependent countries were advised not to accept any capital investment in the form of subsidies or loans, because this would only result in exploitation and would not serve the interests of the countries concerned.[34]

More important, perhaps, were the organizational decisions aiming at propaganda campaigns, the establishment of a council, a permanent secretariat (to be made up of the Egyptian secretary-general and ten members, and to be located in Cairo), and the publication of a magazine.[35]

In Cairo, the Soviet government and the Communist parties were willing to accept a policy they had rejected thirty-five years earlier for fairly obvious reasons. When the idea of a Colonial International was first presented, Pan-Islamism was still a disruptive force in Russia, and Moscow could not rely on Moslem Communists such as Sultan Galiev, let alone fellow travelers like Enver Pasha, who deserted at a decisive moment and joined the opponents of Soviet rule in Turkestan. By 1958, Central Asia had been tamed and partly de-Islamized. For the first time in Soviet history, a Communist of Moslem origin, Nuritdin Mukhitdinov, was made a member of the Presidium. As far as the Soviet domestic scene was concerned, there was no longer any reason to shun close contact with the national movements in Moslem countries. The basis of the new organization was the Soviet-Arab alliance, for not a single non-Arab country was officially represented, and the Colombo powers, in particular, had misgivings about the attempt to relate the Cairo "Conference of the Peoples" to the Bandung Conference of heads of governments. Nevertheless, the new organization offered certain possibilities from the Soviet point of view: it was not in a position to make any important political decisions, but it provided a convenient propaganda outlet under the cover of anti-imperialism, positive neutralism, and other respectable causes. The new organization was certainly not intended to be a new Comintern. It merely constituted a new center for the backward countries of Asia and Africa where strong Communist parties did not yet exist, and where the straight Leninist line could not be applied. The new "Colonial International" was to provide a pre-Communist ideological and organizational framework which combined nationalist and anti-Western motifs with some Leninist conceptions (notably the Leninist theory of imperialism) and support of the Soviet Union, the "best friend of the Asian and African peoples." In time, it was presumed, this would lead to something along more orthodox Communist lines. Egypt's interests were somewhat different: "Egypt has now entered the field of leadership, not only in the Arab world and Africa, but also in that Asia which is turning away from Europe."[36] It is probably true to say that Russia and China did not dictate a party line in Cairo, for those assembled at the conference had reached the same, or in any case very similar, conclusions themselves. "If Russia leads at all, she does it from behind," wrote a sympathetic observer.[37]

9. Some Recent Developments

The Communist movement in Iraq received a strong impetus in the wake of the Baghdad revolution in July, 1958. The Iraqi party reported in its first manifesto (published on July 14) that it had participated fully in the revolutionary movement. Pro-Communist leaders who had returned from emigration or emerged from illegality soon attained positions of command in the nation's political life. Abdel Fattah Ibrahim was appointed director general of the oil refineries administration. Dr. Ibrahim Kubbah became Minister of Economics, and Major Salim al Fakhri was made director general of broadcasting. More important than the appointment of individual leaders were the opportunities that came to exist for the party as such. Owing to their superior technique of organization, the Iraqi Communists emerged on the day after the Baghdad coup with their "cadres" intact, in contrast to the other political groups. The Communists made the most of their advantage, organizing local militias, people's resistance groups, Committees for the Defense of the Republic, etc., which brought them into conflict at an early date with the new government, which, in its majority, was then not Communist-inspired. Administrative measures taken by the new government somewhat impeded Communist activities at first, but did not prevent the growth of the party into one of the country's leading political forces. The Communists, on the other hand, did not want a showdown with the new government at that early stage but pledged their support to the nationalist government and chose to infiltrate the new administration. The situation in Iraq in the summer of 1958 resembled the state of affairs in Syria in early 1954, after the downfall of the Shishakli regime; political conditions in Baghdad were even more conducive than in Damascus four years earlier to further Communist progress.

In the United Arab Republic, meanwhile, the Communist front organizations had received freedom of action but the party itself had not been officially permitted to resume its activities. This in itself was, from the Communist point of view, a considerable advance in comparison with the state of affairs in 1955, but the Communists demanded more than that. In an article in the first issue of the new central organ of the United Egyptian Communist Party, *Itihad al Sha'ab* published in June, 1958,[38] they complained that the dissolution of political parties in Syria (in contradistinction to Egypt) was a step backwards, a disservice to the cause of democracy. They argued that Colonel Nasser's "Liberation Movement" was a state party rather than a national front uniting various "progressive" groups; the Communists, needless to mention, were in favor of the former. Quoting with approval a recent statement by Ali Sabri, Colonel Nasser's chief aide, they declared that "the most intelligent representatives of the national bourgeoisie in Egypt" had already drawn the obvious lesson, namely, that Egypt would have to follow the "Chinese way." In China, the Communists and the parties of the national bourgeoisie "cooperated just as amicably in the construction of socialism as they had collaborated in the anti-imperialist struggle." Egyptian Communists assume that the present national union in their country is a temporary alliance of basically incompatible elements, and that they will gradually gain control by winning over the nationalist "left wing," by neutralizing the "center," and by outmaneuvering and eventually defeating the groups opposed to cooperation with the Communists.*

NOTES

1. For Communist policy in the Middle East in the early fifties see W. Z. Laqueur: *Communism and Nationalism in the Middle East* (New York, 1956), pp. 154-64.

2. Khaled Bakdash, "Oktyabrskaia Revoliutsiia i Arabskii Vostok" (The October Revolution and the Arab East), *Pravda*, November 11, 1957.

3. L. Vatolina in *Sovetskoe Vostokovedenie* No. 1, 1956; translation in *The Middle East in Transition* (W. Z. Laqueur, ed., New York, 1958), p. 488 *et seq.*

4. L. Vatolina (ed.): *Araby v Borbe . . .*, (Moscow, 1957), p. 18.

5. L. Vatolina, see note 3.

6. *Unità* (Rome), September 14, 1956. Spano had been in Egypt as a political émigré from Fascist Italy.

* Khaled Bakdash, writing in the first number of the international Communist journal *Problems of Peace and Socialism* (September, 1958, p. 70), stressed the same point: the ban on the Communist party in the United Arab Republic was an absurdity; the Communists would continue their work for the ultimate aims, the hegemony of the proletariat and the Communist party. Bakdash returned to Damascus in October, 1958, but was again compelled to leave his native Syria in late December, following new restrictions on Communist party activities imposed by President Nasser's government. See Appendix III, "Iraq, Nasser, and the Communists."

7. This manifesto was originally published on July 1, 1957. The references to the "parliamentary life of a new type" were somewhat premature, for only a handful of Communists were eventually elected to the new parliament (and not under that label); some known Communist candidates were debarred.

8. *World News*, November 23, 1957. This was in reply to an interview given by President Nasser to the American magazine *Look*.

9. *World News, loc. cit.*

10. *Unità*, February 1, 1958, quoted in *Neue Zürcher Zeitung*, February 8, 1958.

11. L. Vatolina (ed.): *Araby v Borbe* . . . , p. 234.

12. *Ibid.*, p. 245.

13. Resolution of the Central Committee of the Syrian Communist Party adopted in May, 1956, in L. Vatolina, *loc. cit.*, p. 246.

14. *Al Talia*, May 9, 1955.

15. *Al Musawwar*, February 1, 1957.

16. After November, 1956, the Syrian Communist press began to call for the destruction of the state of Israel.

17. *Al Talia*, May 9, 1955.

18. L. Vatolina (ed.): *Araby v Borbe* . . . , p. 303.

19. See E. A. Lebedev: *Iordania v Borbe za Nezavisimost* (Jordan in the Fight for Independence) (Moscow, 1956), p. 96 *et seq.*

20. *Al Jamaheer*, Rushdi Shahin (ed.).

21. *Al Difa'a*, February 4, February 8, 1957.

22. For the history of the Iraqi Communist Party prior to 1955, see Laqueur, *op. cit.*, pp. 173-203.

23. A. F. Fedchenko in *Araby v Borbe* . . . , p. 391.

24. *Iraq Times*, April 5, 1955.

25. Fedchenko, *op. cit.*, p. 363.

26. Tareq Mohammed in *Sovremennyi Vostok* 5, 1957, p. 15.

27. See Saad ed Din Fawzi: *The Labor Movement in the Sudan* (London, 1957).

28. *Al Sudan al Jadid*, January 27, 1957.

29. For interesting details about the way the Amsterdam Congress was financed and controlled, see Margarete Buber Neumann: *Von Potsdam nach Moskau* (1955). Mrs. Buber Neumann was the sister-in-law of Willy Muenzenberg, a leading German Communist in charge of organizing popular- and national-front initiatives at the time. For similar Soviet protests against allegations of Communist inspiration at the Cairo conference see *Novoe Vremia*, January 9, 1958, and E. Zhukov in *Mezhdunarodnaia Zhizn* 2, 1958, pp. 69-76.

30. Further details about Sultan Galiev are found in A. M. Arsharuni and Kh. Gabidullin: *Ocherki Panislamizma i Pantiurkizma v Rossii* (Essays on Pan-Islamism and Pan-Turkism in Russia) (Ryasan, 1931), and Alexandre Bennigsen: "Sultan Galiev—The USSR and the Colonial Revolution,"

in W. Z. Laqueur (ed.): *The Middle East in Transition* (London, 1958), pp. 398-415.

31. *Al Mujahid* 14 and 15, 1957, translated and discussed in *L'Observateur*, January 9, 16, 23, 1958.

32. George Crawford (of the *Egyptian Gazette*) in *Middle East Forum* (Beirut), March, 1958. See also the semiofficial report: *Afro-Asian Peoples Solidarity Conference* (Moscow, 1958).

33. The resolutions were published as an appendix to *Sovremennyi Vostok*, January, 1958.

34. *Ibid.*, p. 17. There were some contradictions, however, for elsewhere, on p. 15, foreign loans were approved in principle—on condition that no strings were attached.

35. Russia and China had an assured majority in the permanent secretariat, for the delegates of five other countries (India, Cameroon, Syria, Indonesia, and the Sudan) in this body were not governmental representatives but either Communist Party members or fellow travelers.

36. Crawford, *op. cit.*, p. 33.

37. *Ibid.*

38. The English translation of this article was published in *World News*, August 9, 1958. See also Maxime Rodinson, "Les Problemes des Parties Communistes en Syrie et en Egypte," *Cahiers Internationaux* 93, September, 1958, pp. 76-86.

CHAPTER EIGHT

COMMUNISM AND ARAB NATIONALISM

For the last few years radical nationalism has been the strongest political force in the Arab world. Like an irresistible tide, it has swept everything before it. It has successfully defied the West and restored to many Arabs a feeling of dignity and confidence; the decisions about the future of the Arab world that were once made in London and Paris are now taken in Cairo. According to many Western observers, the Soviet alliance with the Arab world has been so successful because it was concluded with Arab nationalism rather than with any individual or government. Arab spokesmen, on the other hand, maintain that dynamic Arab nationalism is now the only barrier in the Arab world against the spread of Communism or the expansion of the Soviet orbit.[1] An appraisal of Arab nationalism is, therefore, of crucial importance for any examination of Soviet policy in the Middle East.

Such an appraisal is a thankless task, for Nasserism, as one astute Arab observer has put it, is "not an ideology but an attitude of mind,"[2] and it is notoriously more difficult to analyze states of minds than ideologies. To paraphrase a well-known definition of a nation: Arab nationalism is a political fact corresponding to a state of mind.*

* Colonel Nasser, his colleagues, and his regime have variously been defined as "left wing" and "rightist" in the West; he has been acclaimed as a new Garibaldi and denounced as a second Hitler. He was hailed in the Communist press as a great liberator and staunch anti-imperialist while certain extreme right-wing publicists in the United States, Britain, and Ger-

Writings on the relationship between Communism and Arab nationalism are not plentiful, are usually confused, and suffer from a lack of knowledge of at least one of the factors involved.[3] The proponents of Arab nationalism are very definite about the foreign political aims of their movement: they want Arab unity, they oppose the imperialist and colonialist West, they stand for "positive neutralism," and they would like to see a progressive transformation of Arab society. Unfortunately, it is almost impossible to receive authoritative answers to most of the remaining questions, such as the relationship between Arab nationalism and Islam, the social and economic structure envisaged by Arab nationalism, its stand between democracy and dictatorship, its economic conceptions, and so on.[4] Some argue that Arab nationalism is so potent and vital a force that it need not justify itself by providing replies to all kinds of topical and specific questions. Others believe these issues to be of secondary importance. But most say that "we shall cross these bridges when we reach them." The primary task of Arab nationalism is to achieve unity and the other national aspirations; afterwards, the domestic problems will have to be tackled. Most of the speeches and writings on Arab nationalism deal with foreign affairs rather than domestic issues.

The three basic concepts of Arab nationalism are independence, unity, and neutralism. There is no need to define inde-

---

many have approved his policies with almost equal enthusiasm. Some liberals, too, have given him critical support. The radical movement in the Arab world combines ideas and policies of the extreme left and right wing without acknowledging a basic contradiction between them. Historical comparisons with nineteenth- and twentieth-century Europe are of limited value, because conditions in the Arab world are so completely different. Nationalism in the Middle East is post-liberal—any comparison with the liberal-democratic spirit that imbued, say, the Italian *risorgimento* is wishful thinking, at best. It is neither pro- nor anti- but pre-Communist; a confrontation on the ideological level has not yet taken place. Nasser's regime does contain Fascist elements but, for the time being, at least, it is a more genuine movement of "national liberation" than the Fascist regimes in Europe. It is a modern dictatorship in the sense that it has realized the need for popular support, a radical social program, and an "activist" foreign policy. But, on the other hand, it can not be totalitarian, because the prerequisites for such a regime do not yet exist in Egypt or Syria.

pendence in the present context; numerous problems are involved, but these are mostly intra-Arab issues that have no direct
bearing on the relationship between the Arabs and the rest of
the world. The struggle for Arab unity is based on the belief
that there is one Arab nation, and that the artificial dividing lines
drawn by the West after disintegration of the Ottoman empire
should be eliminated at the earliest possible moment. The precise
limits of the united Arab state envisaged have never been clearly
outlined. At present the struggle for Arab unity is an internal
Arab affair, chiefly involving the mobilization of popular feeling
in some of the smaller Arab countries, with a view to overthrowing the ruling forces that oppose a merger with the United Arab
Republic. If radical Arab nationalism should retain its "dynamic"
character, there is reason to anticipate trouble between a united
Arab nation and its neighbors (in North Africa, in the Sudan,
with Abyssinia over Somaliland, with Turkey over Alexandretta,
with Persia over Bahrain, with Israel, of course, and perhaps elsewhere). This will mainly depend on the success or failure of
the unity movement in coming years, and on the ambitions of
the movement's leadership; it would be premature, however, to
comment on potential sources of conflict in a part of the world
where there is an abundance of very real present conflict. The
whole issue has been greatly complicated, in addition, as the
result of the rift between Nasser and the Ba'ath, on one hand, and
the Communists and their allies in Baghdad and elsewhere, on the
other. The protagonists of both camps appear as authentic spokesmen for Arab nationalism. The following survey is chiefly concerned with Nasserism—for the time being still the stronger
faction.

The main issue at stake is the origin and character of Arab
neutralism, or "Positive Neutralism." It is, as Arab spokesmen
admit, a somewhat one-sided affair; the anti-Western theme is
dominant in the Arab concept of neutralism. It would perhaps
be more to the point to define it as "Cold War Non-Belliger-
ency"; but this also is unsatisfactory on second thought. For
the weapons of the cold war are propaganda, and it would be
difficult to argue that anti-Western propaganda emanating from
the UAR is much milder than that coming from the Soviet

Union. "Positive Neutralism" ultimately means negative identity, the wish of the leaders of the UAR (and presumably a large segment of public opinion throughout the Arab world) to continue its struggle against "Western imperialism and colonialism" in collaboration with the Soviet Union—while preserving their own national independence. For this hostility toward the West there are, according to Arab spokesmen, good historical reasons. Hostility toward the West has been latent for many years, but the conflict entered its acute stage with the peace treaties that followed World War I, for they disappointed and greatly offended Arab opinion. Frustration over Palestine followed, and when World War II ended, "bitterness against the West had been so deeply entrenched in the Arab heart that the partial fulfillment of some of the Arab national aspirations failed to ease it."[5] Nevertheless, even in 1954-55 this neutralism was latent and potential rather than a real political factor; it was a "practical neutralism" rather than a profound political reorientation. However, Western attitudes, far from being sympathetic and understanding, stiffened; instead of averting further alienation, there were threats, economic pressure, and punitive sanctions. This in turn accelerated the drift toward neutralism, and transformed what was an isolated event and could have remained so (according to some Arab sources) into a firm trend in Arab foreign relations. What had originally been a pragmatic act then became a doctrine, because the West had "pushed the Arabs into the Russian arms."

Another Western attitude that was claimed to have stimulated an Arab-Soviet *rapprochement* was what was described as the reprehensible practice of "international McCarthyism," namely, the labeling of bona fide Arab patriots as Communists or Communist stooges.

Some of this criticism may be justified, while some of it is either exaggerated or simply wrong. It could be argued, for example, that the charges of pro-Communism made by the West had a certain restraining influence, since the Arab nationalists did want to preserve their freedom of maneuver between East and West and knew that they would lose that freedom if the West wrote them off altogether. It has been argued, therefore, that these charges, whether justified or not, acted as a deterrent, and that in the absence of these accusations the flirtation with the Soviet Union would have proceeded much further than it actually did.

There is some doubt, however, about whether all these arguments and counterarguments are really relevant. Assuming that the West had not made any mistakes, and assuming that it had supported all the demands of Arab nationalism in the Middle East and Africa—would that have radically affected the Arab stand? Would Arab nationalism have joined the West or would it at least have maintained an attitude of friendly neutrality? According to the spokesmen of the Arab national movement, neutralism would have prevailed in any case, because it was the logical and natural orientation of their camp. And there are two good reasons why it would not have been a neutralism friendly to the West. One is the fact that in a Soviet-Western competition for the favor of the Arab world, the Soviets would have prevailed anyway, since totalitarian regimes are better equipped than democracies both for wooing and for making war. The second reason is that from the Arab point of view any alliance with or sympathetic attitude toward the West would have been purposeless, for alliances and friendly relations in politics have to be based on common interest or a common outlook. The political ideas of radical Arab nationalism were not identical with, or similar to, those of the West, and while they were not identical with those of the East, either, Soviet political techniques proved to be more attractive. Most Arab contributors to recent debates on fundamental political issues have been critical of Western democracy—not merely because of its "anti-Arab policy" but because it is seen as an unsatisfactory system *per se*, one that "paralyzes the dynamic forces of the nation." "Liberty is not necessarily identical with democracy . . . Liberty is synonymous with sufficiency of food, clothes, housing, hygiene . . . ," one of them has declared.[6] Such a definition is clearly nearer to the Eastern, than the Western, idea of democracy and liberty.

If the Arab arguments about the true character of Arab nationalism are accepted, then the Soviet attitude toward the movement becomes incomprehensible. If radical Arab nationalism is indeed, as Colonel Nasser and many other spokesmen maintain, the only effective barrier against Communism in the Middle East, it would not be very intelligent for Soviet statesmen to support such a movement and give it more than platonic, temporary assistance. Why should Russia deliver great quantities of arms and give hundreds of millions of dollars to a regime that wants to stem Soviet and Communist influence in the Middle East? The differences between this regime and the West may be only temporary, and in a few years a strong "bourgeois" Arab state hostile to Communism could indeed constitute an effective barrier to Soviet ambitions in the Middle East.

One possible line of argument is that the Soviet leaders are very stupid, that they do not see how events are developing, that they are basing their policy on a miscalculation, and so on. This assumption can hardly be taken seriously, for evidence from all over the world indicates that Soviet statesmen are quite realistic and do not, as a rule, act against their own interests.

A more likely resolution of the apparent paradox is the assumption that the Soviet leaders do not pay too much attention to official Cairene and Damascene declarations about the policy and aims of Arab nationalism and are mainly concerned with the objective results of these policies. As one Soviet Asian expert put it succinctly: "These parties and groups may set themselves, and actually do set themselves, as history shows, very limited aims . . . for the Marxist-Leninist, what is important is not so much the subjective tendencies as the objective consequences of those actions and their real historic importance."[7] At this juncture there is a surprising parallel between the Western and Eastern appraisals of radical nationalism in the Arab world. Both sides believe that what the Arabs think about their own policy is of only limited interest and that what matters is not the speeches and articles, but the objective results of this policy and the general direction of developments in the Arab world. There are apparently no great differences of opinion between the West and the Soviet bloc as to the general direction of this trend. The main difference is that the West has been viewing this development with considerable alarm, and the Soviets with hardly disguised enthusiasm. Both West and East could be wrong in their appraisal. To find out more about the reason for Soviet optimism, a closer look at the political, social, and economic ideas of Arab nationalism may be necessary.

Radical Arab nationalism is so strong and vital a force, many of its proponents say, that all Arabs take it for granted; there is no need to justify it, to think about it, and to define it. It is based on religious mystagogy and certain Islamic ideas—and yet it is not essentially religious; it has borrowed from Fascism, Communism, and Kemalism, and yet none of these terms actually fits it. It occasionally uses Pan-Islamist motives (that go back to Amir Shakib Arslan) and, at times, racialist argumentation first evolved by Kawakebi. Sometimes it bases its arguments on the theory that everyone who speaks Arabic is a member of the great Arab nation (Sati al Husri) and sometimes on the conception of a manifest cultural destiny (such as developed by Constantine Zurayk). It would be mistaken to look for consistency and originality in this curious mixture. But similar difficulties have been faced by many nations, not only the Arabs, and a clear definition of nationalism is by no means an urgent prerequisite for a strong national movement. On the contrary, the vague ideological character of Arab nationalism is a distinct advantage, for by its very vagueness it accommodates a considerable variety of views and outlooks.

What is more interesting here is the social philosophy of radical Arab nationalism. People can exist without a precise definition of what makes them a nation distinct from others, but the absence of clear ideas in the social and economic field will have more immediate and graver consequences—especially in backward countries. Colonel Nasser gave the fullest exposition of his social philosophy in a long programmatic speech at the General Cooperative Conference in Cairo (on June 1, 1956). It could be summarized as follows. In the past Egyptians felt that they were feudal serfs, dominated, exploited, and tyrannized, that the entire country was the property of a small clique of exploiters. Then came the revolution, which proclaimed its intention to exterminate feudalism, initiate agrarian reform, and limit ownership. The revolution declared that it was against the domination of government by capital, not against capital itself. Capital had begun to depart from its natural function of regulating investment and increasing production and the national income—instead, corrupt capital had been seeking to dominate the government. The revolution aimed at converting an opportunistic and reactionary society into a new one free of opportunism and reaction, founded on cooperation, work, and production. The social philosophy of the revolution should be given a chance to develop, and the nonexistence of parties did not mean that social thinking or even class thinking was prohibited. Social thinking (i.e., socialism) should develop, provided it was based on law and the constitution. The ideal was a community in which worker cooperated with proprietor, a community free from monopoly, political despotism, foreign influence, and social injustice. All the sons of the homeland were to work in one united national bloc without dissension, free from envy and hate. The entire homeland was to cooperate, all working for the benefit of the community.

Eighteen months later Nasser provided several further explanations and amplifications:[8] the social revolution was a long revolution, and one had to proceed by stages. Each stage determined the commitments and detailed plans to be pursued in the next. One should not jump stages, and should not import foreign methods—one should proceed according to the particular inspiration of the Arab nature. Prosperity could not possibly prevail in a society if exploitation remained in any form, whether it was exploitation of man or social, political, or economic. He wished to build a socialist, democratic, and cooperative society, free of exploitation. The socialism he had in mind aimed at raising the standards of the majority of the people, not the minority which had profited in the past. He wanted to destroy opportunist individualism, but did not want state capitalism. The state was to play its role together with the people. He did not want to destroy or liquidate capitalism, and considered national capital a necessity for the development of production and the national economy. But to prevent exploitation, one had to keep an eye on capital. His aim was not the elimination of ownership, which was safeguarded by the constitution. He believed in national, rather than opportunistic, individualism.*

There are other social and economic views within the radical Arab nationalist movement that are not quite identical with Colonel Nasser's opinions. The Ba'ath party, which was originally founded in Syria and later spread to other Arab countries, is slightly to the left of Colonel Nasser. It has been more outspoken in stressing its social program and in the past has attacked the conservative stand of the *ulema,* whereas Colonel Nasser has shied away from any direct clash with Islam and its representatives. According to the old Ba'ath program, the basic principle was "liberty in all its forms," and the party was in favor of a republican regime and parliamentary democracy. Administration was to be decentralized, and the state "socialized"—i.e., presum-

* There are some interesting parallels in the attitudes of Arab nationalism and the early Kuomintang toward social and economic doctrines. In his third principle (*min shêng*) Sun Yat-sen advocated modernization and industrialization, land reform, state capitalism, and confiscation of unearned increment (while permitting private ownership of land); he wanted to thwart the accumulation of large private capital and envisaged a Communist society as the end goal. At the same time, he opposed the class struggle and believed that the supreme loyalty of the Chinese was to their race-nation. His attitude toward Communism was full of contradictions. A Marxist critic noted that "objectively, this was not socialism at all but something else entirely. Lenin had coined the formula 'subjective socialism' for it . . . It was a 'social' economic policy, that is, a policy friendly to the masses." (Karl Wittfogel: *Sun Yat-Sen, Aufzeichnungen eines chinesischen Revolutionaers* [Berlin, n.d., ca. 1927], pp. 67-68.) See also P.M.A. Linebarger: *The Political Doctrines of Sun Yat-sen* (Baltimore, 1937). The vague character of *min shêng* was a source of much exasperation to Western observers. One of them, friendly disposed to Sun Yat-sen, wrote: "The doctrine of *min shêng,* with respect to its positive social-economic content, may appear vague to the Western student, and he may surmise it to be a mere cloak for unscrupulous demagogues. It could easily do that in the West, or in the hands of insincere and unscrupulous leaders. In China, however, it need not necessarily have been formulated more positively than it was, because, as we have seen, the intellectual temper of the Chinese makes any strict adherence to a schedule or a plan impossible" (Linebarger, *op. cit.,* p. 152). And yet more recently the Chinese intellectual temper has accommodated itself to very strict adherence to plans of all kinds. The advantages of vagueness in economic and social thinking in the Arab world today are as doubtful as they were in China thirty-five years ago.

ably to be taken over by the Ba'ath. However radical the slogans, the party never stated clearly what it really wanted, what sector of the national economy it wished to nationalize, what kind of economic planning should be introduced, nor how much of it. Its propaganda was essentially anti-imperialist and antifeudal, and though it did stand for some kind of agrarian reform, its program remained exceedingly vague in other respects. Until 1957, Colonel Nasser was criticized by the Ba'ath for the lack of democracy in Egypt, but this did not prevent the Ba'ath from asking Nasser, in January, 1958, to accept their new program for immediate and complete unity between Egypt and Syria. This tends to indicate that the ideological differences were not really very important. There is a left wing within Colonel Nasser's movement, consisting of former Communists or former members of the junta who have embraced a diluted form of pro-Communism or *progressisme*. In their occasional writings, these men have called for a larger measure of planning, nationalization, and state intervention. But on the whole, this wing has also distinguished itself more by its support for the policies of the Soviet Union in world affairs than by any clear ideas about what should be done in Egypt.

Before trying to evaluate the social ideas of radical Arab nationalism, credit should be given to the positive achievements of Nasserism in Egypt. Colonel Nasser's regime was the first to carry out a number of progressive (without quotation marks) and long-overdue reforms. His government was the first to carry out a major land reform in the country. True enough, this reform has affected only a small percentage of the peasants, because Egypt's agrarian problem cannot be solved by the redistribution of land—there is simply not enough of it. But it was politically important, for it broke the political power of the big landowners. The regime established hundreds of new schools. It gave a fresh impetus to industrialization. It abolished antiquated titles (Pasha, Bey) and carried out a program for the embellishment of the Egyptian capital.

This was more than any previous Egyptian government had done for many a year, and one could ask whether these achievements alone were not enough to justify Nasser's policy and create a solid basis for his regime. The answer is in the negative, for, despite all these necessary and welcome reforms, the economic situation of the country continued to deteriorate, and living standards remained stationary or declined. These achievements might have been enough for any other government, but not for Colonel Nasser's, for he had promised a radical transformation of Egyptian society, and he had unleashed social and political forces that regarded his reforms as a mere prelude to the future.

Nasserism was quite unprepared to solve the pressing internal problems of the Arab world. Thirty years earlier, an Egyptian party had declared that it wanted socialism without Communism plus Fascism without despotism, plus democracy without anarchy. Most party programs in the Arab world in the last generation had been similar, promising everything to everybody. The Syrian Ba'ath had also been famous for its sweeping promises: it had promised land to the landless peasants and credits to the rich peasants, higher wages to workers, and credits to "national capital," better pay to the army and to state employees, and more investments in the productive sectors of the national economy. It had promised better and more extensive social services, greater economy in the nation's budget, higher living standards, and rapid economic development. It could be argued that such slogans need not be fatal if the men behind them are cynics who know that they are intended to gain votes and political support, and that it would be possible (at most) to realize *one* of these aims to the detriment of the others. Unfortunately, they tried to tackle them all at the same time, but none in earnest.

The economic and social doctrine of Nasserism is made up of many conflicting and mutually exclusive ingredients. The style is reminiscent of the rhetoric of the French revolution: violent attacks on separate party and economic interests and calls for national unity (*amour sacré de la patrie*). There is more than an element of Bonapartism, or, to give its more modern name, Peronism, the Colonel being the only patron of the Egyptian *descamisados* against their exploiters. There is also the solidarism of Othmar Spann, Professor Salazar and others, calling for class collaboration instead of class struggle.* Then there is the Islamic socialism of Khaled Mohammed Khaled—himself a confused though sincere thinker—and an enthusiastic acceptance of Mao Tse-tung's ideas, the bowdlerized Asian version of Marxism. In addition, there is an invocation of the spirit of Bandung, a few quotations from Aneurin Bevan, the "genius of the national revolution," and the *Protocols of the Elders of Zion*. This combination is called "Arab Socialism."[9]

Such a conception, though neither consistent nor practical, could perhaps work in some other part of the world, less beset by immense problems calling for urgent solution. To someone faced with tremendous, immediate problems, as Colonel Nasser is, this strange mixture of half-baked ideas cannot be of much help. In these circumstances, good will and enthusiasm are not enough, and the Communists, who possess a practical social and economic program, have a great advantage over "Arab Socialism" in the long run.

This is why the Soviet leaders have not hesitated to support radical Arab nationalism. They are apparently convinced that this movement will not be able to build a sound economic and social basis for a strong state that would somehow act as a "barrier to Communism." They have expressed their belief that Colonel Nasser's regime (alternatively defined as "national bourgeois" or petty bourgeois) will be unable to solve the basic

* There are great differences, both as to origin and character, between the various movements that go under the name "solidarist" in the West. French *solidarisme* (such as developed by Alfred Fouillée and others) was notably influenced by Herbert Spencer and social Darwinism. The solidarism of Othmar Spann and Professor Salazar was based, *inter alia*, on the social teachings of the Catholic Church. The solidarism of the NTS, a Russian émigré movement, has still a different origin. Common to all these movements, however (and to the Egyptian variety), is the attempt to reconcile conflicting class interests and clashing doctrines. Their position squarely reflects (as a historian of French *solidarisme* has put it) "the interests of the petty bourgeoisie midway between the big bourgeoisie and labor; it wants to head off the revolutionary movement by a policy of partial reform." Egyptian solidarism is more radical in character; the need for reform was more urgent in Egypt in 1952 than in the France of *la belle époque*. Nor is the big bourgeoisie a social or political factor of importance in present-day Egypt.

internal issues of the Arab world. They know that these problems are most urgent, and that there may be an explosion and a general breakdown, or both, in the foreseeable future unless something drastic is done. If this happens, as they expect it to, political power will pass from Colonel Nasser into the hands of more radical forces, a process that will continue until a (Middle-Eastern-style) Communist regime emerges.

But is not the Soviet view too pessimistic about the future of Arab national socialism? Is it altogether inconceivable that Nasser could somehow muddle through? Are not the Russians unduly dogmatic in their anticipations? The Soviet leaders are not concerned with what may happen in the immediate future; they are thinking now in terms of a decade or two. It is quite possible that Colonel Nasser's rule may alleviate the situation temporarily. It has done so already in some respects, and its chances would increase if it could get hold of the Saudi and Kuwaiti oil revenues.

But this is counterbalanced by a "dynamic" foreign policy that may precipitate, rather than delay, an explosion. The forces that have come into motion in the Arab world seem too strong, the expectations too high, the pressure of unsolved economic and social questions too overwhelming, for temporizing and muddling through. Soviet expectations regarding the future of radical Arab nationalism are by no means unrealistic.

Arab nationalism has not yet produced a serious critique of Leninism—in fact, it has hardly taken notice of it. This is not altogether surprising, since these two ideologies have been moving on different levels and have not had to clash so far. Arab nationalists have argued that Soviet Communism developed in conditions very different from those of present-day Egypt, and that its methods are, therefore, not applicable on the whole. They have pointed out that Chinese Communism might be more helpful as a model for Egypt and the Arab world. But they have never explained in detail what features of Soviet Communism were not applicable to Egypt, and why, nor have they discussed or shown how Chinese Communist achievements could be transplanted to the Arab world without adopting Leninism-Maoism in the political field as well.

Communist ideology has been criticized in the Middle East for not making a serious attempt to accommodate itself to Arab nationalism: "Of nationalism itself, it is acutely aware; but it is a stereotype of nationalism, an abstract, lifeless, colorless phenomenon, related only incidentally and casually to the aspirations of a specific people, inhabiting a specific geographic territory and sharing a unique cultural heritage," says Nuseibeh.[10] This point is well made, but since these lines were written, Arab Communism has made great efforts to accommodate itself more and more to the nationalist movement. This has not proved too difficult, for it merely involved paying lip service to (or even sincerely embracing) a few slogans about a great heritage and a collective destiny. The Communists have no quarrel with the Arab nationalists as long as the latter concentrate their efforts on the struggle against the West. They would find it difficult to be accepted in the Arab national movement only if the movement had a positive social content that conflicted with Communist ideology.

A closer examination tends to bring out certain nuances in the radical Arab nationalist attitude toward Communism. There is a right-wing conservative group that subscribes to the Soviet alliance but is not too enthusiastic about Communism in the Arab world. The writers who have propounded these views belong mainly to the older generation, and it is difficult to say whether they have much public backing, though there is some reason to assume that they have the support of several members of the Cairo junta.[11] There is a left-wing, or rather pro-Soviet, group that suggests Communist solutions for Egypt, while, of course, strongly emphasizing its attachment to the ideals of Arab nationalism and the leadership of Gamal Abdel Nasser.[12] And there is a "centrist" group that (without being Marxist) favors an adaptation of certain Soviet policies and methods, but not others, and dislikes Communist competition at home.[13]

In view of the "non-ideological character" of Arab nationalism, these differences are probably less important than they would be elsewhere; in addition, the common struggle against the West has hitherto overshadowed their very existence. An internal differentiation along these lines seems, however, extremely likely at some future date, and the Communists undoubtedly believe that their sympathizers will carry the day. The right-wingers have nothing with which to oppose Communists but a few general slogans about the great destiny of the Arab nation and the need to preserve Islam; in a country like Egypt, the most important question, however, is "What should we do now?" and to this, the Abbas Mahmoud al Akkads have no answer. In addition, Communists have learned since Hitler that they must never neglect nationalist agitation, and it can be taken for granted that they will be second to none in their zeal for the Arab cause. As for the "centrist group," it is apparently assumed that they will have to borrow more and more from Communism, whereas the Communists will show considerable latitude about the local application of Communist solutions. While only the future will show whether these Communist assumptions are overoptimistic, it is true that at present the Communists do not have much to fear from competition.

The Soviet attitude toward Arab nationalism has been analyzed elsewhere in the present study. It should suffice to say, in this context, that Soviet students of Asian affairs have seldom commented on this subject. This absence of comment, especially in recent years, is certainly not accidental: the Soviet authors realized, of course, that the subject would be an extremely ticklish one in view of possible foreign political complications. Arab Leninists have on occasion made no secret of their conviction that all the talk about a national philosophy and the special character of Arab nationalism was mere idealist nonsense;[14] there was no special Arab mission, they said, there were only special Arab needs. Of late, Arab Communists have refrained from such polemics in order not to offend nationalist sensibilities and to avoid leaving themselves open to attack.

By and large, Communist policy toward the national movement in such countries as Egypt and Syria has been surprisingly consistent in the long run. The very first Communist documents dealing with these issues, published almost forty years ago, give authoritative advice that is still followed today vis-à-vis the Arab national movement. In his first draft of the theses on colonial policy for the Second Comintern Congress, Lenin wrote that "lower-middle-class prejudices, national egoism, and narrow-mindedness" are particularly developed in backward countries, that these prejudices could be eradicated only very slowly, and that the Communists would have to compromise in order to remove them.[15] On another occasion, at about the same time, a group of Middle Eastern Communists was told that the time for Communist revolution had not yet come in their country. They would have above all "to exploit the nationalist movement," and only later would the internal class differentiation emerge within the nationalist movement.[16]

In some Asian countries this internal differentiation has taken longer to develop than the Communists expected at the time, and they have made greater tactical concessions than they perhaps originally anticipated. But on the whole, they still follow the guidance given in 1920, and not without success.

Radical Arab nationalism has set out under unfavorable circumstances—despite all contrary appearances. It could be argued that it is unfair to expect this movement to solve the social and economic problems of the Arab world. Most national movements have arisen to solve national, rather than domestic-social, issues. It is the historic misfortune of radical Arab nationalism that it appeared on the scene when the solution of the social issues had become so urgent, when a purely "national revolution" had become impossible. A national revolution alone, in other words, would have accomplished little, and could not have a lasting effect unless it were accompanied by drastic social changes and economic reconstruction. If the national movement is unable to provide guidance and leadership in this field, then it will ultimately fail in its "national aspirations" as well.* It could be argued

* This has been (partly) realized so far only by the "left wing" of Nasserism. Ahmed Baha ed-Din, writing in *Rose al Yussef* (September 15, 1958), says that it is "essential, and possible, that these two revolutions proceed simultaneously. Successful national revolutions in modern times must have a clear social content; it has been proved that the social revolution serves the national revolution to a very great extent, since it rallies more and more of the masses around the nationalist movement . . . and those are the masses which have a stake in social progress and reform.

"But although the two revolutions should go together, they do not do so to the same degree under all circumstances. The social revolutionary must that the Turkish and Mexican revolutions of a generation ago, though perhaps somewhat more fortunate in their leaders and their political ideas, had much in common with the radical Arab nationalism of the middle fifties. They succeeded in their task, established a powerful revolutionary mystique, and made success for their political adversaries (including the Communists) extremely difficult.

If the outlook for the Arab national movement is much less promising, it would be unjust to put the blame entirely on the failings of its leaders. It must be admitted that the economic and social tasks facing this movement are much more formidable and urgent and that for historical and geographical reasons the conditions for success are far from ideal. A latecomer among the "national revolutions," Arab nationalism has had much less time before it to accomplish its tasks.

NOTES

1. Fayez Sayegh, "Arab Nationalism—the Latest Phase," in *Middle East Forum*, November, 1957. *Idem: Arab Unity* (New York, 1958).

2. W.K., "Political Trends in the Fertile Crescent," in *The World Today*, June, 1956.

3. Cf. Abdel Salam al Ajili, "Al Arab wa'l Shiyu'iya fi'l Ahd al Jadid" in *Al Adab* (Beirut), November, 1957, and Abbas Mahmoud al Akkad: *la Shiyu'iya wa la Istamar* (Cairo, 1957).

4. Cf. Hazem Zaki Nuseibeh: *The Ideas of Arab Nationalism* (Cornell University Press, 1956).

5. Sayegh, *loc. cit.*

6. Ali Baddour quoted in Nissim Rejwan, "Arab Nationalism," in *The Middle East in Transition* (W. Z. Laqueur ed., New York, 1958), p. 163.

7. E. M. Zhukov in *M. Zh.* 9, 1957.

8. This is a summary of a long speech, on the basis of the English text

---

discard a lot of reforms in the interest of the national revolution, since, before any social theory can be put into practice, it is essential first to have a free homeland in which to do this. It is the national revolution that furnishes us with this free homeland! When this revolution is accomplished and safeguarded, the only basic duty becomes to push the social revolution to its utmost limits. But while the national revolution is proceeding, the progressive has two fronts to consider."

in *BBC Summary of World Broadcasts*, Part IV, Daily Series No. 421, December 7, 1957, pp. 1-20.

9. See the discussions on Arab nationalism reviewed in Rejwan, *op. cit.* Also *Al Qawmiyya al Arabiyya* (*Ikhtarna-laka* series, Cairo, 1957) and Abdel Moneim Shemis: *Nahwa Mujtama Ishtiraki, Dimokrati, Ta'awuni* (Toward a Socialist, Democratic, and Cooperative Society) Kutub Siyasiyya (Cairo, 1957).

10. Nuseibeh, *op. cit.*, p. 177.

11. The writings of Mohammed Hassanein Haikal and Abbas Mahmoud al Akkad are typical of this trend.

12. See, for instance, Fathi el Ramli: *Anta Muttaham bi'l Shiyu'iya* (You are Accused of Communism), (Cairo, 1957), and Mohammed Kamel al Bindari and Abdel Rahman as Sharqawi: *Rad ala Mabd'a Eisenhower* (A Reply to the Eisenhower Doctrine), (Cairo, 1957).

13. Typical of this "centrist" thinking are, for instance, Mustafa al Sakharati: *Idiologiya Arabiyyah Jadida* (Cairo, 1957) and Fakhry Labib and Mahmoud al Mistiqawi: *Al Ittihad al Sovieti wa Misr al Mustaqilla* (The Soviet Union and Independent Egypt), (Cairo, 1957).

14. Raif Khouri in his controversy with Constantine Zurayk in the late thirties.

15. *Die Kommunistische Internationale*, No. 11, 1922, p. 1698.

16. Sultan zade at the first Congress of the Persian Communist Party "Adalet" in Enzeli as reported in *Die Kommunistische Internationale*, No. 14, 1922, p. 2939.

CHAPTER NINE

CONCLUSION

A survey of Soviet-Middle Eastern relations would be incomplete without at least some brief reference to recent events. One of these was the outbreak of civil war in Lebanon early in May, 1958, sparked off by the assassination of a journalist. Widespread demonstrations turned into riots and, eventually, into guerrilla warfare. After a week of this sporadic fighting, Soviet reports described it as "an anti-government insurrection of an anti-imperialist and anti-U.S. character." From then on, the Soviet reactions followed the pattern they had developed in the Suez crisis of 1956 and the Syrian crisis of 1957. Statements by the Soviet leaders and TASS were mainly warnings against any military intervention by the West, accompanied by appeals for high-level meetings, declarations of support for the just cause of the Arab liberation movement, and, of course, sharp attacks against the West and its supporters in the Middle East, including threats against Turkey, Israel, and other countries.

On May 18, in the first major official statement on the subject, the West was warned that any attempt to intervene in Lebanon would imperil world peace. The Soviet press noted with gratification the successes of the opposition's forces, and reported the emergence of quasi-Soviets ("People's Committees") all over northern Lebanon. When reports of infiltration from Syria and the smuggling of arms were received by the outside world, the Soviet press and radio issued counterreports about threatening intervention from Iraq and Jordan, and the alleged presence of American officers masquerading as tourists, who were said to be actually directing the fighting on the government side in Beirut. Early in June, the idea of a United Nations force was first mentioned—and bitterly opposed by the Soviet Union as a design by the United States and Britain to occupy Lebanon under the United Nations flag. Moscow opposed the strengthening of the group of U.N. "observers" which had been introduced by decision of the Security Council and charged with a "fact-finding mission." Still, Soviet spokesmen welcomed this group's report, when it said the observers had been unable to find much evidence of intervention by the United Arab Republic.

With the Iraqi coup in mid-July, 1958, and the prompt landing of American troops in Lebanon and British troops in Jordan, Beirut ceased to be the storm center of the Middle Eastern crisis, which shifted to Amman and Baghdad. Fighting went on in Lebanon, but on a diminished scale, until the grounds for a temporary compromise between the rival parties had been found.

The civil war in Lebanon was the result of a deep internal division, not of the traditional (Western) kind between Left and Right, but between attitudes of approval and dissent towards Arab nationalism as personified by Colonel Nasser, and what this meant for the country's orientation in world politics. At the same time it was obvious that, without encouragement and help from abroad, the civil strife could not have attained such proportions nor have continued so long. The Christians in the country, with few exceptions, favored a pro-Western orientation and the continuance of national independence vis-à-vis the Arab world, while most Moslems stood for solidarity, if not union, with the United Arab Republic.

The Lebanese government had been democratically elected, in contrast to the governments of most other countries in the Middle East. But revolutionary movements have never been much deterred by legal considerations: what mattered in the last resort was that those who opposed the government were more willing to fight in the streets for their opinions than were the supporters of the regime. Soviet support for the opposition could be counted upon in view of the government's pro-Western orientation; it would also serve to prop up the alliance between Nasser and the Soviets, in which some cracks had by then become noticeable.

Nasser and some of his colleagues had visited the Soviet Union late in April and during the first half of May in this same year,

1958, and had received a most cordial welcome. In their many meetings with Soviet leaders, Communist sympathy with Arab aspirations had been continually emphasized, hospitality had been lavish, and promises of material aid no less impressive. A "common declaration" published at the end of this state visit announced that unanimity had been reached upon all questions discussed.[1] "Nasser is not a Communist," said Khrushchev on a subsequent occasion, "but I understand him, and he understands me." The political agreements (or understandings) arrived at were not made public, but were no doubt upon such subjects as the aims of the United Arab Republic in the Arab world, toward Israel, and in North and Central Africa. That Nasser could be sure of general Soviet support in these directions was obvious enough; the question was how far the Soviet Union might be willing to commit itself. Had Khrushchev really pledged material aid for the unification of the Arab world under Nasser's leadership? If so, what did he expect in return?

There was some evidence that the Soviet leaders expected something beyond "positive neutralism." Shortly after Nasser's return from Moscow two incidents occurred that were noted as signs of irritation or dissatisfaction on the part of the Soviet government. One was an article in *Trud*, early in June, attacking an Egyptian editor who had accompanied Nasser on his return trip, and who had then published, in an otherwise undistinguished article, some supposedly uncomplimentary remarks about the prevalence and quality of ice cream in Russia and other subjects. *Trud* angrily denounced him for spreading "calumnies about the Soviet Union."[2] If it were true, as the Soviet paper added, that all other Egyptian journalists were reporting "objectively and honestly," it did not make sense to be so touchy about this single exception at a moment of ostensibly excellent relations between the two countries: for two years past no such criticism of Nasser's Egypt had appeared in the Soviet press. It looked as though the attack were meant as a warning to persons in higher authority than the editor, Mustafa Amin—perhaps to those who permitted the publication of any such slanderous remarks.

And there was more to come. Relations between Belgrade and Moscow had again deteriorated during the first half of 1958 and reached a new breaking-point in the early summer of that year. Yet Colonel Nasser did not cancel his long-planned visit to Yugoslavia. True, the Communists put the blame upon Belgrade as the seducer, rather than on Cairo, the seduced. Speaking at the Congress of the Bulgarian Communist Party, Khaled Bakdash, the exiled Syrian party secretary, complained bitterly of the disruptive activities of "Yugoslav revisionists" in the Arab East, who not only tried to divide the Arab Communist movement and isolate it, "but . . . also did their utmost to destroy the friendship between the Arab peoples and the Soviet Union."[3] However, the revolution in Baghdad on July 14, of course, overshadowed these misunderstandings and cemented the alliance anew—temporarily, at any rate.

On that day the Hashemite monarchy and the Nuri as Said government were overthrown in a coup by a number of army officers: the new government stood for radical Arab nationalism; most of its leaders had belonged to extremist right- or left-wing groups and had joined forces in order to supplant the old regime. This was immediately hailed in Moscow as a victory of the people;[4] the Soviet delegation at the United Nations called upon the United States not to proceed with the armed intervention which had been the immediate response of America and Britain to this new situation. The Soviet reaction again followed a familiar pattern: *Pravda* denounced the action of the U.S. as "a direct act of war and open aggression";[5] it was hinted that, unless this was stopped, volunteers would arrive from the Soviet bloc countries, and the announcement was made that Soviet land and air forces had begun maneuvers in the military districts of Turkestan and Transcaucasia. Meanwhile Nasser had turned back on his way home from Belgrade and flown to Moscow; and there, according to a semiofficial communiqué, his meeting with Khrushchev had been of exceptionally great importance and would have far-reaching consequences.[6] Details about this, it is needless to mention, were not revealed at the time. Whether Nasser had implored Khrushchev (as Cairo reports suggested) to take no action in the Middle East that might jeopardize peace, and whether Khrushchev told him that "volunteers" were standing ready at Soviet airports for immediate departure if requested, is rather doubtful. For the Soviet attitude in the U.N. and elsewhere was one of moderation. The United States request for a U.N. police force was vetoed; instead, the Soviets appealed for a special session of the General Assembly and an immediate five-power conference in Geneva to prevent the crisis from developing into a world war. *Pravda* called for a solution to be sought in a spirit of "reason, calm, and thorough negotiation."[7]

The subsequent wrangle over a "summit" conference is of no direct interest in the present context. For several days Soviet propaganda constantly accused the West, and above all the United States, of trying to prevent a summit meeting by procrastination. But after Khrushchev's visit to Peking at the beginning of August, the Soviet Union retreated from its own "summit" proposal, presumably because of Chinese objections: Peking doubtless resented the prospect of so important a big-power meeting being held without its being invited.* By that time, too, the immediate danger of war was past, although the war of words continued between the West on the one side and the Arab Republicans and the Communists on the other. The Baghdad Pact Powers were convened in London (and described in *Pravda* as "a conclave of conspirators designing fresh acts of aggression against the Arab countries"), while Turkey received its traditional note from Moscow, accusing it of planning to attack Iraq and sharply warning it of consequences if it did. However, the new Iraqi government was formally recognized by both Washington and London, and in Lebanon General Fuad Shehab, a compromise candidate, was elected President. The midsummer crisis of 1958 had been overcome, or rather, things were temporarily patched up when the Arab delegates to the United Nations announced in mid-August that they would solve their internal conflicts within the framework of the Arab League.

The Iraqi revolution can be assigned to no single cause; it was produced by events upon several different levels. There was the revenge of the army commanders against Nuri as Said, who had hanged some of their fellow officers for taking part in the pro-

---

* There had been some earlier evidence of a more violent Chinese reaction to the Middle Eastern crisis. *Pravda* (July 19, 1958) reported a vast mass meeting of indignation, thirty-four hours long, in Peking.

Axis putsch of 1941. There was also rebellion against the pro-Western orientation of the government, and the movement in favor of Pan-Arabism. Last, but not least, there was the social revolution—or at least the beginning of it—the old-fashioned, long-overdue "bourgeois revolution."

The opposition brought to power by this revolutionary wave was far from homogeneous in thought or character. In Nuri as Said's days almost the entire middle class—certainly all of the intelligentsia—had belonged to the opposition; and their situation had been made worse by the indiscriminate use of the term "Communist" by Nuri and his henchmen against their opponents. The opposition that became the ruling stratum in July, 1958, consisted of four or five groups who were jockeying separately for power and positions almost from the very beginning. Political parties were bound to play a bigger part in Baghdad than they had done in Cairo, for the Egyptian officers' revolt had been, among other things, a rebellion against the traditional parties, which had failed or had been discredited; whereas in Baghdad the parties had been formed to oppose the regime, had been suppressed, and thus came to share in the fruits of victory.

The most prominent of these groups was, at first, the "Istiqlal" (Independence) party, one of whose leaders, Mohammed al Kubbah, became a member of the three-man Council of Sovereignty. Another, Sidiq Shanshal, was appointed minister of propaganda. In the thirties and early forties the Istiqlal had been pro-Fascist, and its leaders took part in the Rashid Ali coup in 1941 (Rashid Ali himself, long exiled from his country, returned to Baghdad in September, 1958, only to be arrested by the new regime two months later). After the defeat of the Rome-Berlin Axis, the leaders of the Istiqlal became impressed by the increase in Soviet strength; they adopted a neutralist attitude, and then began to collaborate with pro-Soviet movements in Iraq. None of them could be said to have even a moderately left-wing view of domestic politics, but they were all bitterly anti-Western; they were inclined to believe that the Soviet Union would prevail in the global struggle, and preferred not to be on what they thought was the losing side. The Istiqlal had a fair number of sympathizers in the officer corps, but its organization as a party was weak, its political program vague.

On the Left, the influence of the old "National Democratic Party" had somewhat decreased in recent years, while the "Ba'ath" or "Renaissance" party (headed by Abdel Rahman al Bazaz, Dean of the Baghdad University law school, and subsequently Iraqi Ambassador in London) had gained in strength. Both these parties were represented in the new government. The "National Democrats" had been originally a Populist or Fabian group; but after 1945 is was joined by Communists, who used it as one of several "popular front" organizations while their own party was illegal. It is difficult to say how much freedom of action the party's leaders still had, or to what extent the party apparatus was still in their hands. The Ba'ath group—a branch of the All-Arab movement of the same name—combined a pro-Soviet neutralism with radical Pan-Arab slogans and Socialist demands. Its influence among the intelligentsia in the beginning was stronger than that of the traditional left-wing parties, such as the National Democrats or the proto-Communist groups led by Aziz Sharif, Tawfiq Munir, and Abdel Fattah Ibrahim. (All these leaders had been in exile in Damascus and Cairo, and returned to Baghdad after the revolution; the last-mentioned was appointed Director-General of the Government Oil Refineries Administration.) Subsequently, however, the Ba'ath was outmaneuvered by the alliance between General Qassem, the National Democrats, and the Communists, who emerged as the "dominant voice in the National Union Front" (*The Times*, London, December 16, 1958). The representatives of the Ba'ath in the government were ousted, some of its leaders were arrested, and its newspaper was closed.

There remained the Iraqi Communist party. Riddled by internal dissension and disputes for many years, it had three different leaderships when it emerged from illegality in July, 1958: there was its old Politburo, headed by Baha ad Din Nuri (in prison since 1953); a new leadership which had been continuing the struggle underground; and, lastly, the leaders who had fled or had been sent to Western Europe, such as Tareq Mohammed. Nevertheless, the Iraqi Communist Party retained some cohesion through all its persecutions; it emerged as probably the strongest single party immediately after the coup, and its prospects of further progress were excellent: its organization was superior to that of the other groups, its political program clearer and in some ways more practical. Its influence was not limited to the intelligentsia, for it also had the rudiments of a "mass basis" in the trade unions, among the Kurds, etc., so that its activities in the first days of the revolution caused concern to the government, which demanded—without success—the disbandment of the para-military Communist forces, the "Popular Resistance" squads.[8] In addition, the Communists initiated local councils for the defense of the Republic: in their first manifesto they proclaimed their eagerness "to fight with the nation to the last drop of our blood to defend our national Iraqi Republic, to exterminate the last im-perialist, and to clear the country of their agents in order to attain a free, democratic, and dignified life, Arab Union, peace and progress."[9] It appears, however, that these immediate activities of theirs upon the outbreak of strife were spontaneous, for a subse-quent manifesto of the Iraqi CP called upon the working class to remain calm until the country survived the critical moment;[10] they had no wish to force an immediate showdown with the right-wing forces in the national coalition. They welcomed the action of the "courageous army" which had brought about "a glorious historical event" and prepared themselves for a period of collaboration with some of the non-Communist forces.

The successes of the Soviet Union in the Middle East since 1955 cannot be ascribed to any single cause: they certainly can not be explained by the magic of words, such as "Algeria," or "Israel" or "Arabian oil." It is even doubtful whether they should, or even could, be interpreted solely in terms of foreign policies. One great secret of the Soviet achievement here was merely that Russia was not involved, and could refrain from action whenever, or wherever, the West could hardly avoid it. In the Arab world, Russia was not tarred with the brush of imperialism: for forty years it had been absent from the area, whereas the Western powers had been very much in evidence there. The Western powers sought to "organize" the Arab world, where they established sundry defensive strongholds, whereas Russia could advocate a neutrality which coincided with the desires of the Arab elites. The West, or at any rate Western Europe, was largely dependent on Middle Eastern oil, and believed that loss of it would be a catastrophe, while the Soviet Union could very well do without it. While Western interests clashed everywhere with the rising tide of Arab nationalism, Russia was thus able to appear in the guise of a disinterested and benevolent onlooker. For obvious geographical and historical reasons, the Soviet Union could support the Pan-Arab movement—as it could not, for instance, support a Pan-Turkish movement.

Not that the purest political motive of sympathy and support for Arab national aspirations would have had much effect in itself, but for the circumstances which governed Arab response to it. The Soviet help extended to Turkey in 1921 had had no lasting political effect. But the Soviet encouragement to the Arab world went far deeper, because it quickened ambitions quite other than political. The Soviet Union after World War II was evoking dazzling dreams of speedy modernization and industrialization for peoples of underdeveloped countries.

On this topic recent years have seen much unnecessary argument and speculation. Those who denied the existence, or belittled the significance, of a real Communist movement in the Arab world were certainly fewer in 1958 than ten years earlier; but a number of commentators, including some of the more careful and intelligent, continued to believe and to argue that Communism was so irreconcilable with both Islam and nationalism that it could never come to dominate the Arab movement toward unification. They said that the resemblance between the anti-imperialist slogans of Communism and the anti-Western language of Arab nationalism was superficial; that it was merely misleading ignorant Arabs—and also nervous Western observers—to imagine a community of interest between the Kremlin and the Arabs which events were bound ultimately to expose as fallacious and nonexistent. In short, that all the fears of Communist domination of the Middle East arose from lack of knowledge of the local realities, exploited by malicious slander—a sort of McCarthyism on the international plane.*

A great deal of misunderstanding might be avoided if discussions of this point were preceded by a little semantic investigation. Those who believe that there is no real Communism in the area in question, or that what there is of it has no genuine influence and no future, having nothing in common with Arab aspirations, base their belief upon a certain well-known image of Communism. They conceive it as an ultra-radical leftist movement with the class struggle as its principal weapon, striving to organize the minds of the industrial workers and the discontented peasantry, hostile to all religion and nationalism and preaching "proletarian internationalism."

Communism of that kind would indeed stand small chance of acceptance in the Middle East. It was, in fact, preached among various small sects some thirty-five years ago in Egypt, Palestine, and Lebanon, where nothing of it is left today—nor, one might say, does it still exist anywhere else. The present challenge is of a quite different kind. The Communism that is striving for power in the Arab world today, though imbued with many Leninist motives, functions as an integral part of the nationalist movement, by no means as an opposition sect. It is not a proletarian party but an authentically nationalist party open to all classes. It has dropped the class struggle and replaced it with the anti-Western propaganda of the cold war. Communism in Asia seldom appears, as

---

* More penetrating insights into the relationship between Communism and Arab nationalism have been deplorably few, and all the more welcome. For instance, Mahmoud Messadi, a former minister in the Tunisian government, wrote, after a visit to one of the (ostensibly) nationalist congresses of Arab writers in Cairo, that "la suprême habilité de l'entreprise communiste au Moyen Orient semble avoir été d'agir en sorte que les éléments de doctrine marxiste qu'elle amalgamait à ceux propres à la 'Qawmiya arabiya' et l'orientation communiste qu'elle lui imprimerait, n'apparaissent pas comme d'origine étrangère, et se confondent, soit avec des tendances authentiques et anciennes du nationalisme arabe, soit avec les réactions et les revendications spontanées des masses populaires, victimes depuis des siècles de la misère et de l'exploitation économique" (*Action*, Tunis, January 20, 1958).

it frequently did (and occasionally still does) in Europe, as the heir to the ideals of 1789, democracy, liberty, and equality. Its prestige and attractive power are those of a reputedly sovereign means toward the modernization and industrial enrichment of peoples ruefully conscious of their "backwardness."

The group, or the class, that is most attracted and inspired by this latter-day Asian vision of the meaning of Communism is the intelligentsia. Communist development in a backward country opens up wide opportunities for the multitude who have been educated in the modern ways but largely unemployed and then politically frustrated under the old regime. It promises the promotion of this intelligentsia from a position of little influence, power, or social status, often of small material means, to that of a powerful political and economic bureaucracy—in other words, their elevation into the new ruling class. As one observer (R. Lowenthal) has put it:

> A combination of state-directed industrialization financed by ruthless industrial exploitation, with the ideological monopoly of a revolutionary party opposed to the traditional superstitions as well as to traditional values, is a powerful engine of speedy modernization. Which means that Communist attraction in Asia (with the possible exception of Japan) is based far less than in the West upon fictions which may be destroyed by some dramatic event, and far more on true facts. Where ideological attraction is not chiefly based on lies, there is no scope for an ideological crisis: in Asia the lesson of the Sputniks is more important than the lesson of Hungary.[11]

Communism is an essentially dynamic movement; it does not want to stagnate, and cannot afford to. Applied to the Middle East, this observation means that Communism cannot be satisfied in the long run with its present status in the Arab world, where it has to play second fiddle to "bourgeois nationalism." Probably it will not even have patience enough to rest content with the steady but slow progress it makes within the national movement. It is, therefore, unlikely that the present alliance between Russia and the Arab "bourgeois" nationalism will last. The Arab movement toward unity will be supported as long as it can be used as a weapon against the West but hardly any longer. Nasser and his colleagues may not have developed clear ideas as to the future political and social goals of the Arab peoples but they are certainly not Leninists. The Communists are probably right in thinking that anti-imperialist slogans, leanings toward a planned economy and partial nationalization are no equivalent, in the long run, to a Communist monopoly of political power. To them the present phase of Arab nationalism may be "progressive" but presents obstacles to the complete transformation of Arab society—the consummation that they may be willing to see delayed, but not indefinitely.

A conflict thus seems inevitable in the long run; but when, and under what circumstances is it likely? It is bound to come, at the very latest, if and when the unification of the Arab world within its historic frontiers has been achieved. The center of gravity of Arab affairs would then shift from foreign to domestic politics—where the community of interests with the Soviet Union is rather limited. Years may elapse, however, before such a development,* and it raises several questions that cannot

* Others would regard this as an unduly optimistic assumption. A close observer of the Middle Eastern scene writing in October, 1958, noted that the officers' regime in Egypt had made considerable efforts to overcome the general social backwardness. "The estates of the former royal family were distributed, and a major part of the large landowners were deprived of some of their holdings . . . The Government fixed minimum wages but was not able to maintain them. Industrial projects were drawn up. Public administration was simplified and purged of the elements of corruption insofar as possible. In each village a schoolhouse was to be constructed. But all these measures had no lasting effect. The first few years after the revolution showed a slight improvement of living standards among the simple people. But more recently this standard has probably dropped back again below the level reached in 1952. The pressure of the population increase defeated the measures made by the Government. Perhaps the material foundations for the reconstruction could have been provided, if at great sacrifice; but there was a lack of people qualified to handle these material foundations properly —government officials with a sense of responsibility, industrialists with some heart for the social problems involved, teachers willing to work in the remote rural areas, scholars willing to apply strictly scientific standards to

be answered at this stage: what are the natural or historic borders of the Arab world? And might not a new Arab state or federation be likely to expand, as it did in the past, until it came up against its natural limit—namely an equally strong or superior power?

It depends largely upon the Soviet Union when its collaboration with Arab nationalism will be discontinued; and it may be taken for granted that an attempt will be made to postpone any open conflict until Soviet predominance in the Middle East, and Communist influence there, will be more strongly entrenched. This does not preclude, of course, a possible rift between Moscow and Cairo that is wanted by neither side, but becomes inevitable as the result of the premature emergence of a semi-Communist regime in such a country as Iraq.

Both the deposition of the Egyptian king in July, 1952, and the *coup d'état* in Iraq just two years later, are regarded by Communists, perhaps with some justification, as "bourgeois revolutions" comparable to the February revolution in Russia in 1917. Bourgeois revolutions only pave the way for the second, the decisive change—they cannot of themselves bring it about. The traditional view is that this second and final stage can be attained only by a violent political uprising. In recent years, however, this idea has been partly modified: the possibility of certain countries, notably those of Asia, growing gradually into a loose, more specifically local, form of popular democracy, is no longer absolutely ruled out. The emergence of national Communist regimes

---

their activity, and students interested in real study rather than the acquisition of diplomas. There is a lack among the leading classes not of intellectual qualities so much as of a sense of moral responsibility and integrity—and patience. That is what happened to the regime—it lost patience with its own plans and projects even before the really serious problems had begun to turn up; more and more it began to desert the more tedious task of raising the living standard of the people in order to engage in more tempting 'large-scale' plans. Foreign policy, Pan-Arabism, armaments, propaganda of all kinds, tirades against the 'colonialists,' spectacular but unrealistic industrial projects absorbed its intention increasingly." Arnold Hottinger, "Egypt and Iraq—Two Stages of the Arab Revolution" in *Swiss Review of World Affairs*, October, 1958, p. 8.

in the East is admitted as at least conceivable.* This Asian or Middle Eastern form of popular democracy remains highly unorthodox from the classical Communist point of view. Such regimes would be on an equal footing with Moscow—so long as the international balance of power did not change.

If the Marxist appraisal of the Arab national movement is correct, it is an essentially transient phenomenon, fated to split into left, right, and center groups in competition for political power. How will the present leadership, somewhat inaccurately called "the national bourgeoisie," be likely to react? May it not voluntarily emulate the Chinese example now so much extolled?

Yet this possibility seems remote, at present, and a violent struggle for power between conflicting groups, interests, and ideologies looks more probable. The present leadership of the Arab national movement will try to carry out its own program of uniting the Arab world, of restoring it to its old power and glory. Arab nationalists believe that they are on the threshold of success. But they are not the only, possibly not the strongest, contestants in the struggle for the Middle East. The end of the first act in this drama is in sight. So is the beginning of the second.

NOTES

1. *Pravda*, May 16, 1958.
2. *Trud*, June 8, 1958.
3. Radio Sofia, June 6, 1958.
4. *Pravda*, July 15, 1958.
5. *Pravda*, July 16, 1958.
6. Radio Moscow, July 20, 1958.
7. *Pravda*, July 21, 1958. The various official Soviet communiqués on the Iraqi crisis were published as an annex to *Novoe Vremia*, July 25, 1958.

* "National Communism" is an opprobrious term in the Communist dictionary—but this is true for the time being only of national Communism in Europe, where it developed as a form of resistance against Soviet domination, and connoted a more neutral, if not sympathetic, attitude toward the West in Belgrade and Warsaw. In Asia, national Communism arises under very different conditions; rising nationalism and Communism are united in a common enmity toward the West. Asian national Communists may be among the more backward pupils in the Leninist preparatory school; but they will not be anti-Soviet, which, after all, is the decisive qualification.

8. Proclamation No. 16 of the Baghdad military governor-general over Radio Baghdad, July 20, 1958; also Proclamation No. 54, August 31, 1958.

9. Declaration of the Central Committee of the Iraqi Communist Party, dated July 14, 1958, *New China News Agency*, August 3, 1958.

10. Declaration of the C.C. of the Iraqi Communist Party, dated August 1; published in *Al Nur*, Damascus, August 10, 1958.

11. Richard Lowenthal, "The Ideological Crisis of International Communism," in *The Year Book of World Affairs* (New York, 1958), pp. 47-48.

APPENDIX I

China and the Middle East

An investigation of Chinese relations with the Middle East lies outside the scope of the present study, but it is not out of place to mention that China is potentially a major Middle Eastern power. As far as the economic links (cotton purchases from the UAR) and cultural relations are concerned, it already belongs to the category of powers with a considerable stake in the area. This economic interest is very likely to grow; with the progress of industrialization in China and the apparent absence of major oil fields in that country, the oil resources of the Middle East may become of great importance for Peking's economic planners. An increase in Chinese political interest and activities is equally likely, yet it is not certain that Chinese and Soviet interests will always be identical. There is a great deal of sympathy for China in the Arab world, exceeding perhaps even the feelings of good will toward the Soviet Union. For China, as a purely Asian country (in contrast to Russia), is believed to be altogether free from imperialist designs of domination and exploitation; it is, moreover, much farther away, and, therefore, seems less dangerous than the other big powers. In addition, the Chinese form of government is widely thought to be more democratic and popular than the Soviet regime. It is doubtful whether China's "hard line" will adversely affect this appraisal for some time to come. Reports about the establishment of communes all over the Chinese countryside are not given much prominence in the Arab press, and their implications are not always understood.

APPENDIX II

Israel in the Soviet Mirror: 1958

After an interval of almost thirty years, a book on Palestine (Israel) has again been published in Moscow, in the autumn of 1958.* The situation in Israel is described in this book, as well as in other recent Soviet essays and broadcasts, in terms of a conflict between American (Standard Oil) and British (Shell) oil companies. Whereas Weizmann followed the lead given by Deterding, Ben-Gurion has now joined Rockefeller's empire. Dealing at considerable length with American capital investments in Israel, Soviet authors find it somewhat difficult to provide a satisfactory explanation of the political implications, for Israel is hardly a very profitable source of income for the American monopolistic trusts.

Of more interest than these attempts at economic analysis is the effort made to refute Zionism, and in particular left-wing Zionism, on the ideological level. It is argued, in one of the longest chapters of the Ivanov-Sheinis book (*About a Certain False Contention*), that the Jewish problem can be solved only by assimilation in a socialist state free of anti-Semitism. The Jews are not a single nation; even the Jews in Israel do not act as if they were one. On the authority of Mr. Alfred Lilienthal, of the American Council for Judaism (*What Price Israel*), the Soviet authors ridicule the idea that there is any more affinity in physical features, language, customs, psychology, etc., between Jews coming from various parts of the world than there is between Spaniards and Slavs.

* K. Ivanov and Z. Sheinis: "Gosudarstvo Izrail, ego Polozhenie i Politika," *Gospolitizdat*, 1958; see also G. S. Nikitina, "Izrail i Amerikanskii Imperialism," in *S.V.*, 5, 1958, pp. 71-79. An English translation of lengthy excerpts from the Ivanov-Sheinis book was given in *Jerusalem Post*, November 28, 1958.

Having thus disposed of the "miserable theories of the [Jewish nation's] exclusivity and its messianic mission," Ivanov and Sheinis comment on another line of approach which, they say, is frequently used by Israeli politicians in dealing with the governments of leading (East European) states and left-wing parties. "Assuming a conciliatory, humble mien, and with false modesty, they appeal to Marxism and the democratic ideals they themselves reject: 'If you recognize the right of nations to self-determination and come out in defense of the incomparably larger Arab nation, recognizing the justice of its struggle against colonialism, why then do you deny the same right to the small Jewish nation, only recently and for the first time constituted in the independent state of Israel? Does not such an attitude toward a small (Jewish) nation contradict the principles of democracy and socialism?' "

This, however, is a false dilemma, according to Ivanov and Sheinis, for the attitude of a genuine democrat and Marxist toward national movements depends entirely on the concrete conditions that actually exist in the struggle for liberation of the peoples of the Arab East and in the world as a whole. Marxists, as distinct from bourgeois nationalists, do not regard each national question as being self-sufficient, or as the main or basic problem of its time. Some national movements are "objectively progressive," others are "objectively reactionary." Ivanov and Sheinis quote Lenin to substantiate their assertion that the liberation of some of the large peoples must be placed above the liberation movements of small nations, and that the whole problem must be considered not in isolation, but in a global context. Marx and Engels in 1848 "directly and definitely distinguished between entire reactionary peoples serving as Russian advance posts in Europe, and the revolutionary peoples, such as the Germans, Poles, and Hungarians. In 1848, the revolutionary peoples fought for freedom, whose major foe was then Tsarism, while the Czechs and others like them were indeed reactionary peoples and the advance posts of Tsarism." With this, the authors think, they have provided the necessary ideological justification needed in 1958.

APPENDIX III

Iraq, Nasser, and the Communists

The line dividing one historical period from another is usually less well defined and clear-cut in actual fact than in the textbooks; there is always some overlapping. The struggle between the Hashemites and Nasser was not yet over by late 1958 (though the eventual outcome was hardly in doubt), when a new phase in the struggle for the Middle East opened with the contest between "integral Arab nationalism" (Colonel Nasser and the Ba'ath) and the Communists. Communism in Iraq emerged as the strongest single force in that country—stronger than it had ever been in Syria, which had for many years been considered its most powerful bulwark in the Arab world. Up to 1957, the Arab Communists themselves deprecated their own political importance in order not to arouse doubts and suspicions among their nationalist allies. This traditional modesty was dropped after the Baghdad coup, and in an open letter to President Qassem, the Iraqi party leaders stated, "We are the strongest group, and the one best able to mobilize the broadest forces for the defense of the republic. Nobody can deny this, or refuse to admit it." The Iraqi army officers and the politicians who collaborated with the Communists (the leaders of the Istiqlal party and the National Democrats) opposed unity with the United Arab Republic for reasons of their own. They needed Communist help in order to fight the Ba'ath (much weaker in Baghdad than in Syria) and to arrest Colonel Aref, to organize mass demonstrations, and to create a popular demand for meting out "severe punishment" to the plotters against Iraqi independence. In Syria, the Communists had had to cooperate with the Ba'ath; in Iraq, they felt free to attack them as nationalist adventurers hostile to political freedom, as "pseudo-socialists," etc. By dissolving the Ba'ath in Iraq, General Qassem opened the way to power to the Communists.

This, of course, was not the way he saw it. He was undoubtedly firmly convinced that he had merely been playing off one political group against another, and that he would one day discard the Communists in the same way as he had got rid of the Ba'ath. This was, to say the least, a very optimistic assumption, for behind Qassem there were some army officers and politicians, generals without an army, whereas the Communists had the only efficient political machine in the country.

The Iraqi Communists did not at first launch a frontal attack against Colonel Nasser and his regime, but the very logic of events brought them into sharp opposition to Cairo. In a policy statement in October, 1958, and in several declarations in November and December of that year (such as the one at the Arab Lawyers' Conference in Baghdad on November 30, 1958), it was stated that the "Iraqi people were thirsting for democratic freedom" and that this thirst would not be quenched by a merger with the UAR, where there was no freedom for political parties: "The political system in the UAR has not, in fact, developed to the democratic level which the Iraqi people desire." While attacking the Ba'ath for attempting to split the Iraqi United Front (dominated by the Communists), the party advocated federal relations with the UAR, reserving full autonomy for Iraq over its own internal affairs, including the legal recognition of all political parties supporting the new republic. "The army and its patriotic officers have deep faith in the principles of the democratic liberation movement in Iraq, and this would be endangered by a merger with the army of the UAR."[1]

The situation in Iraq was further complicated by the re-emergence of the Kurdish issue. Mullah Mustafa Barzani returned to Baghdad from his exile in Eastern Europe soon after the coup and promised loyalty and active support to the new government. Kurdish units gave strong support to the alliance between Kassem and the Communists. The two traditional Kurdish parties had disappeared: the NLP (National Liberation Party, a Communist-front organization), which, according to a latter-day,

[1] Quoted from the English translation in *World News*, December 13, 1958, p. 716. See also Alberto Jacoviello in *Unita* (Rome), October 25, 1958, and *Le Drapeau Rouge* (Brussels), November 5, 1958.

pro-Communist historian, "put inadequate emphasis on immediate Kurdish demands concerning the Kurdish language, education, and local administration,"[2] and the PDK (Kurdish Democratic Party), which had "placed excessive emphasis on exclusively Kurdish affairs to the neglect of striving with other patriotic groups for the solution of common problems."[3] In their place, a new group, the UKDP (United Kurdish Democratic Party), had emerged. Whether this group would be satisfied with the Iraqi Communists' promise of full equality, or whether they would in due time press the demand for full national independence, was uncertain. They had their grievances against the Arab left-wing forces, too. Had not the Arab delegates successfully objected, for instance, to the participation of a Kurdish delegation at the Moscow Youth festival in 1956?[4]

In view of the growth of Communist influence in Iraq, the tocsin was sounded in Cairo during the last week of 1958. In a speech in Port Said, President Nasser for the first time attacked the Syrian Communists, who, he said, were separatists opposed to Arab unity and who wanted the northern province to secede from the UAR. Communist militants in Egypt and Syria were arrested, and Khaled Bakdash, the leader of the Syrian party (who had returned from eastern Europe only a few weeks before), was again compelled to disappear from the political scene. *Al Nur*, the Communist daily in Damascus, was closed. Egyptian newspapers criticized the Iraqi Communists, who "did not know anything about the *coup d'état* in Baghdad until after the revolution, and who now brazenly demand to inherit it and who try to destroy all anti-Communist elements. The Arab nationalists should be crushed so that 2,000 Iraqi Communists shall have the chance to rule Iraq" (*Akhbar al Yom*, January 3, 1959). Hassanein Haikal, President Nasser's confidant among Cairo editors, put it in a somewhat more conciliatory manner: "Communist activity has increased a little of late. In the past, Communist organizations have stood by the nationalist forces in the severe

[2] S. S. Gavin: *Kurdistan: Divided Nation of the Middle East* (London, 1958), p. 47.

[3] *Ibid.*

[4] *Ibid.*, p. 50.

struggle against imperialism, pacts, imperialist collaborators, and feudalism. This struggle has ended or is about to end. What will be the attitude of the Communists in the future? Will they be deflected from the clear nationalist line in order to raise red flags in the Middle East? Or will they keep their mouths shut?" (*Al Ahram* January 4, 1959). Even *Rose al Yussef*, an influential weekly that had revealed for years a pronounced pro-Communist attitude, adjusted itself to the new line. "The conflict between Communism and Arab nationalism was inevitable," wrote its editor on December 29, 1958. "The Communists felt they were slipping and therefore opposed unity under Nasser." One week later, the same writer argued that the Soviet Union "would not sacrifice for the sake of the Arab Communists the trust and respect it had won from the Arabs as a whole. The road to Moscow does not lead via the Syrian and Iraqi Communist parties."

The rift between Cairo and Baghdad affected the Arab Communist parties, too. It will be recalled that the major Communist factions in Egypt had decided to make common cause only in early 1958 (see p. 298). The merger had been held up during the last stage of negotiations as the result of ideological and personal quarrels. The majority demanded that Jews and foreign citizens should be removed from the leadership of the Communist movement in Egypt. (There were three Jewish Communists in the Central Committee of one faction, the "Peasants' and Workers'" group.) After this demand, too, had been fulfilled, the road was clear for organizational unity, and a unified Communist party in Egypt supported President Nasser's policy throughout the spring and summer of 1958. In autumn of that year, however, dissension spread as the result of the stand taken by the Iraqi and Syrian Communists against Arab unity under Nasser. The Iraqi party had already indicated in August, 1958, that it opposed Nasser's Arab policy, and the Syrian party, too, revealed its opposition in November. (At the same time Syrian and Lebanese Communists again separated, and the Lebanese members established an independent organization. This separation, however, was a matter of political convenience and had apparently not been caused by any ideological dispute.)

The Egyptian Communists violently disagreed among themselves with regard to the stand taken by their Iraqi and Syrian comrades. One faction endorsed their attitude, while another group thought it profoundly mistaken and harmful. As a result, the Egyptian party split once again, and by late autumn in 1958 there were again two Egyptian Communist parties, one supporting Nasser and the other in opposition to his policy. In the Syrian party, too, there was some criticism of the "Bakdash line"; Elias Morkos, party secretary of the Latakia district, came out against the separatist stand taken by his party. The majority of Syrian Communists, however, endorsed the stand taken by their leadership.

The Iraqi Communists, meanwhile, made considerable progress, mainly through the "Popular Resistance" movement (a paramilitary organization) and the Students' Union, two groups that all but dominated political life in the country six months after the revolution. Whether their alliance with General Qassem and his fellow officers would go on indefinitely seemed uncertain, but while it lasted, they were given the opportunity to build up positions of strength in many government ministries, the police, and especially such channels of mass communications as the press and the radio. Dr. Ibrahim Kubbah, Minister of Economics, Colonel Fadhil al Madawi, President of the "People's Court," Major Salim al Fakhri, Director General of Broadcasting, and the brothers Wasfi and Lutfi Taher (in charge of the political police and press censorship respectively) followed the party line. The list of prosecution witnesses in the trials of the nationalists in the winter of 1958-59 included most of those who had been prominent in the Communist party or in its periphery in 1945-47: Aziz Sharif, Tawfiq Munir, Daud as Sayigh, Kamil al Kazanji, *et al.* In the daily press the official party line was given by Aziz al Haj in *Saut al Ahrar*, by Abdel Kader Ismail al Bustani in *Itihad al Sha'ab*, and elsewhere.

Nasser's anti-Communist campaign provoked criticism in the Soviet capital. Referring to events in Egypt, Krushchev declared at the 21st Congress of the CPSU that it was untrue to accuse the Arab Communists of weakening and splitting the national movement. Everyone knew, after all, that Communists everywhere, including those in Israel, fought Zionism.[5] It appeared, however, that Khrushchev had underrated the sensitivity of the Egyptian leaders with regard to a potential threat to their rule. In the semiofficial Egyptian reply, it was said that Cairo had not leveled charges against Communism as an idea, nor against foreign Communists in general. "Some of them, such as Khrushchev, Mao Tse-tung, Gomulka, and Tito, we regard as heroes."[6] Nasser had acted against the Syrian Communists because they had "deviated"; this, however, was a purely domestic affair, and any outside intervention was unacceptable.

Mukhitdinov, who had been Nasser's guest in Cairo not long before, was more outspoken than Khrushchev when his turn came during the Moscow party congress: the allegation that the Communists did not serve the interests of their countries was a mean calumny, bitterly resented by all "progressive people." Such allegations merely betrayed antidemocratic tendencies and a willingness to compromise with the dollar or the pound sterling. At the same time, the Yugoslav "revisionists" were blamed for poisoning the minds of some of the leaders in the East and for sowing distrust of Soviet foreign policy.[7] The specter of a Middle-Eastern Titoism appeared on the political horizon.

From the Soviet point of view, the unfolding conflict between the Communists and their allies in Baghdad and Colonel Nasser was inopportune, though in the long run unavoidable. To keep the United Arab Republic happy, Moscow, in the autumn of 1958, offered Egypt its assistance in the construction of the Aswan High Dam, after more than two years' hesitation to commit itself. If power in Iraq were to pass into Communist hands, a reconciliation between Nasser and the West appeared at least a theoretical possibility. But Moscow was perhaps not too greatly disturbed by the possible consequences; Egypt's economy had

[5] *Pravda*, January 28, 1959.

[6] Hassanein Haikal in *Al Ahram*, January 29, 1959.

[7] *Pravda*, January 31, 1959. Salim Adil, representing the Iraqi Communists at the same party congress in Moscow, likewise attacked the slogan of a specific "Arab Communism" used by "reactionary circles" in their struggle against the Communist movement in the Arab world. (*Pravda*, February 3, 1959).

become very much dependent on Soviet bloc trade and aid. Economic considerations alone would probably not be decisive—they had not prevented Tito from cutting himself adrift. More important was the general political and psychological climate in the UAR, which made a *rapprochement* with the West rather difficult. After so many years of violent attacks on the West, a *volte-face* would be a complicated political maneuver, and it was not certain whether Colonel Nasser would risk it. The Soviet leaders, on the other hand, certainly did not want to drive Nasser into such a desperate action, and it can be taken for granted that the Iraqi Communists received counsels of moderation and were earnestly requested to share political power temporarily, rather than to monopolize it.

Such compromises may work for a time, but are unlikely to last. Developments in the Middle East have a momentum of their own, and even Moscow's advice is not invariably followed. The provisional alliance between the Communists and the "petty bourgeois" Arab nationalists can be maintained, as the experience of national movements elsewhere has shown, but not for very long. The two are admittedly less sharply divided in the Middle East than elsewhere. There the Communists appear as Arab nationalists, or, at any rate, as national Communists, while the "bourgeois nationalists" have strong pro-Soviet sympathies and frequently talk in what sounds like Communists' language. But behind this façade of a community of interests there is an irreconcilable conflict that cannot be eliminated by any amount of speech-making and political legerdemain. The Communists want to share power, and, ultimately, to take over, while the Arab nationalists have no intention of giving up their positions. Until the Baghdad revolution, this was a somewhat academic dilemma, because Communism had not yet emerged as a major factor in the Arab world. Since then everything has changed, and what was once a long-term perspective has now become a political problem of decisive importance. Arab leaders, to be sure, have buried the hatchet from time to time; even Nuri as Said, King Hussein, and Nasser temporarily patched up their differences. But basic conflicts will out, and the new phase in the struggle for power in the Middle East is already upon us.

BIBLIOGRAPHICAL NOTE

For a variety of reasons, among them that of space, it has been impossible to provide a full bibliography of Soviet publications on the Middle East. Among the selective lists available elsewhere, two ought to be mentioned: the series of four bibliographies by Rudolph Loewenthal ("Russian Materials on Islam and Islamic Institutions," "Russian Materials on Arabs and Arab Countries," "Russian Materials on Africa," "Russian Materials on Turkey") published in *Der Islam* (Berlin, 1957-58). Eudin and North, *Soviet Russia and the East, 1920-27* (Stanford, 1957), pp. 405-55 give an adequate bibliography covering the early period of Soviet-Middle Eastern relations. There is no such Soviet bibliography; N. A. Smirnov: *Ocherki Istorii Izucheniia Islama v SSSR* (Moscow, 1954), lists many books and some articles on Islam and allied subjects published in the Soviet Union between 1918 and 1953. Only after the present study had already been completed did I have the opportunity to see in manuscript the annotated bibliography entitled *Soviet Middle East Studies*, prepared by A. Bolton at the Central Asian Research Center for the Royal Institute of International Affairs.

Abbreviations used in this volume:

B.S.E.   *Bolshaia Sovetskaia Entsiklopedia*
C.I.   *Communist International*
FLP   *For a Lasting Peace, for a People's Democracy*
Inprecorr   *International Press Correspondence*
K.I.   *Kommunisticheskii Internatsional*
M.Kh.M.P.   *Mirovoe Khoziaistvo i Mirovaia Politika*

M.Zh.   *Mezhdunarodnaia Zhizn*
N.V.   *Novyi Vostok*
R.V.   *Revoliutsionnyi Vostok*
S.V.   *Sovetskoe Vostokovedenie*
Sovrem. Vostok   *Sovremennyi Vostok*
V.I.R.K. *Voina i Rabochii Klass*
WNAV   *World News and Views*

The system of transliteration of Russian names used is, with a very few exceptions (e.g., Trotsky instead of the less familiar Trotskii, etc.), that of the Department for Slavonic languages at Harvard University and the Widener Library. Certain names have been transliterated in two different ways, according to the context (e.g. Persian Azerbaijan and Soviet Azerbaidzhan).

INDEX

361